The American West
from Fiction into Film

To Vicki who made it all possible;
to Holly who made it all worthwhile

The American West from Fiction (1823-1976) into Film (1909-1986)

by
Jim Hitt

McFarland & Company, Inc., Publishers
Jefferson, North Carolina and London

British Library Cataloguing-in-Publication data are available

Library of Congress Cataloguing-in-Publication Data

Hitt, Jim.
The American West from fiction (1823–1976) into film (1909–1986) /
by Jim Hitt.
p.   cm.
[Includes index.]
Includes bibliographical references.
ISBN 0-89950-378-0 (lib. bdg. : 50# alk. paper) ∞
1. Western films — History and criticism.
2. American fiction — Film and video adaptations.
3. West (U.S.) in literature.
4. Film adaptations — Stories, plots, etc.
I. Title.
PN1995.9.W4H48   1990
791.43'6278 — dc20
89-42723
CIP

Manufactured in the United States of America

McFarland & Company, Inc., Publishers
Box 611, Jefferson, North Carolina 28640

Table of Contents

Preface

Many studies have dealt with the relationship between literature and films, some on a very esoteric level of theory, others on the more specific level of examining actual adaptations. In this latter category are such works as *The Modern American Novel and the Movies,* edited by Gerald Peary and Roger Shatzkin, and *Screening the Novel* by Gerald Miller, both admirable works that attempt to discuss a small number of novels that have reached the screen.

This work is different. It is a survey that attempts to cover the entire genre of western fiction that has been adapted for the American screen. The novels and short stories discussed herein were all written as fiction before reaching the screen. Novels written to capitalize on the success of movies — novelizations of films — are not included, although this practice is certainly not new. In 1905 *The Squaw Man* was published as a novel after its success as a play. In the 1920s, novelizations of *The Black Pirate* and *The Iron Horse* appeared after the releases of these films. These books are not literature but promotional campaigns based on the idea that people will buy the book if they liked the movie.

In my research, I have consulted critical writings that pertain to both literature and films, and in a few cases where the films were not available for viewing, I have had to rely on these opinions. However, the great majority of critical views, whether on literature or film, are my own, and I take responsibility for them. In some cases, I have found that my opinion goes against the prevailing current, especially on lesser known works. For instance, I believe that the 1939 Paramount version of *Heritage of the Desert* is the finest film adapted from a Zane Grey work, not because of its big name stars and large budget, neither of which it had, but because it captures the feeling and spirit of Grey better than any other film. This is not to say that *Heritage of the Desert* is a work of art, although it may well be, but that, in the light of film adaptations, it does its job remarkably well.

The chapter headings are my own attempt to find some organization to western literature and film. Within each chapter, the organization rests with the date of the author's first published work to reach the screen. It is this date that determines the author's place within the chapter.

In a survey such as this, it is impossible to discuss every single piece of western fiction made into a film. Therefore, I have chosen to limit this work to strictly American adaptations. Except in a few instances, the works of an American author that were adapted for foreign screens have been omitted. I have also chosen to discuss items that were in some way influential within the genre.

Except in that they may appear in the list which comprises Appendix Two, I have inevitably omitted authors or works that some readers may believe should have been included. I freely acknowledge this. Much of the pulp fiction that has been adapted for the screen, however, has had little overall effect on the genre except to give it a bad name. Walt Coburn is an excellent example. Here is a writer whose main output was in the pulps, and none of his works have endured the test of time. Such stories as "Black K Rides Tonight" or "Ride 'Em Cowboy" offer little in the way of lasting value, and even though six of his short stories became films, they were all unimportant "B's." Many other authors and works fall into this category.

Occasionally a writer like Charles Neider ventured into the western field, and although his novel *The Authentic Death of Hendry Jones* became *One-Eyed Jacks,* it is a relatively unimportant fictional retelling of the Billy the Kid legend. Walter Noble Burns' book on Bonney (see Appendix One), written 35 years earlier, was far better and far more influential. Also, *One-Eyed Jacks* was, in reality, Marlon Brando's work. Except for the inclusion of a few character names, the film, under Brando's direction, ignored the novel and invented its own story. Had this novel been part of a complete oeuvre of a writer who was influential within the genre, perhaps it would have been worthy of inclusion, but, although marginally enjoyable, it was a dead end that influenced no one.

I must also say that I have had to make decisions on the amount of space each author deserves within the book. Some may question the inclusion of an entire chapter — and a long one at that — on Zane Grey, but he is America's most filmed author and seems to rate the extra space, despite the fact that many of the films based on his works fail to rise above "B" status. However, they were often very influential "B's."

Any time an author writes a book, he must ask himself who will be his audience. The answer is simple: *The American West from Fiction into Film* is for those who love books and for those who love films. And I hope that, in some small way, I have contributed to the literature of the West as well as the literature of film.

A book such as this owes a great deal to other people, and I would be remiss if I failed to thank the following: Bill Tedder, who gave me valuable advice and caught many of my most grievous errors; Jim Turner, whose friendship gave me encouragement; Bonnie Carpenter, who guided me in research; Simon and Pam Waltzer and Vic Chaney who helped to keep the fire going; my mother, Fanchon Severe, who laid the foundations; Nonnie, who hopefully knows of my successes; my wife Vicki, who helped me find self-fulfillment; and finally, my daughter Holly, who taught me the meaning of love that only a parent can know.

Jim Hitt
Summer 1989

Introduction:
Words and Shadows

There is the story of the fledgling screenwriter who tried to sell his original screenplay, but every agent kept returning the script unread. After a last rejection, he called the offending agent and pleaded for some constructive criticism that would help sell the manuscript. The agent told him that this year Hollywood didn't want original screenplays; this year they wanted screenplays based on novels. The author immediately sat down and began pounding the typewriter. A month later, the young author took his completed manuscript, now a novel, to a printer and ordered one copy, which he sent to the very same agent who had given him the advice. The agent sold the book to a studio, which, in turn, went on to make a very successful movie.

This story may be apocryphal, but it illustrates the long standing love affair between American films and American fiction. From those early primitive days when D.W. Griffith and others experimented with the new medium, American filmmakers have adapted thousands of American novels and short stories. The reasons are many and varied. By linking film with the older and more established medium of fiction, early filmmakers could claim a legitimacy for a new art form which, at the time, really wasn't considered much of an art form at all. Also, by choosing literary works, the filmmakers had a built-in audience, a reason that was as valid in Griffith's time as today. These literary works could be anything from a classic author like Poe or Hawthorne to the lowest common practitioner of popular literature. In some cases, the lower the better, since the vast American film-going public was much more likely to be drawn by *Peyton Place* than *The House of Seven Gables*. There was one other very practical reason for basing a film on a fictional work;

it was a ready made idea. The studio or producer didn't have to go looking.

But the studios were seldom content to let a fictional work stand on its own. Sometimes they added, sometimes they deleted; sometimes they changed the title, sometimes they kept the title and dropped the original story altogether. It didn't matter what the studios or producers did to the fictional work as long as the credits read that the film was based on a novel or short story. That was all they cared about.

One of the earliest and most important filmmakers who realized the value of adapting literature to film was D.W. Griffith. In 1908, his first year as a director, he filmed Jack London's *Call of the Wild,* Shakespeare's *The Taming of the Shrew* and James Fenimore Cooper's *Leatherstocking Tales.* Earlier the same year, the director made *Edgar Allan Poe,* which dramatized some of the events of the author's life, and Poe's writings themselves proved an inspiration for Griffith in 1914 when he made the six reel *The Avenging Conscience,* which drew from both "The Telltale Heart" and "Annabel Lee." It may have been from reading Poe that Griffith began to understand the art of story telling for the camera. Poe began his narrative slowly, then accelerated the action until the climax. Griffith not only copied this method but, in the process, discovered that long static shots, no matter how crammed with movement, slowed down the pace while quick cutting from one shot to another speeded up the pace. This is not to say that Griffith discovered these techniques, but rather he discovered how to use them in order to tell a story on film.

Griffith also discovered a basic rule regarding adaptations. An American story, even an obscure one by an obscure writer, would have more appeal to American audiences than a famous work by a European author. The American public is quite ready to brush aside the Byzantine complexities of European fiction as irrelevant to entertainment. Added to this is the simple fact that much American fiction is very visual, which gives it the added advantage of being more easily adaptable. Much fiction of other countries is simply not visual in the same way as American fiction. Gabriel García Márquez's classic Argentine novel *One Hundred Years of Solitude* is a rich tapestry of Argentine folk history intertwined with a multi-layered family chronicle. There are some wonderfully visual passages in the book, but they are often surrealistic and dreamlike. By American standards, the novel would seem unfilmable, not because it couldn't be done, but because it wouldn't be commercial. Even classic European writers like Tolstoy or Dostoevsky do not translate well to the American screen. Tolstoy simply presents too much philosophy and Dostoevsky too much depth, too much inner soul. The few European authors such as Charles Dickens or Rafael Sabatini who do translate well are those who, like their American counterparts, are also very visual.

D.W. Griffith was also one of the first important filmmakers to realize the importance of adapting the works of popular as well as classical American authors. For *Birth of a Nation* (1915), he adapted *The Clansman* by Thomas Dixon, Jr., which had the advantage of being not only a very successful novel but also a very successful stage play. For *The Love Flower* (1920), Griffith used a short story "The Black Beach" by Ralph Stock. For *America* (1924) he credited a short story by Robert W. Chambers, one of the most popular writers of the twenties. Now these works as well as the authors are obscure and almost forgotten, but in their time, their appeal was widespread and their names easily recognizable to the American reading public.

Other producers and directors also turned to American fiction. In 1912, Edison's studio adapted an obscure Edgar Allan Poe short story, "The System of Doctor Tarr and Professor Fether," retitling it *Lunatics in Power.* In 1920 Maurice Tourneur filmed James Fenimore Cooper's *The Last of the Mohicans,* still the best adaptation of that novel. *Moby Dick* became *The Sea Beast* (1925) starring John Barrymore. Popular novels such as Paul Leicester Ford's *Janice Meredith* (1924) became vehicles for stars like Marion Davies. When sound arrived, the demand of filmmakers for American fiction grew even stronger. Most major authors and a great many minor ones have had at least one of their works filmed. Every genre has been tapped many times over. When a work became popular or useful, Hollywood gobbled it up, spit out what it didn't want, and digested the rest.

As was sure to happen, some American writers became more popular than others with Hollywood, and their works were used over and over again. Zane Grey had *The Lone Star Ranger* filmed seven times, a record unsurpassed by any other author. Melville's *Moby Dick,* despite many difficulties in transformation to the screen, was filmed three times, as was one of the most popular of all American novels, *Ben Hur* by Lew Wallace. Ernest Hemingway had *A Farewell to Arms, To Have and to Have Not* and "The Killers" each filmed twice.

In the process, certain authors became more important for the films adapted from their novels and short stories than for the works themselves. Today, W.R. Burnett is almost forgotten, most of his books long out of print, yet some of the films adapted from his fiction are true classics of cinema. *Little Caesar* became a cornerstone of the gangster film. *Law and Order,* based on *Saint Johnson,* is a gritty western classic. The movie version of Burnett's *High Sierra* helped to make Bogart a star. *The Asphalt Jungle* (1950) created a new trend in the gangster genre. Yet today, despite his impressive output, W.R. Burnett is seldom read and little remembered.

But if some authors achieved an importance on film far beyond their importance as literary figures, the opposite is also true; some very important writers never became important at all on film. Even though Hollywood tried to adapt William Faulkner, most of the attempts were failures. Only *Intruder in the Dust* (1951) can be considered a success. No work by Willa Cather or Taylor Caldwell has ever been filmed, although the latter did have several works done as miniseries for television. Among more contemporary authors, James Purdy and Saul Bellow are conspicuously absent.

In examining the precise relationship of American fiction adapted for the American screen, it is easy to start with that most original of all American genres, the western. Here the influence from abroad is nil, and the fictional works deal with and explore the national character in its purest form. The inward soul searching and deep philosophizing are kept to a minimum. Character and action are at the forefront, and what often emerges is the strongest type of visual literature. No other genre can lay such a claim, which is both a blessing and a curse.

While western literature often translated extremely well to the screen, the fiction has produced very few classics or important authors. Authors like Zane Grey and Max Brand, two very prolific writers, can lay claim to vast popularity both during and after their lifetimes, yet neither produced a book that can be said to be more than entertaining. These writers and others like them show their pulp and magazine origins. In addition, serious western writers such as Eugene Manlove Rhodes or Jack Schaefer or Dorothy Johnson have found little recognition outside the genre. The few western writers who have found their novels accepted on a wider scale have succeeded for reasons that have little to do with the western. Tom Lea, the author of *The Wonderful Country,* an outstanding and beautifully written novel of Southwest Texas in the 1880s, had already found success with an earlier novel about bull fighting. Walter Van Tilburg Clark used the western to examine the issue of lynch law justice; interestingly enough, while *The Ox-Bow Incident* found favor with the critics, it failed at the box office, mainly because it did away with the very conventions that the audience expected from the western.

It is through film that western writers have reached a far wider audience than they ever did through their novels and short stories. It is a rare case where the author's books are remembered more clearly than the films made from them. Zane Grey's books are probably better known than any one of the films made from them, mainly because few films made from any of his novels were truly great. Even one of his most famous works, *Riders of the Purple Sage,* filmed four times, never emerged as more than a "B." On the other hand, while Max Brand had over 80 film adaptations, only one became really important. That one film, *Destry Rides Again,* became a classic in the genre when it was made into the 1939 film starring James Stewart and Marlene Dietrich. What is fascinating here is that the film has very little to do with the book except the title. Otherwise, the film was the creation of scenarists Felix Jackson, Gertrude Purcell and Henry Myers. An earlier version of the novel starring Tom Mix made in 1932 stuck closer to the original source, but once again, it was no more than a "B" used as a vehicle for a fading star. Except for a small clique of fans, this version is almost forgotten today. It is ironic that many remember the author for, in one of those rare instances, a film that is far superior to the original work.

In this instance, Brand's reputation is enhanced by a film adaptation, but for most authors, that was not to be the case. There were so many shoddy productions from good, even outstanding, novels and short stories, that the reputations of many authors had to suffer. How could anyone who has seen the film version of Paul Horgan's *A Distant Trumpet* ever want to read the book? Despite being directed by Raoul Walsh, the film was a travesty of the novel, shredding the delicate characterizations and leveling the plot to the barest outline. Relationships between several key characters were either altered or done away with entirely. What showed up on the screen in place of the Pulitzer Prize winning novel was a cliché-dominated cavalry versus Indians story with cardboard cutouts instead of the flesh and blood characters created by Horgan. Certainly this kind of callous treatment was far more the norm than the treatment accorded Max Brand with *Destry Rides Again.*

Still, even in the worst of adaptations, there is a magic. Perhaps it exists in the attempt to turn literature into film. For those who love books, there is a curious relationship that exists between the medium of the printed word and the medium of film. How often do we read a book that we enjoy and hope the film will do the same? It rarely does. Still we keep hoping. And we keep wanting to see the books come alive on the screen as they did in our heads. We know our minds are ultimately more adept at sustaining our fantasies, that films can never touch good books that somehow reach beyond our visceral pleasure to touch our hearts, to touch our souls. No film can possibly do this. Yet we long to see the physical reality of a cherished novel or short story upon the screen. We want the ethereal to become solid, touchable.

The magic exists even beyond this. For a person who loves western films — for that matter, a person who loves films in general — there is always magic in films, even the worst of them. The only thing we ask is that they never bore us. The western is aptly suited for this. With so much action inherent in the formula, even in the serious western, there is little time to bore. It takes a real failure to achieve such ignominy in a western. Certainly it has been done, far too many times, yet for every crashing bore, there are a hundred westerns that have at least a spark of life. Much of this life is present in the literature, too. The filmmakers took the novels and short stories and molded them into western shadows that flickered across silver screens, shadows that were seldom eloquent. But occasionally words and shadows combined in a fortuitous collaboration, and when they did, the magic of the book became magic on the screen. Let us look at the magic that was and the magic that was not.

I : Red Man, White Man

1. East Is West

The American westward movement began the moment the first explorers set foot on the American soil. Thus, the frontier began in the East and gradually moved west of the Mississippi. This great early migration has proven a fertile ground for some American writers, who often drew their material from the struggle between red man and white, even when these struggles existed in the midst of far larger and more complex historical events such as the French and Indian Wars or the American Revolution.

The fiction of the frontier, that vast, unexplored West full of Indians and other natural barriers, begins with James Fenimore Cooper, who wrote what still remains the most famous novel of the frontier, *Last of the Mohicans* (1826). This is actually the second of five novels in *The Leatherstocking Tales,* and despite the awkward characterizations and the blatant sentimentality, its popularity has endured, primarily because of the inclusion of Indian lore and the descriptive powers of Cooper. Even though James Russell Lowell criticised Cooper for portraying the Indian as "white men daubed red," so well did Cooper blend his research and invention that *Last of the Mohicans* remains among our most memorable fiction. Certainly Cooper romanticized the Indians, but he did not falsify them. What he showed was their acute senses, their belief in omens, their stoicism, their customs, their intense tribal pride, their harsh virtues. In doing so, he created a work that has since become as much myth as novel, a book that people know even when they haven't read it.

Last of the Mohicans centers around the siege in 1757 of Fort William Henry located in northern New York. To that destination Major Hayward is escorting Cora and Alice Munro, the daughters of the British commander. They are accompanied by psalm singer David

Gamet and the villainous Huron, Magua. Hawkeye and his Mohican companions, Chingachgook and Uncas, prevent Magua's attempt to capture the girls, but after the fall of Fort Henry and the massacre of the survivors, Cora and Alice fall into the hands of the Huron. Adventure follows adventure until Magua kills Uncas, Cora is killed by another Huron and Magua meets his death from Hawkeye's long rifle. Alice is conducted to safety, and she and Major Hayward will eventually marry. Hawkeye promises to remain forever with his friend Chingachgook, the last of the Mohicans, and together, the two return to the forest.

Cooper's novel with all its adventure and movement was a natural for screen adaptation. D.W. Griffith directed the first of many, a short two-reeler, *Leatherstocking* (Biograph, 1909). Two years later, another two-reeler, *Last of the Mohicans* (Pat Powers, 1911), appeared. However, because of the short running time of less than twenty minutes each, these adaptations covered only a small part of the novel, and it was left to Maurice Tourneur to direct the first full length version of *Last of the Mohicans* (Associated Exhibitors, 1920), which proved to be not only the best adaptation but also an outstanding silent film. Although Tourneur's version takes various liberties, the narrative is swift and lean and strikes a consistent balance between romance and adventure. Cora has a beau, Captain Randolf, a character created for the film. Major Hayward is engaged to Alice. As the story opens, Cora is playing the harp for the group when Uncas arrives with news that the enemy is on the move. From this point, the film follows the first half of the novel with only minor variations. However, things change when Randolf betrays Fort Henry, thus leaving it open for the attack and subsequent slaughter. The last reel returns to the novel for the fight on the cliffs and the death of Cora, Uncas and Magua.

While these variations are rather minor, a far more important change occurs in the relative importance of Hawkeye and Chingachgook. These are Cooper's central characters, but in Tourneur's film, they play secondary roles, appearing first only after Magua's desertion. During the attack on the Fort Henry and the final chase, they are conspicuously absent, arriving only at the last moment like avenging angels to kill the evil Magua and bury the lovers. By taking this approach, Tourneur is able to focus more clearly on the love triangle of Cora, Uncas and Magua. In the end, Cora goes over a cliff after being repeatedly stabbed by Magua, Uncas rolls down the same mountainside and dies grasping Cora's hand, and Magua falls from the cliff after being shot by Hawkeye. Their falls are both literal and symbolic. Uncas and Cora fall because they threatened to break the taboo against racial mixing, Magua because he lusted after a white woman.

The first sound version of *Last of the Mohicans* (Mascot, 1932) is a twelve-chapter serial and, although the novel is particularly adaptive to this kind of treatment, the film is far more amateurish and primitive than the Tourneur version. Hawkeye is played by white haired Harry Carey, a wonderful actor too often cast in serials and low budget "B" films unworthy of his talent. In this case, the casting was perfect since in the novel Hawkeye is nearing fifty, but as a character in the serial, he is given little to do except provide heroics. The romance between Uncas and Cora disappears, fur trappers after gold get caught up in the plot and, in the end, both the Munro sisters survive and Chingachgook dies instead of Uncas. There is little to praise here.

When *Last of the Mohicans* (United Artists, 1936) returned to the screen four years later, much of the original novel returned with it. The characters of Alice and Cora are rightfully restored. There is the French capture of Fort Henry and the massacre that follows, a wonderful piece of villainy pulled off by the most loathsome of all Maguas (Bruce Cabot). The climax sees Uncas struggling with Magua high atop a cliff, and when the evil Huron knocks the young Mohican over the edge, Cora leaps after her lover. Chingachgook then faces Magua, and the two battle it out with tomahawks until the Mohican chops down his adversary.

While this version has many of the same incidents as the novel and the Tourneur film, it introduces one element not present in either — a romance between Hawkeye (Randolph Scott) and Alice (Binnie Barnes). Chingachgook mutters his disapproval. "Hawkeye's heart like water." At the conclusion, as Hawkeye prepares to march off with the British army to fight the French and Indians, he kisses Alice and promises to return to her.

Color was added for *Last of the Redmen* (Columbia, 1947), an inferior remake on all counts. This time Uncas is Hawkeye's only companion. Hymn singer David Gamut has been replaced by young Davy, a brother to the Munro sisters. The French have been relegated to the background, and Magua's villainy takes charge of the whole proceedings. Hawkeye is a miscast Michael O'Shea, but top billing is given to Jon Hall, also miscast, as Major Hayward. Only Buster Crabbe gives a solid performance as Magua. Overall, this film never rises above the level of kiddie matinee.

The Iroquois Trail (United Artists, 1950) claimed to be based on

"Leatherstocking Tales," but in reality seemed to have little to do with the Cooper work. While Hawkeye (George Montgomery) is present, other characters related to *Last of the Mohicans* are conspicuously absent, although Hawkeye does have an Indian stooge called Sagamore. A few characters seem familiar — the lovely daughter of the fort commander, her aristocratic officer fiancé, the stubborn, stiff-necked general, scoundrelly settlers, a Huron renegade. Once again, love finds Hawkeye, but the main thrust is action, and the film moves right along without much pause for characterization or sweeping pageantry. Still, it has its moments, including the climactic Indian attack on the fort, all done with a sense of excitement and verve. For the most part, *The Iroquois Trail* ia a pleasant diversion without any pretensions.

A few other adaptations of Cooper reached the screen. An early two-reel version of *The Deerslayer* (Vitagraph, 1913) was built around a few scenes from the book. In 1941 Republic studios cranked out a version of *The Deerslayer* that the *New York Daily News* called "a refugee from a nickelodeon," an inept film highlighted by a campy performance by Yvonne De Carlo as Wah-Tah, an Indian maiden. Somewhat better is *The Deerslayer* (TCF, 1957) starring Lex Barker as a young white man reared by Mohicans who becomes involved with a trader and his two daughters. The trader has been selling Huron scalps for bounty. When the Hurons capture the old man and threaten to kill him, the Deerslayer arrives to save the day, and for this, is rewarded with the love of one of the of the daughters. Little of the novel made it into the film. *The Pathfinder; or the Inland Sea* (1840) was filmed once (Columbia, 1953), a very loose adaptation in which the Pathfinder (George Montgomery) and Chingachgook (Jay Silverheels) expose French plans to gain control of the Great Lakes. The only other screen version of a Cooper work is *The Pioneers* (Monogram, 1941), a Tex Ritter vehicle that is standard horse opera without any connection to Cooper's novel except the title.

Cooper wrote the most famous novel of the French and Indian wars, but Kenneth Roberts wrote the best with *Northwest Passage* (1937). It tells the story of Major Robert Rogers who in 1759 leads a force of American Rangers against the Indian town of St. Francis in Canada. The journey back is even more torturous than the one going, due in large part to a mixup regarding supplies. Langdon Towne, an artist who becomes a staunch follower of Rogers, narrates the story. Later, Towne accompanies Rogers to England where Rogers schemes to get money to seek the Northwest Passage. Instead, Rogers receives the post of governor of Michilmackinac, but proves unable to handle politics and politicians, and when he finally gets to lead the overland expedition to find the Northwest Passage, it comes to grief. Rogers is thrown in jail on charges of treason and malfeasance. After he is acquitted, he becomes a shady adventurer, drifting from intrigue to intrigue.

Northwest Passage is a brilliant novel. Kenneth Roberts based much of his research on Rogers' own journals and other contemporary histories, and in doing so, created a richly atmospheric work that recaptures an entire period of American history. If there is a weakness, it lies at the expense of Sir William Johnson, who was not nearly so evil and conniving as the novel would have us believe. Also, the first half of the novel with its racing narrative and exciting events is superior to the second half, full of stagey scenes that tend to ramble. Still, all the characters, major and minor, white and Indian, are fully realized.

King Vidor was given the job of filming *Northwest Passage* (MGM, 1940), which was subtitled "Book I: Rogers' Rangers." The title is a misnomer since the action ends long before Rogers begins his search for the fabled passage between the Atlantic and Pacific. Producer Hunt Stromberg and his writers, the talented duo of Laurence Stallings and Talbot Jennings, came up with a fine script for Book I, but when they got around to planning Book II, they couldn't hammer out a workable plot, so the idea of a sequel died.

Northwest Passage opens in 1759 in Portsmouth, New Hampshire, the home of artist Langdon Towne (Robert Young) and his hard-drinking friend Hunk Marriner (Walter Brennan), both of whom are local troublemakers. Langdon has just been expelled from Harvard for drawing a satirical cartoon, and Hunk is constantly ridiculing the local Colonial authorities. At a tavern one night, they are tricked by Major Robert Rogers (Spencer Tracy) into joining his Rangers, an independent American guerrilla force fighting the French and Indians. The first part of the film is strong on comedy, but this changes abruptly as the Rangers prepare for their job, which is killing Indians. The film itself becomes strongly anti-Indian, and Rogers states this forcibly when he says to a British officer, "Those red hellions have come down and hacked and murdered us, burned our homes, stolen our women, brained our babies, scalped stragglers and roasted officers over slow fires for five years. If you were in our place, what would you do?" When the Rangers march into Canada, their stated objective is to kill as many Indians as possible.

In the attack on the village, Towne is wounded, but with Hunk's help, he manages to hang on as the Rangers, their job completed with the destruction of the village, head back for the Colonies. Every step of the way, the men fight the elements, which include Indians and

Iron Eyes Cody smoking a pipe during a lull in the shooting of *Unconquered* (1947), based on Neil H. Swanson's novel.

starvation, and only Rogers' dominating personality keeps the Rangers together. Just as all seems lost and the exhausted men hover on the brink of madness and starvation, a British rescue contingent arrives with needed supplies. Major Rogers receives new orders. He and his Rangers are to search for the Northwest Passage. The final scene shows

Rogers walking toward the horizon and a sequel, which unfortunately was never made.

By 1763 Montcalm had been defeated and the French had been expelled from North America, but before the nation could breathe a deep sigh of relief, Pontiac led a rebellion of eighteen Indian nations, once again setting the frontier ablaze. This is the subject of *Unconquered* (1947) by Neil H. Swanson, which tells of Virginia militiaman Chris Holden who tries to warn the frontier forts of the impending trouble. Many difficulties plague his efforts, including the siege at Fort Pitt and a pesky indentured servant girl Abigail with whom he falls in love and eventually marries. Swanson went to great lengths researching Indian lore and eighteenth century America, but his novel, while highly entertaining, seldom rises above the level of frontiersmen-versus-redskins.

Cecil B. DeMille directed *Unconquered* (Paramount, 1947), and despite the fact that it emerges as campy, overblown and overacted, it is an amazingly satisfying film. The director put Gary Cooper as Chris Holden and Paulette Goddard as Abigail through Indian attacks, torture, burning at the stake, explosions and a plunge over a waterfall. The climactic siege of Fort Pitt is especially well staged with flaming arrows and fireballs criscrossing this way and that, muskets and tomahawks flashing, men dying right and left, all filmed so enthusiastically that 30 extras landed in the hospital. Due to the cliffhanger approach, Hollywood gossips referred to the film as "The Perils of Paulette," but the public loved it. Writing for *Time,* James Agee pointed to the ingredients that made it such a successful film. "*The Unconquered* is Cecil Blount DeMille's florid, $5,000,000 Technicolored celebration of Gary Cooper's virility, Paulette Goddard's femininity and the American Frontier Spirit."

A much better novel of the Colonial frontier, and a novel of real importance, is *The Light in the Forest* (1953) by Conrad Richter. The story opens in 1764 after a treaty between the British and Delaware to repatriate white captives, which includes Johnny Butler, called True Son by the Delaware, who has lived most of his life with the Indians and is himself bitterly anti-white. Conflict arises immediately after his being returned to his real parents when he encounters his Uncle Wilse who, with a group of friends, engages in raids where they senselessly murder Indians. Johnny comes to care about one person in particular, his younger brother Gordie. However, when Wilse kills an Indian friend who has come to see True Son, Johnny flees back to the Delaware. Later, Wilse himself is killed and scalped by Indians. When the Indians try to use Johnny to lure white settlers into an ambush, he sees a young boy who reminds him of Gordie, and he warns the settlers off. For this, Johnny is exiled forever from the tribe.

The film *The Light in the Forest* (Buena Vista, 1958) fails to match the insight of the novel. For one thing, it introduces a romance between True Son (James MacArthur) and Shenandoe (Carol Lynley), a character invented for the film. For another, the character of Del Hardy (Fess Parker) is given a much more significant role. Both of these additions weaken the transformation of True Son into Johnny Butler. Another important weakness is the climax. In the novel, this occurs when True Son fails to lure the boatload of whites into a trap and is cast out by the Indians. In the film, Johnny returns to town where he confronts his uncle Wilse (Wendell Cory), and they battle it out, white man style. As Wilse crawls away licking his wounds, he mutters, "He's white, all right." Johnny and Shenandoe then find an idyllic spot in the forest where they will live with nature.

Obviously aimed at the younger set, *The Light in the Forest* is a simplistic outdoor adventure that fails to match the simple grandeur of its source. None of the novel's beauty or poetry reaches the screen. Most of the characters are flat, wooden and unbelievable. One glaring weakness resides in the character of Wilse, a slimy, despicable man who not only taunts Johnny but also lusts after Shenandoe; yet after the fight with Johnny, he suddenly mends his ways as if he has undergone a religious conversion.

Frontier fiction set during the American Revolution also often uses the Indian rather than the British as the chief antagonist. Such is the case with *The Great Meadow* (1930) by Elizabeth Maddox Roberts, which is less a story of frontier warfare than the study of a woman's problems adjusting to the wilderness. Much of the writing has very poetic touches that compliment the thematic content. Even though the novel takes place from 1774 through 1781, paralleling the main events of the American Revolution, formal history takes a back seat to the life of Diony and Berk Jarvis who marry and then follow the trail of Daniel Boone into Kentucky. There Diony weaves linen during the winter and spins wool during the summer, but in the background lurks danger. One day, Indians swoop down, killing Berk's mother and severely wounding Diony. A few days later, Diony gives birth to her first child. Soon after, Berk goes off to join George Rogers Clarke in his expeditions against the British. A year passes, and word filters back that Berk has been captured and killed by the Indians. Diony is forced by circumstances to remarry. One night, Berk appears at her door. He has been held captive for over a year, but finally escaped, and Diony is now forced by frontier law to choose between the two men, sending one of her husbands away never to see him again. She chooses to reunite with Berk, whom she still loves.

When MGM came to film *The Great Meadow* (MGM, 1931), it assigned Charles Brabin to direct. Brabin had been the first director chosen for the now classic *Ben Hur* (1925), but after disappointing rushes, the studio decided that he was not the man for the job. MGM rehired Brabin in 1930, but three years later while he was helming *Rasputin and the Empress* (1933), Thalburg fired him a second time. It was during these intervening years the he cowrote and directed *The Great Meadow*.

Although the film is a faithful and occasionally moving adaptation, it is at best a lackluster effort; at worst, it is a weakly directed film that, despite its ruggedly authentic look, lacks the poetic fire of the novel. Although many of the stock situations of the pioneering theme have been avoided, the film emerges as no more than soap opera, and the love triangle, a weakness in the novel, is downright silly on the big screen. Eleanor Boardman as Diony and Johnny Mack Brown as Berk show some life, but their scenes together are often trite and unintentionally funny. Worst of all, the film doesn't move. Much of the book is given to Diony's interior monologue, and the exterior events themselves are not enough to keep the film moving. Certainly, it is not always easy to judge an older film by contemporary standards, but the plain truth is that *The Great Meadow,* while appreciated by critics of the time, is terribly dated today.

The Revolutionary frontier is also the subject of *Drums Along the Mohawk* (1936) by Walter D. Edmonds. The novel recounts the efforts of Gil and Lana Martin and their friends and neighbors of the Mohawk Valley in New York to protect their lives and property against attacks by the Indians and Tories. Although the novel occasionally suffers from a lack of focus as the events are dispersed over a number of years, it remains one of our best novels of the American Revolution, a story full of warm, human individuals who are unique and diversified.

In 1939 John Ford made *Drums Along the Mohawk* (TCF, 1939), his first film in color. Previously that same year he had directed *Stagecoach* (United Artists, 1939) and *Young Mr. Lincoln* (TCF, 1939), the latter marking the first time Henry Fonda and Ford collaborated. Now they again joined forces. Although not great John Ford, *Drums Along the Mohawk* is a highly polished and enjoyable film with some vivid touches.

The film opens in Albany where Gil (Fonda) and Lana (Claudette Colbert) are getting married in the home of her wealthy family. After the wedding, they leave in a wagon leading a single cow and head west into the wilderness. They spend their wedding night in an inn where they encounter a sinister man with a dark patch covering one eye (John Carradine), a Tory who is overly concerned with the politics of the Mohawk Valley. The next evening amidst a drenching thunderstorm, they arrive at Gil's cabin, a small, dark hovel compared to her father's mansion back in Albany. In addition to this, Lana is frightened by a friendly Indian who wanders in out of the storm. Such is her introduction to the Mohawk Valley.

Just as Lana is adjusting to her new home, Mohawks force them to flee to the fort for protection, and the savages burn their house and crops. Lana suffers a miscarriage. Homeless and without money, Gil and Lana hire themselves out to work for Mrs. McKlennar (Edna May Oliver), a strong-willed, robust old woman who comes to think of Gil and Lana as her children. Gil marches off to war, and when the soldiers return, Mrs. McKlennar sets up her house as a hospital. Lana finds Gil wounded and unable to walk, and she helps him back to the safety of the house. In a moving monologue, he describes to her the horrors of battle and men dying around him.

In the following spring, Lana delivers their first child, and life seems to be improving for the Martins, but war intrudes once more as the Indians led by the Tory with the eye patch invade the Mohawk Valley, and once again the settlers flee for the protection of the fort. Here the movie makes an important change in the story. In the novel, Gil learns all the necessities of being a hunter, and he is a good shot, but his occupation is farmer, and to woodsmen like his friend Adam Helmer, he is too noisy and clumsy. So, when the fort is under attack, the defenders send Adam through enemy lines to bring back help. However, the film gives the job of saving the fort to Gil. Leaving under the cover of darkness, he is spotted by three Indians who give chase. For most of the night, they seem to be gaining, but as dawn breaks, Gil drops over the horizon and disappears from sight. The next time we see him, he is leading troops back to save the fort.

On most points the novel and film contain the same philosophy regarding the Indians and settlers. With the exception of the Christian, Blue Back (Chief Big Tree), the Indians are demons without any evidence of humanity. Even Blue Back himself serves little purpose except as a comic figure without any attachment to the community. On the other hand, the settlers are shown to be decent, God-fearing people who have a perfect right to take the land from the Indians. These are the people who will make America great.

However, the novel and film deviate in the settlers' view of the Revolution. According to the novel, the people of the Mohawk Valley were an ill equipped rabble whose main concern was the preservation of their farms. They fought only to protect what was theirs and to maintain civil order. But the conclusion of the film shows the Stars and Stripes being hoisted atop the fort as the amazed Adam Helmer (Ward Bond) says, "So that's what we've been fighting for." A warm patriotic glow fills the screen at fade out, which mirrored the political climate of 1939.

An unusual and offbeat story of the early American frontier is the fine short story "Rachel" (1945) by Howard Fast. The story opens in 1788 just after the death of Sam Harvey's wife. The narrator is Sam's young son Davey, who is ten. (A similar viewpoint and structure would later be used by Jack Schaefer in his magnificent *Shane.*) After a period of mourning, Sam takes young Davey in tow and goes to Murry's Fort in search of a new wife, and there for $22 he buys the bondservant Rachel and marries her. From that point, he ignores her and little Davey is outright hostile. Life becomes cold and lonely for Rachel until Jim, an itinerant hunter, shows up and begins to court her. Then Sam's interest in her is piqued. By the time Davey comes around, Jim sees the writing on the wall and moves on to greener pastures. Rachel knows she is accepted when Sam tells his son, "You mind your Ma, Davey."

"Rachel" was transformed into *Rachel and the Stranger* (RKO, 1948). Changes included moving the time to 1820 and Davey's father being called Big Davey (William Holden). Jim (Robert Mitchum) is more of a womanizer than the short story makes him out to be, but Rachel (Loretta Young) is the perfect embodiment of the story's character, a quiet, demure woman who is far stronger on the inside than she first appears.

Rachel and the Stranger is a warm, humorous historical drama. The film sticks to the simplicity of the story and, except in the climatic Indian fight, it is restrained and intelligent, taking its time to develop characters and avoiding the trap of settling for a tale of flamboyant derring-do. Most historical films dealing with pioneers, such as *Unconquered,* have shown them to be either brave, noble heroes or despicable villains, but in *Rachel and the Stranger* they perform as normal people whose foibles are as clearly evident as their strengths. Also, the film suggests the difficult and strenuous life of the frontier and, in conjunction with its restrained characterizations, it becomes a better historical document than most.

Occasionally the exploits of real frontiersmen inspired novels. Such is the case with *The Iron Mistress* (1951) by Paul Wellman, based on the life of Jim Bowie. In New Orleans in 1817, Bowie finds himself entangled in the affairs of an aristocratic Creole family, including their attractive but coldhearted daughter Narcisse. Disappointed in love, Bowie moves on to Texas, becoming involved with the revolution, finally ending up at the Alamo where he is the last defender to die, his knife buried to the hilt in a Mexican soldier. Wellman gives the reader a quasi-biography in which he fills in gaps that history has left blank. However, the book slows when it strains to get inside Bowie's head. On the other hand, when our hero swings into action, the novel is first rate, especially during the great fight against the Indians on the San Saba and the climactic battle of the Alamo. The novel's main fault lies with the characters who are shallow and stereotypical; its main strength is that, as entertainment, it succeeds admirably.

When it came to casting *The Iron Mistress* (Warner Bros., 1952), Warner Bros. made an odd choice. In the novel, Bowie is described the first time he sees Narcisse, the Creole girl with whom he becomes infatuated:

> With discontent he glanced down at himself, for she reminded him of his own vastness and clumsiness, matters of which he had not even been conscious before coming to this city where a tapering hand, a small wrist, and a slight and elegant figure were esteemed as much in a man as in a woman, as marks of gentility.

The film cast Alan Ladd as Bowie, and the "vastness" of Bowie disappeared. The character of Bowie also went through a change. In the novel, he is a ruffian whose very physical presence insures him the role of outcast in New Orleans society, but as portrayed by Ladd, he emerges as the archetypal romantic matinee idol. When Bowie falls in love with the unworthy Narcisse (Virginia Mayo), she rejects him, and he turns to gambling and land speculation. After a battle with a bear, he invents the Bowie knife, a blade of immense proportions that, in the hands of a director more astute than Gordon Douglas, might have come to represent a phallic symbol dominating the film, but very little tension of any kind, including sexual, exists here. Later, Bowie wanders off to Texas where he is reformed by the Governor's daughter (Phyllis Kirk), whom he marries. The film ends with fully one half of the novel—the better half—left untold.

Another frontier figure, Andrew Jackson, surfaces in *The President's Lady* (1951) by Irving Stone, although most of the frontier episodes, including an encounter with Indians, occur during the first third of the novel. Stone also shifts the novel's emphasis to Rachel, who is romantic and subdued, which is the book's fatal flaw. It tries to see Jackson's life through the eyes of Rachel, a passive spectator. The story opens with Rachel returning home with her brother after being divorced by her first husband. It ends with her death in 1826. The bulk of the novel deals with her courtship by Jackson, their marriage and relationship. There are no fictional characters here, and as usual, Stone's research is commendable. But this is closer to biography than fiction; only Rachel's interior monologues and various dialogue sequences seem invented for the book. Still, neither Rachel nor Jackson come fully alive, and the whole thing was done much better in Marquis James' excellent biography of Jackson.

Like the book, the film *The President's Lady* (TCF, 1953) rhapsodizes the love between Jackson (Charlton Heston) and Rachel (Susan Hayward). When they first meet, she is the wife of a philandering businessman, who she leaves for Jackson. After she has been divorced by her first husband for adultery, Jackson and Rachel marry, but two years later they discover that the divorce has not been finalized. They are faced with various humiliations, and at one point, Jackson almost dies defending her honor. Just before Jackson is elected president, Rachel expires in her husband's arms.

The best parts of the film are the early scenes wherein Jackson, a young lawyer, arrives at the frontier station where he meets Rachel, and they make a hazardous journey down the Mississippi. The Indian attack is appropriately tense and exciting. But far too much of the story is taken up with long-winded, wooden dialogue. Added to this is the unimaginative direction of Henry Levin, which can best be described as functional. He tells the story but never allows his camera to comment on or to shade the events. What should have been the emotional highlights of this film, the tearful reunions of Jackson and Rachel, are simply bland and redundant. An attempt at sentimentalized biography, *The President's Lady* is only mildly interesting frontier soap opera.

All attempt at historical accuracy was ignored in *The Mark of Zorro* (1924) and its sequels by Johnson McCulley (1883–1958), which supposedly chronicled daring deeds in early California. The story first appeared as a serial entitled "The Curse of Capistrano" in *All Story Weekly* in 1919, and only after the success of the 1920 film starring Douglas Fairbanks did Grosset and Dunlap issue it as a novel. McCulley was nothing more than a hack with no pretensions at anything other than writing successful adventure stories, and he possessed no originality. His style was bland and functional, his characters transparent and unbelievable. Even the character of Zorro is nothing more than a copy of the Scarlet Pimpernel, created by Baroness Emma Orczy in 1905. The Pimpernel took his name from a flower, Zorro from the fox. Where the Pimpernel protected the aristocracy, Zorro protected the peasants. However, Zorro seems closer to the Lone Ranger than the Scarlet Pimpernel, just another masked man riding around the country trying to right the wrongs of the bad guys. McCulley's novels, including *The Mark of Zorro,* have been out of print for years, and it is just as well. The novels didn't made Zorro famous; it was motion pictures.

The first film version, *The Mark of Zorro* (United Artists, 1920), directed by Fred Niblo, opens with a foreword that declares, "Oppression—by its very nature—creates the power that crushes it. A champion arises—a champion of the oppressed." In early nineteenth century California, Don Diego Vega (Douglas Fairbanks) returns from Spain to discover that his father has been replaced as Governor by the tyrannous Alvardo and his henchmen Captain Ramon and Sergeant Garcia. Diego immediately adopts the disguise of an effeminate fop who displays squeamish distaste of violence. Using this masquerade, he covers his activities as the masked avenger Zorro, a devil of a fighter who constantly embarrasses Ramon and Garcia whenever they cross swords with him. Indians and the Church are his particular objects of protection. At one point, he carves a Z on the forehead of a soldier who has mistreated an Indian; he has another flogged for sentencing a priest to be flogged. When the lady Lolita's family tries to arrange a marriage between her and Diego, she balks at his cowardly ways. Even Diego's own father is disappointed in his son. At last, Diego as Zorro leads a revolution that overthrows the wicked governor, and he regains the respect of his father and wins the love of Lolita, the woman who has spurned him as Don Diego Vega but loved him as Zorro.

The Mark of Zorro began the swashbuckling career of Douglas Fairbanks, Sr., and set the style for many subsequent swashbucklers such as *The Scarlet Pimpernel* (Alexander Korda, 1934) and *The Son of Monte Cristo* (Edward Small, 1940). Also, the film is directed with flair. There are several spectacular swordfights and a fast paced, exciting chase sequence during which Zorro outmaneuvers the Governor's soldiers with fantastic acrobatics, swinging from balcony to balcony, vaulting over walls and under wagons, sliding through windows and leaping from roof to roof. The lighthearted approach to the action carries through to the end when Sergeant Garcia, one of the chief villains, frustrated at being unable to defeat Zorro, joins him. Also, Fairbanks added to the atmosphere with his nonchalant, devil-may-care performance, dashing through the film with a contagious enthusiasm.

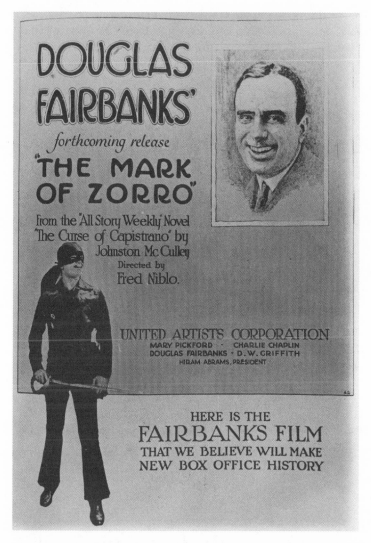

Ad in *Motion Picture News* of Nov. 20, 1920, for *The Mark of Zorro* (1920) based on the Johnson McCulley serial, "The Curse of Capistrano."

In 1936 Republic Studios began a whole cycle of films devoted to Zorro and his imitators. The first was the twelve-chapter serial *The Vigilantes Are Coming* (Republic, 1936), the story of the Eagle (Robert Livingston), a masked avenger who tries to save California from the Russians in 1844. It is credited as an original story, and McCulley is not given credit, yet for all intents and purposes, it is the Zorro story. The success of the serial inspired the studio to make the *The Bold Caballero* (Republic, 1936), this time claiming the McCulley novel as its source. Even though filmed in color, it was a low budget action feature wherein Zorro (again Robert Livingston) once again fights the evil Commandante (Sig Rumann). Republic followed with two more twelve-chapter serials aimed at entertaining the kids. *Zorro Rides Again* (Republic, 1937) is a modern western wherein a descendant of Don Diego Vega (John Carroll) rides as Zorro to oppose the evil intentions of railroad magnate Marsden (Noah Beery); *Zorro's Fighting Legion* (Republic, 1939) is set in old California with Zorro (Reed Hadley) fighting a mysterious villain known as Don-del-Oro, who wants to control Southern California for its gold mines on Indian lands. While each was typical of Republic Studios, fast-paced and smoothly done, they exposed the pulp origins of the original McCulley story.

Then, in 1940, 20th Century–Fox decided to remake *The Mark of Zorro* (TCF, 1940) as a vehicle for its top male star, Tyrone Power. Instead of using the Fairbanks version as a model, the studio looked to Errol Flynn's *The Adventures of Robin Hood* (Warner Bros., 1938), opting for less acrobatic stunts and more story substance. Even the music score by Alfred Newman sounded suspiciously like a Korngold score. Also, straight from *Robin Hood* came Basil Rathbone to play the chief villain, Captain Estaban Pasquale. Sergeant Garcia became Sergeant Gonzales, and in doing so, suffered a considerable demotion in importance, no longer the comic foil for Zorro that Noah Beery had played so cleverly in the 1920 version. Also, the writers showed more concern for the downtrodden peasants, which may have mirrored the concern of liberal and left wing writers over the Spanish Civil War.

Certain touches make this an outstanding swashbuckler. For one, it invokes a good deal of humor as Power alternates between swishing and swashing, first appearing as the scented popinjay who flutters about waving his handkerchief and sniffing his snuff, then donning his black mask and cape to ride the countryside carving his Zs hither and yon with *macho gusto*. For another, there are some excellent action sequences, including the finest bit of swordplay ever put on celluloid. In tight quarters, the blades clammer and clash, cold steel resounding within the four walls, until at last Diego penetrates the Captain's defenses, running him through.

After the Governor discovers Diego's identity and throws him in the dungeon, Diego returns to his foppish ways to escape. He dupes the jailer into believing that he can change a copper coin into gold, and when the jailer insists that Diego do it for him, Diego steals his gun and forces the man to open the cell door. At this point, the hidalgos are brought under guard before the Governor, who tells them that he has captured Diego who is in reality Zorro. "Have you seen this trick, father," asked Diego as he whips out the pistol. The fight is on! Diego breaks free, and while the hidalgos hold off the Governor's men, he fights his way across the rooftops, drops to the gate and throws it open, allowing the peasants to flood through and win the day. At the conclusion, Diego embraces Lolita (Linda Darnell) and announces that he will settle in California and raise fat children. Taking his sword, he hurls it into the ceiling where it will hang until needed again. It's a rousing finish to an adaptation that is far superior to its source.

In name only, Republic brought Zorro back in *Zorro's Black Whip* (Republic, 1944), a twelve-chapter serial that never once mentioned Zorro, and the masked rider called the Whip was really a woman (Linda Stirling). Four years later, the same studio followed up with another twelve-chapter serial, *The Ghost of Zorro* (Republic, 1949), in which a grandson of the original Zorro (Clayton Moore before he became the Lone Ranger) battles outlaws who are trying to prevent a telegraph company from completing a line. It was economy all the way with much stock footage from previous entries. Each chapter was relatively short, and it moved right along at a fast clip. Two other Zorro-like serials, *Don Daredevil Rides Again* (Republic, 1951) and *Man with the Steel Whip* (Republic, 1954), ended the cycle, each one deteriorating further because of dwindling budgets. By the time these last two serials were made, Republic had lost the right to use the Zorro name, so they dropped all reference to the McCulley character and created replacements, yet cannibalized footage from the previous Zorro films. Except in name, they were the Zorro character.

In 1960 Disney released *The Sign of Zorro* (Buena Vista, 1960), but this was only a compilation of several of the television shows and looked extremely embarrassing on the big screen. The plot is the now familiar one where Don Diego (Guy Williams) returns home to California and finds it in the hands of the unscrupulous Commandant. He plays the fop while at the same time donning the disguise of Zorro. If the film has a redeeming factor, it lies in its sense of humor, especially in the characters of Bernardo (Gene Sheldon) and Sergeant Garcia (Henry Calvin). Otherwise, it is bland and without distinction.

To date, the last American film incarnation of Zorro is the spoof *Zorro, the Gay Blade* (Melvin Simon/FOX, 1981). Here there are two Zorros (both George Hamilton), Don Diego Vega and his twin brother,

Bunny Wiggleworth, the latter who is gay. Due to an unfortunate accident, Diego is injured and Bunny takes his place fighting Estaban (Ron Leibman), a cruel dictator who is oppressing the people. The film is played for laughs with most aimed at the gay Zorro, a stereotype that is more offensive than comical. Overall, the film is predictable and boring. The sense of parody might work if were a parody of the McCulley story, which it is not. It is, instead, a parody of the previous Zorro films. What the screenwriter and director fail to understand is that, in the best of the Zorro films, a subtle element of self-parody already exists.

In one way or another, all historical fiction is distorted and inaccurate — by the very fact of its being fiction. A writer like Johnson McCulley simply dispensed with any attempt at reality and created his own imaginary world. Who's to say his motivations were bad? After all, he wrote with a specific audience in mind, and he probably did not have the talent to rise above hack. On the other hand, writers such as James Fenimore Cooper, Kenneth Roberts and Walter D. Edmonds attempted, within boundaries limited by their own conceptions of reality, to give us accurate pictures of the early American frontier. Much of our conception of this period of American history is certainly influenced by these fictional narratives as well as the film adaptations, regardless of whether those adaptations followed the books.

2. Mountain Men

Before the settlers, even before the explorers, came the Mountain Men, that hearty breed of hunters and trappers, who opened the West to the very civilization they sought to escape. In the end, they were either driven deeper into the mountains or were assimilated by onrushing civilization. The mountain men have provided material for a number of writers whose fiction made it to the screen in adaptations of varying quality.

Harvey Fergusson wrote one of the finest novels of the mountain men when he penned *Wolf Song* (1927). In his introduction to *Followers of the Sun* (aka *The Santa Fe Omnibus*) which included *Wolf Song,* Fergusson stated, "What ails the huge and infantile body of our conventional western romance . . . is not that its stories are melodramatic but that its heroes and heroines are lifeless." Fergusson's style is a blend of the realistic and romantic, but his main concern is always on the characters and their relationship to the land.

Wolf Song opens with Sam Lash and two companions coming down out of the mountains to sell their furs at Taos, buy their supplies, and have a good time, which includes sexual escapades with the señoritas. At a dance, Sam meets Lola Salazar, the daughter of Don Solomon Salazar, owner of a large rancho and a man who hates all gringos. Sam and Lola immediately fall in love, and in the night, Sam and his companions steal her away. Sam takes her to Bent's Fort where they are married, but soon, despite her fears that he will be killed, Sam returns to his beloved mountains. However, his mind is no longer on what goes on around him but on Lola, and he lays himself open for tragedy. A Cheyenne, Black Wolf, steals Sam's outfit, and Sam trails the Indian. In a hand to hand struggle, Sam gets the upper hand, and drives his knife into Black Wolf's belly.

Sam surveys his own wounds and finds a cut under one shoulder blade, long but shallow. He will lose blood, but he isn't "rubbed out." He manages to make his way back to Taos and Lola. Accepted by her father, he will begin a new life, no longer a mountain man but rather a son for the old Don, a son who will help to tame the wild land he once roamed.

Fergusson did not believe that his novel lent itself to a motion picture, but nevertheless Paramount filmed *Wolf Song* (Paramount, 1929), casting Gary Cooper in the role of Sam Lash and Lupe Velez as Lola. While the surface story remains, the problem is that much of the novel's interior dialogue explains the actions of Sam and Lola, and when the film fails to give us any insight into their actions, their motivations seem unclear and insignificant. In the novel, Lola is at once afraid of giving up her life of comfort and at the same time irresistibly drawn to Sam. It is almost a spur of the moment decision to flee with him. In the film, Sam crawls through Lola's window, and without a second thought of how this wild-looking specimen of humanity is going to care for her, she permits him to spirit her away. Lola's final victory over Sam, a victory of the civilizing instinct, comes in the novel when she realizes that Sam, wounded and alone, has returned to her because he needs her. "Just as before, it was his weakness that softened her." In the film she takes him back because she feels sorry for him. He is a pathetic, wounded animal. The father, who holds a gun on Sam as he lies bleeding on the steps of the hacienda, relents because he sees how much his daughter loves the mountain man. His own feelings and needs do not enter into his decision to spare Sam's life.

Additional changes were made in the script. A kindly Mexican priest who befriends the lovers has been dropped. In the novel his presence is important because he helps Sam bridge the gap between his world and Lola's. The conclusion of the novel hinges upon the priest's explanation of why the old Don has had a change of heart regarding Sam. Without this, the Don's sparing of Sam's life and his acceptance of the mountain man seems incomprehensible. In the novel, Sam confronts only Black Wolf, but in the film, the challenge had to be much greater. Black Wolf has several braves with him on a raiding party. Sam kills Black Wolf's companions, but not without receiving a couple of wounds himself. Then he fights Black Wolf, knives flashing in the sun, until Sam emerges victorious. Only then does he go crawling back to Lola.

Originally made as a silent, the film was advertised as a "part-talkie" because the studio added two songs for Lupe Velez, who is downright silly when she warbles. During her singing, all action stops, but the film is so slow, the deliberate change of pace isn't apparent. Harvey Fergusson was also displeased by Velez's — as he called it — "pneumatic bosom" bouncing through the picture. He also felt that the script concentrated too much on romance and missed the main thrust of the novel. Certainly the love scenes are played with too many smoldering looks and slow embraces, and whenever Cooper is about to kiss Velez, he studies her forehead, her eyes, her nose, her lips, while his own face is twisted in pain as if he has a bad case of gas. "Lupe Velez," said *Motion Picture News,* "indulges in a flock of respiratory acrobatics whenever she has a love scene with Gary." One nude bathing scene that might have enlivened the proceedings was left on the cutting room floor. In addition, director Victor Fleming used too many close ups, and whenever he attempted to stress a point, people turn their heads so slowly that they appear half asleep. The sluggishness of the characters is carried over to the story, which moves slower than Sam crawling down the Rockies. Amazingly enough, the film proved to be a hit, although the story and acting had little to do with its success. The off-screen romance between Gary Cooper and Lupe Velez plus a cross-country publicity campaign helped to deceive an unwary public.

The most popular novel about mountain men remains *The Big Sky* (1947) by A.B. Guthrie, Jr. This is not a romantic novel, not Leatherstocking, but a mature, even *noir* examination of a way of life that has since become a part of the American experience. The story opens in 1830 in Kentucky where seventeen-year-old Boone Caudill runs away from home. On the way to Louisville, he meets Jim Deakins, and together the two make their way to St. Louis where Boone hopes to find his Uncle Zeb. Boone and Jim join a keel boat, the *Mandan,* owned by the Jourdonnais, who is going up the Missouri to trade with the Blackfoot. On board is Teal Eye, a ten-year-old Blackfoot maiden who Jourdonnais hopes will be his ticket to trading with her people. Indians attack the boat and kill most of the crew. Only Boone, Jim, and Dick Summers, a mountain man, escape. Several years elapse while Boone and Jim learn from Dick Summers the ways of the mountains, and all the time, Boone wonders about Teal Eye, who disappeared from the *Mandan* just before the raid. Boone finds Teal Eye, and they settle down with her people, many of whom have been rubbed out by small-pox. But Boone's brooding nature causes friction between Teal Eye and himself, and his inability to deal with the situation causes her to turn to Jim. When Boone bursts into his tepee and finds Teal Eye in the arms of his friend, he shoots Jim, killing him. Distraught, Boone goes to see

Lobby card for *The Big Sky* (1952). Notice that director Howard Hawks is listed in big, bold type while author A.B. Guthrie, Jr., is relegated to very small type.

Dick Summers to whom he confesses that he killed Jim. "It's like it's all sp'iled for me now, Dick," says Boone. "Teal Eye and the Teton and all. Don't know as I ever can go back, Dick. Goddamn it! Goddamn it!"

Guthrie attempted to portray the trappers and mountain men as they really were, and this forced him to deal with their barbaric vices as well as their romantic resourcefulness and fortitude. The brutality and squalor of the period come through with amazing clarity, but therein lies one of the faults of the novel. Guthrie's mountain men would be more believable if they were more legendary, precisely the way that Vardis Fisher handled them in *Mountain Man*. Though a few tall tales are spun around the campfires and at Rendezvous, they are too few and far between. Also, Guthrie never attempts to plumb the consciousness of the Indians except Teal Eye, and then only when she is drawn into the white man's world.

Even when all the defects are considered, what remains is an extraordinary first novel, a book whose faults are to a large extent compensated for by the author's understanding of the mountain men and their environment. The novel is a celebration of a way of life from the rebellious beginning when Boone runs away from home until its dark conclusion after he shoots Jim and leaves his mountains for good. It is also the story of the land, that great wilderness covered by the big sky under which Boone and the people of his world exist.

When Howard Hawks decided to film *The Big Sky* (RKO, 1952), he chose Dudley Nichols to write the screen play. What emerged was a story that covered only the first third of the novel and even altered those events. In the canon of Hawks' work, this is a significant, although underrated, film; as an adaptation of Guthrie's novel, it goes its own way. After Boone (Dewey Martin) saves Jim's (Kirk Douglas) life in the Kentucky woods, the two head west where they come across Uncle Zeb (Arthur Hunnicutt), who is working for Jourdonnais (Stephan Geray). They join the Frenchmen aboard the *Mandan* and head up river for Blackfoot country. On board is Teal Eye (Elizabeth Threatt), a maiden princess in her early twenties. Boone hates all Indians because he believes that one was responsible for his brother's death, and he treats Teal Eye with contempt. Yet he is also attracted to her. Jim, too, falls in love with her. On the way up-river, the boat is attacked several times by Streak (Jim Davis), a villainous mountain man who works for the fur company trying to keep outsiders out of Blackfoot territory and a character created especially for the film. But the group overcomes all the obstacles, finally reaching its destination. All along, Teal Eye's feelings about the two men remains a mystery, but she finally says that she loves Jim like a brother. That night she and Boone spend together, and the next morning when he emerges from her tepee, Zeb tells Boone that, according to Blackfoot law, he has married Teal Eye. As the boat pulls out heading back down river, Boone jumps aboard, choosing to go with Jim and Uncle Zeb rather than remain. But that night when the boat camps beside the river, he returns to Teal Eye.

In the novel, Uncle Zeb is a minor character appearing in only a few early scenes, but in the film, he takes over the responsibilities of Dick Summers. As off-screen narrator, Uncle Zeb gives the story added warmth and insight. In an especially eloquent moment, Zeb describes how, bringing civilization further and further west, the white man unfailingly spoils the land, and the Indians are rightfully resentful. Despite all of this, he still loves the frontier. He also gives the film the one significant ingredient lacking in the novel—a sense of humor. An excellent example of this is the famous scene when Jim has an infected finger amputated. After getting Jim drunk, Zeb cuts the finger off at an unexpected moment. Jim reacts with laughter, but when he remembers that an Indian believes that he cannot get to heaven if a part of his anatomy is missing, he crawls in the dust looking for the missing digit. However, it is too bad that Dick Summers is dropped because he is such an important character, not only to *The Big Sky* but also in Guthrie's two sequels, *The Way West* and *Fair Land, Fair Land.* Still, the character of Zeb is so original and so important within the framework of the film that the change seems warranted.

Howard Hawks seldom adapted literary works, but when he did, he did not feel compelled to be faithful to the source. Even though filmed in national parks, Hawks pays little attention to the wilderness. To Hawks, the relationship between Boone and Jim is more important than scenery. It is this relationship which ultimately drives Boone back to Teal Eye. For Boone, friendship with a man is more important than loving a woman. For Jim, the opposite is true. Jim would have gladly stayed with Teal Eye, but she loves Boone. When Boone chooses to go back with the men, the friendship between the two is ruptured, and the only way Boone can repair it is to return to Teal Eye.

While *Wolf Song* and *The Big Sky* are both important novels of the mountain man, the best is Vardis Fisher's *Mountain Man: A Novel of Male and Female in the Early American West* (1965), a magnificent book that won the Wrangler Award from the National Cowboy Hall of Fame for the Best Western Historical Novel of 1965. The central character, Sam Minard, is based on the legend of John "Liver Eating" Johnson, a mountain man who supposedly killed over two hundred Crow Indians in a bloody vendetta after the killing of his Indian wife. Sam is an interesting character, playing Bach and Mozart on his mouth organ as he wanders through the mountains, singing arias and quoting poetry, but when the time comes, he can be as vicious and barbaric as any Indian. After Crow Indians kill his wife and unborn child, he declares war on the whole Crow nation and proceeds to kill any and all braves sent against him. To identify his handiwork, Sam cuts off the right ear of each of his victims. When he is captured by the Blackfoot, a chief spits in Sam's face, and the mountain man vows vengeance. Escaping from the Indians, Sam crosses two hundred miles of frozen wilderness to safety, a feat that in itself becomes a legend. When Sam and the Blackfoot chief meet again on the battlefield, Sam "was then on top of him, bloody knife in hand, and while the stunned chief lay helpless Sam took his scalp."

Incorporated into the story of Sam Minard is also the story of Kate, a woman whose husband and three children are slaughtered by Indians and who becomes crazed with grief. Finding her, Sam builds the woman a cabin, and she lives a dreamlike existence unable to communicate with anyone except her dead children. It is to Kate's place that Sam crawls when he escapes from the Blackfoot. After her death, Sam makes peace with the Crows, and then heads deeper into the mountains and valleys he loves.

Mountain Man is more than a story of cruelty and revenge. Even though filled with plenty of blood and guts, the novel is a paean to the freedom of the Old West, full of myth and legend, bigger than life. Fisher carefully recreates the self-sufficient daily routine of the mountain man, but he encompasses more humor and more barbarity than either Fergusson or Guthrie, and the novel is not nearly as dark and as brooding as *The Big Sky.* The major impression here is the heroism of the mountain man to whom self-reliance and freedom were the norm.

On the screen, *Mountain Man* became *Jeremiah Johnson* (Warner Bros., 1972). Much of the early part of the film explains how Johnson (Robert Redford) arrives from the East and heads into the Rockies, an inexperienced novice who meets up with Bear Claw (Will Geer) who teaches him the ways of a mountain man. These scenes were invented for the film. From this point on, there are certain surface similarities with the novel, but the depth and insight of Vardis Fisher's novel completely vanishes. After Johnson learns his trade and leaves Bear Claw, he happens upon a woman and her son whose family has been massacred by Indians. Driven mad by her experiences, the mother insists that Johnson take her boy. Having acquired a son, Johnson then takes a wife, an Indian maiden called Swan. Leading a rescue party to free settlers trapped in the mountains, Johnson is forced to cross a sacred burial ground of the Crows. Upon returning home, he discovers that the Crows have killed his wife and the boy in retaliation. He sets out to exterminate the Crow nation. In one scene, he bursts into a Crow encampment, killing all but one Indian who escapes. Afterward, he lies down among the corpses to rest. At last, sick of the killing, Johnson makes peace with the Indians, and then heads deeper into the wilderness that he loves.

The differences between the novel and film are quite vast. The wonderfully barbaric Sam Minard who plays the mouth organ and sings opera but who is capable of incredibly savage deeds is replaced by a flat, romantic, back-to-nature symbol that never emerges as a fully developed character. A far more innovative film would have followed the lead of the novel by giving us a fully matured mountain man as protagonist. Along with the disappearance of Sam has also gone the mythic nature of the novel, the interplay and tall tales of the mountain men. Also, much of the terrible violence of the novel, so necessary to the scheme of things, is toned down until it is almost nonexistent. Still, the movie draws some strengths from the novel. Both offer sympathetic and accurate portraits of the Indians. But the main strength is that in both the landscape is so effectively presented that it often begins to dominate the characters and the plot.

Similar in plot to *Mountain Man* is *Yellowstone Kelly* (1957) by Henry Wilson Allen, written under the pseudonym of Clay Fisher. Like Vardis Fisher, Allen based his novel on an actual historical personage, Luther Sage Kelly, a genuine mountain man who General Nelson A. Miles called "a hero in war, a true American patriot in times of peace," who the Sioux called "The Little Man with the Strong Heart" and who other scouts called Yellowstone Kelly. Born in 1849, Kelly lived to be 79, and his life was full of many adventures including his time as scout for General Miles, as an Alaskan explorer and as a government official in the Philippines where he led the inhabitants of the province of Suriago in defense of an attack and siege by escaped convicts and outlaws. But *Yellowstone Kelly* takes place only during 1875–76 while Kelly is a wolf hunter and later a scout in the Yellowstone Basin. Here he comes in contact with Hunkpapa Sioux led by Gall from whom he rescues a young Crow girl. When she is retaken by Gall and his braves, Kelly sets out to get her back. While *Yellowstone Kelly* never matches the power or grandeur of *Mountain Man,* the final encounter between Kelly and the Sioux chief avoids the cliches inherent in the material and provides a powerful and touching conclusion.

The film *Yellowstone Kelly* (Warner Bros., 1959) is a disappointment. Kelly (Clint Walker) is a big, beefy scout who manages to fall foul of both the army and the Sioux, but he survives both and prevents an Indian outbreak. He also finds true love in the arms of his Indian maiden (Andrea Martin). In the novel as well as in reality, Kelly was a small but powerfully built man, thus when the Sioux call him "The Little Man with the Strong Heart," it makes sense. When he and Gall battle in hand-to-hand combat, the more muscular Indian wins in a titanic struggle, but Gall spares Kelly's life becuase he so admires his adversary's fighting spirit. As far as romance goes, the novel's ending is rather downbeat. The Indian maiden, Crow Woman, is driven almost insane from hunger yet chooses to stay with Gall and his warriors rather than go with Kelly. If the film had stuck more closely to the novel, it might have avoided the standard cliches that relegated it to the second half of double bills.

A darker version of the mountain man cum Indian scout is explored in *The Gilded Rooster* (1947) by Richard Emery Roberts. Set in 1863, it chronicles the exploits of Jed Cooper, an uncivilized mountain man who becomes entangled in the lives of the individuals in an unnamed fort somewhere in the Rockies. Jed is drawn to Corinna Gunne, the wife of the newly arrived Captain Gunne, and finds himself in conflict with the commander of the fort, Major Bonwitt, who is also attracted to her. Even though Corinna and Jed come close to consummating their desires, she holds back, frightened by his wild nature. In a battle against the Sioux, Jed kills Captain Gunne, then returns to the fort. Later, to atone for his deed, he rides to Fort Laramie in the dead of winter in order to get help. His feet frozen, he faces amputation, but with pistol in hand, he holds off the doctor and others for days until he finally dies. His death is symbolic of the death of the mountain man, the death of a way of life.

Early in *The Last Frontier* (Columbia, 1955), the film version of *The Gilded Rooster,* the old fur trapper Gus (James Whitmore) says, "Civilization is creeping up on us, lads." What keeps creeping up in this film are events and characters created for the big screen. Major Bonwitt becomes Captain Riorden (Guy Madison), second in command to the new Col. Marsden (Robert Preston), whose very name foreshadows his warlike attitudes. Col. Marsden's wife Corinna (Anne Bancroft) becomes the main attraction for Jed (Victor Mature), who has taken a job as army scout after being forced out of trapping by the Sioux. When Jed leaves Marsden after the latter has fallen in a bear trap and returns to the fort, Capt. Riorden, Gus and Corinna persuade him to go back after the Colonel. Marsden later is conveniently rubbed out by the Sioux, and Jed settles down to be civilized by Corinna.

The film has some intriguing touches, the most interesting of which is the character of Jed. In the novel, although he is a man of honor and some sensitivity, he is brutish and sulking, often failing to understand the ways of civilization. In the film, Jed is comically naive, a noble savage who is civilized by the love of a good woman. Only slightly less interesting is Robert Preston's portrayal of Marsden, a martinet of a colonel who wants to make up for his Civil War blunders but instead presents the Sioux with an easy victory. Least interesting is the substitute happy ending, which finds Jed emasculated by civilization, a corporal in the army, dismissing his men and rushing into the arms of the waiting Corinna.

The days when hunters wiped out the great buffalo herds are chronicled in *The Last Hunt* (1954) by Milton Lott, a book that Carlos Baker called the best American novel of the year. Like Jed in *The Gilded Rooster,* Sandy McKenzie helps to destroy the world in which he lives, slaughtering the buffalo for their hides and leaving the carcasses to rot. Sandy takes on a partner, Charley Gilson, and together with a half-breed youngster, Jimmy, and an old skinner called Woodfoot, they set out after the buffalo. When Charley forcibly takes an Indian mistress, tensions develop over the girl. Sandy is too kind and sensitive to accept Charley's callous treatment of the woman, and he also finds himself falling in love with her.

The bare bones outline of the novel makes it sound melodramatic, but Lott handles the characters, atmosphere and action so well that it always rings true. The same cannot be said for the film *The Last Hunt* (MGM, 1956), mainly because the studio, believing that director Richard Brooks's savage indictment of the buffalo slaughter meant death at the box office, mutilated the final cut. Still, what remains is an intriguing film despite the additional handicap of bad casting. Robert Taylor as the Indian-hating Charlie Gibson is too old for the part, and Stewart Granger as the older hunter who has wearied of all the killing seems out of place with his British accent. Both the roles of Jimmy (Russ Tamblyn) and the Indian Maiden (Debra Paget) cry out for Indian actors, especially in light of the film's concentration on authentic details. Only Lloyd Nolen as Woodfoot seems perfectly cast in light of the novel, displaying all the complexities, emotional as well as physical, of the character created by Lott.

The strong points of the film far outweigh the negative ones, however. Buffaloes have never been shown to such advantage. The great shaggy beasts roam majestically across the prairie, sometimes stampeding, their hooves pounding like thunder, and it is a definite shock to see them actually slain before our eyes. Bullets crash into their heads, and they collapse into heaps. Filmed during the "thinning" at Custer State Park in South Dakota, which is done to keep the herd from getting too large, the sequences are appalling and disturbing. The slaughter also sets a climate for the rest of the film. The demoralizing influence of the slaughter upon the characters takes its toll. When Charley pursues the Indians who have stolen his horses, he slaughters them just as he does the buffalo, and we understand just how far he has fallen.

The climaxes of the novel and film diverge considerably. The novel's climax happens in two parts, years separating each. Sandy searches for the Indian girl who has long ago run away from Charley, and when he wanders into an agency of starving Indians, he finds her, and together they ride out. A year later, while still hunting buffalo, Charley, half out of his mind, freezes to death, wrapped in the hide of a buffalo he has killed. In the film, Charley hunts down Sandy and the Indian maiden, finally trapping them in a cave. Because night is almost upon them, Charley warns Sandy not to come out, that they will settle their differences with morning's first light. During the night, a storm comes up, and the temperature plummets. Sandy and the girl huddle in robes by a fire inside the cave. Charley is freezing when he manages to kill a sacred white buffalo, skin it and wrap himself in the hide. When morning comes, Sandy leaves the cave knowing that he is no match for Charley with a gun. But when he finds Charley, there will be no showdown. Charley is dead, frozen during the night, the ice encrusted hide hugging him in a deadly embrace.

The film is often very good, and the scenes of the buffalo slaughter are especially powerful. Considering that MGM did not know how to handle *The Last Hunt* and mutilated the film before its release, it is a wonder that it retains the power it does. Despite the film's failure at the box office, director and screenwriter Richard Brooks must be commended on his fine adaptation of Lott's novel, a chilling and somber indictment of the nature of man.

3. Cavalry to the Rescue

James Warner Bellah wrote a number of short stories picturing the cavalry on the frontier, most of which appeared in *The Saturday Evening Post*. This magazine had a long standing policy against showing the Indian point of view, and Bellah's own feeling toward Indians paralleled the *Post*'s. In his novels and short stories, the Indians were usually no more than a force of nature to be subdued by the American military. Often the tribes are not even mentioned. In "Massacre," a typical Bellah story for the *Post*, his description of the Indians is unappealing and unromantic:

> The smell of an Indian is resinous and salty and rancid. It is the wood smoke of his tepee and the fetidity of his breath that comes of eating body-hot animal entrails. It is his uncured tobacco and the sweat of his unwashed body. It is animal grease in his hair and old leather and fur, tanned with bird lime and handed down unclean from ancestral bodies long since gathered to the Happy Lands.

The central character of Bellah's cavalry stories is Flintridge Cohill, an officer from Virginia who has come to understand the frontier and its ways. He often finds himself in conflict with his superior officers who fail to see clearly what their actions will cause.

John Ford adapted four of Bellah's stories into three films, his cavalry trilogy. Typical is *Fort Apache* (RKO, 1948), based on "Massacre" (1947). As in the case of most short stories adapted for the screen, the story itself became only an outline. Major Owen Thursby, who is obviously patterned after Custer, ignores the advice of his junior officers and leads his men into battle against the forces of Stone Buffalo. Cohill is one of the men who advises against the rash move but who obeys his commander's orders. The result is that most of Thursby's men are wiped out by a superior Indian force, and Thursby, understanding the magnitude of his defeat, commits suicide on the battlefield. First on the scene, Cohill covers up the suicide by removing the gun from Thursby's hand. In the end, Cohill is left with the understanding of life's inevitable defeats.

Ford and scenarist Frank Nugent opened up the film and introduced many new characters. Lieutenant Colonel Owen Thursby (Henry Fonda) and his daughter (Shirley Temple) arrive from the East to take over a Western outpost. Thursby immediately brings a new discipline to Fort Apache, and he comes into conflict with Captain Kirby York (John Wayne). When the Apaches leave their reservation, York persuades the Apache leader that he will be listened to and treated with respect if he meets with Thursby, but Thursby's rigidity forces a conflict. In a speech taken almost directly from Bellah's story, Thursby says of Cochise and the Apaches, "They are recalcitrant swine and must be made to feel it." Then to his translator, he says, "Tell him I find him without honor. Tell him they're not talking to me but to the United States Government. Tell him the government orders them to return to the reservation. And tell them if they have not started by dawn, we will attack."

Even though the feeling persists of two opposing forces moving toward an inevitable confrontation, Ford gives the Indians far more humanity than Bellah. Thursby forces the Indians into a fight, one in which the Apaches will win, yet as Cochise stands on a hilltop and gathers a handful of dirt, then tosses it away, the tragedy is etched on his face. He understands that in the end, he and his people will lose. Against Captain York's advice, Thursby leads his men in a reckless charge against what he considers to be the retreating Apaches. Instead, he bungles his way into a trap, and he and his whole force, with the exception of York and a few men left with the supply wagons, are massacred. It is a useless gesture, one which should never have happened.

In another scene lifted from the story, Thursby is wounded, and York rides to the rescue, picking him off the ground and offering to carry him to safety. Thursby refuses and says, "When you lead this troop, mister, and I expect you will shortly, then lead it." He then takes York's horse and rides off to die with his men.

However, the conclusion reached by the film is far different from that of the story. Thursby does not commit suicide but rather is killed by the Apaches. In the last scene, York, now commander of Fort Apache, speaks of the heroic "Thursby's charge," maintaining the lie for the good of the service. His rigid stance and the same desert cap that Thursby wore earlier show us that York has learned from Thursby.

Thursby may have ignored opinions and made bad decisions, but his men always knew he was in command. This is why they stood by him in death, and this is the lesson that York has learned from him.

After the success of *Fort Apache,* John Ford looked around for another property that would work commercially and also express his vision of military glory. Once again he turned to James Warner Bellah, selecting two more stories, "Command" (1946) and "Big Hunt" (1947), both of which had also appeared in *The Saturday Evening Post.*

"Command" relates the story of Captain Nathan Brittles, a veteran of 43 years in the cavalry, who must deal with an Indian uprising. Once again, the events are seen through the eyes of Lieutenant Flintridge Cohill. The troops, led by Captain Brittles, find a squad of dead cavalry who have been tortured and mutilated. At first, Cohill believes a party of Cheyenne encamped on a nearby river are to blame, and he wants to charge off and attack them. Brittles waits until he has more proof, and he soon discovers that the culprits were Apache, not Cheyenne. He sets an ambush and wipes out the offending Indians. After the battle, Cohill apologizes for doubting Captain Brittles, who replies, "Mr. Cohill, never apologize. It's a mark of weakness." This is the only piece of dialogue to make the transition from the story to the film, although the Indian uprising did become the central conflict.

"Big Hunt" concerns the efforts of Major Allshard to stop the flow of repeating rifles to the Comanches. He tricks Rynders, the Indian agent who is the guilty party, into leading him to the cache of arms where he captures the rifles and kills Rynders and his men. This is another in Bellah's continuing stories of Flintridge Cohill, although in "Big Hunt," he is only mentioned and never seen. In the film, the story became only a small segment where Capt. Brittles confronts a crooked Indian agent.

Three writers were given the assignment to write *She Wore a Yellow Ribbon* (RKO, 1948). First, Bellah himself attempted to adapt his own stories, and he proved adept at creating certain kinds of characters and emotions. However, he proved unable to handle a love interest or to develop complex exposition. Laurence Stallings was brought in to write the next draft. Stallings' main contribution rests in two specific scenes he developed. First, he created the scene in which Captain Brittles (John Wayne) passes by the post graveyard where his wife is buried, and he stops to talk with her as if she is still very much alive. Stallings also created the scene where Brittles is presented by his troop with a gold watch and chain on which is inscribed, "To Captain Nathan Brittles from the men of his Company. Lest we forget." When this scene was filmed, John Ford added an extra touch. As Nathan Brittles receives the watch and tries to read the inscription, he fumbles for an old pair of bifocals hidden away in his tunic. It was a perfect comic touch to keep the scene from becoming maudlin. The final polish was added by Frank Nugent who tied the exposition together and reworked the dialogue, making it more authentic to the times. He also added an omniscient narration that tied together the rambling story.

Many additional plot complications were added, foremost among them a romantic conflict between Lieutenant Pennell (Harry Carey, Jr.), a character out of "War Hunt," and Cohill (John Agar) over the affections of Olivia Dandridge (Joanne Dru). Also, Stallings and Nugent added a real sense of humor to the proceedings with the character of Sergeant Quincannon (Victor McLaglen), who blusters and bellows and gets drunk, all cleverly arranged by Nathan Brittles to keep the good sergeant safely out of the last action.

Bellah's anti-Indian bias disappeared from the script. The film's action takes place immediately after the Indian victory at Little Big Horn, but there is no hint that the cavalry is making the West safe for white democracy. Even the narration describes the Indian action as a war against the United States Cavalry, not against white settlers who build churches and raise families. When Brittles goes into the Indian camp in an attempt to prevent the outbreak, he meets with his old friend Pony That Walks (Chief Big Tree). There is a real sympathy between the old men. When Brittles says it is up to the old men to stop wars, Pony That Walks says, "Too late, Nathan, too late." Even though the Indian war is averted, it is too late for Nathan and Pony That Walks; their time is past, and lesser men have taken over.

The third James Warner Bellah story used by John Ford was "Mission with No Record," which tells of Colonel Massarne, a by-the-book officer whose son enlists in the army after flunking out of West Point. The son turns up in his father's regiment, but the Colonel is so dedicated to duty that he refuses to recognize the boy as his son. Once again, Flintridge Cohill is a character, this time the company commander under whom the young Massarne serves. Of all of Bellah's stories adapted for the screen, more was retained from "Mission with No Record" than all the others put together. (Bellah's novel, *Sergeant Rutledge*, was written after the screenplay.)

As scripted by James Kevin McGuinness, the central character of *Rio Grande* (Republic, 1950) became Lieutenant Colonel Kirby Yorke (John Wayne). Except for the addition of an "e" on the end of York, Wayne plays the same role as he did in *Fort Apache*. Carried over from

She Wore a Yellow Ribbon were Sergeant Quincannon (Victor McLaglen) and Trooper Tyree (Ben Johnson). None of these characters appeared in the Bellah story. Also added was Kathleen Yorke (Maureen O'Hara), who comes west attempting to buy her son out of the service. Therefore, the main thrust of the film became not only the gradual acceptance of Jeff York (Claude Jarman, Jr.) by his father but also the rekindling of the love between Kirby and his wife.

Since he was much more interested in presenting a realistic picture of the frontier cavalry, Bellah seldom cluttered his stories with romance. It was the relationship between men that interested the author. He saw the American Indian only as a savage who had to be chastised and subdued. Although he wrote well and told a well-crafted tale, it is too bad that his racist ideology overwhelms his fiction; it limits his humanity and diminishes his achievement. In his adaptations of Bellah's stories, John Ford allowed his own romanticism and his love for his people to dominate. His cavalry trilogy is filled with warm humanism, often giving the Indians dignity in a time when such sentiment was not popular.

Throughout most of the 1930s and 40s, *The Saturday Evening Post*'s anti–Indian editorial policy was outright racist, as exemplified by James Warner Bellah. On the other hand, others found ways of working within the editorial policy without expounding a virulent racism. Such an author was Ernest Haycox, who tended to portray the American Indian as a malevolent force that occasionally threatened his protagonists, but he never advocated eradication or extermination. On the other hand, he seldom showed them as individuals, and in his fiction, they remain ominous figures of violence and death.

Haycox's best novel, *Bugles in the Afternoon* (1943), specifically concerns Custer and the Seventh Cavalry, climaxing with the Battle of Little Big Horn. Like Bellah, Haycox was saddled with the *Post*'s policy regarding the portrayal of Indians, and while he made them ambiguous, using them only for dramatic interest, he did not make a hero out of Custer. And unlike Bellah, he had no racist ax to grind, and today his novels and short stories remain as readable as the day he wrote them.

The routine film *Bugles in the Afternoon* (Warner Bros., 1952) stresses action for the sake of the story, and while the whole things moves at a fast clip, it is unsatisfying in comparison with the novel. Custer becomes a peripheral figure, occasionally mentioned and glimpsed only once or twice, the last time from far atop a hill as the hero watches the last moments of the Battle of Little Big Horn. In the novel, Haycox made

Custer a central figure, even though Custer is never aware of the hero's existence.

The main action of the film revolves around Kern Shafter (Ray Milland) who has come west to find solace from a woman who betrayed him. Once he enlists in the Seventh, he discovers that the officer Garnett (Hugh Marlowe), who seduced the woman Kern loved, is at the fort, and the rest of the film revolves around the struggle of these two men over the attentions of another young woman. Garnett is a mean, despicable cad who is not above murder, and more than once, he tries to eliminate Kern. Even during the Battle of Little Big Horn, he attacks Kern, only to be shot and killed by the Sioux.

While the conflict between the two men remains at the center of the novel, it never dominates. Always there is the impending conflict with the Indians and the sense of doom that pervades the whole proceedings. While Garnett is a weak man, Haycox never makes him an outright villain as the film does. He is far more complicated. There is no showdown between these two—only the fight against a common enemy during which Garnett is fatally wounded. On the other hand, the hero Kern is the more inflexible, unforgiving, and unable to feel sorry for Garnett as the latter lies dying, even after he admits to Kern that, if he could live his life over, he would lead it differently. Garnett seems to have the measure of Kern when he says of him: "You always were a fellow who hated to change. You would rather burn your bridge than go back over it."

Whereas the film is only an exercise in mediocrity without scope or depth, Haycox's *Bugles in the Afternoon* may be the best novel written about Custer and the disaster at Little Big Horn, and also one of the best novels ever written about the cavalry, a complex work filled with a sense of the epic and populated with real people, including Custer, Reno and other historical personages.

In marked contrast to *Bugles in the Afternoon* is "Sergeant Houck" (1952) by Jack Schaefer, an offbeat, almost gentle cavalry story which is reminiscent in style and tone of Dorothy Johnson at her best. The plot is simple enough. Sergeant Houck, a professional soldier who is near retirement, takes part in a raid on an Indian camp. He rescues a white woman, Cora, and her halfbreed son. Houck is assigned the task of taking the woman and boy back to her white husband. On the trip, he grows close to both, and more than once he stands up for the boy, endearing himself to both Cora and her son. When they finally reach their destination, the husband demands that Cora give up the boy, but she refuses. The husband rejects both and kicks them out of the house.

Houck suggests that Cora wait four months until his enlistment is up, and the three of them will go away together.

The film became *Trooper Hook* (United Artists, 1955) and sported a title song sung by Tex Ritter, *à la High Noon,* which dates it badly. However, even though the script is too talkative, this is an important film because of its examination of sex and racism, the very issues on which critics attacked it at the time of its release. The film begins much as the story, then it goes its own way, ultimately to reach the same conclusion. Hook (Joel McCrea) discovers a white woman (Barbara Stanwyck) and her halfbreek son among a band of captured Apaches. Ordered to escort her home to her white husband, Hook soon finds himself pursued by Chief Nanchez (Rudolfo Acosta), Cora's Indian husband, who is bent on regaining his son. When the Apaches attack the stage carrying the trio, Hook threatens to kill the boy if Nanchez doesn't pulll back. Finally, they reach Cora's husband, Trude (Royal Dano), who rejects the halfbreed boy. Nanchez shows up, and he and Trude conveniently kill each other, leaving Hook, Cora and the boy to begin a new life together.

Obviously the ending is contrived, but the film dealt with controversial issues in an unflinching manner. Even Hook, a compassionate and sensitive man, wrestles with the fact that Cora cohabited with an Indian. Yet, he protects the halfbreed boy, and even when he threatens to kill the boy in order to force Nanchez to break off his attack, Hook is incapable of pulling the trigger, Hook also must face and overcome his own innate prejudice. But racism exists on both sides. Nanchez himself is not above it, and he is appalled that his wife would return to her white husband. *Trooper Hook* is not a great western, but it goes well beyond rudimentary action to explore important issues and present characters who struggle with the issues and against them.

A novel that chronicles the last cavalry charge in United States history is *They Came to Cordura* (1958) by Glendon Swarthout, which is similar in plot to Jack Schaefer's *Company of Cowards.* Here, an officer, Major Thomas Thorn, sees his first action in the punitive expedition against Pancho Villa in 1916. In the attack on Columbus, Thorn turns coward and hides in a ditch, and because of his conduct, he is put in charge of selecting men for the Medal of Honor. After he chooses five such men from various encounters, he is assigned the task of getting the men safely out of the combat zone and to Cordura so that they will be alive to receive their medals. The government wants heroes for recruiting purposes since those in power are aware that the country will soon be involved in the war in Europe. A political prisoner, Adelaide

Geary, an American who is living in Mexico and has given aid to the enemy, is also assigned to the detail. As the group crosses over a hundred miles of desert full of hostiles, Thorn comes to question the meaning of heroism. In facing the elements and facing his own men who turn against him and, in the end, kill him, he finds an inner strength and a heroism far greater than of the men who are about to be decorated.

While *They Came to Cordura* is a well written, it eschews the normal heroic and stereotypical characters of action fiction. Even a possible romance between Thorn and the woman never develops, although they do discover mutual respect and admiration. There is also a lack of an outside threat to the group except in one scene where they are attacked by a group of Villistas. The real threat comes from within. The downbeat ending also put the novel outside the parameters of the traditional western. More a historical novel than true western, it is nevertheless a story about the end of the West, the story of a time when the old world of the cavalryman was ending and about to be replaced by mechanized warfare already in full swing in Europe. More importantly, however, the novel is an examination of the meaning of courage.

Except for the end, the plot of the film (Columbia, 1959) remains basically the same. Major Thorn (Gary Cooper), because he has shown cowardice in battle, is assigned the position of Awards Officer. When he is detailed to conduct the men and one woman prisoner to Cordura, he must overcome his own fears and also the resistance of the five men under his command. Along the way, all the men as well as Thorn and Miss Geary (Rita Hayworth) are given ample opportunity to show their true mettle. In the end, Thorn successfully leads his men to Cordura without loss, dragging themselves into the town and safety.

The upbeat ending was the complete antithesis to Swarthout's purpose, but in reality it did little to hurt the film, which was a failure both critically and financially. Gary Cooper was miscast as Major Thorn. It was simply too hard to believe that a man with such a world weary look could be so unknowledgeable about himself. The only credible performance is Van Heflin as Sergeant Chawk. But performances alone did not destroy this film. For an action picture, it is extremely slow and uninvolving. Where the book contained a good deal of interior monologue, especially from Thorn, the film, by its very nature, had to concentrate on action, of which there is very little. Director Robert Rossen also argued with the studio over the editing, insisting his cut was better. As usual, the studio won and released its version. After its initial release, Rossen gained the rights to the film with the intention of cutting it to his original plan. However, the director died before he could accomplish this, and the only version that remains is the studio version, a complete disaster on all counts.

Along with *Bugles in the Afternoon,* the finest novel of the American cavalry out west is undoubtedly *A Distant Trumpet* (1960) by Paul Horgan, parts of which were also serialized in *The Saturday Evening Post* under the title "The Captain's Lady." By 1960, the editorial policy of the magazine had shifted, allowing Horgan some latitude in dealing with his Indian characters, and he shows great understanding in his portrayal of them, especially the Apache scout White Horn.

However, while the Indians are an important ingredient, they are only one; the novel is really about Matthew Hazard. The story opens with the birth of Hazard and his life through the Civil War, his time at West Point, his assignment to Fort Delivery in Arizona, his affair with Kitty Mainwaring and his marriage to Laura Greenleaf. Hazard and his wife begin their married life at this remote army outpost where life is, on the whole, uneventful, although the threat of Apache warfare is constantly present. After hostilities break open, Hazard is assigned the job of gaining the surrender of the Apaches, which he does with the aid of the loyal scout White Horn, but the army breaks its word and has all the Apaches, including White Horn, shipped off to Florida. In disgust, Hazard resigns his commission over the treatment of the Indians.

This is a grand historical novel, highly readable and consummately researched, that evokes with beauty and affection the life of a cavalry officer in the 1880s. The early scenes of the Civil War during which Matthew Hazard's father is killed as well as the later scenes on the arid Arizona landscape full of skulking hostiles come vividly alive, so much so that the environment often dominates and determines the actions of the characters. Of the characters themselves, they are fully realized. Matthew Hazard is a man who knows himself, a good honorable man capable of doing the deeds recounted in the novel, yet he is more complex than a simple stereotypical hero. White Horn is a loyal yet tragic figure caught in the mechanisms of the white man's decisions. There are also the two women in Hazard's life: Kitty, with whom he has the affair at Fort Delivery and who later dies at the hands of the Apaches; and Laura, whom he loves and marries. There is also the general who keeps spouting Latin phrases and then explaining them. All these characters and more are given in-depth stories that make each and every one a real, breathing individual. Therein lies the key to the action of *A Distant Trumpet;* there, also, lies its greatness.

It is hard to imagine that the film version of *A Distant Trumpet*

(Warner Bros., 1964) could be so dull, even in the scenery and stunts, yet that is exactly the case. All the introductory material that makes flesh and blood people out of the characters has been excised, and only the cavalry versus Indians is left with the insipid love story, which even itself has been altered. Laura (Diane McBain) is a femme fatale, an insincere and shallow woman, out to latch on to Matthew Hazard (Troy Donahue). It is Kitty (Suzanne Pleshette) who ultimately wins him. Actually, the film's tension is so weak and dissipated that one really doesn't care who gets him, including the Chiricahua Apaches. As for the Indians, they are the usual mock villains, and even the character of White Horn has been replaced by a white scout called Seely Jones (Claude Akins). The only concession to the Indians is that during the scene where Hazard asks Chief War Eagle to surrender, the scene is played in subtitles and the Apache is not forced to speak in pidgin English.

Scenarist John Twist and director Raoul Walsh threw out most of the plot and character development. The actors and actresses, all from the studio's stagnant pool of television talent, walk through the events as if they had sleeping sickness. If this is not enough, the action scenes are played with little excitement and imagination. All in all, this adaptation is a travesty of a great novel, a film that should never have been made in such a slipshod fashion, and once made, should never have been released. It is hard to believe that this version did not, in some way, damage the reputation of Horgan's novel.

A comic treatment of the cavalry emerged in *Hallelujah Train* (1963) by Bill Gulick. Based on an actual event, the novel traces the path in 1867 of 80 freight wagons carrying 2700 cases of imported French champagne and 1600 barrels of Philadelphia-brewed whiskey and escorted by a troop under the command of Colonel Thaddeus Gearhart. The train is trying to reach Denver so the miners there will have plenty to drink over the long winter months, but along the way the train is beset by Indians, thirsty Denver citizens, striking teamsters, and worst of all, temperance-minded suffragettes who are intent on destroying the evil cargo. Told as a flashback by a government agent giving a report to the hard-drinking President Grant, the events jump from one subplot to another with such rapidity that not one character rises above the stereotypical. The cargo of spirits loosely holds the whole proceedings together, but it is a slight novel that provides, at best, only a chuckle or two. It is certainly not "one of the funniest westerns ever written" as the promotional flyleaf would have the reader believe.

The novel became *The Hallelujah Trail* (United Artists, 1965), a turgid, overblown dud. At least Bill Gulick had sense enough to keep his novel relatively short, but director John Sturges, brother of Preston Sturges, allowed the proceedings to drag on for 165 minutes. Perhaps because it was originally shot for a road show engagement in Cinerama, a super wide screen process, the producers reasoned that the film must be long to draw the crowds. All they got at the box office was a bomb.

The story remained basically the same with cavalrymen leading a wagon train beset by all sorts of divergent groups wanting to dispose of the cargo of whiskey. In this version, even a few road agents were thrown in for good measure. Some additional comic scenes were added, such as the lead suffragette (Lee Remick) bursting in on Colonel Gearhart (Burt Lancaster) while he is taking a bath. These scenes succeeded only in lengthening the film. A slam bang shootout finale where not one person gets shot was also created for the film, but it is a silly, contrived climax. The characters remain basically the same, and as a result, not one emerges as anything more than cardboard except for Brian Keith as Wallingham, the loudmouth guardian of the whiskey. Everyone else looks bored. Again, there are a few chuckles along the way, but the basic idea is simply too slight to carry the ponderous story developed by screenwriter John Gay. Unfortunately, the script also lacked the comic insight of much better comic westerns like *Cat Ballou* or *Little Big Man*. Had the film been cut to ninety minutes or so, it might have been bearable, much like Gulick's novel, but at just under three hours, it is an interminable bore.

In direct contrast to Haycox and James Warner Bellah, T.V. Olsen wrote a formulaic romantic novel of cavalry versus Indians, *Arrows in the Sun* (1969). Somewhat lighter in tone than the same author's *The Stalking Moon* but not the burlesque of *Hallelujah Train,* it tells the story of Honus Gant and Cresta Lee, two survivors of a Cheyenne attack. Alone and isolated on the prairie, they try to make their way back to civilization. Although the novel has plenty of action, the main thrust is the relationship between the two, an ordinary soldier and a white captive, who also happens to be the wife of Chief Spotted Wolf. At first, the two are hostile toward each other. Because Cresta is so outspoken and willful, Honus Gant comes to believe that he hates her, even though her levelheadedness and knowledge save their lives more than once. She despises him for his puritanical virtuousness. Yet, they draw closer, so much so that when Cresta is recaptured by Spotted Wolf, Honus goes into the hostiles' camp to rescue her. In the Indian camp is also Cumber, a renegade selling rifles to the Cheyenne. A final showdown finds Honus eliminating the gunrunner and finding happiness in the arms of Cresta.

If *Arrow in the Sun* sounds familiar, it is because the idea of whites trapped inside Indian territory had been used before in both novels and films. Louis L'Amour had used a similar plot for *Last Stand at Papago Wells*. Films such as *Bad Lands* (RKO, 1939), a "B" version of *The Lost Patrol* out west, and *Escape from Fort Bravo* (MGM, 1953) had previously covered the same ground. Only the interplay between Honus Gant and Cresta Lee made the novel offbeat, and it is their constant bickering even in the face of danger that adds some spark of life to the novel. Otherwise, it was fast-paced but pedestrian.

Arrow in the Sun became *Soldier Blue* (Avco-Embassy, 1970), an overly violent film that climaxes with the Sand Creek Massacre. Some of the novel remains. Honus and Cresta survive the Indian attack. Even though her personality is strident at best, it is her knowledge that constantly saves them as they slowly try to make their way back to civilization. But the tone of the novel is never present in this film. What was a standard adventure novel with humorous overtones becomes a film that invites comparisons between the U.S. Cavalry's treatment of the Indians with American atrocities in Vietnam. The overly violent end focuses on hacked off limbs and spouting blood, one of the most tasteless climaxes ever to appear on American screens. While the intentions of *Soldier Blue* may be admirable, the execution deserves nothing but scorn. The fault does not lie in the fact that screenwriter John Gay and director Ralph Nelson reshaped the novel for the screen but rather how they reshaped it. Actually, certain changes such as deepening the content might have helped, but Gay and director Nelson went overboard. Certainly the Sand Creek Massacre was a terrible atrocity, but the way this film handles it turns the audience's collective stomach, not at the massacre, but at the film itself. Far better was the similar scene in *Little Big Man,* which evoked the desired anger and shame without resorting to the sensationalism of special effects. *Arrow in the Sun* is a shallow but enjoyable novel; *Soldier Blue* is shallow but offensive film.

The cavalry in *Soldier Blue* is a far different cavalry than the romantic, idealized cavalry envisioned by James Warner Bellah, Ernest Haycox, and John Ford. It has evolved into a mean-spirited apparition of Ralph Nelson. This is not to suggest that a revisionist picture of the American cavalry wasn't needed, but Paul Horgan provided such a revisionist picture with *A Distant Trumpet*. To date, *Soldier Blue* is the last American film to deal with the American cavalry, and it is a sorry end for an interesting and entertaining subgenre of American western literature and film.

4. Scouting for the Army

Civilians who scout for the army is a common motif in many western novels and films. Typical of this subgenre is *Ambush* (1948) by Luke Short, a pseudonym for Frederick Glidden. Protagonist Ward Kinsman is a heroic Westerner without apparent blemish, a man who loves the desert and its ways, so much so that the land itself becomes as strong a character as anyone in the novel.

> Ward sat slack and somnolent in the saddle, feeling the hourly increase in heat. It was dry, savage, merciless, and he liked it. The land, of a sameness that was soporific, was a dun-colored waste of rock and sage clumps and mesquite tangles, and it was never wholly level, so that the twisting road accommodated itself to an endless upthrust of eroded mesa and slope of canyon floor.

When an army unit is assigned the task of freeing a white woman held by the renegade Apache Diablito, Kinsman at first refuses to be drawn into the fight, but he soon comes to realize his responsibility and joins the pursuit. Because he admires the Apaches, he remains ambivalent about his decision throughout most of the ensuing action. "I like the way Apaches live," he says, "and I think it the way a man is meant to live." In this aspect, the novel is progressive and admirable, especially in a time when such magazines as *The Saturday Evening Post* had editorial policies against showing native Americans in a favorable light.

The film *Ambush* (MGM, 1950) eschews all talk of noble Apaches. For the most part, the Indians are seldom seen except at a distance and represent a force of nature to be subdued rather than a proud people fighting for survival. Their culture and life style is occasionally vilified by Kinsman (Robert Taylor) who speaks of their teachery and their treatment of captives. He mistrusts them, too, and when a captured

50

Apache, Tana (Chief Thundercloud), agrees to lead the army to Diabilto, Kinsman tries to warn stubborn Captain Lorrison (John Hodiak) of treachery. When Tana attempts to sneak off and warn his people, Kinsman kills him. Still, the film must be complimented for using actual Indians to play the Apaches. Charles Stevens, who played Diablito, was a grandson of Geronimo.

The film is cluttered with the same plot complications as the novel, which weaken both. Kinsman falls in love with Ann Duverall (Arlene Dahl), an Eastern woman who has come west to find her sister, captured by Diablito's band. Captain Lorrison is also attracted to her, and this sets off the one humorous scene in the book and film. The two rivals battle it out in a barn, and the supercilious officer thoroughly whips the hero. A further complication involves a likeable officer in love with the wife of a drunken enlisted man. These extraneous subplots slow the action and divert attention from the main thrust of the story, the pursuit of Diablito and his band. However, when the story finally gets down to business, it is a gritty tale of pursuit and ambush, often capturing the harsh realities of conflict with the Apaches.

Very similar to *Ambush* is *Adobe Walls* (1953) by W.R. Burnett. This time Walter Grein, the best scout in the Arizona Territory, helps to squelch the last Apache uprising led by Toriano. Burnett patterned Grein in part after the army scout Al Sieber, Toriano after Apache war chief Victorio, but this is not a novel that sticks to historical fact. The title itself is misleading. The first battle of Adobe Walls occurred in 1864 and the second in 1874, both in Texas. Very few, if any, Apaches were involved in either siege. Al Sieber was not present at either. The final showdown in the novel is really only an ambush that results in the death of Toriano and the destruction of the Apache rebellion.

Burnett makes no attempt to portray the Apaches as anything other than a force of nature to be wiped off the landscape as one would eradicate rattlesnakes. When a character says that perhaps the scout has been harsh in his judgment of the Apaches, Grein replies, "They laugh at kindness, think it's weakness. They understand only one thing; force. It's the only way to handle them." Most of the novel concerns itself with political problems as do-gooders from Washington hamper Grein's job, but they finally see the errors of their ways and give the scout permission to punish the offending Indians. There is very little action until the last few pages when Grein leads his ragged band into the mountains to confront the dreaded Apache leader and his horde.

Already a noted screenwriter, Burnett had six previous novels made into films including *Little Caesar* and *Asphalt Jungle,* but it was Charles

Marquis Warren who wrote the screenplay for the film, which became *Arrowhead* (Paramount, 1953). In addition to the title, Warren made other changes. Walter Grein becomes Ed Bannon (Charlton Heston), and there is the addition of a love interest. In *Adobe Walls,* Grein considers a relationship with an officer's wife, but it is never consummated. In *Arrowhead,* the woman is a widow, and although there is competition from an officer, the hero eventually wins her over.

The character of Toriano (Jack Palance) becomes a major character. In the novel, Toriano is a shadowy figure who appears only at the end of the novel to be killed off quickly, but in the film Ed Bannon and Toriano hate each other, stemming from the time when, as young men, Ed cut a deep scar across the cheek of the Apache. The scout hates all Apaches, believing that the only good one is a dead one, and he refuses to change. Once Toriano arrives on the scene, he begins to prove the correctness of the theory by killing every white person in sight, including the local Indian agent who is Toriano's own blood brother.

The novel's climax takes place in the mountains where the scout and his men track Toriano, and in a violent battle, the scout shoots the Indian, then sits around while the dying Apache sings his death song. On the other hand, the film's climax finds the soldiers and the scout surrounded by the hostiles, and the only way the hero can save them is a hand-to-hand encounter with Toriano during which he breaks the Indian's back. The climax of *Arrowhead* is weaker for the changes, missing the gritty realism and symbolic intent of the novel. It also suffers from the same inflexible anti–Indian stance as the novel, a jaundiced view that turns the film into a dour, sour diatribe in which it is hard to pull for either side.

The Apache was treated with more respect in Louis L'Amour's *Hondo* (1952). The author himself in a 1982 introduction to a reprint of the novel wrote of the Apache:

> He was no poor, pathetic red man being put upon by whites, but a fierce warrior, a veteran of many battles, asking favors of no man. He did not fear the pony soldiers but welcomed them, for they brought into his harsh land the horses, the food, the clothing, and the weapons he could take from them. Often he admired the men he killed, often he was contemptuous of their ignorance and lack of skills.

The Apache chief Vittoro keeps appearing and reappearing throughout the novel, and his presence, or lack of, often dominates and determines the actions of Hondo Lane and those around him. Vittoro is L'Amour's ideal Apache, an honorable man and a fierce warrior, a rebel of sorts, a defender of his homeland intent upon pushing the white man out. The treaty has been broken by the white man, and as Hondo points out, "There's no word in the Apache language for 'lie,' and they've been lied to."

Hondo Lane is part Indian himself and has lived among the Mescalero Apaches for five years, even taking an Apache wife, Destarte. When he is asked what her name means, Hondo gives an eloquent, poetic speech.

> It means like Crack of Dawn, the first bronze light that makes the buttes stand out against the gray desert. It means the first sound you hear of a brook curling over some rocks — some trout jumping and a beaver crooning. It means the sound a stallion makes when he whistles at some mares just as the first puff of wind kicks up at daybreak. It means like you get up in the first light and you and her go out of the wickiup, where it smells smoky and private and just the two of you there, and you stand outside and smell the first bit of the wind coming down from the high divide and promising the first snowfall.

Yet the Apaches are warriors, and their society can be cruel. When he is captured by Vittoro and his braves, Hondo is threatened with an excruciatingly slow death, and for a start, hot coals are poured over his hand. Only an old tintype that Vittoro recognizes saves Hondo's life.

The film *Hondo* (Warner Bros., 1953) retains most of the novel's plot and dialogue. The story opens in 1874 with Hondo (John Wayne) riding dispatch for the cavalry when he comes across Angie Lowe (Geraldine Page) and her son Johnny, abandoned on their small ranch. Equal time is then divided between the growing romance of Hondo and Angie and the constant incursions of the Apaches. Some incursions are benevolent, some not. More importantly, however, the novel's attitude toward the Indian's is not only left intact but expounded upon. The entire sequence explaining Destarte's name is lifted straight from the book, and Hondo's admiration of the Apache extends far beyond his dead wife. After Vittoro's death and the defeat of the Apaches, Hondo says, "It means the end of a way of life. Too bad. It was a good life." His eulogy are the last words spoken in the film.

Two major scenes from the novel have been omitted. The first is the massacre of Company C by Vittoro and his warriors, which is the only section of the novel that shifts the action away from Hondo, and while it may illustrate the tactical skill of the Apache, it weakens the story. The film's exposition speeds things up by having Hondo mention finding the dead troopers and presenting the ragged guidon flag as evidence. A more important scene omitted is when Hondo and Johnny are threatened by four mountain Apaches not associated with Vittoro. Hondo is forced to kill one, and immediately thereafter Vittoro rides up. The mutual respect between these two men is never more evident than in this scene, and as Hondo and Johnny ride back to the ranch, the depth of their relationship is exposed when the young boy jumps in Hondo's arms and cries.

Although *The Burning Hills* (1956) by L'Amour uses Indians to resolve part of its plot, it is really a formula western. When Trace Jordon's partner is killed, he goes looking for the men who did it and winds up killing Bob Sutton. Immediately, he is on the run from Sutton's relatives. Along the way, he meets Maria Cristina, who joins him. By clever tricks and ruses, Jordon avoids his pursuers, managing to kill many of them, and leads them into an ambush by Apaches. Eventually, Jordon captures the wounded Ben Hinderman, the leader of the pursuers, who realizes that Jordon has been in the right all along, and he calls off the vendetta, allowing Maria and Jordon to escape. It is all pretty standard stuff with much action and very little characterization. As with so many of L'Amour's women, Maria never comes alive, and her accent reads as phony as it sounds on the screen. The only interesting thing about her is that she is no starry eyed heroine, but a woman who has lost one husband and who has been pawed by so many Gringos that she is sick of the sight of men. However, L'Amour's strong point has always been his ability to tell a fast paced, lean story without too much extraneous interferences like character and meaning. *The Burning Hills* fits the mold.

The movie *The Burning Hills* (Warner Bros., 1956) was scripted by Irving Wallace before he became a popular novelist, and it sticks fairly closely to the novel. At first, it is Trace Jordon (Tab Hunter) who seeks revenge on the men who killed his brother, but soon he becomes the hunted. After Trace shoots the head of the Sutton clan (Ray Teal), his son West (Skip Homeier) leads his men in pursuit of Jordon. Wounded, Trace is befriended by Maria (Natalie Wood) who nurses him back to health and then is forced to flee with him into the hills. Slowly Trace decimates the men after him, wounding and killing them one by one and finally leading the last dozen or so into an ambush by Comanches. Wes and one of his henchmen escape along with their guide. In the final confrontation on the cliffs high above a rushing river, Trace stands his ground and wins his victory. The guide, half Indian himself, says that he promised to lead Wes to Trace but that he had no part in the fighting, and he rides off leaving the young lovers in a clinch.

The Burning Hills is an important western in that it signalled a move toward youth in westerns during the 1950s. In addition, Skip Homeier is a fine villain, chillingly cold, who backshoots his foreman without a second thought. The script helped to flesh out a thin plot, except that Maria became a virginal Mexican girl completely worthy of the blond hero's love. But the real problems lie with Tab Hunter who gives his customary wooden performance as the hero, and Natalie Wood, whose accent is so unbelievable as to defy description. Even though the film tried to copy the theme and style of *Hondo,* it lacked all the qualities that made the earlier film a superior work. Where *Hondo* showed sympathy and understanding of the Indians, this film, like the novel, relegated them to the role of *deus ex machina,* a force which, at the moment of decision, becomes the hero and Maria's salvation. Like the novel, the film moves quickly and tells its story with economy, but also like the novel it is standard fare, despite its influence on other westerns.

Louis L'Amour wrote another novel involving Apaches that became a film, *Last Stand at Papago Wells* (1957), also one of the author's weaker efforts. There is not one sympathetic character among the Indians. They are simply savages who attack a disparate group of travellers at Papago Wells, New Mexico. The defenders are led by Logan Cates, a Hondo-like character who once scouted for the army, and only his knowledge and courage keeps the group together. Much of the tension comes from the relationships within the group rather than from the Apaches without. The film became *Apache Territory* (Columbia, 1958), a undistinguished oater. The plot, including the love interests and the film's attitude toward the Indians, remains basically the same as the novel. It is an obvious attempt by the studio to cash in on the success of *Hondo,* but too much of the basic premise of both the novel and film depends upon coincidence. There are also too many plots and subplots cluttering things up, and the basic simplicity of *Hondo* is missing.

The Indian as enigma has never been more clearly articulated than in *The Stalking Moon* by T.V. Olsen. Once again Toriano shows up, although in name only, as the hero Sam Vetch ends his last days of scouting for the army by helping to capture a small band of squaws and children belonging to the famous chief's band. Among the prisoners is a young white woman, Sara Carver, captured ten years earlier, and her two children by the Indian Salvaje. Taken back to the army post, the woman asks to be sent back east, and Sam agrees to accompany her and her children to Silverton. In Silverton, Sam is rejected by Vangie Armitage when he asks her to marry him and move to his ranch in New Mexico. Afterward, he realizes that Sara has nowhere to go, and he invites her and her children to come with him to his ranch. Nick Tana, a half breed Apache and close friend of Sam, goes with them. Despite the great distance between San Carlos and Sam's New Mexico ranch, Salvaje tracks them down. Nick is killed and Sam barely escapes death before shooting the rampaging Indian.

Apaches themselves are often spoken of derisively. "It ain't good water, but a critter or a 'Pache can keep it down," says Sam, and his comparison of an Apache with an animal is clear. The Apache's cruelty is also alluded to. "'Paches will mutilate a dead body, not to say a live," says one character. "They don't cotton to watching a live one die fast." Even Salvaje means "savage" in Spanish, and before the end of the novel, the Indian lives up to his name. He is a spectre, a shadow haunting the background, never seen, although his body count mounts until he finally emerges like some vengeful ghost. He kills Nick without a sound and almost does the job on Sam. Only the timely intervention by first Sara and then her young son, Jimmy Joe, prevents it. When Salvaje confronts Sara for her betrayal, he not only beats her but also prepares to cut off her nose before Sam puts a stop to it by killing him.

It is in the character of Jimmy Joe, Sara's oldest child, where the novel is ambivalent toward the Indians. When he first meets the boy, Sam sees the typical Apache. "They never show you a thing. Not a damn thing," he thinks. Yet, when a miner insults the boy, Sam beats the white man senseless. Sam starts out believing that one day, after his mother's hold is gone, Jimmy Joe will return to his people. He is already too old and the Apache blood too strong. But when Salvaje is beating Sara and threatening to mutilate her, Jimmy Joe attempts to stop him, going so far as to try to shoot his father. It is then Sam realizes the boy has the blood of both races in him, and that Jimmy Joe can grow strong from this.

The film *The Stalking Moon* (National General, 1968) never fully articulates the book's viewpoint of the Indians. Instead, it settles for enigma without insight. We never see Salvaje until the very end, but we know he is coming for his son by the telltale signs—a dead animal, a twanging arrow, dead bodies. In the novel, Salvaje spoke one word, and that as he lay dying, his eyes focused on his son. "Enju," he mutters. "It is well." In the film, he does not even have this to say nor does he utter one sound as our hero puts bullet after bullet into his pesky hide. The character of Jimmy Joe fares no better. He is a silent miscreant, stealing a knife from one settler and causing a fight. Later, when Salvaje attacks, he runs out to meet his father, causing Sam (Gregory Peck) to catch a bullet in the arm. At no time does Jimmy Joe seem to realize that his blood is also part of his mother's blood, and he never tries to help her when Salvaje carries her off. At the end, it is easy to believe that the boy will someday return to the wild life, forsaking his mother and the white man's way.

The script made a couple of other important changes. The first strengthened it. Sam's love interest in Silverton is dropped, and he and Sara (Eva Marie Saint) head straight for the New Mexico ranch with little delay. In a deliberately paced film such as this, such a cut speeded up the action. However, a second change proved far more important and somewhat damaging. In the novel, Sam is a grubby, gritty hero, often unsure of himself, and his weaknesses make him far more vulnerable than the Sam of the film. As a result, the film's tension is somewhat dissipated. Peck plays Sam as far more the romantic hero, often clean shaven and striking statuesque poses, stalwart to the end and without a prejudiced bone in his body. A main character a little weaker would have made a much stronger film.

5. Wagon Trains and Settlers

As the settlers crossed the Great Plains in their canvas-covered wagons, the migration appeared to them as one continuous flow, a river of moving people, but the various novels and films that have tried to capture this great movement, despite whatever strengths they may possess, often appear episodic and disoriented. Even a writer as talented as Zane Grey, whose novels were more heavily plotted than most, could not escape this problem.

Grey displayed more than a casual interest in the plight of the American Indian amidst this great migration. His first novel to deal with them, *The Thundering Herd* (1918), did so rather indirectly. Tom Doan is a buffalo hunter, one of the vast number of professional hunters who were ultimately responsible for the almost complete annihilation of this massive beast. As the buffalo herds declined in number, so did the threat from Indians. Millie Fayre, Tom's sweetheart, implores him to stop the slaughter, but he refuses to quit until he has earned enough to buy a ranch. However, after a particularly brutal killing of a young motherless calf, Tom sees that the killing degrades him as a man and he gives it up. This was one of Grey's novels with a message, certainly an appealing one of conservation of our wildlife. However, the human characters, never a strong point of the author, proved to be particularly weak, and when Grey submitted the book for publication, the editors of Harper's wanted him to change the ending for greater emotional depth.

The first film of *The Thundering Herd* (Paramount, 1925) failed to resemble the novel in any way although it was exciting. Tom Doan (Jack Holt) is a buffalo hunter out to stop Randell Jett (Noah Beery) from stirring up trouble between the Indians and white settlers. To complicate matters, Doan is in love with Jett's daughter, Milly. The

58

Lobby card for *The Thundering Herd* (1934), based on the Grey novel. In the middle is Noah Beery, who played various roles in many silent and sound adaptations of Grey's works.

climax comes with covered wagons stampeding across a frozen lake. The remake (Paramount, 1934) was almost the exact same story, including the race across the frozen lake, a scene lifted from the earlier film and inserted into this one. This time Randolph Scott took the role of Tom Doan, and Noah Beery repeated his role as the villain, Randall Jett. The film was directed in workmanlike fashion by Henry Hathaway, who directed eight "B" features in all for Paramount based on the novels of Zane Grey, of which *The Thundering Herd* ranks among his best, despite the overabundance of stock footage. However, neither of these adaptations are the Grey novel; on the contrary, both films made every effort to stay away from the message and constructed films with more commercially viable plots.

The serial *The Overland Freighter* appeared in 1928 in *Country Gentleman,* but by the time it appeared in hardcover the title had been changed to *Fighting Caravans* (1929). It told the story of Clint Belmet, a famous freighter and Indian fighter who on his various trips between Kansas and New Mexico searches for his true love, May Bell, who was captured by Indians at an early age. The novel is filled with gruesome episodes as Cling is constantly harassed by Kiowas and Comanches. After a huge offensive against the Indians and white renegades, Clint finds May Bell, and their reunion closes the novel on a poignant note. As Grey novels go, this was standard in its depiction of hero and heroine, but the descriptions of the wagons crossing the plains and the daily life of the pioneers are superb.

When *Fighting Caravans* (Paramount, 1931) came to the screen, it was a big budget effort that had little to do with the Grey novel. Bill Jackson (Ernest Torrence) and Jim Bridger (Tully Marshall) convince Felice (Lily Damita), a French girl travelling alone, to pose as the wife of Clint Belmet (Gary Cooper) in order to get him out of jail. They all join a wagon train on which is Lee Murdock (Fred Kohler), a renegade who is planning an Indian attack on the pioneers somewhere on the plains. Clint falls in love, much to the chagrin of his friends, but luckily for all, the Indians attack, and Jackson and Bridger are killed. Also killed is Murdock when Clint dumps kerosene in the river and sets it ablaze, thus thwarting the attack. This was a big but disappointing production, sluggish at the start and resembling *The Covered Wagon* more than the Grey novel.

Fighting Caravans had so much unused footage left over that it was put to use in *Wagon Wheels* (Paramount, 1934), which once again purported to be based on Grey's novel. In this version, Clint Belmet is leading a train of settlers to Oregon, but Murdock, who is employed by vicious fur traders, wants to keep out settlers, and he tries to stir up trouble with the Indians. In the climactic battle, Clint kills the renegade, and the attack is defeated. Like the preceding film, *Wagon Wheels* has little to do with the Grey novel. Although entertaining and interesting, it seldom rises above "horse opera" status. Far too much time is spent on a love story between Clint and Nancy Wellingham, one of the settlers travelling on the train, and the main plot of the renegade out to destroy the wagon train is standard stuff. It simply lacked the epic sweep that might have raised it above the average.

Perhaps the best known of all novels concerning the westward migration is *The Covered Wagon* (1922) by Emerson Hough, who, as a boy, had traveled the plains in a covered wagon himself. In order to lengthen his novel, Hough cluttered the proceedings with a very conventional and stereotypical romance between Will Banion, the natural leader of the wagon train, and Molly Wingate, the daughter of the man voted to lead the settlers. A love triangle is added when Woodhull, the villain, spreads lies about Banion in order to gain favor with Molly. As the train crawls slowly westward, dissensions arise, and when news is received of a gold strike in California, many of the adventurous are attracted southward. Only a few reach their final destination. However, the strength of this novel does not lie in its story but in the description of the daily life of a community on the march, incidents of which, such as the buffalo hunt and the Indian attack, are told with skill and dash.

While riding a train, producer Jesse Lasky read the Hough novel, becoming absorbed in the struggles of the pioneers, and later he stated: "Superimposing the past on the present by reading about that trek while actually retracing it myself, as I looked out the window of a speeding luxury train at the same scenery my grandfather viewed from a lumbering conestoga, was an emotional, almost mystical experience." Lasky's enthusiasm for the novel probably contributed to its faithful adaptation to the screen.

Although the great westward migration had been treated earlier in *Wagon Tracks* (1919) starring William S. Hart, *The Covered Wagon* (Paramount, 1923) was the first film to deal with the epic nature of the subject. Even the titles used in the film add to this impression: "The blood of America is the blood of pioneers — the blood of lionhearted men and women who carved a splendid civilization out of an uncharted wilderness." Filming on location in Utah and Nevada under conditions that were often as hard on the participants as it had been for the original pioneers was in itself a departure from the closely supervised studio work that had preceded it. A river crossing was accomplished by caulking the wagons just as the pioneers themselves had done before. Over 750 real Indians were used, and also 1,000 of the local inhabitants. A buffalo herd of 200 head was imported and used for the stampede sequence.

Originally a ten-reel film, *The Covered Wagon* no longer exists in its original form. The most common print is only six reels (approximately sixty minutes), although the Museum of Modern Art has an eight-reel version. The missing footage includes the dramatic prairie fire and some other documentary-like footage, which is too bad since this is the strongest part of the film. This trimming was originally done to add prominence to the characters and plot, but the only originality here is that Molly (Lois Wilson) shows unusual spirit. The rest of the characterizations are rudimentary. Banion (J. Warren Kerrigan) is too stoical in not countering the accusations of Woodhull (Alan Hale), although there is a moment at the end of their fight when he is tempted to gouge out his opponent's eyes, just as his character was tempted in the novel.

Lois Wilson and Chief Yellow Calf in "THE COVERED WAGON"—Criterion Theatre

(Above) Lois Wilson and Chief Yellow Calf pose during a break in the filming of *The Covered Wagon* (1923), based on the novel by Emerson Hough. *(Opposite)* Some native Americans pose for a still during the making of *The Covered Wagon*.

However, these drawbacks are not solely the film's problems; they stem from the novel.

Just as with the novel, the film's strength lies with the documentary approach to the 1848 trek. Director James Cruze seldom exploited action, and combined with the immobile camera, the viewer often feels as if he is watching actual historical scenes filmed at the time the events happened. When Molly's horse runs away and Banion rides to the rescue, the episode is seen from a single long shot and is disposed of in a matter of seconds. Its importance lies not as action but as a device to further the enmity between Molly and Banion, much the way Hough used the incident in the novel. Even the massive Indian attack is quick and concise, its purpose to show the stupidity of Wingate's leadership. The Indians themselves are without humanity and, like fire and flood, are only hazards of the trail. Certainly Cruze's decision to avoid the sensational slowed the film but added to the antiquated look; yet today it is the look of *The Covered Wagon* that is remembered and not the irrelevant story.

A far better novel of the trek westward is *The Way West* (1949) by A.B. Guthrie, Jr., a sequel of sorts to *The Big Sky*. It tells of a journey in 1845 of a wagon train headed for Oregon and led by Dick Summers, one of the characters from *The Big Sky,* who says of himself, "I'm bound to chase my tail, I reckon, like a pup." But the novel centers on relationships between husbands and wives, examining five in detail. Irving Tadlock from Illinois has organized the wagon train in the hope of finidng a place in the West where he can enter politics and also bolster his faltering marriage. Charles Fairbanks and his wife are taking their son to Oregon for his health. Henry McBee and his woman are trying to escape their creditors in Ohio. Amanda Mack, a beautiful but frigid woman from Kentucky, is afraid to become a mother; thus she unwittingly drives her husband Curtis to adultery with Mercy, one of the McBee children. Lije and Rebecca Evans discover along the way the depth and strength of their relationship and reliance upon each other. Guthrie emphasizes the social conflicts within the wagon train, and although some of these arise from natural obstacles, they test the courage, endurance and characters of the people. It is the group that unifies the novel; otherwise, it is an episodic story of a number of people told through a number of viewpoints and without much plot.

The first part of the novel is dominated by politics as Tadlock tries to keep his position as captain of the train but is replaced by Lije Evans. At Fort Laramie, Curtis Mack seduces Mercy McBee, with whom young Brownie Evans has already fallen secretly in love. At first, Lije is reluctant to approve of a connection between his family and the McBees. But Mercy's need for affection and love, her gentleness despite her hard life, her naivete, raise sympathy rather than condemnation toward her. Mercy proves herself worthy of Brownie's love, Mack attempts to make up for her earlier indiscretion, and Mercy and Brownie are married at Fort Hall.

Although the land and climate put serious obstacles in the way of the immigrants, the more serious problems originate from the immigrants themselves. Once greed, lust, jealousy and aggressiveness are tamed, the mountains and rivers can be crossed. The only protection that couples like Lije and Rebecca Evans have is provided by each other. It is this defense that not only gives Lije and Rebecca a happy married life and promises one for Brownie and Mercy, but also insures that the wagon train under Lije's guidance will safely reach its destination at the mouth of the Willamette. Where most western writers are content to show what the characters do, Guthrie concentrates on what they think and feel, and by doing so, brings a far greater sense of depth and reality than is to be found in *The Covered Wagon.*

As a film, *The Way West* (United Artists, 1967) is just about as bad as any epic western ever made. Big stars and big landscapes come together in a neurotic script that includes a sex starved teenage girl, a virginal wife, rape and self-flagellation. The characters bear little, if any, resemblance to those in the novel. Mercy McBee (Sally Field) is so horny that at one point her lusty father points out that if she doesn't get a husband pretty soon, they'll have to mate her to an ox, which is all well and good, considering oxen, like mules, don't mate. Her constant flirtations end when she is raped, not seduced, by Johnnie Mack (Michael Whitney), who pays for his sin by being hanged. When his son is killed in a buffalo stampede, Tadlock (Kirk Douglas) orders his Negro servant to flog him. Dick Summers (Robert Mitchum) just seems bored by the whole proceedings.

The revolt by the train that puts Lije Evans (Richard Widmark) at the head comes late in the film after Tadlock has already hanged Mack. Tadlock has pushed the train and those in it to a breaking point, and as they have become more and more exhausted, he has become more obsessed. Sometime after the revolt, Tadlock is making a descent by rope down a steep gorge, and Mack's widow cuts the rope, dropping Tadlock to his death. This sobers the train, and everyone agrees to finish the trip just as Tadlock had planned, thus legitimizing his dream and his actions.

All of these events are consciously absent in the novel and illustrate just how far the film has strayed from its source. Crowded into a two hour movie are enough bizarre plots and subplots to keep a television soap opera going for a year. In the right hands, this might have been a good, even great, film, but the lack of a decent script and solid direction turn this into a regrettable adaptation.

It may be that the episodic quality *The Covered Wagon* and *The Way West* prevented these novels from adapting well to the screen. Other types of stories dealing with settlers and their encounters with the Indian fared much better, in large part because of tighter plotting. An excellent example of this is Ernest Haycox's most famous short story, "Stage to Lordsberg," which is typical of the author's treatment of the American Indian within his fiction.

Although it appeared in *Collier's* in April 1937, *The Saturday Evening Post's* influence was evident. The story opens:

> This was one of those years in the Territory when the Apache smoke signals spiraled up from the stony mountain summits and many a ranch house lay as a square of blackened ashes on the ground and the departure of a stage from Tonto was the beginning of an adventure that had no certain happy ending.

Thus the author sets the stage for the events to follow. The Apache lurk among the mountains waiting to pounce on the unweary and unlucky. Lives will be lost.

On the stage to Lordsberg are representative types of the frontier. Happy Stuart is the driver, John Strang the shotgun guard. Among the passengers are a young woman going to marry an infantry officer, a whiskey drummer from Kansas City, a cattleman, an Englishman and a gambler. They are not given names; they simply are types. The protagonists are Malpias Bill, on his way to Lordsberg to settle an old debt, and Henriette, a woman of dubious past and through whose viewpoint the story is seen.

The story is simple and direct. As the stage rolls across the desert toward Lordsberg, Malpias Bill and Henriette are drawn to one another. Throughout the journey, the constant threat of Indian attack hangs over everyone, and just as the danger seems past, the stage is attacked. During the chase the gambler is killed, but the others make it through safely. Once in Lordsberg, Bill pays his debt by killing two men, and he and Henriette are united.

In the Haycox story can be found traces of "Boule de Suif" by Guy de Maupassant, which tells of a prostitute during the Franco-Prussian war of 1870 who gives herself to an enemy officer in order to arrange safe passage for a coach load of bourgeois passengers who, in turn, despise her for her act of self-sacrifice. When John Ford bought "Stage to Lordsberg" for $2,500 and he and screenwriter Dudley Nichols wrote the screenplay, they focused on the hypocrisy of class distinction that so intrigued de Maupassant.

The prostitute in *Stagecoach* (Walter Wagner, 1939) is Dallas (Claire Trevor), a girl with a heart of gold who is being forced out of town by the Law and Order League, a group fo sexually repressed women threatened by the likes of Dallas. Her self-sacrifice comes when she stays up all night to help the virtuous army wife deliver her child. There are two other outsiders on the coach. Doc Boone (Thomas Mitchell) is also kicked out of town for being the town drunk. When Dallas asks him what they have done to deserve their fate, Doc says, "We have been struck down by a foul disease called social prejudice, my child. These dear ladies of the Law and Order League are scouring out the dregs of the town. Come, be a proud, glorified dreg like me." As the coach pulls out, he makes an off-camera, obscene gesture, which makes some of the ladies cry out and others avert their eyes. The third outsider is the Ringo Kid (John Wayne), who joins the coach along its journey to Lordsberg. Having just broken out of prison and heading to Lordsberg to kill the man who framed him and killed his brother, the Kid also feels the sting of rejection. When he and Dallas seat themselves at the way-station table, the army wife, the gambler and the banker get up and move away. "I guess you can't break out of prison and into society in the same week," he says.

The other passengers are themselves flawed characters. The army wife, Lucy Mallory (Louise Platt), is a cold, class-conscious Southern woman finally warmed by Dallas' generosity. The gentleman gambler, Hatfield (John Carradine), hides his good family name and is not above shooting a man in the back, yet he, too, looks down on the outcasts. The villain of the coach, however, is Gatewood (Burton Churchill), who is absconding with the bank's money, but he keeps up the class distinctions more virulently than anyone. Even after the birth of Mrs. Mallory's child when many of the barriers have broken down, Gatewood persists in building them up again, much to everyone's annoyance. When the coach pulls into Lordsberg, it is Gatewood who insists that Ringo be put in chains, only to be restrained himself and led away to jail. Only Peacock (Donald Meek), the meek whiskey drummer and sometimes comic relief, shows humility and understanding to all, and it is he who bridges the gap between the outcasts and the socially acceptable. Hypocrisy is not part of his makeup, so it is doubly ironic when he is the first to fall in the Indian attack.

The two remaining people on the coach are the good-hearted driver, Buck (Andy Devine), and the courageous sheriff, Curley (George Bancroft). Buck ably handles the six-in-hand team as it rolls and plunges across the mountains and desert, but he has trouble with his mouth that constantly gets him in trouble and makes him seem slightly stupid. On the other hand, Curley is laconic. Words come less frequently, but they mean something because he is the authority figure.

The main outside threat to the stagecoach and passengers is the Indians led by Geronimo. "That old Apache butcher," says Doc Boone. Other than this one statement, the Apaches are regarded more as an uncontrollable force of nature than as savages to be eradicated. Actually, part of the titles that introduce the film point to Geronimo as a rebel fighting against tyranny: "At the time no name struck more terror into the hearts of travellers than that of *GERONIMO* — leader of those Apaches who preferred death rather than submit to the white man's will."

As Dallas is being run out town, she is advised that the Indians are on the loose and her life may be in danger if she takes the stage. Glancing at the ladies of the Law and Order League, she says, "There are worse things than Apaches." The Indians' one act of savagery is the massacre of a family at the way station, although we see only a glimpse of a woman's arm just before Hatfield covers her with his coat. The feeling is much more of pity for the woman than hatred for the Apache. Even when the Apache are first seen high atop a bluff watching the coach rolling along down below, they seem a part of the landscape, part of nature. When they attack, their movements are quick and beautiful, their skill in riding extraordinary. But it is not the Apache Dallas fears; it is hypocrisy.

On the way to Lordsberg, the passengers will meet their fate or redemption. Both Doc and Dallas find renewed hope in the birth of Mrs. Mallory's child, Doc because his skills have been reinforced and validated and Dallas because she is able to give herself unselfishly and have her act accepted graciously by Mrs. Mallory. In addition, love gives Dallas and Ringo something neither expected nor hoped for. The whiskey drummer and Hatfield fall to the Indians, the banker is arrested, and in a final showdown, Ringo takes revenge for the murder of his brother. Curley allows him go free with Dallas to flee across the border, where, as Doc says, they will be spared "the blessings of civilization."

When *Stagecoach* (TCF, 1966) was remade 27 years later, the story remained basically the same, although it ran nine minutes longer and was in color. The Indians became Sioux rather than Apache and the location became Colorado rather than the Southwest, which in a sense, violated the intent not only of the previous version but also of the Haycox story. The film seldom comes alive, and as is usually the case with remakes, it invites comparison with the original, emerging a distant second, if for no other reason than Ford managed to capture the spirit of the Haycox story while at the same time adding depth and character; the remake evokes little feeling of any kind.

Settlers and their trouble with the Indians are the focus of a number of western short stories and novels, one of the best of which is *Canyon Passage* (1945), also by Ernest Haycox, which was serialized in *The Saturday Evening Post.* The setting of the novel is atypical of the western genre. While many western novels have used Oregon as their place of destination, few have used it as their main locale, and although Haycox was to return to it several times, he never used it to better advantage than here. Note the rich, vivid texture from the opening paragraph in which the protagonist, Logan Stuart, crosses a Portland street during a downpour:

> The plank walk-ways across the street intersections were half afloat and sank beneath his weight as he used them; at two o'clock of such a day the kerosene lights were sparkling through drenched panes and the smell of the saloons, when he moved by them, was a rich warm blend of tobacco, whiskey and men's soaked woolen clothing.

In many ways the novel seems more a historical romance than a western. There are no gunfights *per se,* although at one point Logan is ambushed by his arch enemy Bragg. There is a fight in a saloon between Logan and Bragg, a knock-down, drag-out barroom brawl. The stereotypical fast gunfighter or roving cowboy or army scout are nowhere to be found. Although Logan Stuart is not above fisticuffs and chasing Indians, he is really a frontier entrepreneur, a freight-line owner with a restless urge to keep moving and opening up new territories. There are two women in his life: Lucy, who is engaged to his friend George; and Caroline, the settler's daughter. Haycox tended to overuse the love triangle in his novels, but it works perfectly here. The characters' strengths and weakness are mirrored in the various relationships.

As in "Stage to Lordsberg" and *Bugles in the Afternoon,* the Indians are hazards much like the weather, something to be borne and endured. As the novel opens, the Indians are peaceable, perhaps responsible for the death of one miner but no more. Only after Bragg kills some unarmed squaws do the Indians go on a rampage, and in a fitting conclusion, Bragg himself is killed and scalped as Logan watches from a safe distance. Other than as the *deus ex machina,* the Indians serve little purpose.

The film *Canyon Passage* (Universal, 1946) is a remarkably faithful adaptation of the novel. Filmed in Technicolor, it captures the wild setting and makes it as much a part of the plot as the characters. The early scenes in Portland and later in the wilderness are equally stunning. Also, there are some excellent vignettes of frontier life, the most impressive of which is a cabin-raising that has the look of the real thing. But among all these superior production values also resides the story, kept intact, and therein lies another of the film's strengths. Director Jacques Tourneur and scenarist Ernest Pascal took time to delve into the dark side of their characters. This is not to say they made any drastic changes; only that they were content to allow Haycox's novel to work for them. The characters are all here: Logan Stuart (Dana Andrews), the sturdy hero who doesn't allow little things like attempted murder and Indian uprisings to get in the way of business; Bragg (Ward Bond), the hard drinking villain; George (Brian Donlevy), Logan's banker friend who is embezzling money; Lucy (Susan Hayward), the heroine with enough fire to match Logan's drive. *Canyon Passage* is an excellent and underrated film, and along with *Stagecoach* must rank as the very best of the adaptations made from Haycox's fiction.

Indians were also a threat to those cowboy entrepreneurs who attempted to drive their cattle first to Missouri and then to Kansas. Such material was used by Bordon Chase, whose greater fame is that of a screenwriter rather than a novelist. *The Chisholm Trail* was serialized in *The Saturday Evening Post* in 1946, but when it was published as a hardback, it was retitled inappropriately *Blazing Guns on the Chisholm Trail* (1947), which made it sound like a hackneyed formula western. The novel followed the standard policy of the *Post* and presented a straightforward, no nonsense story, but it was certainly not formula. Thomas Dunsun, an Englishman, crosses the plains in a train headed for the gold fields of California, but he leaves the other wagons and turns south toward Texas. Along the way, he picks up Matthew Garth, a young boy left alone after an Indian attack. Years later find them on a ranch in Texas and needing to move their cattle to market. On the hard and dangerous drive to Missouri, the men hear of a market in Kansas. At first, when the drovers complain and turn against Dunsun, Matthew stands beside him, even to the point of joining him in a gunfight and killing three of the cowpunchers. But even Matthew comes to see the folly of pushing on to Missouri, and he and the others take the herd away from Dunsun and head toward Kansas.

Along the trail, Matthew and the men come to the aid of a wagon train besieged by Comanches. On this train is Tess Millay who Matthew had previously met in Memphis. In love with Matthew, she wants to join the drovers and go with them into Kansas, but Matthew forbids it because he knows that Dunsun is on his trail. Later, after Matthew and his men have gone, Dunsun arrives, and she persuades him to take her along into Kansas, even though Dunsun knows that she is in love with Matthew. They run into Cherry, who shoots it out with Dunsun. Cherry is killed and Dunsun wounded, but still he pushes on, determined to kill Matthew. At last, the showdown comes, but as the two men reach for their pistols, Matthew halts his draw, unable to shoot at the crucial moment. Dunsun has no such compunction; he fully intends to kill Matthew for the betrayal. But the wound that Cherry has inflicted on him finally takes its toll, and he collapses. Dunsun hangs on just long enough for Matthew and Tess to get him back to Texas where he dies.

Many formulary elements are present in *Blazing Guns on the Chisholm Trail*, yet it constantly avoids the pitfalls and clichés of the genre, remaining a novel with far more depth than the average formula western. The writing is slick, but Chase tells a good story, and an early jump in years is smoothly handled. Also, the characters, especially those of Dunsun and Matthew Garth, are sharply drawn. Even the minor characters such as Cherry Valance and Groot come alive. Only Tess Mallay seems forced, especially in her early meeting with Matthew, and her dialogue often sounds unconvincing. She seems a superficial character created solely to achieve the needed turns of plot. Also, the Indians who attack the wagon train are never really defined, faceless entities that help to bring the lovers together and then disappear off stage. However, considering the restriction that Chase worked under writing for the *Post*, this novel is an underrated minor classic in the genre.

The novel became *Red River* (Monterrey, 1948), a seminal western and one of the best in the long canon of John Wayne classics. Bordon Chase worked on the screeplay; as a consequence, much of novel remains intact. However, several changes proved important. Dunsun (John Wayne) is no Englishman but rather a frontiersman knowledgeable in the ways of the Indians. The opening has Dunsun leaving the train and the woman he loves and striking out for Texas with Groot (Walter Brennan). After the wagon train is attacked and everyone is massacred, including Dunsun's love, the two men pick up Matthew Garth, who was out hunting for a stray cow when the attack occurred. That night, the Comanches attack them, but Dunsun and Groot kill them all. This opening segment has been enriched by the addition of the love interest for Dunsun, and thus his later attraction for Tess Millay (Joanne Dru) and his offer to make her rich if she gives him a son makes even more sense than it did in the novel.

The script also drops the early meeting between Tess and Matthew, instead jumping right into the organization of cattle drive and the drive itself. For almost two-thirds of the film, the drive is the centerpiece as Dunsun slowly becomes a tyrant, pushing his men beyond all limitations. By the time Matthew (Montgomery Cliff) rebels, the film has taken on all the aspects of a western *Mutiny on the Bounty*. Unfortunately, just as Chase was forced to pander to the dictates of the *Post* and include a love interest, so the movie finally introduces Tess Millay, and what has been a brilliant script quickly degenerates into a standard love story. Just as in the novel, Tess never seems real but rather a character forced upon the stage against her will. However, what has gone before is so strong that even her presence cannot ruin the film.

The weakest element within the structure of *Red River* is the climax. Chase was forced by Hawks to alter the conclusion where Cherry inflicts a wound on Dunsun and then is taken to Texas by Matthew and Tess where he dies. Instead, there is an artificial ending where Dunsun and Matthew are prevented from killing each other by the intervention of Tess, a comic ending that is totally inappropriate to all that has gone before. Chase complained bitterly, but to no avail. Hawks didn't want the Wayne character to die. A lesser film would have been ruined by such treatment.

There are so many things to praise in this film — the beginning of the cattle drive, the stampede, the funeral under the darkening landscape, the complex relationship between Dunsun and Matthew. Much of the praise must go to Howard Hawks who directed so magnificently. Yet, Bordon Chase must also be singled out, first for the novel on which the script is based and second for the script itself, despite the changes Chase was forced to make. In retrospect, the author's judgment on the ending must be respected. The story seems to demand the death of Dunsun, a man out of step with the times, a man of the old West who must give way to the man of the new West. What is amazing is that the film retains so much power despite the weak ending.

Comanches are also present in *The Comancheros* (1952) by Paul Wellman, an entertaining albeit undistinguished novel. Here New Orleans gambler Paul Regret flees trumped up charges of murder and drifts into Texas where he is forced to join the Texas Rangers in order to save his skin. He is paired with Gatling, a crusty veteran who takes an instant dislike to the young upstart. The two men are sent by Sam Houston into the Staked Plains to make contact with the Comancheros, outlaws who, with the Indians, prey upon outlying settlements and ranches. Once at the Comanchero camp, Paul discovers the leader Musketoon has a daughter, Eloise, who Regret knew and loved in New Orleans. Musketoon is killed by one of his followers, a malevolent lieutenant has Regret and Gatling tortured, and the Rangers arrive just in the nick of time. In the ensuing struggle, Gatling is killed, and Paul turns the tide of battle by killing Iron Shirt, the Comanche chief.

The Comancheros (TCF, 1961) proved to be the last film directed by Michael Curtiz, although most of the action sequences were actually directed by second unit director Cliff Lyons. It is a rousing film, although like the novel, undistinguished. It might have been better had it stuck more closely to the novel; where it diverged, it weakened the story.

Paul Regret (Stuart Whitman) engages in a duel, killing a judge's son, and flees to Texas. Along the way, he encounters a beautiful adventuress, Pilar (Ina Balin), with whom he has a quick affair. When he reaches Texas, he is immediately arrested by Ranger Jack Cutter (John Wayne). After various plot manipulations including an escape by Regret and a shootout between Cutter and a Comanchero (neither incident is in the novel), Regret becomes a reluctant Ranger and is forced to go along with Cutter to find the Comanchero camp. Once there, he discovers that Pilar is an active participant in the outlaws' activities; yet, she does not betray Regret and Cutter, even though she knows the latter is a Ranger. When she finally helps them escape, the situation seems helpless until a Ranger detachment arrives to save the day. In the end, Cutter gives Regret and Pilar horses and allows them to ride away to Mexico.

In the novel, the relationship between Regret and the girl is built on coincidence, and as such, rings hollow, and the film does nothing to ease this strain. On the contrary, Pilar's sudden first interest in Regret is inexplicable, and later at the Comanchero camp, their blossoming love is even harder to accept. Even though Sam Houston is the only authentic historical character in the novel, his presence is important in that he makes the decision to allow Regret to remain in Texas as a Ranger, and it is he who sends the former gambler and Gatling off on the mission. It is on the mission that the mutual respect between the two men grows. With the single exception of the mention of his name, the film drops Houston from the story. Also dropped are the scenes before the mission when Regret learns the ways of the Rangers and begins to develop strengths that make him a better man and that make Gatling finally come to accept him.

One area in which the novel and film agree is in their depiction of Indians. The Comanches hover in the background, villainous and deadly savages led by ruthless outlaws. When Iron Shirt arrives on the scene, he is wined and dined by Musketoon (Nehemiah Persoff), finally collapsing in a drunken heap. It is Musketoon and his ruthless Comancheros who take center stage, and the Indians are only window dressing for the plot, without individuality and without dignity.

In *Canyon Passage* by Haycox, *Blazing Guns on the Chisholm Trail* by Chase and *The Comancheros* by Wellman, Indians were only a small part of the plots, minor irritants that the settlers and trail drovers had to deal with. The main thrust of each novel was elsewhere. However, in *The Searchers* (1954) by Alan LeMay, Indians become not only the main focus of the story but also an obsession of the two central characters. The story opens in Texas Panhandle in 1868 and recounts the seven year quest by Amos Edwards and Martin Pauley for a girl who has been captured by Comanches. Amos is a complex, neurotic man and an Indian hater, a common enough character on the frontier, and when he finds Debbie, his niece, he plans to kill her because of her contamination by the Indians. Martin hopes he will be able to stop Edwards when the time comes. Eventually, Debbie is found, but only at a high cost. Martin sacrifices his romantic relationship with his girl Laurie, and Amos is killed.

The Searchers is a subtle and powerful story. Underlying the central story are certain psychosexual implications that motivate the characters. Amos has been in love with his brother's wife for years, and much of his life previous to the opening of the story has been dictated by his feelings. Even his search is wrapped up in the feelings for Martha. Because the novel was first serialized in *The Saturday Evening Post,* that magazine's anti-Indian editorial policy influenced the depiction of the Comanches as a savage and cruel people. When Brad tells Amos that he has seen Lucy in the Comanche camp, Amos tells him, "I found Lucy yesterday. I buried her in my own saddle blanket. With my own hands, by the rock. I thought it best to keep it from you as longs' I could." When Brad presses for more information, Amos yells, "Shut up! Never ask me what more I seen!"

The Comanches are also clever, and their cleverness provides an ironic commentary on the events. Early in the search, Amos explains why they will eventually find Debbie:

An Indian will chase a thing until he thinks he's chased it enough. Then he quits. So the same when he runs. After a while he figures we must have quit, and he starts to loaf. Seemingly he never learns there's such a thing as a critter that might just keep coming on.

For five years, the Comanches keep feeding Amos and Martin false information, leading them from one place to another, and it is only when the Comanches finally understand that Amos and Martin will not give up, they set a trap and allow them to find Debbie.

The machinations of the Comanches is the one thing missing from John Ford's version of *The Searchers* (Warner Bros., 1956). Thus, at the end, when the Indians return to the same place the story opened, the site of the murder raid, and allow Ethan (John Wayne), changed from Amos in the novel, and Martin (Jeffery Hunter) to find Debbie, it seems more a manipulation of plot than anything else. But this is the film's only weakness.

The novel *The Searchers* was too grim for director John Ford's taste, and when he and screenwriter Frank Nugent set out to make a workable script, they added several comic characters. The top-hatted Texas Ranger, the Rev. Samuel Clayton (Ward Bond), was invented for the film, a military clergyman in the same tradition as Father Rosenkranz (Arthur Shields) from *Drums Along the Mohawk*. There is a significant difference, however. Rosenkranz was a chaplain of a military unit; Clayton commands one, moving from one job to another with no clear demarcation. Ethan is constantly asking him if he is speaking as a reverend or a captain of the Rangers. At the river, he hands a Bible to a wounded man. "Hold it. It will make you feel better," he says, then goes right back to killing Indians with a cry of "Hallelujah!" One other military man, the young lieutenant (Patrick Wayne), is also made the butt of several jokes, most regarding his father, the colonel. When the Texas Rangers attack the Indian village, the young lieutenant inadvertently stabs the Rev. Clayton in the behind. Another comic figure is Ol' Mose Harper (Hank Worden), a simple minded old man who borders on insanity. It is he who finally brings news of Scar's encampment and enables Ethan and Matt to find Debbie. However, the most comic of all the comic figures is Charley McCorry (Ken Curtis), a Texas Ranger and Laurie's suitor. In the novel, Charley is a straight character, bright enough and brave enough to eventually win Laurie's hand and marry her. Even the first draft of the script failed to change his basic character. While on location, Ford changed Charley into a slow-witted, stammering country boy after hearing Ken Curtis use a hillbilly accent he had used in a radio routine.

Curtis, however, protested that he would look like a fool. Ford convinced him otherwise, arguing that Curtis' part was insignificant as it was, and especially since he wouldn't get the girl in the end. Carrying the thought further, Ford felt it would be best to make Curtis' part funny if he couldn't be made to look good, and that the hillbilly accent would make the character stick out in people's minds.

Ford also made the character of Look, the rotund Comanche squaw who Martin unknowingly buys, a comic figure when she first appears. When she crawls into Martin's bedroll, he unceremoniously kicks her out and she rolls down the hill. Her fate, however, is tragic. She runs off in the night after being confronted with Scar's name, and Ethan and Martin discover her body in the village destroyed by the soldiers. "Why did they have to kill her?" yells Martin. The novel offers no such tragic death. Instead, she simply disappears one night, probably carried off by an Indian lover who had been trailing them.

Ford and Nugent also added a sense of warmth to the grim, violent story, a sense of family and community. As Martha Jorgenson tells Ethan and her husband Lors,

> A Texan is nothing but a human man way out on a limb. This year, and next year, and maybe for hundred more. But I don't think it'll be forever. Someday this country will be a fine good place to be.
> Maybe it needs our bones in the ground before that time can come.

In the novel, this speech is given, almost word for word, but by Amos, not Martha, as he, Martin and Brad search for Debbie. For Ford, Martha becomes the symbol of hearth and home, and therefore she is more fitting to utter such a statement.

The underlying motivation of Ethan Edwards and his love for his brother's wife is also subtly handled. As Martha goes to get Ethan's Confederate coat, she pauses a moment and strokes it lovingly. From the outer room, Clayton notices the tender scene, and quickly looks away, realizing that he has intruded upon a very private moment. There are no such subtleties in the novel. From the way Amos talks of Martha, Martin figures it out himself, and since the point of view is through Martin, the reader learns it as he does.

Ford made an important change in Debbie's fate. In the novel, Scar has taken Debbie for his daughter, and while it is true that she will be forced to marry a warrior sooner or later, she is unspoiled at the time of her rescue. By the time Ethan and Martin locate her in the film, she is Scar's wife, a squaw, and as such, has been polluted by the Comanches both psychologically and sexually.

The novel concludes with the raid on Scar's camp where Amos is killed by a squaw whom he mistakes for Debbie. When a search of the camp fails to find her, Martin continues the search alone. He finds her late the next day out on the plains, dehydrated and exhausted, but otherwise fine. When Martin tells her that he is going to take her home, she says, "It is empty. Nobody is there." Martin replies, "I'll be there, Debbie." However, the film ends quite differently. The final scene of Ford's *The Searchers* is justly revered by critics as well as film buffs. Jorgenson and his wife escort Debbie through the door into their house, followed by Martin and Laurie. For a moment, Ethan, who was not killed in the raid, stands framed by the door, the eternal outsider, then he turns and walks away as the door closes.

In retrospect, it may be that both the novel and film of *The Searchers* are tainted with racism as both book and film dwell on the brutality and barbarity of the Indian without any insight into motivating forces. Only when Scar briefly mentions the death of his sons do we get an inkling of what might lie inside the man. Even so, the story is so strong and powerful, in LeMay's case so well written and in Ford's so well directed, that the fault appears minor.

Alan LeMay came up with in interesting variation on *The Searchers* with *The Unforgiven* (1957), also serialized in *The Saturday Evening Post*. Where the former novel had Indians kidnapping and raising a white girl as one of their own, *The Unforgiven* reverses the idea by having a white family on the Texas plains, circa 1875, raising a girl who may or may not be a Kiowa. Interesting in concept, the novel suffers from a diffused narrative structure. The largest portion of the story is told through the point-of-view of Rachel, the girl raised by the Zachery family. However, part of the action is also seen through the perspective of her adopted brothers, Ben, Cash and Andy. An occasional flashback sequence often seems to have no point-of-view at all. Still, the narrative drive and the character of Rachel are enough to provide an entertaining story, although one that has little lasting power.

The Kiowas are depicted as brutal as the Comanches in *The Search-ers*, yet the author, despite his anti–Indian bias, attempted to deal dramatically with the cultural differences between the races, placing most of the blame on tradition and exposing the basic hypocrisy of the white position. When the Kiowas come to reclaim Rachel, they use white man's logic:

> We many times take your people. You come, you want them, you buy. You pay us. We let you take them back. Many times. All friendly. All good. Long ago you take a child of ours. You take my sister. We look for her very long. Now we find. Now we come. We

want her back now. She is ours. We pay. You pay us, now we pay
you. All friendly, all good.

The fact that Rachel is "white" is cultural only; born a Kiowa, she has
been raised by the whites and is therefore "white." The thought that she
could be returned to the Kiowas is both repellant and unrealistic to the
Zacherys. To the white characters, it seems perfectly logical to
repatriate a white from the Indians. On the other hand, returning
someone who is culturally "white" to the Indians is a completely un-
natural act.

When John Huston came to film *The Unforgiven* (United Artists,
1960), he and scriptwriter Ben Maddow, who had previously helped the
director adapt *The Asphalt Jungle,* made some basic changes in the plot.
They gave Rachel (Audrey Hepburn) a beau, Charlie Rawlins (Albert
Salmi), who is killed by the Kiowas as he returns home one night from
courting. Zeb Rawlins, angered over the death of his son, renounces his
partnership with the Zacherys and leaves them to face the Kiowas
alone. Ben (Burt Lancaster) and the rest of the Zachery clan gather at
their house to face the Indian threat where Mattilda tells them that the
story of Rachel's origin is true. Cash (Audie Murphy), who hates Indians with a vengeance, denounces Rachel and leaves. The Zacherys
then fight the Kiowas through the night during which Andy (Doug
McClure) is wounded and Mattilda is killed. Just as the Indians seem
to be gaining the upper hand, Cash returns to sway the tide of battle.
Rachel kills her own brother, the Indian who has led the war party to
get her. As the film ends, Ben announces his plans to marry Rachel.

In many ways, Huston improved upon the novel and made the
story far richer. While he concentrated less on the Indians than Ford
in *The Searchers,* he emphasized the search for a truth hidden in the past,
a truth that reveals something about the present. This idea Huston was
to explore in more depth in *Freud* (Universal-International, 1963) and
The List of the Adrian Messenger (U-I, 1963). There are also numerous
references to the Old Testament and often the dialogue has a Biblical
sound. Such dialogue shows up even more prominently in Huston's
other western, *The Life and Times of Judge Roy Bean* (National General/
Famous Artists, 1972).

The Unforgiven is also filled with a strange mysticism. Cash seems
to have special powers wherein he is able to sense the presence of Indians. During the siege of the Zachery house, he is ten miles away with
the Rawlins' daughter. Even so, he is able to tell her exactly what is happening. It is only with Rachel that his senses fail. Never once before his
mother reveals the truth does he grasp that his adopted sister is an

Indian. Another mystical character is Kelsey (Joseph Wiseman), whose ghostly character keeps appearing throughout the film until he is finally hanged when the crazy prophet reveals the truth about Rachel's origin and forecasts doom.

The most striking scene in the film does not even occur in the novel. During the night before the attack, the Indians play their war flutes. Ben and Andy move the piano outdoors, and their mother counters with light classics. The Indians are so threatened by the white man's instrument, six braves are killed in a frenzied attack on the piano.

In a 1965 interview in *Film Culture,* John Huston said, "I don't want to put my brand on a Western; it has its adequate style already." However, when he made *The Unforgiven,* he did put his own brand on it, and it emerged as a visually impressive and well acted film. Where he failed to make strides was in his presentation of the Indians, who remain only shadows without substance. The Zacherys band together to save their sister from the savages and to save her from being an outcast by the whites. That is the *raison d'être* for the Kiowas' existence. Although *The Unforgiven* is good-looking and enjoyable, its underlying racist attitude ultimately makes the film less satisfying than it should have been.

Also very similar in content to *The Searchers* is *Comanche Captives* (1959) by Will Cook, which also first appeared as a serial in *The Saturday Evening Post.* It is the story of a town sheriff, Guthrie McCabe, and a young army lieutenant, Jim Gary, who band together in an attempt to rescue white captives from the Comanches. In many ways, McCabe shares many of the same characteristics with Amos Edwards from *The Searchers,* especially in his cynical outlook on life, although he is not personally involved in the action as was Edwards. McCabe agrees to help the relatives of the captives for money, a thousand dollars for each returned captive. Jim Gary plays the foil, the same as Martin Pauley, and even though under orders to bring back the captives, Gary is far more a humanitarian than McCabe. Duty and moral responsibility are one in the same for him; he believes that bringing back the captives is a positive act. In the downbeat ending, he realizes that his actions have brought only more heartache and suffering.

When John Ford was offered *Comanche Captives,* his first impulse was to turn it down; yet, the more he thought about it, the more it appealed to him. He agreed to direct the film only after an agreement with the producer that he could rewrite the script and add some humor. He also insisted on a more upbeat ending. In the planning stage, Ford must have been intrigued by the similarities between *Comanche Captives* and Alan LeMay's *The Searchers,* but the Will Cook novel, although pleasant enough, is far weaker. By the time the story reached the screen as *Two Rode Together* (Columbia, 1961), an adequate novel became a disappointing John Ford film, and the director himself referred to it as "the worst piece of crap I've done in twenty years."

The novel's point of view is through the army lieutenant, Jim Gary, but Ford made Gary (Richard Widmark) and McCabe (James Stewart) of equal importance. In their basic characters, they are much as Will Cook created them, but to Ford, neither is the hero; both have weaknesses and strengths that evoke sympathy and identification from the audience, yet they are also opposites. Gary is an army man who will follow orders even if it means death, but he lacks the depth of understanding to see things as they are. It is only after the visit to the Indian camp that he fully realizes the fool's errand on which he and McCabe have been sent. On the other hand, McCabe has allegiance to no one but himself, a cynical, charming mercenary who has seen too much to have illusions about anything. In the end, his compassion and faith in people match Gary's; each has learned from the other.

In the novel, Gary and McCabe bring out only two captives, a young boy who has grown up with the Comanches and is as much Indian as any brave and a young woman who has been taken as a wife by a chief. Furious at Gary for bringing the woman along, McCabe strikes out alone with the boy leaving Gary to make his way back by himself with the woman's Indian husband trailing them. In *Two Rode Together,* Ford reversed the teams, having Gary take the boy and McCabe staying behind with the woman, Elena (Linda Cristal). When Stone Calf (Woody Strode) attempts to recapture his wife, McCabe kills him. After he returns Elena to the fort, she is mercilessly hounded by the officers' wives, and McCabe lashes out at them, telling them what hypocrites they are. Giving up his badge, McCabe takes Elena and they leave for California and a new beginning.

One particularly impressive scene remains from the novel which aptly illustrates the folly connected with Gary's and McCabe's task. The boy who is brought back is first caged, then finally turned over to a half crazed woman who believes him to be her son. When she lets him out, the boy kills her, but before he can escape, he is captured and lynched. Just as the noose is dropped over his head, he hears a music box that belonged to Marty Purcell (Shirley Jones), and it registers in his mind. He is her brother, captured by the Comanches when only a small child, and the Indians have turned him into a savage. Civilization, in turn, kills the savage.

Somewhat of a cross between Wellman's *The Comancheros* and LeMay's *The Searchers,* although not as good as either, is *Guns of the Rio Conchos* (1958) by Cliff Huffaker. A good formulary writer, Huffaker often wrote short novels that, while they had two-dimensional characters, were far too brief to build complete, multilayered individuals. His protagonists usually fell into the prototypical western hero mold and his plots often lacked the intricacies of more important novels such as *The Searchers.* However, his novels are lean and swift, providing a couple of hours of enjoyment, yet he seldom leaves the reader with much to remember or cherish.

Guns of the Rio Conchos tells the story of Riot Holiday, a frontiersman who is wounded by Comanches, an arrowhead buried in his chest as a souvenir of their attack. Given six months to live, he sets out with young Tad McCallister, whose own mother and father have been killed by the Comanches, to take revenge on the Indians responsible. The novel ends on a light note when, after the two have accomplished their mission, a doctor removes the arrowhead from Holiday's chest, thus saving his life.

Rio Conchos (Fox, 1964) is far darker and far more complex. Although Huffaker himself was a coscenarist, the novel completely disappeared, replaced by a story with a central character, Lassiter (Richard Boone), who well may be the most venomously bitter hero ever to ride the range. When a shipment of rifles is stolen, army captain Haven (Stuart Whitman) arrests Lassiter because he is in possession of one of the rifles. Later, Lassiter and a Mexican bandit, Rodriguez (Tony Franciosa), join Haven in an attempt to find the stolen weapons. Lassiter does so because he is anxious to find the Indians responsible for the death of his wife and son. The three men are also accompanied by Sergeant Ben Franklyn (Jim Brown). The group discovers that the rifles are in the hands of Colonel Theron Pardee (Edmund O'Brien), who wants to rekindle the Civil War and plans to hand the rifles over to the Comanches. At the cost of the lives of Franklyn and Rodriguez, the group manages to blow up the rifles before they fall into the hands of the Indians.

The script is far superior to the novel. The characters, especially that of Lassiter, are much more complex. Even the choice of Lassiter as a name is interesting. Lassiter was also the name of the central character in Zane Grey's *Riders of the Purple Sage,* and he, too, was a man on a quest for vengeance. Grey's Lassiter was essentially a man of principle, a stereotypical western hero. However, the Lassiter of *Rio Conchos* is far more crazed, a Lassiter carried to extremes by his hatred of the

Indians and his desire for vengeance. He is a twisted man, hard and without pity, yet a man who is the perfect embodiment for the task at hand. *Rio Conchos* is an underrated film and also one of those rare examples where the film managed to improve and deepen the book.

Putting all the clichés into one fort, so to speak, was done in *Chuka* (1967) by Richard Jessup, a novel somewhat reminiscent of *Beau Geste.* Since Jessup also wrote the screenplay for his own novel, there are very little differences between the book and film. A gunfighter, Chuka (Rod Taylor), wanders into Arapahoe land and befriends the Indians, giving them food when they are starving. From there he goes into Fort Clendinon, which is under the command of alcoholic Colonel Valois (John Mills). At the fort, Chuka happens to meet his long lost love. Also present are a grizzled but likable army scout (James Whitmore) and a stage driver who hates war because horses get killed. The plight of the Indians is sensibly argued by Chuka but to no avail. The insensitive commander refuses to give in to the Indians' simple demands for food and ammunition. The fort is cut off and the stage is set for tragedy. For once, the Indians act sensibly, attacking at night. In the end, only Chuka and a young Mexican girl are left alive. The chief recognizes Chuka, and turning his horse, he rides out of the fort and allows them to live.

For a man who tries so hard to make a statement of tolerance and understanding toward the Indian, Chuka kills off whole bunches of them as he helps to defend the fort and tries to save his lady love. When the end seems near and only he and the young girl are left alive, he puts the pistol to her head, prepared to blow out her brains rather than allow her to fall into the hands of the Arapahoes. There is a dichotomy here that pulls both the novel and film apart and remains unresolved at the end.

Perhaps one of the strangest novels of Indian and white man is *The White Buffalo* (1975) by Richard Sale. While the paperback edition claims it is "in the grand tradition of *Shane* and *The Ox-Bow Incident*," it comes closer to *The Last Hunt*, although in reality, it fails to approach any of these works in stature. Under the name of James Otis, Wild Bill Hickok returns to the Black Hills. Although only 37 Hickok is already an old man, his eyesight fading and rheumatism settling in his bones. He is also beset by a demon, the white buffalo, that haunts his dreams, and he sets out to rid himself of the nightmares. During his odyssey, Hickok runs into Crazy Horse, who calls himself Worm and is also searching for the beast, the skin of which he needs to wrap around the body of his dead daughter who was killed by the white buffalo. At first, the two men are enemies, then become weary partners, then friends. In the end, they kill the monster only because they have joined forces. Apart, neither would have accomplished the task.

Obviously *The White Buffalo* was meant to be a western *Moby Dick*—Hickok is Ahab, Crazy Horse is Queequeg. It is an interesting experiment and a revisionist western that approaches its story from the perspective of half myth, half history. Sale's prose sets the right tone, making the book read almost like a dream, yet his details are hard and clear. The characterizations are also interesting, especially that of Hickok, the haunted part of his personality taking on a fatalistic aura that adds to the dreamlike atmosphere of the novel.

Despite the presence of Charles Bronson as Hickok, the film *The White Buffalo* (aka *Hunt to Kill;* United Artists, 1977) was universally castigated by critics, many who thought it Bronson's worst film, and it died an inglorious death at the box office. Critics and public alike were too hard on it. It has a few things to recommend. Richard Sale adapted his own novel, and the screenplay is a literal translation. Much of the dialogue is lifted straight from the book, and while it may, at times, delve too deeply into philosophy, it fits the tone. While Bronson was a little old to play Hickok—he was already 56—he appeared properly world weary and exhausted, a man nearing his end and haunted by a nightmare. As Crazy Horse/Worm, Will Sampson is fine, and once again it was gratifying to see an Indian portraying an Indian. As directed by J. Lee Thompson, the film had an additional strength. From the opening amidst one of Hickok's nightmares until the final confrontation with the white buffalo, the Moby Dick of the plains, the surreal tone seldom lapsed. Even the mechanical buffalo, which is never believable, in some strange way adds to the surreal quality.

Of course the film has many weaknesses. At times, the direction is ponderous, and the script takes on pretensions that weaken the overall effect. Too often author Sale and director Thompson are willing to settle for symbols instead of story, which further slows the action and impedes the story. On top of this, the film, like the novel, lacks a sense of humor. In no way can this be considered a great film but, like the book, it is an interesting failure.

6. Shadow Warriors

Occasionally the viewpoints of novels or short stories, and subsequently the films adapted from them, are narrated from the perspective of the Indian. Although not written by native Americans, these fictions have tried to avoid the white man's stereotype and present the Indian as a fully developed character who operates within his own cultural barriers rather than as "white men daubed red."

In 1881 Helen Hunt Jackson published an exposé of the treatment of the American Indian in *A Century of Dishonor*. Echoing the majority sentiment of that time, an irate Theodore Roosevelt said, "The most vicious cowboy had more moral principle than the average Indian." Caught up in her subject, however, Jackson wrote *Ramona* (1884), a novel she completed just a year before her death. It became her most popular and enduring work, going through more than 135 printings.

The central character, Ramona, is a half–Indian, half–Scottish girl who is the ward of Señora Moreno, a haughty Spanish woman with an eligible son, Felipe—all of whom reside in Southern California. Señora Moreno becomes alarmed over a possible romance between Ramona and Alessandro, a full-blooded Indian visiting the ranch. She has cause for alarm as the desperate couple elope. Hounded by the encroaching Americans, the couple moves from village to village. When Alessandro borrows a horse to go find a doctor for his sick child, he is brutally murdered by Farrar, a local ruffian. Bending over the body of her slain husband, Ramona laments, "My Alessandro! Gone to be with the saints; one of the blessed martyrs.... The burdens of grief were too great. He could not bear them!" Ramona's foster brother takes Ramona and her child to the old estate, but they are soon forced to move when Americans force Felipe to sell the ranch. In Mexico, she and Felipe are married, and Ramona is accepted into the society of Mexico City.

Ramona pleaded for racial tolerance, but it is too much the stereotypical nineteenth century women's book to be fully effective. Ramona and Alessandro are both openhearted, generous souls while the settlers are a mean, dispirited lot, an early version of the ugly American. Any serious examination of the Indian's plight is lost in over-sentimentalized romanticism. Far more important than the story and characters are the picturesque scenes and atmosphere of Spanish California.

The first film version of *Ramona* (Biograph, 1910) was directed by D.W. Griffith, who paid the publishers $100 for the rights. It is important for several reasons. It was touted as the most expensive film production of the day, and Biograph called it the director's most artistic film. For the first time in the history of motion pictures, the studio even sent the cast and crew on location to the actual spots where the novel took place. This also forced Griffith to rethink his approach to filmmaking, and the film became the first in which he used very long shots to open up the dramatic horizon. By breaking the rigidity of studio bound productions, Griffith made films more fluid and eloquent, adding to their novel form of expression. One remarkable scene stands out. From a far mountaintop, Alessandro watches the destruction of his village by the whites a mile or more away. The burning huts and scurrying Indians, although mere specks in the distance, are clearly visible.

Most reviewers agreed that the film captured the tone and quality of the novel, and a few even went so far as to proclaim it a trailblazer. The reviewer for the *Moving Picture World* said:

> It is too late now for the reproduction of the novel to exert any influence in the rectification of a great wrong. But perhaps it will be worthwhile to show thus graphically the injustice which preceded the settlement of a considerable proportion of the United States.

Closer examination, however, hints that the message may have been misinterpreted, especially in light of the director's later *The Birth of a Nation*. The theme here may be Darwin's survival of the fittest rather than a genuine concern for the Indian. When Ramona (Mary Pickford) falls in love with Alessandro, it is clearly evident that he is the weaker of the two, and that she sees her lover as some unrealized ideal. When white men take advantage of Alessandro, he weakly submits, deploring his fate rather than fighting against it. In the end, he is eliminated in the coldblooded way that nature removes the unfit.

The film also broke with the novel on several other counts. Since Griffith aimed the film for women, he tried to wring every tear possible from the script. The child of Ramona and Alessandro dies, and the director milked the burial scene for every sniffle. Felipe does not show up in this version to save Ramona and spirit her and the child away to Mexico. Instead, having sacrificed every material object for her husband, Ramona makes the ultimate sacrifice at Alessandro's funeral pyre, ending her own life.

The longest version of *Ramona* (Clune, 1916) came next, a three hour extravaganza full of excellent photography and detail but woefully lacking in pace. Long stretches grind by in which nothing happens. The best part of the film, the sheep shearing scene, comes early, and after that, everything is downhill.

The next version of *Ramona* (United Artists, 1928) is often considered the best. Certainly it is the most interesting on several counts. First, the public's appetite had been strongly whetted by a 78 RPM record on which the star, Delores Del Rio, sang the theme song. Second, Delores Del Rio proved to be the definitive Ramona, looking and acting the part, and as a result, she garnered some solid reviews. The most interesting aspect of the production, however, lay with the director, Edwin Carewe, a former hobo who had bummed around the West with Jack London. Carewe's real name was Fox. He was one-quarter Chickasaw and had spent much of his youth among the Indians. Perhaps this is why he was able to bring a particular sensitivity to the oft-filmed story.

One of the best scenes in this version happens when Ramona discovers that she is part Indian. Her joy is clearly expressed as she runs from one character to another crying that she is an Indian. When she finds Felipe, she shares her joy by telling him that, being an Indian herself, she can now marry Alessandro (Warner Baxter), whom Señora Moreno has just kicked off the ranch. It is with the character of Señora Moreno that the film deviates considerably from the novel. She is too severe, and as she reprimands Ramona for kissing Alessandro, there is a hint of the sinister in her face. When Señora Moreno tries to give Ramona the jewels left to her by her Scottish father, Ramona refuses, and an expression of suppressed glee spreads across the older woman's face.

Other changes include Ramona and Alessandro's baby dying because white doctors will not attend to an Indian child. The atrocities against the Indians mount. In a scene that predates by more than forty years similar scenes in *Soldier Blue* (Avco, 1970) and *Little Big Man* (Cinema Center, 1970), whites attack the village and kill everyone, including women and children. Alessandro is stronger in this version, a man of honor and courage, but he still meets his death by white men, once again because he is accused of being a horse thief. This leaves Ramona to wander through the forests until she finally collapses from exhaustion.

By the time *Ramona* (TCF, 1936) was filmed for the last time, the story was so old that not even sound and Technicolor could save it. Like so many silents remade with sound, *Ramona* needed drastic reshaping, but director Henry King and scenarist Lamar Trotti settled for rehashing the novel and earlier film versions. Ramona (Loretta Young) runs the emotional gamut, but with dialogue, it is an impossible role. Alessandro (Don Ameche) is strong and protective, but his black wig does little to disguise his non–Indian heritage. Once again he is killed for a horse thief, this time shot by Jim Ferrar (John Carradine) when he "borrows" a horse to ride for the doctor for his sick daughter. This version also sees the further hardening of Señora Moreno (Pauline Frederick), far from the loving mother figure of the novel. Here she is an out-and-out white supremacist. It turns out that her sister had spurned Ramona's father, which drove him into the arms of his Indian lover. Also added for this version was the character of Margarita (Katherine De Mille), a smoldering maiden jealous of Ramona. The only things critics found to praise were the color and supporting performance by Jane Darwell as a kindly settler from Tennessee. The plot was recognized for what it was, "unadulterated hokum" as Frank Nugent called it in *The New York Times,* and the characters were straight out of nineteenth century melodrama, no more believable than comic book characters.

Another controversial novel of the American Indian was *The Vanishing American* by Zane Grey, serialized in the *Ladies' Home Journal* in 1922 and brought out in book form by Harpers in 1925. The delay between the magazine and book publication is explained by the furor the story created, especially among religious groups, for the way it depicted treatment of the reservation Indians by the missionaries. Instead of converting them to Christianity, the missionary of the novel, Morgan, a cruel and wicked man, rapes their women and steals their possessions and land, justifying his acts with Bible thumping.

The main action of the novel takes place on the Nopah Reservation around World War I. The chief character is Nophaie, who, when a child, was kidnapped by white men and turned loose in the desert. He is found and reared by Easterners who give him a white man's education. While in college, he meets Marian, and after graduation she comes to visit him on the reservation, which proves to be a miniature version of hell. The Indian agent is Blucher, who is sympathetic to the

German cause and discourages the Indians from joining the army. The head of the missionary cause is the cruel and wicked Morgan. Nophaie speaks out against the system and advocates that the Indian be given land to work, be able to send his children to the school of his choice and allowed to move freely among the whites.

If corrupt officials and missionaries are not enough, the postwar influenza epidemic of 1918 strikes the reservation, and over 3,000 Nophas die. Nophaie himself catches the dreaded disease but recovers. He then goes on a pilgrimage to a sacred natural bridge that had been part of his tribe's religion for generations.

It is at this crucial juncture that the magazine version and the published book go their separate paths. Grey's original ending in the *Ladies' Home Journal* has Nophaie recover completely. Just as he returns to the reservation, a group of Indians try to kill Blucher and Morgan, but Nophaie intervenes and saves them. The gratitude of the two villains is to shoot Nophaie and leave him for dead. But he recovers again, and in the end, despite his misgivings, he and Marian are to be married. Says Nophaie:

> They are vanishing — vanishing. My Nopahs! Only a question of swiftly flying time! And I too — Nophaie, the warrior! In the end I shall be absorbed by you — by your love — by your children... It is well!

Grey came under a great deal of pressure from Harper & Brothers, who refused to publish the novel unless he made substantial changes and remove a great many of the offending passages. They also insisted that he change the ending so that Nophaie did not marry his white sweetheart. In that day, a white man marrying an Indian woman was acceptable, but not a white woman marrying an Indian. The revised ending has Nophaie returning to the reservation, but he is so exhausted from his pilgrimage and the ordeal of saving Blucher and Morgan that he has a relapse of influenza. This time he does not recover. Says Marian,

> It is — symbolic... They are vanishing — vanishing. Oh! Nopahs! ... Only a question of swiftly flying time! My Nophaie — the warrior — gone before them! ... It is well.

The film *The Vanishing American* (Paramount, 1925) chose the second ending. The studio also demanded additional changes, especially in the missionary angle, fearing that to film it as Grey wrote it, even in the revised version, would anger too many religious groups. Grey himself was used only as a consultant, and screenwriting credit went to Ethel Doherty. The changes the studio demanded upset Grey:

As to the motion picture, I have eliminated entirely the missionary element. This I was forced to do by the influence brought to bear upon the Will Hays office, by missionary powers. This is the first time in my life that I have been driven away from the turth, from honor and ideals, and in this case, from telling the world of the tragedy of the Indian. [Quoted from the Preface of the restored version of Zane Grey's *The Vanishing American*, Pocket Books, New York, 1977.]

The film opens with a prologue, not found in any version of the book, that shows that while the Indian is a vanishing species, he took the land from those who came before him and ends with the white race overwhelming the Indian, which seems to justify the demise of the red-man. The body of the film opens on a reservation just prior to America's entry into World War I, real Navajos substituting for Grey's manufactured Nophas. Some whites such as the school teacher Marian Warner (Lois Wilson) bring the benefits of white man's civilization, while the majority, led by Booker (Noah Beery), the unscrupulous Indian agent, seek only to exploit the Indians. When Booker forces his attention on Marian, Nophaie (Richard Dix) attacks him and must flee to the hills. When war is declared, Nophaie and many of his tribe join and are shipped to France. Nophaie distinguishes himself, but many of the Navajos perish. When they return to the reservation, they find appalling conditions due to Booker's tyrannical rule. Open war breaks out during which Nophaie is fatally wounded. As he lies dying, Marian reaches him with the news that Washington has dismissed Booker.

The film is a disappointment on several levels. For one, it is too tied to the melodramatic plot of the novel. In addition, the casting of Richard Dix is a mistake. The film cries out for an Indian to play Nophaie, but since the studio had so much invested, it wanted a name it could bank on, and Dix was Paramount's most popular star. While Grey's novel may have been partially to blame for the movie's inadequacies, Paramount must bear the major blame. They added and subtracted until much of the original story was so transformed as to be unrecognizable. They further weakened the story by removing all references to the missionaries, one of the prime concerns of the novel.

However, on two counts the studio and Grey must be complimented. In the author's contract with Paramount, it was stated that his stories must be filmed on the actual locations where they were supposed to happen. In the case of *The Vanishing American*, this meant Monument Valley, Utah, which later John Ford was to make so famous. The second, and by far the most important, is that no other silent film deals so clearly with the plight of the American Indian. What

is amazing is that, given the attitude of the American public at the time, this film was made at all, even in such an abbreviated form.

A pedestrian remake of *The Vanishing American* (Republic, 1955) also included a prologue of race succeeding race, which culminates in the white man's take over. However, this film added a quotation from Herbert Spenser on the survival of the fittest that comes close to claiming superiority of the white race. Scenarist Alan LeMay, who would later write the magnificent *The Searchers,* concentrates on action as Nophaie (Scott Brady) is out to stop land grabbers, and the context of the prologue is lost as quickly as the Grey novel. In this version, Nophaie vanquishes the bad guys and survives at the end.

Although not nearly as famous as *Ramona* or *The Vanishing American,* Paul Wellman's *Bronco Apache* (1936) is a far better novel than either, an intense and realistic portrait of Massai, the last fighting Apache. This Apache would never wander off to the white man's school or fall in love with a white woman. He is Apache through and through, an unrepentant savage in the best sense of the word. Wellman based his novel on an actual incident found in *Personal Recollections* by General Nelson Miles that tells of an Apache who escaped from Geronimo's band as they were being shipped to Florida. Somewhere east of the Mississippi, Massai jumps the prison train, and in a heroic and impossible journey, makes his way back to the San Carlos Mountains in Arizona, only to be betrayed by his own people and recaptured. Once again Massai escapes, this time killing three soldiers, and he begins a reign of terror throughout Southern Arizona.

Massai captures one Apache woman and takes her into the mountains with him, but when she betrays him, he slashes her Achilles tendons, and she dies. Later, he captures another woman, Nalinle, the daughter of old Santos who had been the first to betray him. This time, love comes to Massai. When Nalinle becomes pregnant and is near term, Massai takes her back to her people because he believes that he will soon be hunted down and killed by the white man, and he wants to insure the safety of his woman and their unborn child. As Massai attempts to leave the reservation, Al Sieber and his Indian scouts corner him. In a desperate fight, Massai kills several of his attackers, and as he makes a break, Sieber shoots him. Massai falls into a clump of bushes. By the time Sieber and his Indians gather enough courage to investigate, they discover a trace of blood where Massai fell, and prints

(Opposite) **Navajos threaten in a scene from** *The Vanishing American* **(1925), based on the Zane Grey novel.**

in the dust of two horses heading for the mountains, and among the prints, the outline of a woman's small foot.

Massai is a brutal savage who is not above killing defenseless and unarmed people. When he captures Nalinle, he calmly shoots her old mother. However, Nalinle doesn't seem to mind. She is an Apache herself, a woman worthy of a warrior like Massai, and she understands the ways of the warrior. When Massai coldbloodedly kills Fritz and Mina Ziernnstein, even Al Sieber isn't overly concerned. Fritz was a weakling who didn't belong in the West, and his wife was a shrew. On a foray into Mexico, Massai wipes out Miguel Duran and his entire band of renegades. Whoever Massai kills, they seem in the need of killing, as if he is some sort of avenging angel.

The film *Apache* (United Artists, 1954) opens with these words:

> This is the story of Massai, the last Apache warrior. It has been told and retold until it has become one of the great legends of the Southwest. It began in 1886 with Geronimo's surrender.

As Geronimo (Monte Blue) walks toward the soldiers to give himself up, Massai (Burt Lancaster) rides up and a fight breaks out. Despite the assistance of Nalinle (Jean Peters) who brings him extra ammunition, Massai is captured and shipped off to Florida with the rest of Geronimo's band under the control of Weddle, a corrupt Indian agent who taunts and berates the Indians. On the journey east, Massai escapes and heads back for Apache land. Along the way, he wanders through the city of St. Louis where he sees the white man's civilization up close, a fast paced, acerbic society that pursues him through the dark streets. This interlude stands in sharp contrast to Massai's later life among the mountains of Arizona.

Another stop on his journey occurs in the Indian Territory where he meets a friendly Cherokee who not only feeds him and gives him a place to stay for the night but also passes on to Massai a small sack of seed corn along with the advice to give up the warrior's path and adopt the white man's ways by learning to farm. Even though Massai sneaks out in the middle of the night, he takes the seed pouch.

Once back on the reservation, he goes immediately to see Santos and his daughter Nalinle. While Massai rests peacefully for the first time in months, Santos ties up Nalinle and goes to fetch the soldiers, who once again put Massai in chains. Escorted off to the prison train by Weddle and his friend, Massai again escapes, this time killing both white men. Returning to Santos, Massai kidnaps Nalinle. Believing that she participated in the betrayal, he treats her harshly until he discovers that she is innocent. Moving into the high country, Massai and Nalinle settle down to married bliss, even growing the corn while expecting a little Massai. But army scout Al Sieber (John McIntire) tracks them down. Trapped in his own corn field and surrounded by troopers, the wounded Massai manages to get the upper hand on Sieber. As he is about to kill the army scout, Massai hears the wail of his newborn son, and without further violence, he stands and walks calmly out of the corn field and unmolested into his wickiup.

The optimistic ending was forced upon director Robert Aldrich by the studio. Originally, Massai is senselessly killed by one of the soldiers as he stands up, but United Artists demanded an upbeat ending, so the troopers and Apache scouts allow Massai to saunter back into his abode to meet the little Massai. Much of the film has pointed to Massai's death, another vanishing American, and the ending weakens all that has come before. Actually, the ending of the novel, ambiguous as it was, would have sufficed.

Much from the novel had been omitted or changed. During the long trek back to Apache land, Massai is careful not to set foot near a white man, and in fact, is never glimpsed until he is already in the Southwest. He never strolled through St. Louis. There is not Cherokee to give him corn seeds, and never does Massai attempt to plant anything except bodies. Paul Wellman's Massai was too much the Apache warrior to be led astray by such foolishness. There is no Weddle or any corrupt official to clutter the picture. There is only Massai, the warrior, who seeks to return to his homeland, and once there, to stay there.

Only one scene from the novel remains intact. When Massai decides to go into the mountains for good, he forbids Nalinle to follow, and when she does, he firsts beats her with a stick, then he takes her moccasins and throws them away. Still she follows him, until her feet are bleeding so badly that she cannot walk. Then she crawls, inching her way forward on bloody fingers. At last, Massai comes back, and sweeping her up in his arms, carries her off to care for her. From that point on, their love is solidified.

Apache is not a great film, although it is a good one and an important one. Burt Lancaster looks physically right for the part, except that his black wig often seems slightly skewed and his blue eyes often dominate the screen. The fact that he is not an Indian and the overly optimistic ending ultimately combine to keep the film from greatness. An occasional line of dialogue may sound a bit corny, but scriptwriter James R. Webb managed to insert enough colloquialisms to make it, on the whole, sound vaguely authentic. Still, the most important aspect is the fact that this film, like the earlier *Devil's Doorway* (MGM, 1950), tells its story from the perspective of the Indian and not from that of the white man. The problem lies in the film's attempt to turn Massai into a docile Apache by having him learn that the only way he can survive is by settling down, building a home and planting corn. First the Cherokee in Oklahoma warns him, and later Nalinle reinforces the idea. And once the army and Al Sieber see that Massai is truly domesticated, they allow him to live. So, the Apache vanishes, assimilated into the white man's world just as Nophaie was in Grey's novel. However, Paul Wellman's Massai was never assimilated nor rehabilitated; he roams the mountains now, proud to be an Apache, proud to be a warrior.

In 1909 near Banning, California, a Paiute Indian named Billy Boy killed the father of his girlfriend, a distant cousin, and dragged the girl off into the mountains. The white man immediately set out to make Billy Boy, who was renamed Willie Boy, a good Indian. This true incident is the subject of *Willie Boy* (aka *Tell Them Willie Boy Is Here*, 1960) by Harry Lawton, a novel that reads like narrative history rather than fiction.

After Billy Boy kills the father and heads into the mountains with Lolita, his woman, the white population rises up in pursuit. The Paiute is hounded by posses until, rather than allow Lolita to fall into the hands of the whites, he kills her. The posse continues to give chase. Days later, the men come across Billy Boy, lying among the rocks, his chest blown open, his body bloated and blackened by the elements. A Winchester lies beside him, and his right foot is bare, a toe curled around the trigger. "We've been hunting a ghost," says one of the characters.

While Billy Boy is at the center of this novel, he is not the hero. He is simply a modern Indian who reverts to the old ways, and civilization ultimately destroys him. The problem with the novel is that it is too much like history. Except for the pursuit of Billy Boy, there seems no center to the novel, and while various members of the posse show heroic qualities, they never come fully alive. Still, it is an interesting book in that it brings to light a long forgotten incident in the history of white and Indian relationships.

The film *Tell Them Willie Boy Is Here* (Universal, 1969) threw away most of the book except for the basic idea of the hunt. Christopher Cooper (Robert Redford), a character invented for the film, is the sheriff in charge of hunting Willie Boy (Robert Blake). A romance was also invented for Cooper with a white doctor on the reservation, Liz Arnold (Susan Clark), who equates hunting Willie Boy with hunting deer. Lola/Lolita (Katherine Ross), is found dead by the posse, and she may have killed herself or may have been killed by Willie Boy. When the final confrontation comes, Cooper faces Willie Boy alone. Willie Boy holds up his rifle but doesn't fire. Cooper kills him, then discovers the Indian's rifle is empty.

While the whole thing looks good on the big screen, it has a feeling as if it is a social message disguised as a western. Too often the script settles for preaching rather than action, and it often bogs down in its own verbosity. However, the film has far worse faults than this. First, it is too much a starring vehicle for Redford, and this weakens the original story adapted from Lawton's novel. However, the second fault is the most damaging. The film was shot in Thousand Oaks, California, and utilized various Indian tribes as extras, which was all well and good, but the film cast Robert Blake as Willie Boy. The part cried out for a real Indian, and one more closely resembling the physical appearance of the real Willie Boy, who was tall and lanky. Although Blake looks good as an Indian — after all, he was Little Beaver in all those Red Ryder movies of the forties — his New Jersey accent too often surfaces. He was just another white actor playing an Indian.

The modern Indian is the subject of Hal Borland's *When the Legends Die* (1963), a sensitive portrait of the coming of age of a young Ute, Thomas Black Bull. Much like *Tell Them Willie Boy Is Here*, the story opens in 1910 on the Ute reservation in southern Colorado where George Black Bull is provoked into killing Frank No Deer, and he and his wife flee into the mountains, there to live in the manner of their ancestors. A child, Thomas Black Bull, is born. After the death of his parents, Thomas lives alone with only a tame bear. Brought out of the mountains by Blue Elk, Thomas attends the reservation school. Eventually, he is taken under the wing of ex-bronc buster and alcoholic Red Dillion, and they travel the small-time rodeo circuit. After Red's death, Thomas turns to the big time, and his pent-up anger explodes when he kills a horse in the arena. By the time he appears at Madison Square Garden, he is known as "Killer" Tom Black. After he is seriously injured in a spill, he returns to the reservation.

Within this novel is displayed the biting injustice of white man against red, just as found in such earlier novels as *Ramona* and *The Vanishing American*, although *When the Legends Die* is superior to both. Here the love of animals and nature, which has always been part of the Indian heritage, is interwoven into the fabric of the story, deepening it considerably. Also, Thomas Black Bull and Red Dillion are completely realized characters, far more so than those created by Helen Hunt Jackson or Zane Grey. Only Paul Wellman's *Massai* ranks with Hal

Borland's creation. The novel is weakest in its Horatio Alger aspect of the Indian boy making good in the white man's rodeo and also in the brief, romantic interlude with nurse Mary Redmond; it is strongest when it deals with the timeless riddle of identity, grappling so successfully with this theme that the novel deserves to be ranked as one of the half dozen greatest novels about the American Indian. The last three chapters where Thomas once again returns to the reservation and then to the mountains are especially thrilling, ending on an upbeat note when he pledges to himself that he will never again forget his heritage. "It was an old chant, a very old one, and he sang it not to the evening but to himself, to be sure he had not forgotten the words, to be sure he would never again forget."

Along with dropping "the" from the title and calling it simply *When Legends Die* (Sagoponack, 1972), the film also dispensed with the whole episode where Thomas' father kills Frank No Deer and runs off with his wife to the mountains. Instead, the story opens with Thomas already a young boy of fourteen living in the mountains with only the tame bear for companionship, his parents having recently died. Carried out of the wilderness by Blue Elk, he is sent to a Ute reservation school where he is forced to diagram sentences that seem as if they were composed by Bulwer-Lytton, and when he rebels, he is locked in a room with wire windows. Years later, Thomas (Frederic Forrest) is spotted by Red Dillon (Richard Widmark), a hard drinking, former rodeo rider, who teaches him how to ride well and how to ride badly in order to throw a contest, the better for Red to hustle bets on the side. Red wastes most of the money on booze and women. When Thomas gets fed up with playing Red's game, he goes his own way, calling himself Thomas Black, and after he kills several horses in the arenas, gets the moniker "Killer." After his fall and recovery, during which time he has his brief affair with Mary, his nurse, he returns to see Red. On the night of Thomas' return, Red goes on one last binge and drinks himself to death. After that, Thomas returns to the reservation, and in front of the council, he tells them that he wishes to return to be with the horses.

Certainly, saving Red's death for the climax makes the film more cinematic, yet it misses Thomas' renewal and self-awakening. His identity crisis is resolved strictly in terms of the white man's world, and without touching the roots of the Utes and of Thomas himself, the film misses the point. In addition, the film may be a little too intelligent and gentle for its own good; the small betrayals, the hurt feelings, the interior resolutions all contribute to a film of calculated good taste, and yet, the film is rather distant and emotionless. It is not a bad film; on the contrary, it is a very good one. Where it fails is in the area of involvement, the very area that makes the book a minor masterpiece.

Completely different in tone is Cliff Huffaker's *Nobody Loves a Drunken Indian* (1967), a seriocomic novel of the modern Indian, in this case a tribe of Paiutes in Arizona, and of one Indian in particular, Flapping Eagle, who organizes a rebellion that includes an attack on a bulldozer, lassoing a helicopter and, finally, the takeover of Phoenix by the Paiutes. There are times when the novel is wildly comic, such as the whorehouse scene where Flapping Eagle almost loses his life for being unfaithful to an Indian whore. However, underneath all the laughs is a serious subject — the treatment of Indians by the white majority. As second class citizens, the Indians, led by Flapping Eagle, strike back, not with any real malice, but out a sense of frustration and injustice. The downbeat ending, although seemingly in conflict with the rest of the novel, has been adequately foreshadowed and should come as no surprise to the perceptive reader. Fortunately, Huffaker never degenerates to propaganda, and therefore the story of Flapping Eagle and his friends remains involving to the very end.

Nobody Loves a Drunken Indian is not a great novel, certainly not in the same league as *When the Legends Die,* but it is an entertaining, fast read, as if it were written with the screen in mind. That doesn't detract from the importance of the novel. Huffaker makes clear the plight of the American Indian by putting us on the inside of his skin — the novel is narrated by another Paiute and friend of Flapping Eagle, Eleven Snowflake — yet these are not the downtrodden Indians of Zane Grey or Helen Hunt Jackson. These men may be the descendants of defeated warriors, but they are not beaten men. They are, however, slightly crazy. Nevertheless, we come to root for the success of Flapping Eagle's rebellion.

The studio had trouble coming up with a title, first calling it *Nobody Loves a Drunken Indian,* then changing it to *Nobody Loves Flapping Eagle,* finally settling on *Flap* (Warner Bros., 1969). After the film was completed, it remained on the shelf for eighteen months while the studio tried to decided what to do with it. In this case, the studio should have let it stay on the shelf.

When Brian Garfield reviewed the novel for *Saturday Review,* he said that *Nobody Loves a Drunken Indian* would make a better film than book. As he later admitted, he was wrong; *Flap* became a $6 million flop. As directed by Carol Reed, the outstanding British director, *Flap* is a sluggish, ludicrous comedy too heavy handed to make anyone laugh. One of the best scenes in the novel is the lassoing of the helicopter, a marvelously visual highlight that is thrown away on the screen in a most uninvolving manner. Huffaker himself wrote the screenplay and followed the events of his novel closely. The only real change comes in the character of Dorothy Bluebell (Shelly Winters), the mistress-whore of Flapping Eagle. In the novel she is a Paiute who works for the madame, but in the film she is the madame herself, a long suffering woman who has waited in vain for Flapping Eagle. The miscasting here throws the film askew. For that matter, the miscasting of the entire film throws it askew. Not one real Indian has a lead or supporting part. Anthony Quinn is totally miscast as Flap. The same is certainly true of the rest of the cast, the most outrageous example of which is Tony Bill as Eleven Snowflake. Another fault lies in the inability of the film to take a stand, as if the producers were afraid to step on anyone's toes. Yet, while these faults are numerous, they pale by comparison to the last fault. Despite the engaging source material, *Flap,* as a story, is a bore.

Although told from the perspective of a white Bostonian in the 1840s, "A Man Called Horse" by Dorothy Johnson, which originally appeared in *Colliers* and was later anthologized in the wonderful *Indian Country* (1953), tells a story of a white man who learns to see through the red man's eyes. The unnamed young man travels west out of some vague desire to feel equal. When he and his party are captured by Crows, he survives by emulating a horse, a valuable animal to the tribe. He is turned over to an old hag named Greasy Hand, whose daughter Pretty Calf he finds attractive and appealing. Slowly, he begins to learn the ways of the Indians, first by associating with the young boys who themselves are learning. When the Crow take him on a hunting expedition, he manages to kill a dying man from another tribe and take his horses. Back in the Crow camp, Horse is accepted as a hero, and using his new wealth, he buys Pretty Calf in marriage. As the months pass, Horse falls more in love with his wife and soon they are expecting a child. During the same period, Old Greasy Hand keeps cutting off a finger every time one of her children dies or is killed. During childbirth, Pretty Calf and the baby both die, and Horse thinks about returning to Boston. Old Greasy Hand begs him to stay, for to be without relatives is the worse thing that can happen to a Crow. He calls her mother and stays. Only after her death does he return to the East, and then "he did not find it necessary either to apologize or to boast, because he was the equal of any man on earth."

The film *A Man Called Horse* (Cinema Center, 1970) bears little resemblance to the Dorothy Johnson short story. Here Lord John

Morgan (Richard Harris) — from England, not Boston — is captured by the Sioux, not Crow, and not only does he survive his initial captivity but he also goes on to become a super hero, more fitting to come from the pen of Edgar Rice Burroughs than Dorothy Johnson. In order to win his Indian bride, he goes through the ritual of having bones poked through his flesh and then being lifted off the ground by rawhide attached to the bone. Later, he leads the Sioux against an enemy tribe, and even though greatly outnumbered and outmanned, he carries the day because he has taught his Sioux the disciplined tactics of the British army. All in all, it is a macho-masochistic western that went on to inspire two inferior sequels.

The producers and writers claimed accuracy in their presentation, stating in their production notes that 80 percent of the dialogue is in Sioux and that all the rituals had been meticulously researched. Unfortunately, the accuracy did not carry over to casting. Dame Judith Anderson as Buffalo Cow Head, the film's Old Greasy Hand, looks ridiculous in her fright wig, and most of the other actors and actresses look as if they came right out of the studio casting office. *A Man Called Horse* is not a bad movie; it is, however, an absurd one, and one with little connection with its source.

In an attempt to portray the interaction between the white man and the red man's cultures, Elliot Arnold chose a lofty theme that all men are brothers and produced an important, albeit imperfect tale of Cochise and Tom Jeffords in *Blood Brother* (1947). The story constantly moves back and forth between Indian and white viewpoints. The first third of the novel tells of Cochise and his band of Chiricahua Apache who try unsuccessfully to make peace with the Americans. By the time Jeffords arrives on the scene, the Civil War is in progress, and the Apaches have banded together to terrorize the Southwest. General Canby sends Jeffords to Tucson to assess the situation, and on the way, he rescues a young girl named Terry, who falls in love with the scout. After receiving a wound while scouting, Jeffords recovers with a determination to put an end to all the killing. Taking an Indian boy with him, he goes into Cochise's stronghold. There the Indian chief, seeing that Jeffords is indeed a brave man, agrees to listen to him. They talk of peace and become friends. While in the camp, the scout sees the puberty rite of an eighteen-year-old maiden, Sonseeahray, and he is struck by her beauty.

Although their first meeting fails to bring about total peace, it does bring a promise from Cochise to allow the mail riders to go through Apache country unharmed. Back in Tucson, Jeffords' agreement with

Cochise brings on hostility with the local citizenry. When Jeffords returns to Cochise, an Apache, Nahilzay, tries to kill him, and in the middle of the camp with everyone watching, Jeffords and the Indian fight it out to the death. When the white scout kills his adversary, Cochise says to his people, "The duel was fair. It is over and finished. There will be nothing of this to remain in the heart of any man."

Jeffords marries Sonseeahray, and for a while, they settle down to a life of bliss. Soon, however, he is going back and forth between the Apache stronghold and Tucson. It is during one of his trips to Tucson that soldiers raid the Indian village, and the Camp Grant Massacre takes place. Sonseeahray is killed. It is after this that Cochise and Jeffords go through the ceremony to become blood brothers. This time Jeffords brings General Howard to see the great Indian chief, and together the men make peace. Jeffords is appointed Indian agent for the Chiricahuas. A love affair blossoms between Jeffords and Terry, the girl he once rescued. Cochise dies and is buried secretly by his followers in the Stronghold with Jeffords at the graveside.

When the novel first appeared, some reviewers proved actively hostile toward it. Hoffman Birney, himself a novelist, wrote in the *New York Times*,

> If the theme of the book is the blood brotherhood of all men and all races, Mr. Arnold should have selected an exemplar as Indian such as Joseph of the Nez Perces, or Wovoka, the Piute "messiah." The Apaches were the scourge of the Southwest for centuries before the white man came.... As a novel, *Blood Brother* will delight those who believe that all Indians were as noble as Hiawatha. As biography it is inaccurate; as history it is often distorted; as ethnology is is balderdash.

Mr. Birney misses the point. Just because the Apaches were such fierce fighters and warriors, the fact that a man of stature and vision such as Cochise should arise among them and should come to stand for universal brotherhood makes the message all that more appealing. Other reviewers were impressed. Historian Stanley Vestal called Arnold's research "hard and intelligent" and an "important contribution to history of the Southwest."

On the screen, *Blood Brother* became *Broken Arrow* (TCF, 1950), the first of a cycle of western films appearing during the 1950s that discarded previous caricatures of the American Indian. Just as in the novel, the Apaches are depicted as intelligent men with a culture of their own that is worthy of respect. The fact that the film romanticizes the Apaches and especially Cochise can be forgiven for years of neglect by the film industry. Not since the inferior *Ramona* in 1936 had Hollywood treated the Indian so sympathetically.

Broken Arrow opens in 1871 and drops all the events previous to that date. Tom Jeffords (James Stewart) narrates the story, and he informs us that everything we see will be just as it happens, except that the Indians will speak English "so that you can understand them." The story opens as he is en route to Tucson to act as scout for the military. In the desert, he finds a wounded Apache boy, whose life he saves, and when a war party discovers them, the boy talks his people into sparing Jefford's life. Still, they tie him to a tree and force him to watch an ambush of miners. When the Apaches discover the miners possess Apache scalps, they torture the survivors.

Disgusted by the war, Jeffords attempts to make contact with Cochise (Jeff Chandler). Once in the camp, Cochise agrees to allow the pony riders safe passage. In a scene taken straight out of the novel, Jeffords sees Sonseeahray, and on his second visit to the stronghold, he asks her to marry him. Some film critics unfamiliar with the novel attacked the love affair as being nothing more than a sop to a rising young star, but in reality this becomes Jefford's ultimate expression of a belief that there must be peace between the two races.

Terry, the young girl rescued by Jeffords in the novel, has been dropped. Added to the proceedings is Slade (Will Geer), an Indian-hating miner, and his son, who at one point try to lynch Jeffords because of his friendship with the Indian chief. Saved at the last minute by General Howard, Jeffords is persuaded to take the army man to meet Cochise. A truce is arranged, and dissident Indians under Geronimo bolt the Stronghold to continue the fight.

Historically, the treaty that followed destroyed the Chiracahua way of life. Eventually the government would move them to the San Carlos Reservation, and although Arnold alluded to the fact in the novel, the film ignores it. The climax of the film occurs when Slade and other whites set a trap for Cochise and Jeffords. During the fight, Sonseeahray is killed trying to prevent Slade from killing her husband. This is certainly more cinematic, having Jeffords not only engage in the fight but also be at the side of his wife at her death. Sonseeahray's death unites the two sides in determination to make the truce work. The film closes with Jeffords riding alone into the desert and the voice-over narration saying that the memory of Sonseeahray will live with him forever.

Much of the novel has been dropped or changed, yet it is amazing how much of the spirit of the book remains. Some of the important dialogue between Cochise and Jeffords has been lifted straight from the novel, and even though stylized, it remains believable and moving. The dialogue also adds a certain poetic cadence to the love scenes, which are spoken simply, honestly and with feeling. The wedding scene, again taken straight out of the novel, is both mysterious and beautiful as the two lovers mingle their blood and then ride off on beautiful white horses to their honeymoon wickiup. A longer film might have been more faithful, but as it stands, *Broken Arrow* is a fine adaptation that ably represents the novel from which it sprang.

There is no denying the importance of *Blood Brother*. It featured the first sympathetic portrait of Apaches since *Apache* (1931) by Will Levington Comfort and *Bronco Apache* (1936) by Paul Wellman, and it became the first novel to fully explore the interaction between the two races. But the great American novel on the American Indian was still to come — *Little Big Man* (1964) by Thomas Berger, a novel of immense depth and meaning. The story opens with a "Foreword by a Man of Letters," Ralph Fielding Snell, who explains that the story that follows is that of one Jack Crabb, a 111-year-old man who claims to be the only white survivor of Little Big Horn. The rest of the novel, except for a brief epilogue, are the reminiscences of Jack Crabb, former frontiersman, mule skinner, gambler, gun fighter, Indian scout and adopted Indian of the Cheyenne tribe.

The opening line spoken by Crabb sets the tone of the book. "I am a white man and never forgot it, but I was brought up a Cheyenne from the age of ten." In 1852 when he is only ten, his father decides to move to Utah, but somewhere west of Laramie, the wagon train encounters a small band of Cheyenne led by Old Lodge Skins. When the white men serve the Indians liquor and get them drunk, disaster strikes. The Cheyenne kill all the men and rape all the women, except for Crabb's mother and sister Caroline, the latter who looks so masculine that the Indians mistake her for a boy. The next day, the Indians return to bring horses in payment of their depredations, and Caroline mistakes their intentions, believing they have come for her. She returns to their camp, taking Jack along. Once she realizes that the Cheyenne are not interested in her, she runs off, leaving Jack. Jack grows up with the Cheyenne, and Old Lodge Skins becomes his foster father.

At the age of fifteen, Jack is captured by soldiers, and he claims that he has been held captive for five years. The army assigns him to the Reverend and Mrs. Pendrake, and he comes to adore his foster mother, until he discovers her in the arms of the local druggist. Running away to St. Louis, he signs up with a wagon train heading west.

On this journey he is captured by Comanches but escapes and makes his way to Santa Fe where he takes up with a Mexican woman. Later, he pans for gold in Colorado, and after another short stay with the Cheyenne, goes to Denver where he marries Olga, a Swedish immigrant, and fathers a boy. He loses his wife and child in an Indian attack, becomes a drunk and is rescued from saloon rowdies by his sister Caroline. For the next two years, he helps to build the Union Pacific. During this time, he acquires an Indian wife and foster son during a raid, and with them, he returns to the Cheyenne and Old Lodge Skins.

When Custer and his troops attack the Cheyenne in what became known as the Battle of the Washita, his Indian wife and their new son are killed, and Jack blames Custer. Returning to Kansas City, he meets Wild Bill Hickok who teaches him to shoot. Also while there, he meets Sue Ann, who he believes is his niece, the daughter of Caroline, and he places her in a fashionable school and turns to hunting buffalo to earn enough money to keep her there. Ultimately, his attempt to turn her into a lady succeeds when she marries a son of a state senator.

When Jack finally meets Custer in 1876, his desire for vengeance has worn off, and he unofficially joins his command. He is at Little Big Horn, surviving only because he is carried from the field by an Indian whose life he once saved. He is back with the Cheyenne when Old Lodge Skins goes up on the mountain to die.

Little Big Man is a most American novel, not just in its setting and story but also in its thematic structures — savagery and civilization, the virgin land and the city, nature and the machine, the individual and community, innocence and knowledge, all the unifying and divisive themes of the American experience. In his desire to explore all these varied ideas and themes, Berger chose the picaresque form. Jack Crabb, antihero, a man in search of himself, is at one time or another all the figures of the western hero except the cowboy. Within this form, the novel is a comedy, yet it grows more serious as it progresses.

The novel opens when Jack Crabb is ten and ends 24 years later with him among the Indians, obviously for the last time. Their world is ending. In between, he alternates back and forth between the white civilization and the red, the period with the Indians always ending violently, a way of life in the midst of dying. The periods with the whites is more disconcerting and discouraging to Crabb's wish for a decent and honorable solution to the conflict between Indian and white. In this conflict, Old Lodge Skins has the final word on the white man's victory.

There is no permanent winning or losing when things move, as they should, in a circle. For is life not continuous? And though I shall die, shall I not also continue to live in everything that is? . . . But white men, who live in straight lines, do not believe as I do. With them it is rather everything or nothing. . . . Winning is all they care about.

The film *Little Big Man* (National General, 1970) made some drastic changes in the story. For one, the story opens with Jack Crabb (Dustin Hoffman) and his sister Caroline (Carole Androsky) the only survivors of an attack on a wagon train. The attack is not made by the Cheyenne but by the Pawnee, and Old Lodge Skins has nothing to do with it. It is obvious why this particular change occurs. In making the film, director Arthur Penn was very concerned about drawing parallels with the treatment by the United States government of the American Indian with our government's involvement in the Vietnam War. To show Old Lodge Skins (Chief Dan George) involved in the death of Jack's family and the raping of the women would make him seem too much the villain. Penn's Cheyennes had to be purer than the ones in the novel.

Once Jack gives himself up to the soldiers and is turned over to the Rev. Pendrake and his wife (Faye Dunaway), he quickly learns that a white man seldom does what he says, and when he sees Mrs. Pendrake making love to the druggist, he runs away. In the book, this is the last we see of Mrs. Pendrake, but in the film she shows up later as a whore who is also Wild Bill Hickok's mistress.

After his religious period, Jack takes up with a traveling medicine man (Martin Balsam), in a role created especially for the film, only to be tarred and feathered by a group of irate citizens led by Caroline. She then takes him under her tutelage and teaches him the art of gunfighting, at which he proves to be a natural. Along the way, he meets Wild Bill Hickok (Jeff Corey), but when Jack sees Wild Bill actually kill a man, Jack sells his gunfighter's outfit.

Jack marries Olga, a Swedish immigrant, and when they go bankrupt, General Custer (Richard Mulligan) happens along and suggests that Jack and his wife head west to the land of opportunity, and he guarantees their safety from Indians. Indians attack the stage and carry off Olga, although there is no baby as there was in the novel. Jack joins the army as a scout in order to find Olga, but instead he rescues Sunshine, who he takes for a wife, and together they move back with the Cheyenne and Old Lodge Skins. But the Seventh Cavalry under Custer arrives for the Battle of the Washita, a massacre of men, women and children. Sunshine and her baby are killed, but both Jack and Old Lodge Skins escape.

Lobby card for *Little Big Man* (1970), based on the novel by Thomas Berger.

Surprisingly, Jack returns to civilization and becomes a drunk, only to witness the death of Wild Bill. Fleeing civilization once again, he becomes a hermit, and then, just as he is about to commit suicide, he sees the Seventh Cavalry and rides to join them. Using the truth as a weapon, he leads Custer and his men to Little Big Horn and destruction. As in the novel, Jack is saved by an Indian whose life he has once saved.

The historical personages of Wyatt Earp and Calamity Jane who Jacks meets in the novel disappear in the film. So, too, does the niece Amelia. In reality, these omissions fail to hurt the story or change it drastically in any way. However, this is not true in regard to the conclusion. "Take care of my son here," Old Lodge Skins says to the Great Spirit, "and see that he doesn't go crazy." Then he lies down on the damp rocks and dies. However, in the film, Jack accompanies Old Lodge Skins up on the mountain, but as the old man lies on the buffalo robe, rain begins to fall, and the drops splash on the old man's face.

Reluctantly, the old man opens his eyes. "I was afraid of this," he says. "Sometimes the magic works and sometimes it doesn't." Arm in arm, Jack and Old Lodge Skins stumble back toward the village.

An interesting contrast between the novel and film lies in the approach each takes toward the Indians. The novel treats them alternately as children, very dangerous ones to be sure, and as Human Beings, which they call themselves, cruel, reserved, wise in the ways of nature, yet doomed. Jack Crabb says of Old Lodge Skins, who comes to represent the whole Cheyenne nation, that he "started out as a buffoon in this narrative. Let me say that was true only around white men. Among the Cheyenne he was sort of genius. It was him who taught me everything I learned that wasn't physical like riding or shooting." On the other hand, the film is definitely pro-Indian, and it avoids all sense of criticism. Other than Jack Crabb, the only sympathetic characters in the film are the Indians. The society of the Human Beings is all good, the society of the whites is all bad.

Another interesting point of contrast is in the portrayal of George Armstrong Custer. In the novel, Thomas Berger made him a man of splendid paradoxes — compassionate yet odious, brilliant yet vain, impatient yet magnanimous, rational yet cruel — much as Ernest Haycox had done in *Bugles in the Afternoon*. Berger has made Custer an ordinary fellow, neither a saint nor a villain. The film sees Custer in a different light. He is a pompous buffoon out to secure his political ambition, which happens to be the presidency of the United States, and he believes that one more victory over the Indians will insure his desire. His inevitable defeat is fully justified by the previous atrocities performed by the Seventh Cavalry.

Despite the fact that the film *Little Big Man* goes its own way, it remains a stunning achievement, a great film that, like the novel, forces us to reevaluate many western myths. It accomplishes on celluloid what Berger accomplished on paper.

Most fiction dealing with the American Indian has been prejudicial, often showing him as only a savage to be justifiably eradicated by the white man. In this category, the stories of James Warner Bellah stand out as the most blatant example of this racist attitude among writers. Even when racism was not so blatant, the Indian was seldom an individual character worthy of respect. The novels and short stories that did treat him with respect are few, and fewer still are those fictions that put the American Indian at center stage and show him in relationship to his own culture. When these works reached the screen, they were often truncated or the leads were handed over to non-Indian actors or both. Two films rise above this. Although not a particularly good book, *The White Buffalo* had a white man and an Indian as protagonists, each of equal importance, and the film cast a native American to costar with Charles Bronson. While the lead character in both the novel and film *Little Big Man* was white, Indians play key roles, and the studio cast real Indians, even in the pivotal role of the grandfather. Of all American literature and American film to deal with the Indian, *Little Big Man* must rank among the greatest as well as one of the most honest. However, these two films are in the minority; far too often films were even more conservative than the novels, and whatever grudging respect the novel or short story may have had for the Indian disappeared on the screen.

II : Six-Gun Heroes

7. The Creation of a Myth

The western story outside the white man and Indian confrontation—the story of the cowboy, the gunfighter, the farmer, the railroader, the miner, the stagecoach driver, the outlaw, the gambler—began with an Easterner who saw the West when it was still wild. Bret Harte wrote a series of short stories of the mining camps and the men and women who inhabited them based on his real life experiences, and many of these were adapted for films.

Before he wrote his most famous short stories, he apprenticed himself on a number of short sketches and one longer work entitled "The Work of Red Mountain," which became more famous under the title of "M'liss." Here, for the first time, the author made use of his experiences in the mining camps and told the story of Melissa Smith, the daughter of old Bummer Smith who discovered Smith's Pocket. Her father believes he has struck the mother lode, but comes to realize he has only hit an isolated pocket, and his fortune soon vanishes. M'liss herself is a half wild girl who the local schoolmaster almost manages to civilize.

Under the title of "M'liss," this novelette became a standard repertory and stock item for years to come, as well as being adapted into three silent films, the first of which (Paramount, 1918) starred Mary Pickford romping around the woods, playing a wild girl who is never quite so wild as to offend the paying public. Uncontrollable until she meets schoolmaster Mr. Gray, she allows herself to be taken under his guidance for instruction and finally marriage, but not before he is falsely accused of murder and almost lynched, which of course, never happened in the Harte story. As it stands, this version of *M'liss* is far too romantic to be anywhere near a faithful adaptation. The film was remade twice more as a silent, first as *The Girl Who Ran Wild* (Universal, 1922) and later as *The Man from Red Gulch* (PDC, 1925), neither of which improved upon the first version.

Although called *M'liss* (RKO, 1936), the only sound version also bore little resemblance to the Harte story. Gone is the turbulent old mining camp of Smith's Pocket, full of saloons and sin, repaced by a commonplace small town squabbling over its new schoolteacher, Stephen Thorne (John Beal). Meek M'liss (Anne Shirley) is a friendly, uneducated lass, far too trustful to remain unprotected, especially since a distasteful rival lurks in the wings. At one point, M'liss wanders into the saloon and sings "I'll Hang My Heart on the Weeping Willow Tree" in order to get enough spare change to equip her for school. Naturally, the relationship between schoolteacher Thorne and M'liss ripens into love in this idyllic reworking, forsaking all the hard edge in Harte's story.

Throughout the silent period, Harte's stories continued to be popular with filmmakers. "Salomy Jane's Kiss" was filmed twice as *Salomy Jane* (Alco Films, 1914, and Paramount, 1923). "In the Carquinez Woods" became *The Half Breed* (Triangle, 1916), a Douglas Fairbanks vehicle directed by Alan Dwan. The short novel *Cressy* became the action-oriented *Fighting Cressy* (Pathé, 1919).

In 1868, Bret Hart published his most famous stories, "The Luck of Roaring Camp" and "The Outcasts of Poker Flat," in the pages of the *Overland Monthly,* a San Francisco based publication that the author also edited. "The Luck of Roaring Camp" (1868) was very daring for its time, including as it did Cherokee Sal, a camp follower in a remote mining camp who dies in childbirth. What made the story palpable to Victorian audiences was the biblical theme "A little child shall lead them." Christening the child Thomas Luck, the miners are regenerated and find prosperity by the communal decision to rear the child born in their midst in more proper surroundings. There is less swearing and shouting, and mining claims begin to turn enormous profits. Then, tragedy strikes when winter floods inundate the camp, and the child drowns. The story could have been mired in bathos had it not been for Harte's skill at blending humor into the action.

While other lesser known Bret Harte stories have been filmed, some more than once, only one film version of *The Luck of Roaring Camp* (Monogram, 1937) reached the screen, a cheap, penny-ante production from a studio that specialized in such product. The best that can be said for the film is that it is based on Harte's story, although even that did not keep it from being corny and slow. It even tacked on a happy ending.

Far better were the adaptations of "The Outcasts of Poker Flat" (1869), the story of a group of undesirables kicked out of a miners town and forced to cross the Sierras in the winter. There are four of them: Uncle Billy, sluice robber and drunkard; Oakhurst, the gambler; the Duchess, and Mother Shipton, whose "impropriety was professional." After Uncle Billy runs off with the horses and mules, the others take shelter in a cabin with a young couple, Tom the Innocent and Pliny, on their way to be married. Caught there by a snow storm, most die from cold and exposure except for the gambler John Oakhurst, who, "at once the strongest and yet the weakest of the outcasts of Poker Flat," shoots himself.

The first film of *The Outcasts of Poker Flat* (Universal, 1919) was directed by John Ford, his most ambitious film to date. It was the director's first literary adaptation, and although it also proved to be the first of Ford's films to find favor with the public, it was self-conscious and pretentious. Ford himself was not happy with the results. It certainly bore little resemblance to the Harte story. Using the plot within a plot technique, with the principal actors playing dual roles, the story told of a gambling hall owner in Arizona (Harry Carey) who cannot make up his mind whether to sacrifice his love for his pretty ward (Gloria Hope), who he believes is in love with his best friend Tommy (Cullin Landis), or tell her of his own feelings. Coming across a copy of Harte's story, he reads it. He sees that Oakhurst had the same problem. After befriending a girl on a steamboat, Oakhurst relinquishes her when another and younger man steals her attention. The gambler reading the story then decides to fight for his lady love, and it turns out that she has been in love with him all along. There is a sequence where the three are snowbound, and the set piece done on a sound stage looks patently phoney. Ford did much better handling the exterior scenes of the mining camp, circa 1850, full of bristling action and authentic details. However, the main problem lies in the slowly developing and awkwardly structured plot that never comes alive and never captures the Harte story.

The first remake and first sound version of *The Outcasts of Poker Flat* (RKO, 1937) not only takes ingredients from the original story but also throws in a few from "The Luck of Roaring Camp." Tom, Pliny, Mother Shipton and Innocent are missing, replaced by a school marm, a preacher, Kentuck and a small fry named "Luck," the mascot of the rough mining camp. In this version, Oakhurst (Preston Foster) drinks, a habit he forsakes in the story because he didn't want it to cloud his head and get in the way of his gambling. Duchess is his greedy "associate."

Lobby card for *The Outcasts of Poker Flats* **(1952), based on the short story by Bret Harte.**

Helen, the school marm, is out to reform Oakhurst, unsuccessfully, but the Reverend Samuel Woods (Van Heflin) is around to pick up the pieces after Oakhurst's death. The strength of Harte's stories often lay in his feeling for his people, but this film reduces them to one dimensional and uninteresting caricatures. The *New York Times* reviewer asked, "An interesting experiment, but is it Harte?" It wasn't.

Harte's story is simple and tragic, and although he felt for his people, he did not dig too deeply into their characters. However, the last version of *The Outcasts of Poker Flat* (TCF, 1952) attempted to rectify this omission; the result didn't improve the story any. The opening sequence shows Ryker (Cameron Mitchell) and his henchmen stealthily sneaking up a dark street of a mining town, the tinny music from the background the only sounds. They rob the assay office-bank, kill two men and ride off with the money. The townspeople, rightly upset over the whole thing, take out their frustrations by ejecting from town four individuals of dubious character: Oakhurst (Dale Robinson); Jake (Billy

Lynn), the town drunk; Duchess (Mariam Hopkins); and Cal (Anne Baxter), who also happens to be Ryker's wife. When a snowstorm catches them high in the mountains, they take shelter in a cabin occupied by Tom and Pliny, two young lovers on their way to be married. This whole group is joined by Ryker, who holds them at gunpoint and eats all their food. Along the way, Cal agrees to give up the man she really loves, Oakhurst, and go with Ryker if the outlaw will just let everyone go free, but he kills Tom, and when Duchess tries to signal a posse, he kills her, too. This gives Oakhurst the chance to jump the outlaw and kill him. The film then ends on a happy note as Cal and Oakhurst ride off together to a better future.

In many ways, this adaptation has even less Harte than the previous version. At least in that one, Oakhurst died. In this one, he survives and is turned into a stereotypical hero. There was no Ryker in the original story, no outlaws, only the outcasts and the lovers, who meet their deaths in the mountains. Even though the film is grimly dramatic, and in many ways enjoyable, especially in the opening sequence where the assay office is robbed and also in the performance of Cameron Mitchell as Ryder, a brutally vicious and selfish murderer, it is not Bret Harte.

One of Harte's favorite themes, the loyalty of a miner to his partner, is characteristically exaggerated in "Tennessee's Partner" (1875). The partner is like a faithful dog in his dumb, dogged devotion to Tennessee, making him a comic figure and, simultaneously, pathetically appealing. He forgives Tennessee for running off with his wife; he compromises himself after Tennessee becomes a highwayman, and finally, he offers his savings to the judge, not even realizing that he is breaking the law by offering a bribe. After Tennessee is hanged, his partner provides him with a proper funeral, then pines away and dies.

The story was filmed twice, the first time as *The Fighting Forties* (PDC, 1924). The second version at least restored the title, *Tennessee's Partner* (RKO, 1955) and was directed by Alan Dwan, who way back in 1916 had directed *The Half Breed,* based on Harte's "In the Carquinez Woods." That film had been notable for Douglas Fairbanks' playing the title role; *Tennessee's Partner* is notable as being one of the last films starring Ronald Reagan, who played Cowpoke, Tennessee's partner. Otherwise, the film is ludicrous.

Tennessee (John Payne) is a slick gambler with a fast gun in the town of Sandy Bar, where his lady friend the Duchess (Rhonda Fleming) runs the local saloon. When a disgruntled prospector tries to kill Tennessee, Cowpoke steps in and saves his life, and the two become fast

Tennessee's partner (Ronald Reagan) administers a beating to Tennessee (John Payne) in an adaptation of Harte's short story "Tennessee's Partner."

friends. Cowpoke has come to Sandy Bar to marry his girl Goldie (Coleen Gray), appropriately named since she is a golddigger in the worst sense of the word. In order to save his friend, Tennessee woos her, much to Cowpoke's consternation. Despite the conflict between the two men, when Tennessee is accused of murder, Cowpoke comes to his aid and is gunned down in the final fight. The grateful Tennessee gives his partner a fine funeral, then marries the Duchess, who understands the ruse to save Cowpoke from Goldie.

The best parts of the film are the scenes of the mining camps, rampant with gold fever, excitement and shady characters. Here it comes closest to Harte; still, the film falls far short of its mark. This is not Harte, no more than any of the other films based on his stories. In each and every case, the filmmakers settled for the romantic west and turned the centers of their films soft; thus, they missed Harte's hard edge and artistry.

In "The Bride Comes to Yellow Sky," Stephen Crane used the setting and characters that Harte might have used, except that Crane's treatment is the antithesis of Harte's. Almost everything that Harte would have played up, Crane played down. The characters are neither glamorized not made to seem odd or unusual. Jack Potter's bride is neither pretty nor very young. By the end of the story, Potter, the town marshal, is revealed as a man of great courage, but until then he seems ordinary and not particularly heroic.

On the train ride into Yellow Sky, the Potters feel the happiness mingled with self-consciousness of a newly married couple, yet Potter's nervousness is occasioned by something more. He failed to consult the town before hurrying off to San Antonio to marry, and he does not know how they will accept his new bride. On arriving in Yellow Sky, Jack and his wife are accorded quite a different reception than he anticipates. The streets of the city are deserted because Scratchy Wilson is on the warpath. When sober, Scratchy is "the nicest fellow in town," but from time to time, he goes on a drunk and shoots up the town, and on these occasions, Jack Potter has had the task of subduing him. When the newlyweds arrive, they are confronted by Scratchy. Potter shows Scratchy that he is unarmed, then announces that he has just gotten married. "Well," said Scratchy at last, slowly,

> "I s'pose it's all off now." He was not a student of chivalry; it was merely that in the presence of this foreign condition he was a simple child of the earlier plains. . . . He went away. His feet made funnel-shaped tracks in the heavy sand.

This lighthearted yet bitter meditation on the death of the Old West made the second half of an anthology film *Face to Face* (RKO, 1952), the first half being an adaptation of Joseph Conrad's "The Secret Sharer." Sticking very close to the original story, James Agee, who wrote the screenplay, shows up briefly in the proceedings as a prisoner. Agee varied from Crane on one minor point. As Scratchy (Minor Watson) is shooting up the town, he vows to shoot Jack Potter (Robert Preston) because the marshal is the only man around who Scratchy respects. When the confrontation comes and Scratchy discovers that civilization has beaten him to the draw, he tosses his guns into the dust and walks off. Other than this, there are so significant changes, and this segment of *Face to Face* emerges as pure Stephen Crane, a fine and faithful adaptation that captures the essence of the story as well as the events.

Whatever faults Bret Harte may have had as a writer, he took pains with the plots while still providing local color. Not so with

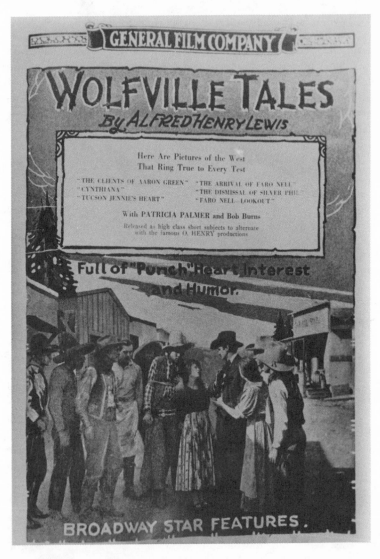

General Films advertisement of 1918 announcing a series of two-reelers based on *Wolfville Tales* by Alfred Henry Lewis.

Alfred Henry Lewis, who long ago wrote the "Wolfville" stories under the pseudonym of Dan Quin. Lewis created a narrator, the "Old Cattleman," who narrated his stories in the vernacular, and while he created local color, he did so at expense of plot. "These yere obsequites which I'm about to mentionin'," begins the Old Cattleman in *Wolfville* (1897), and the narration seldom improves, making the whole series, six books in all, a hard task for modern readers. Two silent films emerged from Lewis's fiction, *Dead Shot Baker* (Vitagraph, 1917) and *The Tenderfoot* (Vitagraph, 1917), both directed by and starring William Duncan. The ads for both acclaimed in bold print that they were based on the Wolfville stories of Alfred Henry Lewis, but in reality, they were low budget action features that exploited the popularity of the author without using his material. In 1917–18 a series of reel shorts called collectively *Wolfville Stories* from General Films played around the country, and while the stories were often drawn straight from the books, they were undistinguished. As a writer, Alfred Henry Lewis rests in obscurity; the films based on his work have long ago turned to dust.

An important writer in his time, Stewart Edward White wrote several early novels, the first of which, *The Westerners* (1901), originally serialized in *Munsey's Magazine,* had a character called The Kid and indirectly involved Custer and Little Big Horn, although it is essentially a story of wagon trains and mining camps. It became the first of the large scale westerns when it reached the screen in 1919, and White himself participated in writing the scenario, and the story, improbable as it is, moves along at a fast clip. Other silent films adapted from White's work included *The Call of the North* (Paramount, 1921), based on *Conjuror's Horse; The Killer* (Pathé, 1920), later remade as *Mystery Ranch* (Fox, 1932); *The Grey Dawn* (Hodkinson, 1922); and *Arizona Nights* (FBO, 1927), based on a collection of short stories loosely strung together as a novel.

One short story from *Arizona Nights,* "Two-Gun Man," was a reasonably well told story with an O. Henry twist. Cattle rustlers are bleeding rancher Buck Johnson dry, who tries to find a man who knows the country and is not afraid to pursue the rustlers. He discovers there is no one to fit the mold until he runs across the two-gun stranger who promises to bring back the cattle and the man responsible for the rustling for $5,000 in gold. The stranger rides off and returns over a week later with the cattle at which point the stranger draws his pistols and announces, "Your stock is in the corral. I'll trouble you for that five thousand. I'm the man who stole your cattle."

Michael Curtiz directed an adaptation of "Two Gun Man" entitled *Under a Texas Moon,* which had the distinction of being an early Technicolor production. It was pleasant enough and had a sense of humor. However, like all the films based on White's novels and short stories, it is easily forgettable, like much of White's writings. It tells the story of bandit Don Carlos (Frank Fay) who keeps crossing the border between Texas and Mexico and the two women, Lita Romero (Myrna Loy) and Raquella (Raquel Torres), who vie for his love. The story is cluttered with romantic clichés, a villain (Noah Beery), chases and enough songs that one reviewer considered the film a musical.

While both Harte and Crane were better artists, it was left to Owen Wister to popularize the formula western. An early book of Owen Wister, *Lin Mclean* (1900) was filmed as *A Woman's Fool* (Universal, 1918), billed by the studio as one of "Harry Carey's and Jack [John] Ford's Just Plain Westerns," but it was nothing more than one of the many westerns the team churned out at the rate of one every six weeks and had little to do with Wister's fiction except for the central character. Far more important, of course, were the four versions of *The Virginian.*

Originally, seven short pieces about the Virginian appeared in *Harper's* and *The Saturday Evening Post* between 1893 and 1902, and these were incorporated into the novel, without any effort on Wister's part, to provide continuity. What may help to explain the novel's enduring appeal is that it presents two different but equally appealing Virginians in two separate but equally appealing success stories. These two stories bring together James Fenimore Cooper and Horatio Alger, Jr., merging the values of East and West.

First, the Virginian is a romantic primitive who rejects the traditional values of civilization in favor of a free life in the West. This part of the novel is told in a first person viewpoint of an easterner who has come west for the first time and has fallen in love with the great wide open spaces. From this story comes an enduring line of dialogue. During a poker game, the Virginian has made Trampas look bad, and Trampas says, "Your bet, you son-of-a- — ." With that, the Virginian removes his pistol from the holster, and holding it unaimed, says to Trampas, "When you call me that, smile." Trampas is responsible for the estrangement between the Virginian and his friend Steve and Steve's involvement in rustling. The Virginian's ultimate triumph comes when he kills Trampas in a shoot-out.

In the second story, told through an omniscient viewpoint, the Virginian readily accepts eastern society and civilization which brings with it culture and technology. Here the Virginian's triumph takes the path from cowhand to ranch foreman to partner in a cattle ranch and to marriage with a young, refined New England woman. In place of the wild man from the first story, this Virginian is hard working and industrious, qualities necessary for an upwardly mobile businessman.

A stage production of the novel featured Dustin Farnum as the lead. When Cecil B. DeMille in his solo directing debut came to casting the film (Paramount, 1914), he choose Farnum, and the scenario that the director wrote proved to be so viable that it would be followed more closely than the novel by the succeeding film versions. When pretty Molly Wood arrives in Beer Creek, Wyoming, she meets and is attracted to a happy-go-lucky cowboy called the Virginian. Of course, the Virginian tangles with Trampas when he calls the hero a vulgar name. The Virginian draws his gun, and the screen reads, "When you call me that—smile." He is also forced by circumstances and his own western code to assist in the hanging of his friend Steve. Eventually, the entire outlaw gang is run down and captured or killed, and the Virginian and Trampas have their showdown. Afterward, the Virginian wins the hand of the pretty school teacher.

In its review of the film, the *New York Dramatic Mirror* said, "The strength of the dramatic and spectacular elements were to be expected; but comedy is a less familiar attribute of virile tales of the West. Needless to say, it adds immensely to the entertainment value of the film." One scene showed Molly (Winifred Kingston) and villain Trampas (Monroe Salisbury) seated on the ground talking. The Virginian rides up and shoots straight at Trampas. When the camera focuses on Trampas' feet, there is a dead rattler sprawled out instead of Trampas.

The second version of *The Virginian* (Preferred Pictures, 1925), produced independently by B.P. Schulberg, stuck even closer to the stage play than the 1918 film. This time, Molly rejects the Virginian (Kenneth Harlan) when he leads the posse after cattle rustlers and participates in the hanging of Steve. When the Virginian is wounded while trailing Trampas, Molly nurses him back to health, then rejects him once more when he goes off to face Trampas. Once the showdown is concluded and Trampas is dead, the lovers are reunited.

When Schulberg joined Paramount in 1929, he was determined to film the novel once more, this time as a talkie. The third version of *The Virginian* (Paramount, 1929) proved to be lethargic, verbose and slow, yet it also proved exceedingly popular at the box office. Except for the addition of dialogue, there are few changes in the story. When the film opens, much of the earlier part of the novel has already been done away with and the Virginian (Gary Cooper), already a foreman, is leading a trail herd into the town of Medicine Bow, Wyoming. In the saloon, the confrontation with Trampas (Walter Huston) develops over a saloon girl rather than a card game. There is one comic episode added that has become a classic. At a christening, Steve (Richard Arlen)

Lobby card for the 1946 version of *The Virginian*.

exchanges the clothes of several babies and hopeless confusion follows as the parents try to figure out who belongs to whom. In addition, the conclusion in which Molly (Mary Brian) tries to dissuade the Virginian from facing Trampas anticipates a similar scene twenty-five years later in *High Noon*.

The Virginian (Paramount, 1946) was remade once more, and there was nothing new added except color, although Joel McCrea made the most believable Virginian of the lot. By this time, the plot line was too hackneyed and overused to impress anyone. Even though a different pair of screenwriters were given credit, this film is almost identical to the 1929 version.

In 1902, the same year that Wister published *The Virginian*, William Sidney Porter moved to New York City and began to publish short stories under the pseudonym O. Henry. In the collection *Heart of the West* (1907) appears "The Caballero's Way," the only story about the Cisco Kid. It is a brilliant short story that is coldly told and free of the author's usual sticky sentimentality.

Gary Cooper and Mary Brian strike a pose in the 1929 version of Owen Wister's *The Virginian*.

The Cisco Kid was O. Henry's most attractive villain who "killed for the love of it — because he was quick-tempered — to avoid arrest — for his own amusement — any reason that came to mind would suffice." As the story opens, he has already "killed six men in more or less fair scrimmages, had murdered twice as many (mostly Mexicans), and had winged a larger number whom he modestly forbore to count." His reason for killing in this instance is to avenge the insult to his honor. His mistress, Tonia Perez, has conspired to turn him over to her new lover, Texas Ranger Sandridge. The Kid's way of paying back Tonia for her unfaithfulness is the "caballero's way" of tricking the ranger into shooting Tonia by mistake.

The Cisco Kid (Warner Baxter) came to the screen in the first major sound western, *In Old Arizona* (Fox, 1929). In the O. Henry story, the Kid's real name is Goodall, and he was not Mexican, but this film set the pattern for all the others to follow. The Cisco Kid is a Robin Hood of the border, a happy-go-lucky bandit who is as apt to turn over his loot to the poor as visit his girlfriend Tonia (Dorothy Burgess). When Sergeant Mickey Dunn (Edmund Lowe) arrives on the scene, the film turns into a western *What Price Glory?* with the Kid and Dunn substituting for Flagg and Quirt. When Tonia betrays the Kid almost costing him his life, he gets his revenge, but no one gets killed.

Twenty-two sequels of varying quality followed with a number of actors playing the Kid, although only *In Old Arizona* claimed to be based on "The Caballero's Way." All the others simply acknowledged that they were based on a character created by O. Henry. Even this was not true. The character O. Henry created has never been put on film; the films used only the name.

Another O. Henry story, and one of the author's most tightly knit plots, was "The Double-Dyed Deceiver." A desperado known as the Llano Kid shoots a man in Texas and flees to South America where an unscrupulous American consul persuades him to pose as a long-lost son of a wealthy couple with the idea of bilking them of their money. Under his hard exterior, the Kid has a heart of gold, and he is so moved by the joy of the woman who believes him her son that he refuses to go through with the plan. Furthermore, it seems the man the Kid killed back in Texas was the real son, and to make restitution, he will take his place permanently.

The first film of "The Double-Dyed Deceiver" was *The Texan* (Paramount, 1930). In a Texas town of 1885, run by scripture-quoting Sheriff John Brown (John Marcus), the Llano Kid (Gary Cooper) gets himself in trouble when he shoots a young man in a poker game and flees town on a stolen horse. On board a steamer headed for South America, he meets Thacker (Oscar Apfel), who offers the Kid a sure-fire proposition. Thacker has been hired by Señora Ibarra to find her long-lost son, a runaway at the age of ten. Thacker persuades the Kid to pose as the son, and the Kid easily fools the old woman. Complications quickly arise. First, Señora Ibarra is kind and generous, and this tugs at his conscience. Also, he realizes that he was responsible for the death of her real son. Then he falls in love with his lovely "cousin," Consuelo (Fay Wray). The Kid calls off his deal with Thacker, who immediately hires some thugs to take care of the Kid. Just as Sheriff Brown shows up to take the Kid back, Thacker and his henchmen attack the ranch. The Kid is wounded, but Thacker is killed. The sheriff, realizing the Kid has reformed, agrees to let the dead Thacker assume the identity of the Llano Kid.

With certain modifications, this was a faithful adaptation. The addition of Consuelo as the obligatory love interest failed to damage the film. Stronger on atmosphere than action, it was a picturesque version of the O. Henry story, and its success inspired a loose remake, *The Llano Kid* (Paramount, 1939), which was much lighter in tone. The Llano Kid (Tito Guizar) is hired by a couple of con artists (Alan Mowbray and Gale Sondergaard) to defraud an innocent Mexican girl (Jan Clayton), with whom he falls in love. Except for the skeleton plot, the film has little to do with O. Henry.

Irony is always a strong point in the work of O. Henry, and certainly irony is present in "The Passing of Black Eagle," a tale of a drifter who, while riding the freights, inadvertently gets mixed up with an outlaw gang, takes control and becomes known as "Black Eagle." The drifter is a man who wants to escape commitment, and in the end, he simply boards another freight and rides away, leaving his career as bandit chief behind.

The film *Black Eagle* (Columbia, 1948) attempted to keep some of the irony, although it changed the story around and padded it to a 76 minute running time, probably about 15 minutes too long. Jason Bond (William Bishop) is the drifter who wants to avoid contact with people because they cause him trouble. He becomes involved in a range war, first joining good guy Benjy Laughton (Gordon Jones) and then switching sides to greedy Frank Hayden (James Bell). All works out well in the end as the drifter finally returns to his boxcar and privacy. *Black Eagle* is nothing more than a "B" film from a studio that churned out such product on a regular basis, but it is an entertaining little film.

8. Zane Grey

As a novelist, Zane Grey was a writer of romances in the tradition of Sir Walter Scott, Victor Hugo and Robert Louis Stevenson, and the time-honored devices present in these literary figures are present in Grey: the larger-than-life hero, the innocent heroine, the chase, the duel, the triumph of good over evil. Whatever faults his works may have had, and they were many, Grey was seldom boring and, more often than not, presented his readers with wonderful stories full of atmosphere. Grey wrote over 70 novels, many of which were made into films, often more than once. *The Lone Star Ranger* was made seven times under different titles, *The Border Legion* (1916) was made five times, four others were made four times each, and fifteen were made three times each. In all, 104 films were credited to Grey, making him the most filmed author in the history of American cinema.

Grey began his writing career with a trilogy of the Ohio frontier, the conclusion of which was *The Last Trail* (1906). Essentially it is the story of the Ohio frontier after the Indian threat has been extinguished. White rustlers have to be cleared out by Wetzel and Jonathan Zane, heroes of the previous two novels, *Betty Zane* (1903) and *Spirit of the Border* (1906), before the border can be truly civilized.

The various film adaptations of *The Last Trail* had little to do with the novel. In the first (Fox, 1921), a stranger (Maurice Flynn) rides into town and is immediately mistaken for a bandit known as "The Night Hawk." He is protected by Winifred Samson (Eva Novak), but her fiancé, dam engineer William Kirk (Wallace Beery), tries to have him arrested. When Kirk attempts to steal the company payroll, the stranger, who is an undercover agent, prevents his escape. The remake (Fox, 1927), a Tom Mix vehicle, follows the previous film rather than the novel and adds an Indian attack as well as comic relief in the form of an indolent bloodhound. Also included is a stagecoach race that compares favorably with the chariot race in *Ben-Hur* two years earlier. The only sound version (Fox, 1934) was a George O'Brien vehicle that has an outlaw gang plan to swindle the hero of his land but inadvertently hire the hero, not knowing who he is. The crooks are soon brought to justice. Of these three films, not one came close to using the Grey novel. Fox Studios never showed much interest in the book; it was, however, interested in Grey's name.

Grey's first major success as a novelist came with *The Heritage of the Desert* (1910), a book that would set the tone and voice the themes prevalent in most of his romantic westerns. The main character, like so many of Grey's heroes, is an easterner who comes west, in this case for his health. In Salt Lake City, John Hare is mistaken for a cattleman's spy by outlaws and becomes a hunted man. Before Dene, the leader of the outlaws, can find him, Hare is rescued by Mormon August Naab. Taken into Naab's home, Hare finds himself drawn to two things: Naab's touching piety and Mescal, the young daughter of a Navajo woman and a Spanish father. Although she has been promised to Snap, August Naab's son, she finds herself attracted to Hare. At the same time, Naab begins to transfer much of his fatherly affection to Hare as his own son drifts slowly into the world of the gunman.

When Naab sends Hare into the mountains accompanied by Mescal, Hare finds both his health and hidden strengths that make him more of a man. Later, on the eve of her wedding to Snap, Mescal runs away into the Painted Desert. Soon afterward, Snap goes to work for Holderness, the arch enemy of August Naab. One day, Snap shoots the unarmed Hare, causing his father to disown him. Then, a year after she ran away, Mescal returns. A final showdown occurs in which one of Naab's son's is slain, Dene is killed, and Hare and Mescal are captured by Holderness. Holderness argues with Snap, and Holderness kills him. During the night, a masked man known as Nebraska sets Mescal and Hare free. In a final shootout, Hare guns down Holderness, and Nebraska turns out to be the son of a local bishop. Naab then gives his blessings to the planned union of Hare and Mescal. Certainly, *The Heritage of the Desert* is a melodramatic novel full of too many coincidences, but its universal themes of humanitarianism and courage found a waiting audience and launched Grey on the road to fame and fortune.

The earliest adaptation of *The Heritage of the Desert* (Paramount, 1924) sticks very close to Grey's novel. August Naab (Ernest Torrence) owns a ranch called "The Oasis" where he lives with his son Snap and his adopted daughter Mescal (Bebe Daniels). The Naab ranch is coveted by the villain Holderness (Noah Beery). Into this fray wanders tenderfoot Hare, who is promptly shot full of holes while in Holderness' town. Of course, Snap proves to love whiskey too much to capture Mescal's heart, and Mescal and Hare are inevitably drawn together. In the end, Holderness kidnaps Mescal and sets a trap for Naab, in which he will raise his hands in surrender while his henchman kills Naab from ambush. Before Holderness can accomplish this, he is shot down by Hare. Even though the film displays nice location photography and some good individual scenes, it never quite latches on to the story, and as a result, it is often vague and halting.

Far better are the two sound versions. The first (Paramount, 1932) was directed by Henry Hathaway, his first job as a director on any film. In his first starring role, Randolph Scott played Jack Hare. Some changes occur in the story. The character of August Naab became Adam Nash (J. Farrell MacDonald), and the characters of David Naab and Nebraska were dropped as was all reference to the horse Silvermane that played an important role in the novel. Also, a new character, Lefty (Guinn "Big Boy" Williams), Holderness' righthand man, was added. What is special about this film is not so much the action sequences, which are well done, but rather the slowly developing love between Jack Hare and Judy (Sally Blaine), full of a gentleness seldom found in westerns of the period. It is in the relationship between the two lovers where the film comes closest to capturing the spirit of Grey.

Even though the 1932 film was good, it is the third and last *Heritage of the Desert* (Paramount, 1939) that is truly a fine film. In fact, it may well be the best of all adaptations of Grey as well as the greatest "B" western ever made. This film not only sticks closely to the novel, retaining characters like Nebraska and David Naab as well as the horse Silvermane, but it also captures the feeling of a Grey novel better than any film before or since.

Despite the scenario's taking a few liberties with the plot, it remains faithful to the book. John Abbott (Donald Woods) is a young Eastern lawyer who heads west to check up on his mine holdings managed by Holderness, who has been cheating him. Holderness, fearing he is about to be found out, has Abbott shot and left for dead in the desert. Rescued by Andrew Naab (Robert Barrat) and his son, David (Russell Hayden), Abbott is at first reluctant to divulge his true identity and to let it be known that he owns the land that Holderness is trying to take from Naab and his family. Of course, Abbott falls in love with Naab's daughter, Miriam (Evelyn Venable), who Naab has promised to Snap

Thornton (Paul Guilfoyle), an orphan who has been adopted by Naab. Unknown to Naab, Snap joins forces with Holderness when he sees Miriam drawing closer to Abbott. When ranchhand Nosey (Sidney Toler) takes Abbott up into the mountains, Abbott discovers strengths in himself he never imagined. When Naab forces Miriam to go through with the wedding to Snap, she runs away and is captured by Holderness. When his henchman Nebraska tries to prevent it, Holderness shoots him. David Naab rides to save his sister, and he, too, is gunned down by Holderness. Later, when Snap shows up to claim Miriam, Holderness shoots him. Abbott and Nosey lay siege to Holderness' hideout, but they are greatly outnumbered. All the while, Naab, consumed by Christian forgiveness, has refused to ride after Holderness, but with the death of David, he rides with a vengeance, arriving just in time to save Abbott and dispatch Holderness with his bare hands. Afterward, Abbott and Miriam are united with Naab's blessings.

Certainly, the film retained many of the melodramatic elements of Grey's plot, but director Lesley Selander underplayed the melodrama and concentrated on the influence of Grey's beloved desert on the characters and action. Also, the characters, except for the villain Holderness, avoid the stereotypical and emerge as well-rounded individuals. By today's standards, the film may be too romantic, but then so were Grey's novels and so were the vast majority of "B" westerns.

One of Zane Grey's best novels is certainly *Riders of the Purple Sage* (1912), a novel marred only by its extremely prejudicial view of Mormons. The structure of this novel is really two stories in one, either of which might have been a complete novel in the hands of another author.

Jane Withersteen, whose father was Mormon, befriends Berne Venters, a non–Mormon. Also, Jane has taken in a child, Fay Larkin, whose non–Mormon mother has died. Not only is Elder Tull incensed over Jane's humanitarian treatment of non–Mormons, but he also wants Jane as one of his wives. As the story opens, Venters is about to be horsewhipped by Elder Tull and his followers, but they are prevented when Lassiter, a well known gunman, arrives on the scene. Lassiter has been searching for eighteen years for his sister, Millie Erne, who had been lured away from her husband by a Mormon. When he discovers that Millie is dead, he sets out to kill the man responsible, even though Jane tries to dissuade him. In the meantime, Venters wounds a member of the outlaw Oldring gang known as "the masked rider" only to discover she is a girl, Bess, who turns out to be the daughter of Millie Erne, and the man who defiled Millie is Bishop Dyer,

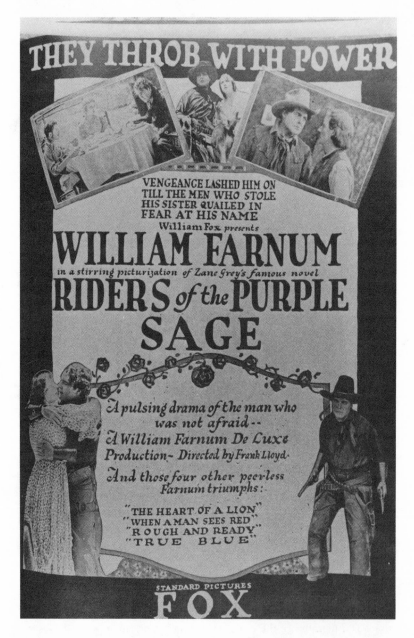

Magazine ad for the 1918 version of Zane Grey's *Riders of the Purple Sage* with William Farnum as the first Lassiter.

a leader of the community. After Lassiter methodically kills Dyer, a Mormon posse takes out after him. The classic climax has Venters and Bess escaping into the desert while Lassiter, Jane and little Fay climb the steep mountain into Surprise Valley, the Mormon posse right behind them. Lassiter rolls the balancing rock down on the pursuers, killing them all and sealing Surprise Valley from the outside world.

Grey's novel was important in the development of the western on at least two counts. First, he formulized the position of the frontier woman. Jane represented the civilizing instinct, and it is her efforts to tame the wildness in Lassiter that ultimately brings him to love her. Second, Grey emphasized the importance of the fast draw to the taming of the West. As Lassiter himself says, guns are still necessary: "Gun-packing in the West since the Civil War has growed into a kind of moral law."

There were two silent versions of *Riders of the Purple Sage*. The first (Fox, 1918) starred William Farnum as Lassiter, and the scenario followed the plot of the novel very closely. However, in this and all succeeding versions, all references to Mormonism were dropped. A more important version (Fox, 1925) followed seven years later. While it was really only a vehicle for Tom Mix, it again stuck closely to the Grey novel and managed to be both coherent and entertaining in a quick, action-packed sixty minutes. When his sister and her child are abducted by a vengeaceful judge, Lassiter (Tom Mix) leaves his job as Texas Ranger and sets to find them. After many years, he comes to Jane Witersteen's ranch where he takes a job. He soon learns that his sister is dead and that Bess, the woman Venters has rescued, is her daughter. Jane (Mabel Ballin) informs him that Judge Dyer (Warner Oland) is responsible. At that point, Lassiter rides into town and kills Dyer. A posse led by Metzger (Fred Kohler), the film's stand-in for Elder Tull, gives chase. The final flight up the cliff and the destruction that Lassiter wreaks on his pursuers is a wonderful visualization of Grey's finale. Overall, this is a good adaptation except on one point, but that one point is quite devastating. By the time Tom Mix made this film, his flamboyant screen persona was already too well established, and he was ill suited to play the hard and stoic Lassiter.

Both sound versions of *Riders of the Purple Sage* had more convincing actors play the central character. The first of these (Fox, 1931) starred George O'Brien, who certainly fit the Grey characterization. Once again, the plot remains basically the same, although the dialogue sounds a bit stilted. The fine action scenes, especially the chase up the cliff, attempt to make up for this deficiency. The last version of *Riders*

William Fox presents a new star—
Fox Special Features   TOM MIX

Tom Mix was the second Lassiter.

of the Purple Sage (Fox, 1941) changed the plot a bit. Judge Dyer
(Robert Barrat) is cheating his niece, Jane Withersteen (Mary
Howard), of her rightful inheritance. He is also the secret leader of an
outlaw gang that poses as vigilantes. Into this situation rides Lassiter
(George Montgomery) to put things right as the rest of the plot follows
the main outline of Grey's novel. By the time this last version was made,
the story itself and its implausible plot complications had begun to creak
with age, yet this is still a model "B" that takes only 56 minutes to tell
a very complicated story in a very straightforward and logical manner.
Also, Montgomery was the best looking of all the Lassiters, and his dry,
laconic delivery aptly suited the character.

Even before *Riders of the Purple Sage* was printed, Grey was busy
working on a sequel, *The Rainbow Trail* (1915), serialized in *Argosy* as *The
Desert Crucible,* which deals with a disillusioned reverend, John Shefford
of Illinois, who travels to Cottonwood where Jane Withersteen, Lassiter
and little Fay once lived. In almost a repeat of the previous book,
Shefford discovers Fay Larkin, now a grown woman herself, living

George O'Brien as the third Lassiter.

among the Mormons who are tormenting her. Fay and Shefford are driven out of the village and flee to Surprise Valley where they find Jane and Lassiter, who have been living there for many years. The four escape across the desert to a trading post where they make plans to return to Illinois where Berne and Bess Venters await them.

Once again Fox cast William Farnum in the first film version (Fox, 1918), followed seven years later by another Tom Mix vehicle (Fox, 1925), released only two months after Mix's *Riders*. Changes abound. John Shefford (Tom Mix) is a nephew of Jim Lassiter (Doc Roberts). He rescues Fay Larkin (Anne Cornwall) from an unwanted marriage

Lobby card for the 1941 version of *Riders of the Purple Sage* with George Montgomery as the final Lassiter.

to Jake Willets (George Bancroft); saves a squaw from the unwanted attention of Shadd, a half-breed; and manages to get Fay safely away from the villains. The film concludes with Shefford and Fay in love, and the union between Lassiter and Jane Withersteen formally legitimized. However, the film suffers from lack of continuity, and without knowledge of the prior film or of the Grey novel, much of the action makes little sense.

The only sound version of *The Rainbow Trail* (Fox, 1932) was another sequel for George O'Brien who played Shefford, a man who is searching for his Uncle Lassiter. While the plot followed the same path as the previous films, it did have one interesting feature. Dyer (W.L. Thorne), a character left over from *Riders of the Purple Sage* and the main villain of this story, wears a mask over half his disfigured face. A strange fact about all these versions is that the hero of *Riders* is, in a sense, searching for himself. Also, as in the film versions of *Riders,* all references to Mormonism are dropped, and the villains are villains simply because they are evil, not because they are Mormon.

When Grey wrote *Desert Gold* (1913), he set the action in the Sonora Desert along the Arizona-Mexico border. The novel opens in the late nineteenth century when two men, Cameron and Warren, son-in-law and father-in-law, become lost in the desert and die. Just before he expires, Cameron finds a lost treasure in gold and marks the place of reference on a certificate proving his marriage to Nell Warren. The action then shifts to 1911 when George Thorpe enlists the aid of his friend, Richard Gale, to help him rescue a girl from Rojas, a Mexican bandit. Gale is an easterner who has come west to prove his manhood. Along the way, Gale saves the life of a Yaqui Indian and also falls in love with Nell Burton, who is in reality Cameron's daughter. It is the Yaqui who teaches Gale the way of the desert, a far more rigorous life than he had faced in the East. When Rojas attacks the ranch, Yaqui leads Gale and his party into the desert where he tricks the Mexican bandit over a cliff. Later, Yaqui takes Gale into the desert where he shows him the fortune in gold and the certificate proving that Nell is not illegitimate, which allows her the freedom to marry Gale.

Desert Gold was filmed three times. The first (Zane Grey Productions, 1919) was from Zane Grey's own company and starred Elmo Lincoln, the screen's first Tarzan. It tried to cram a very complex story within seven reels, approximately 70 minutes, and much of the novel, including the prologue, was omitted. When it was remade (Paramount, 1926) seven years later, the length remained the same, but the story had been simplified. George Thorpe (William Powell) enlists the aid of his adventurous friend Richard Gale (Neil Hamilton) in capturing a murderous Mexican bandit who has carried off his sweetheart. The only sound version of *Desert Gold* (Paramount, 1936), cut down to 58 minutes, has Nell (Marsha Hunt) kidnapped by bandits and rescued by a Yaqui Indian (Larry "Buster" Crabbe) before she is finally reunited with her fiancé (Tom Keene). Just as the villain (Monte Blue) is about to kill Thorpe, the Yaqui shoots him, thereby avenging an earlier insult. In this film, the easterner (Robert Cummings) is played strictly for comic relief and could easily have been dispensed with since the character offers little more than padding to fill out the story. Although it is an above average "B," the only originality here is the role of the Yaqui, which bears a close resemblance to Massai, the character created by Paul Wellman in *Bronco Apache*. He is stoic and full of hate — hate that explodes when he coldly shoots the villain and then, without a second thought, rides away.

Another of Zane Grey's desert novels, *The Light of Western Stars* (1914), takes place along the Arizona-Mexico border during the Mexican

Revolution. Madeline "Majesty" Hammond, a New York society girl, buys a ranch, which becomes entangled in the struggle between Mexican leaders Francisco Madero and Victoriano Huerta. Gene Stewart, who works for Majesty, joins the Huerta faction. The climax of the novel occurs after Stewart is captured and sentenced to death. Majesty manages to get a pardon for the cowboy, but she must cross a hundred miles of desert in a car in order to save him. There are several good scenes in this novel. The first is a golf game between cowboys and Easterners that is played for comedy. The second is the autombile race to save Steward, a high octane ride across wild and rough terrain in which Majesty arrives just at the moment the cowboy is to be executed.

The Light of Western Stars was filmed four times, and not one followed the Grey story. Although the novel first made it to the screen with Dustin Farnum as the lead (Sherman/United, 1918), a far better adaptation appeared seven years later (Paramount, 1925). This time Jack Holt took the role of the hero, Stewart. The story dropped all references to the Mexican Revolution and put its action further back in the past when automobiles were yet to be invented. Despite its slow beginning, the film included a suspenseful climax as Stewart walks the streets of the town, unarmed and prevented from escaping by the villain's henchmen who will shoot him if he tries, knowing that if the ransom money fails to arrive by sundown, he will be killed anyway. In 1930, the first of three sound versions appeared (Paramount, 1930) with Richard Arlen as Dick Bailey, the cowboy with whom Ruth Hammond (Mary Brian) falls in love. It was also Paramount's first sound Grey adaptation. Ruth has come to take charge of the ranch because her father has been killed by Stack (Fred Kohler), who is out to get the ranch. Bailey saves Ruth's ranch and brings the culprits to justice. Overall, it is an entertaining film although it occasionally strains credulity. The last remake of *The Light of Western Stars* (Paramount, 1940) has the distinction of Alan Ladd in an early role. About the only thing left over from the novel is confrontation between East and West in the love affair between the girl (Jo Ann Sayers) and the cowboy (Victor Jory), although Ruth's race to save Stewart is also included. However, the pace is a little too leisurely, and the skimpy budget gives the film a look of a "B," which is not the case with many of the earlier Grey adaptations, especially the Randolph Scott series.

Often in Grey's novels, the gunman, such as Lassiter in *Riders of the Purple Sage,* was the strongest of all his characters. This was once again the case in *The Lone Star Ranger* (1915). On the run from Texas Rangers for killing a man in a fair fight, Buck Duane soon acquires a far-flung reputation, one he would like to forget. When Captain McNelly of the Rangers offers the gunman a pardon in return for helping to capture an illusive outlaw called Chilsildine, he invades the outlaw's stronghold. There he meets Granger Longstreth and his daughter Ray. Duane finally exposes the outlaw leader, and in a climactic gunfight, downs Poggin, the main henchman, although not before Duane receives five bullet wounds himself. Ray's father agrees to give up outlawry and return to Louisiana, and Duane and Ray are married. While most of the characters in his novel are wooden and unbelievable, this is one of the novels that helped to mold the stereotypical western hero, silent, steely eyed, and fast on the draw.

The Lone Star Ranger was adapted seven times for the screen. The novel is divided into two distinct sections. The first details Duane's flight from the law and his life as a gunman. The second half details his acceptance into the Rangers and his infiltration into the outlaw gang. If there are differences between the film adaptations of *The Last of the Duanes* and those of *The Lone Star Ranger,* and they are minor, they lie in emphasis. The various versions of *The Last of the Duanes* pulled more of their plots from the first half of the novel, usually having Duane on the run from the law. The versions of *The Lone Star Ranger* relied more on the second half where Duane is already a Ranger or becomes one almost immediately.

William Farnum became the first to play Buck Duane in *The Last of the Duanes* (Fox, 1919). Farnum portrayed Duane as a two-gun hero, a good-bad man in the same vein as those made famous by William S. Hart. The second adaptation returned to the original title, *The Lone Star Ranger* (Fox, 1923), a vehicle for Tom Mix, who gave his standard portrayal as Buck Duane. A year later, Mix made *The Last of the Duanes* (Fox, 1924), again playing the same character. With slight variations, the stories were the same. At this time, Fox as well as other studios such as Paramount and Universal were churning out westerns at a rapid rate, so there was little concern over the fact that these two films, both based on the same Zane Grey novel and both starring Tom Mix, appeared within less than a year of each other. While both followed the basic outline of the Grey story, the real value to the studio and to Mix was Grey's name above the title rather than the story itself. It was this combination of actor and author that propelled Tom Mix to the zenith of his popularity.

The Lone Star Ranger (Fox, 1930) became Fox's first all-talking remake of a Grey western. Once again, the basic Grey story remained. Buck Duane (George O'Brien) is an outlaw turned rancher who is given a pardon for past sins when he agrees to go after cattle rustlers. He falls in love with Mary Aldridge (Sue Carol) only to discover that her father is the leader of the gang. This film was released in January of 1930, and a mere eight months later, the studio released *The Last of the Duanes* (Fox, 1930). This time Buck Duane (George O'Brien) kills the man who killed his father and must flee the law. While on the run, he learns that Ruth Garrett (Lucile Brown) has been kidnapped by a gang of outlaws, and he sets out to rescue her. He defeats the gang that framed him and captures the leader, Bland (Walter McGrail), thus squaring himself with the law. An interesting subplot involves Bland's wife (Myrna Loy) and her attempt to seduce the hero. Both of these remakes were almost identical in plot to the Tom Mix vehicles which, by now, had begun to suffer from overuse, although this version not only had some good photography but also fine performances and plenty of action.

Still, the studio wasn't finished, resurrecting *The Last of the Duanes* (Fox, 1941) one more time. An honest cowboy on the run from the law, Buck Duane (George Montgomery), is persuaded by the Texas Rangers to infiltrate an outlaw gang and discover the identity of Chilsildine, the mysterious leader, who turns out to be saloon girl Kate (Eve Arden). Duane also rescues Nancy Bowdrey (Lynne Roberts) from the outlaws' clutches. As "B" films go, this is a well done effort, given a bit of freshness by the mystery angle. Seven months later, Fox released its last remake, *The Lone Star Ranger* (Fox, 1943), perhaps the weakest of the seven adaptations, mainly because the lead, football star John Kimbrough as Buck Duane, could play football but couldn't act. In this version, Duane is a Texas Ranger on the trail of outlaws who are scaring off potential buyers of land so they can get it for themselves. He becomes involved with Barbara Longstreet (Shelia Ryan), whose uncle proves to be part of the gang without her knowledge. Eventually Duane brings the gang to justice. (One interesting sidelight on these last two adaptations. William Farnum, who played the very first Buck Duane, was in both films playing Major McNeil, the captain of the Texas Rangers.)

When Zane Grey wrote *The Border Legion* (1916), he stated that he believed the novel (1916) would make a "strong photo-drama," the kind of story that would be read in one sitting. Certainly the story had all the melodramatic elements common in Grey's novels, including a wild shoot out of a climax. It opens in Alder Gulch in 1860. Joan Randle quarrels with her sweetheart, Jim Cleve. Angered and hurt, Cleve runs off and joins a group of outlaws headed by Jack Kells. Dressed in a mask and a man's clothes, Joan sets out to find Jim and is captured by the

Kells gang. When Jim discovers who she is and finds that she has not been despoiled, he manages to sneak in a pastor who secretly marries them in the outlaw camp. Soon afterward, a gold rush ensues, and Jim and Joan attempt to escape. Kells and his gang shoot it out with one another over the gold, leaving only Jim and Joan alive at the end. Even though Kells himself had been taken with Joan, it is greed rather than love that drives him to destruction. While the book fails to rank among the very best Grey, it is entertaining, and the character of Kells is complex and believable.

The first film version of *The Border Legion* was by Goldwyn Studios in 1918. It was also the first of all Zane Grey adaptations to reach the screen. Perhaps Jim Cleve (Eugene Strong) appears a little too disheveled, but otherwise the film sticks closely to Grey's original story. However, it is the character of Kells (Hobart Bosworth), the leader of the Border Legion, who emerges as the strongest character, so much so that Joan Randall (Blanche Bates) is even drawn to him, although by story's end, she has seen the light. After Kells and his brigands are wiped out, she rides off with Cleve. The second silent version, (Paramount, 1924), and far more impressive, was a large scale adaptation directed by William K. Howard, who wound up directing four other Grey productions for the studio. Again, the main plot complications were carried over from the novel, but this time, the film had a far more expensive look as much of the action was filmed on location.

The Border Legion proved so popular that it was filmed three more times as sound features. A further shift of emphasis came in the first sound version (Paramount, 1930). Jim Cleve (Richard Arlen) joins the outlaws after the friendly Kells (Jack Holt) rescues him from a false murder charge. Shortly thereafter, the gang captures a young girl, Joan Randall (Fay Wray), and imprisons her in a hillside cabin, leaving her under the watchful eye of Cleve. Love soon blossoms, and Kells sacrifices himself for the lovers, whom he calls "the kids," becoming the hero that Grey never intended. At one spot in the novel, Jim Cleve ponders killing himself and Joan when he fears that she has been despoiled by Kells and his men, but in this adaptation the hero faces no such dilemma. The outlaw leader is far too honorable to force Cleve into such a decision. The next version changed the title to *The Last Round-Up* (Paramount, 1934) in order to capitalize on the title song. Once again Kells (Monte Blue) leads a gang of desperadoes known as the Border Legion, and Joan Randall (Barbara Fritchie) is so smitten with him that she comes close to throwing over Jim Cleve (Randolph Scott) for the outlaw. As a matter of fact, this film so weighs the story in Kell's favor that he actually emerges as the hero rather than Cleve, who seems rather slow thinking. During the final shootout when Kells' loyal lieutenant lies dying, Kells appears on the verge of tears. Before this embarrassment can happen, the outlaw leader is himself dispatched by a bullet, and Cleve and Joan Randall ride off into the sunset.

Each successive film adaptation whitewashed Kells' character more than the preceding version, and this trend reached its logical extension in Republic's bowdlerized *The Border Legion* (Republic, 1940), turning it into a vehicle for Roy Rogers. Gone are the characters of Jim Cleve and Joan Randall. Instead, Steve Kells is a doctor framed for a crime he didn't commit and on the run from the law. While clearing himself, he manages to wipe out an outlaw gang led by Gulden (Joe Sawyer), one of Kells' henchmen from the novel. If Paramount played around with the story, Republic Studios sanitized and butchered it. As a Roy Rogers vehicle, this was an enjoyable little "B," far better than the overblown musicals he would do later. It just wasn't Zane Grey.

The same year that *The Border Legion* appeared in book form, 1916, the novel *Wildfire* was serialized in *The Country Gentleman*. The story concerned horses, one of Grey's favorite subjects, plus it also predated the later and better *To the Last Man* by introducing a feud between families. In this case, Bostil and Creech, who at one time were friends, become bitter enemies over horses. Bostil himself is a fanatic on the subject. While basically a good man, he is quite capable of lying and cheating to get the horse he wants. His daughter, Lucy, taunts him into accepting the challenge of a race between his horse, Sage King, and Wildfire, owned by Sloane, a dealer in horses. When the race ends in a draw, Bostil is so intent on possessing Wildfire that he even hints to Sloane that he will trade his daughter for the horse. However, Lucy is kidnapped by Creech and his son, Joel. When the two men argue over Lucy, Joel shoots his father, then strips Lucy naked and ties her on the back of Sage King. He sets fire to the prairie to prevent pursuit just as Sloane arrives on Wildfire. A chase ensues, and Wildfire eventually overtakes Sage King. Lucy is rescued, but Wildfire has exerted himself beyond all endurance, and the great beast dies. However, the sacrifice is not in vain as Bostil, overjoyed to have his daughter returned safely to him, renounces his selfish ways and blesses the union of Sloane and his daughter.

This book, like most of Grey's fiction, contains no great insights. Neither are the characters particularly deep or convincing. Even the use of the name Wildfire conveys no real symbolic meaning, despite the fact that the end of the novel takes place in the midst of an inferno. Still, this is one of the author's more enjoyable books, mainly because it is well plotted and the action moves at a nice pace. Also, Grey's love of horses shows throughout, investing the proceedings with some emotional intensity.

Wildfire was made twice into moving pictures. The first was *When Romance Rides* (Goldwyn, 1922). While Zane Grey may have lacked a great deal of depth as a writer, he was at least sincere, but *When Romance Rides* injects unfunny humor and false sentimentality. The race becomes the pivotal part of the plot, and the Bostil-Creech feud is dropped. Also dropped is the climactic race across the burning plains. A better film was *Red Canyon* (Universal, 1949), even if it didn't exactly follow the novel. Lin Sloane (Howard Duff) is chasing a wild stallion when he comes across Lucy Bostel (Ann Blyth). Sloane wants to run the stallion in a race that Lucy's father (George Brent) also wants to win. Additional conflict comes from Sloane's family, the Cordts, notorious horse thieves and outlaws. Sloane clears his name in a shootout where he guns down his father and brother. It is interesting to note that Cordt was a horse thief in the novel, often discussed but little seen, but he bore no relation to the hero. In addition, this film lessened the importance of Wildfire, and once again, the climactic chase and prairie fire vanished from the story. While it certainly was not Zane Grey, the outstanding color photography and great shots of wild horses add to the film's appearance, and the leads gave acceptable performances, all adding up to an enjoyable minor "A."

Grey turned to the modern world with *The Desert of Wheat* (1919), which opens in the Bend country of Washington in 1917 just after the outbreak of World War I. There Kurt Dorn first struggles with both his German born father over the United States' entrance into the war and also with his own guilt about his German background. He goes off to war, becomes a hero and is wounded so badly that he is given a short time to live. Returning to Washington to die, he is nursed back to health by Lenore Anderson, who marries him and becomes his major source of strength.

Zane Grey himself had very little interest in films, although as early as 1912 he saw the financial possibilities of filming his own novels, but it was not until 1919 that he invested in them. That year saw the formation of his own production company and the release of his first feature film based on *The Desert of Wheat,* which became *Riders of the Dawn* (Zane Grey Productions, 1919), and Grey's novel, just as in so many productions done by other companies, disappeared in the transition. The story becomes one of a war hero (Roy Stewart) who returns home to Washington State only to discover a crooked lawyer and his henchmen trying to take control of the wheat. The hero removes his uniform, dons his cowboy outfit and roars into action. The film failed to impress critics, and the *New York Times* said it would probably "seem much like a comedy to many real westerners," but it did well enough at the box office for Grey's production company to adapt four more of his novels: *Desert Gold* (1919); *The U.P. Trail* (1920), again with Roy Stewart; *The Man of the Forest* (1921); and, *Mysterious Rider* (1921).

Although these films all proved financially successful, Grey soon tired of movie making, complaining that it took away too much time from his writing. Grey sold the whole business to Jesse Lasky, who merged it with his own company, Famous Players–Lasky. Lasky also gained the Brunton Studio from Zane Grey Productions, all of which later became the basis for Paramount Studios.

The 1920 Grey novel, *Man of the Forest,* was the first of the author's attempts to expound his Darwinian philosophy. At one point, a characters says, "If you're quick to see, you'll learn that the nature here in the wilds is the same as that of men — trees fight to live — birds fight — animals fight — men fight. They all live off one another." The story is of two sisters, Helen and Bo Rayner, who come to Arizona to oversee their ailing uncle's ranch. There Helen meets Milt Dale, a gifted mechanic, who people of the area like but consider shiftless because he refuses to work on a ranch. But when Milt kidnaps the two sisters to keep them from harm at the hands of the villain, he teaches Helen to understand the value of life, and of course, the two fall in love. Despite its predictability, this is an enjoyable Grey novel.

Any reference to Darwinism is conspicuously absent from the first film version of *Man of the Forest* (Zane Grey Productions, 1921), although the scenario followed the novel very closely. The uncle (Harry Lorraine) sends for his two nieces, Helen (Claire Adams) and Bo (Charlotte Pierce), to take over his land empire which is coveted by Lem Beasley. Milt Dale (Carl Gantvoort) hides the girls until he can settle with the villain. The first remake (Paramount, 1926) trimmed the story to a single heroine (Georgia Hale). When Helen arrives to take the ranch from her dying uncle, Milt Dale (Jack Holt) kidnaps her and takes her to his forest retreat to keep her from being murdered by Clint Beasley (Warner Oland). Helen suspects that Milt's motives are not pure, and she runs away and has him jailed. But Milt escapes and, with the aid of his pet cougar, ends Beasley's villainy. Helen realizes that Beasley was behind her uncle's death, and she and Milt are together at last.

The final version of *Man of the Forest* (Paramount, 1933), the only sound version, was directed by Henry Hathaway with a real feeling for the characters, although the melodramatic elements of the story, especially the scene where a pet mountain lion helps the hero escape from jail, are difficult to accept. Also, the comic relief, a staple in "B" westerns of the period, seems an intrusion, especially the scene in which Guinn "Big Boy" Williams wrestles with a sitting mule. However, these are minor complaints because this is a superior Grey entry. For the most part, the story follows the first remake rather than the novel. The only heroine, Alice Gaynor (Verna Hillie), discovers her father, Jim Gaynor (Harry Carey), murdered by Clint Beasley (Noah Beery) who frames Brett Dale (Randolph Scott). One particularly effective scene occurs when Beasley calmly slits the throat of Jim Gaynor, then delivers a monologue with the dead body at his feet. Beasley is finally done in by his housekeeper who is jealous of the attention he shows Alice. Perhaps the film is a little hokey at times, but so much of it is good entertainment that the film survives its drawbacks.

The year 1921 saw the serialization of *The Mysterious Rider* in *The Country Gentleman*. In some ways the plot was reminiscent of Grey's earlier *The Heritage of the Desert*. Set in late nineteenth century Colorado, the novel tells of Bill Bellounds, who loves his spoiled son, Jack, so much that he cannot see what everyone else sees — that the boy is thoroughly rotten. Like August Naab who saved Mescal for his rotten son Snap, Bellounds expects Columbine, a girl he has reared after rescuing her from Indians, to become Jack's wife. Columbine loves Wilson Moore, a cowboy, and all seems lost until Hell-Bent Wade arrives on the scene. Eighteen years before, Wade wrongly accused his wife of infidelity, and as a result, she ran away, taking their young daughter with her. So Wade became a wanderer, dooming himself to a life of self-punishment. Wade takes a job on Bellounds' ranch and tries in vain to reform Jack. When Wade discovers that Jack is rustling his own father's cattle and laying the blame on Wilson, he shoots it out with the boy, both of them dying in the process. At the same time, Columbine finds out that Wade is her real father. The novel ends with Columbine and Wilson planning their marriage.

The Mysterious Rider (Zane Grey Productions, 1921) was the last from Grey's own production unit before he sold out to Jesse Lasky. The story finds Columbine (Claire Adams) in love with Wilson Moore (Carl Gantvoort), but to please her foster father (Walt Whitman), she marries Jack (James Mason). Later, Bellounds becomes friends with the Mysterious Rider, Hell Bent Wade (Robert McKim). When Jack is drawn into a rustling scheme, Wade discovers the head of the gang is Ed

Smith (Frederick Starr), who murdered his wife. Wade also discovers that Columbine is actually his daughter. In a showdown, Wade kills Smith, and Jack is sent off to jail. Columbine and Wilson are then united in marriage. This film failed to find much favor critically as most reviewers faulted the lack of originality and the contrived plotting.

After the appearance of the film, Grey turned the novel into a play, calling it *Hell Bent Wade.* Much of the main action happened off stage, making the motivations of the characters unclear. Grey himself changed the plot, allowing Bellounds to discover the truth about Jack and banishing him. Wade is left alive at the end to go about helping people.

The first remake of *The Mysterious Rider* (Paramount, 1927) ignored all previous versions and substituted its own story. Homesteaders in the California desert learn that their claims are superseded by a Spanish land grant owned by Cliff Harkness (Charles Sellon). When Harkness offers to sell his claim for $25,000, Hell Bent Wade (Jack Holt) suggests that the homesteaders take it. Accordingly, they collect the money and turn it over to Wade to purchase the claim. When a power company owner offers Harkness more money, Harkness tricks Wade out of the homesteaders' money and sells his land to the magnate. After he is almost lynched, Wade manages to break jail and forces Harkness to confess. He then marries Dorothy King (Betty Jewel), the daughter of the power company owner. Except for the character of Hell Bent Wade, Grey's novel disappeared, perhaps for the better considering the unanimously hostile reviews the first version had received.

The first sound adaptation of *The Mysterious Rider* (Paramount, 1933) followed the previous Paramount entry with Cliff Harkness (Irving Pichel) out to dupe homesteaders of their money. In rides Wade Benton (Kent Taylor), the young hero, to set things right and win the heart of ingenue Dorothy (Lona Andre). Although the typical dialogue and story reduce this film to a rather ordinary "B" western, the camera work and lighting give the film an appearance of a bigger budget. However, it is a routine action drama with more connection to the previous film version than the Grey novel.

By the time of the last remake, the Paramount Zane Grey features had been turned over to Harry Sherman, who was already making the Hopalong Cassidy entries for the studio. Thus *The Mysterious Rider* (Paramount, 1938) became the first of this new series, and Maurice Geraghty was assigned to write the script. Unaware of the previous versions, Geraghty returned to the novel for his source, and at least some of the Grey story returned to the screen. Also, no stock footage from the previous versions was to be used. Sherman did instruct Geraghty to follow the same formula that had been used so successfully on the Hoppy films — open big, forget the middle, and close big. Of necessity, this called for changes in the original story.

Ben Wade (Douglas Dumbrille), who is also the masked bandit Pecos Bill, and his sidekick Frosty (Sidney Toler) return to the ranch where Wade's daughter Collie (Charlotte Field) has been raised by William Bellounds (Stanley Andrews). Though in love with Wils Moore (Russell Hayden), she is promised to Jack Bellounds, who is rustling cattle in league with Folsom (Monte Blue). Wade manages to do away with the villains and unite the lovers by movie's end. While the film sounds and plays as a standard "B," this *Mysterious Rider* has several unique ingredients. Like *Heritage of the Desert* made the following year, it has a fine comic performance by Sidney Toler, noted more for his later portrayals of Charlie Chan. Also, Douglas Dumbrille, who normally played cold, heartless villains, is oddly effective — even warm — as Ben Wade, although it is a little hard to believe him as the two-gunned Pecos Bill. While he may not mirror the desperate loneliness of the Grey character, his face projects a world weariness behind his subdued sense of humor. Wade's relationship with Frosty avoids the silliness and superfluousness that pervades such teaming in most "B" westerns. There is an easy warmth and comradeship between the two. In reality, this is nothing more than Saturday matinee material, but it is a superior example of its kind and only a slight notch below *Heritage of the Desert.*

Also beginning in 1921 was the serialization of another Grey novel, *The Call of the Canyon,* this time in *Ladies' Home Journal.* Once again Grey moved out of the historical West and into the modern era and told the story of Carley Burke who travels to the Arizona desert in search of her fiance, Glenn Kilbourne, who is recuperating from wounds suffered in World War I. The values of East and West soon clash, and when Carley asks Glenn to return to New York, he refuses. Carley goes back east, but there she fails to find happiness, and finally rushes back to Arizona to marry Glenn. Essentially this novel was both an affirmation of the woman's role in American — and especially western — society and also a bitter attack on the new morals of postwar America. While this novel may have taken place in the 1920s, its values were those of nineteenth century Western America.

The Call of the Canyon (Paramount, 1923) was made only once as a film, and neither the dated philosophy nor the lack of action boded well for an adaptation. The film opens with Glenn (Richard Dix) in New York finding himself disgusted with the dress and manners of the moderns, and he packs his bags and heads west to recuperate from his wounds. Carley (Lois Wilson) follows and, once she arrives, the cowboys on Glenn's ranch play all sorts of jokes on her, including telling her that a skunk is a hyacinth squirrel. It is their jokes as much as anything that drives her back to New York only to discover that she, too, can no longer abide the shallowness of modern living. The only suspense generated in this film comes when Carley rushes back to Arizona while Glenn is preparing to marry another woman. She manages to arrive just in time to bust up the wedding. The other woman gives up Glenn and rushes off to marry the ranch foreman, who is far better suited to her anyway. As Zane Grey adaptations go, this film stays very faithful to its source, but despite fine acting and good direction by Victor Fleming, the story's implausibilities and dated material, even for 1923, doom it to mediocrity. After the promising opening of busloads of soldiers returning from the front, the film quickly degenerates into a crushing bore.

Using the Graham-Tewksbury feud that began in Texas and ended in the Tonto Basin in Arizona, known there as the Pleasant Valley War, Grey fashioned *To the Last Man* (1922), a far better and more lasting work than *The Call of the Canyon*. The story begins when, during the Civil War, Lee Jorth courts and marries Gaston Isbel's sweetheart, thus laying the basis for the feud. However, the main story concerns the chidlren of these two men, Ellen Jorth and Jean Isbel. Even though they both want to support their families in the feud, they find themselves falling in love with each other. Certainly the novel bears a striking resemblance to *Romeo and Juliet,* but Ellen and Jean are not doomed lovers. Instead, the feud dies when the last of the major participants dies. The last obstacle standing in the way of the lovers' happiness is an outlaw named Colton, and when Jean kills him, they are free to marry.

Of the characters in this novel, Ellen is certainly the most interesting. She is close to nature, a wild girl who has grown up motherless. The women of the Isbel clan refer to her as a "hussy," but Jean sees deeper than the others and discovers a woman of rare beauty and strength, a woman who aptly represents the moral code of the West. It is in the women of this novel rather than the men where Grey finds his heroes. When the Jorth men sneak up on the Isbel ranch and open fire, they kill two Isbel men. While the bodies lie in the fields, the Jorths open the gates and release the pigs. The Isbel women plead with their men to recover the bodies before the pigs begin to eat them, but the men refuse to jeopardize their lives. Two of the women, risking fire from the enemy, rush from the house and out into the fields where they dig shallow graves to keep their kinfolk from being eaten by the swine. It is a marvelous scene, certainly the best in the novel and perhaps the best in all of Grey's works.

The first film of *To the Last Man* (Paramount, 1923) ran seven reels, a little longer than most of the studio's silent adaptations of Grey. Like the other entries in the series, it was filmed on location, and the action was practically nonstop. However, the emphasis of the story shifted to a feud between cattlemen and sheepmen, thus ignoring the Graham-Tewksbury feud and all its complications. Jean Isbel (Richard Dix) loves Ellen Jorth (Lois Wilson), even though they are on opposite sides of the feud. When Colter (Noah Beery), Ellen's father, discovers their love, he goes crazy and leads an attack on the Isbels. In the end, only Jean and Ellen remain alive, their love legitimized in spite of all the bloodshed and death.

The first sound version of *To the Last Man* (Paramount, 1933) cut ten minutes from the previous version, which failed to damage it in any way. On the contrary, the story seemed much tighter. The story opens in the hills of Kentucky where a feud rages between the Colbys and Haydens. When Jed Colby (Noah Beery, reprising his role from the 1923 film) kills the patriarch of the Haydens, Mark Hayden (Egon Brecher) has him thrown in jail. Afterward, Mark Hayden moves most of his clan to Arizona in an effort to put an end to the feud. Years later, Jed Colby, his daughter Ellen (Esther Ralston) and his partner Jim Daggs (Jack LaRue) move to Arizona in pursuit of the Haydens. There Ellen Colby and Lynn Hayden (Randolph Scott) meet and fall in love, much to the chagrin of Colby and Daggs. A final showdown occurs in which all the Hayden men except for Lynn are killed. As Jed Colby gloats over his victory, Daggs turns on him and kills him. Daggs rushes back to the ranch to take Ellen. In the meantime, Lynn, badly wounded, stumbles to the Colby ranch where Ellen hides him in the loft at the very moment that Daggs rushes in. While Ellen and Daggs struggle below, Lynn manages to pull his knife and roll off the loft, landing on Daggs and driving his knife into the villain, killing him. The last scene shows a newspaper clipping announcing the wedding of Lynn and Ellen.

As directed by Henry Hathaway, this excellent "B" ranks as one of the best adaptations of Grey and a film that is superior to the novel on which it is based. The primitive yet vulnerable character of Ellen is fully realized in Esther Ralston's performance, the finest of her career. Also, the fledgling love affair between Ellen and Lynn is given an erotic angle in a nude bathing scene. While Ellen is swimming in a pond,

Daggs comes upon her and taunts her to come out and get her clothes. Happening upon the scene, Lynn knocks Daggs in the water and then runs him off. In addition, the action scenes are fast and brutal. This is especially true in the scene where Colby and Daggs coldbloodedly dynamite a pass as the Haydens ride through, killing all but Lynn. It is also true of the climactic fight between Ellen and Daggs, a scratching, hair-pulling encounter with Lynn lying helpless in the loft. Even the ambush at the ranch is included, although the incident with the pigs has been omitted.

The last time *To the Last Man* reached the screen it was called *Thunder Mountain* (RKO, 1947), which is the title of another Grey novel discussed later. In this case, another film company had scheduled a feature called *The Last Man,* and to avoid confusion, RKO opted for another Grey title but chose to use the plot ingredients of *To the Last Man.* As it turned out, the planned film never materialized, but by that time, *Thunder Mountain* was already in release.

In this version, Marvin Hayden (Tim Holt) returns home after college to discover that an old family feud has once again erupted. With the help of his girl friend Ellen Jorth, who belongs to the rival family, he uncovers a gang of crooks who have set the families feuding in order to drive them off their land on which the government intends to build a dam. Together, the lovers expose the crooks and reunite the families. While a good little western, as were most of the Tim Holt vehicles at RKO, this had little to do with the Grey novel. Most of the harshness of the feud that existed in the novel as well as the previous films has been dissipated, thus weakening the story considerably. Where the 1933 film ranks among the very best "B" westerns ever made, *Thunder Mountain,* while well made, must be considered rather routine.

Although somewhat unstructured in plot, *Wanderer of the Wasteland* (1923) ranks with the most important of the author's works. It is an idea that Grey would often return to, that of a man wandering the West in search of himself. In this instance, Grey employed a Cain-Abel motif to set the story in motion. Adam Larey and his older brother Guerd quarrel over a woman, and in the ensuing fight, Adam shoots his brother. Believing his brother dead, Adam flees into the desert where he almost dies. Saved by the prospector Dismukes, he once again begins his wanderings, becoming known throughout the territory as Wansfell the Wanderer. In this role, he kills Baldy McKue, who has kidnapped and violated another man's wife. Later, he tries vainly to save the life of Magadalena Virey, who had come to live in Death Valley with her husband to atone for her past sins. One night her husband brings a terrible avalanche down on their cabin, killing both husband and wife. All Adam retrieves from the scene is a picture of their daughter, Ruth. Later he rescues another young woman, Genie Linwood, from kidnappers. When he finally meets Ruth Virey, he refuses to allow himself to fall in love with her because he is unworthy. At last, he returns to face the consequences of killing his brother, only to find that Guerd is still alive and well. The novel ends with Adam's love for Ruth unresolved.

Wanderer of the Wasteland (Paramount, 1924) became Paramount's first feature entirely in two strip Technicolor. Also, the film crew travelled to Death Valley for location shooting. In addition, despite the novel's episodic nature, the scenario stuck fairly close to the original plot. The story opens with Adam (Jack Holt) discovering his brother has gambled away all his inheritance and is in the process of stealing from Adam. They struggle, a gun goes off and Guerd collapses to the floor. Adam flees, leaving behind Ruth Virey (Billie Dove), the girl he loves. As he lies dying in the desert, Adam is rescued by the kindly prospector Dismukes (Noah Beery). Later in his wanderings, Adam comes across Ruth's parents living in the desert. The father (George Irving) wrongly believes that his wife (Kathlyn Williams) has been unfaithful and has moved them there to keep her away from other men. From a distance he sees Adam talking to his wife, and misinterpreting their actions, he scrambles above the cabin and sets off a dynamite blast that brings an avalanche down on the cabin, killing him instantly. Rushing back to the cabin, Adam finds Magdalene clinging to life long enough to tell him to give her love to her daughter. When Adam returns to Ruth, she urges him to find his brother who may still be alive. Once he discovers Guerd alive, he returns to Ruth.

Critics found it an important film, especially in light of the Technicolor process that *Variety* called "perfect tones." Color was even used to enhance the story itself. In one scene, a fight breaks out in the millrace, and when one man is trapped in the revolving wheel, it is obvious he is being cut to pieces as the mill water turns bright red from his blood. In addition, the film left the essential ingredients of the Grey story untouched. The public also greeted the film enthusiastically, standing in long lines to see it when it first opened in Los Angeles and later in New York. Of all the silent adaptations of Grey's films, this is certainly the most important.

Wanderer of the Wasteland was remade twice as sound films. The first (Paramount, 1935) is a tedious affair that takes liberties with the novel. Here Adam (Dean Jagger) once more flees into the desert after he mistakenly believes he has killed his brother. As he lies dying in the desert, he is saved by prospector Dismukes (Edward Ellis), whose daughter Ruth (Gail Patrick) nurses him back to health. She convinces Adam to turn himself in, and when he does, he discovers his brother still alive. The years of wandering that Adam did, the epic proportions of his survival that Grey so intricately depicted, have disappeared, replaced by a rather flat, incomplete story. The last version of *Wanderer* (RKO, 1945) bears little resemblance except in the title to either the novel or the two previous film versions. Here Adam Larey (James Warren) is a young hero on a vendetta to find the killer of his father. When he finally tracks down the villain, he chooses not to kill him because he has fallen in love with the man's niece (Jean Collinshaw). However, the man is killed anyway, and Adam is blamed. In the end, Adam clears his name and wins the girl. The problem with this film is not so much that it fails to follow the Grey story but that it has so little action and a hero without heroics. In fact, the hero is beaten at every turn. As with most RKO productions, the film looks good technically, but it is a static, sterile film. In addition, Adam has picked up a comic sidekick, Chito Rafferty (Richard Martin), a character who would later continue in the Tim Holt series. Chito is the highlight of this turkey.

The same year that *Wanderer of the Wasteland* appeared, 1923, also saw the serialization of *The Code of the West* in the magazine *The Country Gentleman*. Like *The Call of the Canyon* before it, this novel was placed in the modern West and utilized automobiles as part of the plot complications. Also like the earlier novel, it is an attack on modern morals. Shortly after World War I, Gloriana Stockwell joins her sister in the Tonto Basin area of Arizona. Gloriana is a "flapper" interested in the liberation of the American woman, but when she meets cowboy Cal Thurman, the "code" of the West begins to work its magic on her. When Cal forces Gloriana to marry him, he does so to protect her from scoundrels like Bid Hatfield. All ends well. As it turns out, Cal really loves Gloriana and she loves him. Grey himself was pleased with the novel as was the editor of *The Country Gentleman*, who thought the work was an important literary piece.

Code of the West (Paramount, 1925) first reached the screen as an "A" feature, but the rambling narrative of the novel carried over to the film, producing a rather flat story. Even the changes in the plot failed to hasten things along. Soon after Georgie May Stockwell (Constance Bennett) arrives on an Arizona ranch, all the cowboys fall in love with her. At first, cowboy Cal Thurman (Owen Moore) resists her charms, but he, too, is smitten when she flutters her eyes in his direction. However, once she has won his heart, she seems to direct her attention elsewhere, leading Cal to the conclusion that she was only interested in winning a conquest. Cal, who has a head for business, stakes a claim on land opened to settlers, and soon thereafter, he finds himself and Georgie caught in the midst of a terrific forest fire. They escape in a daring leap from a cliff into the water. Trial and tribulation finally bring hero and heroine together by fadeout. The reviewer for the *New York Times* called the film "wavering and tedious" and pointed out that there didn't seem to be much motivation for many of the incidents. If the reviewer had read the novel, he would have discovered the same faults.

The first sound adaptation was called *Home on the Range* (Paramount, 1935), and like the title, the story had little to do with the novel. It is a combination western and race track yarn about the brothers Hatfield, Jack (Jackie Coogan) and Tom (Randolph Scott), who own a stable of horses with one sure winner, Midnight. The bad guys want to foreclose, taking the ranch as well as the horse. At one spot, Tom enters the villain's office, and with gun drawn, says, "Now I got every chamber in this here gun loaded up. I'm agoin' to shoot four bullets careless, and then I'm agoin' to put the last two through the dirtiest coyote in Green Valley, and you're it. That is, unless you open up that there safe and sign over the deed of the ranch you stole off'n us Hatfields, and while that safe is open, you better pay back that money that your boys took off'n me." His eyes turning into slits, Breaty (Addison Richards) threatens, "You'll hang for this." Smiling, Tom replies, "Not while there's honest men in Green Valley." The big race finally comes, and Midnight wins it easily. The ranch is saved, the villains are defeated and Tom is united with his best girl, Georgie (Evelyn Brent). But *Home on the Range* is a western in name only. There is virtually no gunplay and only one good fistfight to enliven the tale, and on the whole, the film just doesn't work. Not only is the script to blame, which failed to improve on either the novel or the previous version, but also the limp and uninspired direction by Arthur Jacobson. Had Henry Hathaway directed, it might have been a different story.

The last remake returned to the original title, *Code of the West* (RKO, 1947), but by now all visible evidence of the original plot, other than the title of Grey's novel, had disappeared. Even Grey's characters, which had showed up in the previous entries, were gone. In this concoction, Bob Wade (James Warren) leads a group of settlers in a battle against outlaws who are trying to prevent them from settling on their land. It is a routine effort, although the film contains a fine performance by Raymond Burr as the smooth and magnetically evil villain.

Zane Grey's love of horses surfaced again in *Wild Horse Mesa,* also serialized in *The Country Gentleman* (1924). While Chayne Weymer hunts for the wild stallion Panquitch, he encounters the Melberne-Longbridge group which captures and sells wild horses. Bent Mannerube, a horse thief, soon becomes foreman for this group. Because of Longbridge and Mannerube's treatment of the horses in which many die, Melberne breaks with his partner. Chayne and Melberne's daughter Sue continue to search for Panquitch, and in doing so, they discover a lost mesa full of wild horses. Soon after, Mannerube and his gang are defeated and the two partners are reunited. Chayne abandons his pursuit of Panquitch because he comes to feel that such a magnificent horse should remain free.

The first adaptation of *Wild Horse Mesa* (Paramount, 1924) followed the novel in broad outline, although it dropped characters here and there while adding others. A sub plot involving an Indian girl named Sosie as well as the character of Longbridge are missing; an Indian sidekick for the hero has been added. While hunting for the stallion Panquitch, Chayne Weymer (Jack Holt) and his Navajo friend are set upon by Mannerube (Noah Beery) and his men. Weymer is rescued by Melberne (George Irving) and his daughter Sue (Billie Dove). When Weymer sees Melberne using barbed wire to catch wild horses, he persuades the old man to cease the cruel operation. Later, when Mannerube attempts to use the same trap, Weymer's Navajo friend dispatches the villain with a rifle shot. The highlight of the film occurs when Chayne Weymer heads off a herd of horses stampeding toward naked barbed wire. No sooner does he accomplish this task, than he learns that hundreds of other horses are rushing toward a cliff, and he dashes off to save them. Unfortunately, the film runs too long at eight reels. Much of the story seems forced and lacks any sense of humor, which is due to the original source. While Grey was writing the novel, he suffered frequent bouts of depression, and he often wrote for extended periods — twelve hours or more a day, completing a minimum of 27 pages each day. As a result, the novel is a slapdash affair, and the film suffered from the same malaise. The titles, often taken right from the novel, are stilted and cliché ridden, reading like something out of *The Drunkard*. At one point, Sue says, "If Benton's plan does not succeed Father will be ruined." When Weymer first meets Sue, he utters, "You must forgive me as I have never had the chance to meet a girl like you."

However, the first remake of *Wild Horse Mesa* (Paramount, 1932) was among the best of all the Paramount Zane Greys, silent or sound. Where the previous version concentrated on large scale action, this version, directed by Henry Hathaway, concentrated on character. Also, further changes were made in the story, and in the end, this film emerged as a much better piece of entertainment than the novel. Chayne Weymer (Randolph Scott) battles the horse trapper (Fred Kohler, Sr.) who cruelly uses barbed wire to trap horses. In the process, Weymer saves Sandy Melberne from the villain. In the end, there is the stampede, which utilizes footage from the previous version, and the crooked horse trapper is trampled to death by an outlaw stallion. What is important about this version is the delicacy of emotions expressed by both the script and the actors. Director Hathaway and his writers added depth of character and incident where none had previously existed.

When *Wild Horse Mesa* (RKO, 1947) made it to the screen for the last time, it changed studios and dropped almost all connection to the Grey novel. Dave Jordon (Tim Holt) and his sidekick Chito Rafferty (Richard Martin) set out to find a herd of wild horses that has been hidden in the mountains of Utah. Also, an outlaw gang has killed Jay Olmstead (Harry Woods) and blamed Dave and Chito. With the help of Sue (Nan Leslie) and Pop Melbern (Jason Robards, Sr.), Dave rounds up the herd, defeats the bad guys and clears himself and Chito. While the plot summary sounds as if the film is full of rousing action, it is rather a sedate western, emphasizing pictorial quality over action. As usual with RKO, it was an impressive "B," but it failed to match the 1932 version.

In 1925, Grey penned a novel, *The Bee Hunters,* which was serialized in *The Ladies' Home Journal.* Because of a similar title by another author, the title was changed to *Under the Tonto Rim.* Again a modern story, it tells of Lucy Watson, a social worker, who comes to work among the residents of the wild Tonto country. At first, she sees herself as a symbol of culture and westerners as people behind in their development. By book's end, she has come to realize the error of her thinking and marries Edd Denmeade, hunter of wild bees. The only real importance of this novel lies in the fact that Grey, within the events of the novel, once again stated his belief in Darwinism.

The three film versions show a complete disregard for the book. *Under the Tonto Rim* (Paramount, 1928) first made it to the screen as a western murder mystery wherein the hero (Richard Arlen), a gold-miner, is framed for the killing of the brother of his girl (Mary Brian). He unmasks the killer and wins the hand of his love. The first remake (Paramount, 1933), although directed by Henry Hathaway, is a weak entry in the series, a silly story of Tonto Duley (Stuart Erwin), a slow-witted cowpoke who proves his worth by defeating a handful of bad guys and wins the hand of the boss's daughter. When *Under the Tonto Rim* (RKO, 1947) made it to the screen for the last time, the story became one of a stagecoach operator (Tim Holt) who goes under cover to get the goods on the gang that killed one of his drivers. The only Grey-like touch has the hero falling in love with the sister (Nan Leslie) of the leader of the gang. Of the three versions, although it has absolutely nothing to do with the novel except the title, this is the superior film, a topnotch "B" western made so by Lew Landers' snappy direction and enhanced by fine camera work. What is surprising about these three films is that they chose to adapt such a nonwestern as *Under the Tonto Rim*. What is *not* surprising is that, in all three cases, the scriptwriters threw out Grey's inferior story and substituted stories of their own. This is certainly a case where the Grey name and title were far more important than the novel itself.

In 1926, *Forlorn River,* also serialized in the *Ladies' Home Journal,* was the first of two novels featuring Ben Ide and his friend Nevada. They are wild horse hunters in Upper California Lake Tule area in the late nineteenth century. Ben's one obsession is to capture the stallion California Red, and this leads the pair into a number of conflicts. Ben loves Ina Blaine, but her father, a rich rancher, is convinced by the story's villain, Lew Setter, that both Ben and Nevada are horse thieves. Nevada loves Hettie, Ben's sister, but because of his shady background, her father forbids any romance. The climax comes when Setter and his men attack Ben at the ranch, and Nevada rides up and dispatches the villain and his men. Exonerated, Ben is able to unite with Ina, but Nevada has been recognized by the dying Setter. He is Jim Lacy, a well-known gunman from Nevada. As the novel ends, Nevada rides off, leaving behind his true love, Hettie.

Forlorn River (Paramount, 1926) was another in the Jack Holt series of Zane Grey silents. The plot was simplified a great deal with Ben Ide *sans* Nevada fighting off rustlers. The double romance was dropped in favor of a single love affair between Ben and Ida, but it was a routine entry in the Holt series. Routine was also the word for the only sound remake (Paramount, 1937) ten years later, which threw out even more of the novel. Here the daredevil hero (Larry "Buster" Crabbe) is on the trail of bank robbers. Others characters include a perpetually hungry sidekick (Syd Saylor) with a perpetually bobbing adam's apple and a wooden love interest (June Martel). The best thing about both versions is the photography, which fills the screen with bleak landscapes. Otherwise, both films are forgettable.

Grey immediately penned a sequel to *Forlorn River, Nevada,* which first appeared as a serial late in 1926 in *American Magazine* and concentrated on the story of Jim Lacy or Nevada. When he is forced to shoot a man in Linville, Nevada, he flees into Arizona where he falls in with a gang of rustlers known as the Pine Tree Gang. In reality, the hero is working undercover for the Cattlemen's Association. In the end, Jim Lacy destroys the outlaw gang and is finally united with Hettie Blaine. While this novel is considerably weaker than some of Grey's other novels, it is interesting to note that it became the best selling western of all time, due in large part to the expiration of the copyright, allowing publishers all over the country to churn out copies without having to reimburse Grey.

Between the time the story appeared in *American Magazine* in 1926 and its appearance in hardcover in 1928, *Nevada* (Paramount, 1927) hit the screen. All mention of the previous *Forlorn River* and the situations created in that story are dropped. This is not sequel but a story that stands strictly on its own. Nevada (Gary Cooper) is a young gunman trying to reform who gets caught up protecting Hettie Ide (Thelma Todd) and her brother Ben (Phillip Strange) from cattle rustlers. It is hardly one of the studio's better adaptations of Grey, mainly because neither the novel nor the screenplay rise above the mediocre. However, it does contain some good performances, rousing action and excellent photography.

While the silent version may have strayed a bit from the novel, the two sound films substituted completely new studio plots and characters. *Nevada* (Paramount, 1936) has the hero (Larry "Buster" Crabbe), a gambler who wins a ranch in a poker game and then joins a group of ranchers to protect themselves from rustlers. Many of the ranchers suspect that Nevada is in with the rustlers, but in the end, he unmasks the real culprit and also wins the love of Hettie (Kathleen Burke), another rancher's daughter. In the last remake (RKO, 1944) Nevada (Robert Mitchum) is a roving cowboy accused of killing homesteader Ben Ide (Larry Wheat) and almost lynched. Complications arise when, while searching for the real killer, Nevada falls in love with Hattie (Nancy Gates), the sister of the murdered man. Neither of these adaptations are exceptional, but both are well crafted "B's" that take a light hearted approach that add a touch of freshness. In addition, the last effort has the distinction of introducing Robert Mitchum in a starring role that established his screen persona of the tough, laconic hero.

Another magazine serial, *The Water Hole,* was published in *Collier's Weekly* in 1927. By the time the book was printed in hardcover as *Lost Pueblo* (1954) fifteen years after Grey's death, the novel seemed antiquated. It tells the story of Janey Endicott whose father makes a deal with Philip Randolph to steal his daughter and take her into the desert because he wants her to know what a real man is like. After various hardships including a fiancé who follows, encounters with a bandit called Black Dick and a mob that almost lynches Philip, the couple returns to civilization where they are united in marriage. While the novel is contemporaneous to the 1920s, the best scenes are those involving the couple's attempts to survive in the desert, a situation somewhat reminiscent of Jack London's "Love of Life," although it lacks London's merciless naturalism. Overall, it is sub-par Grey.

The only film adaptation was *The Water Hole* (Paramount, 1928) and it contained a curious mixture of comedy and melodrama. Judith Endicott (Nancy Carroll) flirts with Philip Randolph (Jack Holt), adding him to her list of conquests, but her father, hoping to cure her of her flighty ways, convinces Philip to kidnap her and take her off into the desert. The early scenes in the desert contain various attempts at comedy, most of which are forced and unfunny. At one point, Philip insists that Judith make breakfast, and the biscuits turn out harder than the desert rocks. Soon, however, more serious events replace comedy. Judith's fiancé, Bert Durland (John Boles), catches up with them and all their horses are stolen. As they wander around the desert trying to find water, Bert goes out of his head and begins to chase a mirage, forcing Philip to shoot him in the leg. Eventually they make it back to civilization where Judith comes to realize that she loves Randolph. Jack Holt as Randolph gives one of his patterned iron jaw performances, and the outdoor scenes are beautifully photographed but, like the novel, the film is sub-par, working neither as comedy nor as drama.

An O. Henry type of irony was used by Grey in "Avalanche," first published in *The Country Gentleman* in 1928, which was among Grey's own personal favorites—he often identified himself as the author of "'Avalanche' and other stories." It told of Jake Dunton and his stepbrother Verde who fight for the affections of any empty headed flirt, Kitty Mains. Once again, the setting is Grey's beloved Tonto Country. Verde runs off and Jake trails him to Black Gulch Canyon where an avalanche strands them and crushes Verde's leg. When gangrene sets in, Jake amputates Verde's infected leg and then sticks with him through the winter until they can make it out in the spring. By the time they finally return home, their father informs them that Kitty has married another local boy just two weeks before. This story differs from O. Henry on two levels. First, it is far longer than anything O. Henry would have written. "Avalanche" is really a novelette rather than a short story. In the beginning, it is overwritten, a common Grey fault, although on the whole, it is charming and enjoyable. Second, Grey stresses sacrifice, a common theme with the author, rather than the irony that O. Henry would have stressed.

Most of Grey's story disappeared in *Avalanche* (Paramount, 1928), although it is a fine western. In this version, Jack Dunton (Jack Holt) is an honest gambler who takes an orphan under his wing and raises the boy as his own. When his ward, Verde (John Darrow), wants to become a mine engineer, Dunton begins to cheat at cards to get enough money. All seems wasted, however, when, after three years, the boy returns only to take up a riotous life. Even his clean living sweetheart, Kitty Mains (Dons Hill) cannot change his course. Finally, Dunton believes the only solution is to take Verde and move away from the town and from his Dunton's mistress, Grace (Barclanova), but before Dunton can accomplish this, Grace vamps the boy in typical twenties fashion, and they elope. Dunton takes after them, utimately saving their lives in an avalanche. All works out well as the boy sees the error of his ways and returns to Kitty, and Dunton and Grace are reunited. While the plot sounds rather silly, it works well on the screen. In addition, the avalanche is particularly well handled, a beautifully staged piece of special effects. If the story is not Grey's, at least it has a sense of style and appearance.

In 1929, Grey finally got around to writing a sequel to *Wanderer of the Wasteland,* calling it *Stairs of Sand.* The story picks up eighteen years after the first novel ended. Ruth Virey has become Guerd Leary's wife, and because of her unhappy marriage, she tends to toward self-pity. Adam Leary, who at one time believed he had killed his brother, returns to the scene, and when he sees what villainy his brother has wrought, decides to kill him this time for sure. Before he can accomplish this, an old prospector called Merryvale shoots Guerd, which allows Ruth and Adam finally to marry.

Neither of the two film versions of *Stairs of Sand* paid much attention to the novel. The first (Paramount, 1929) was an "A" film from Paramount with Guerd Larey (Wallace Beery) a good bad man who helps out young Easterner Adam Wansfell (Phillips Holmes) and dance hall girl Ruth Hunt (Jean Arthur), all of whom get mixed up in a stagecoach robbery. In the end, Guerd sacrifices his own love for happiness of the young couple. While this film's relationship to the Grey novel seems dubious at best, the remake, *Arizona Mahoney* (Paramount, 1936), is even further removed. It is a failed attempt to cross a western with a circus story. As the film opens, Mahoney (Joe Cook) rides up on an elephant accompanied by his piano playing friend Randell (Robert Cummings). With the aid of Talbott (Larry "Buster" Crabbe) and his girl Sue Bixby (June Martel), the group puts an end to a reign of terror by rustlers led by Blair (Fred Kohler, Sr.). Often situations are stretched beyond all credulity in order to fit in various circus performers meeting up with the rustlers. Certainly it is easy to see why these two films strayed so far from their source. *Stairs of Sand* depended too heavily on its predecessor, *Wanderer of the Wasteland,* and in order to make a coherent sequel, too much explanation would have been required. Also, the story was simply not very good screen material. Unfortunately, Paramount's replacement stories were not any better.

Once more in 1929 another Grey novel, *Sunset Pass* , was serialized. It tells the story of loner Trueman Rock who sets out to find the man and his sons who rustle cattle, butcher them and sell the meat. Rock's problems soon multiply as he falls in love with the culprit's daughter. As it turns out, Rock is reformed by her love and puts aside his desire for vengeance. *Sunset Pass* is entertaining enough, although it fails to come close to Grey's better novels.

The first film of *Sunset Pass* (Paramount, 1929), a silent, appeared soon after the magazine serialization. Jack Rock (Jack Holt) poses as a wandering cowboy but is in reality an undercover agent looking for cattle rustlers. He gets the job on a ranch run by Englishman Ashleigh Preston (John Loder), who Rock suspects of being the leader of the outlaws. Before he can take action, the hero falls in love with Preston's sister (Nora Lane). Rock gives Preston a chance to reform, but the villain tries to shoot it out, and Rock kills him. This fails to dampen the spirits of the lovers who are united at fadeout. While a few of the events of the film seem similar to the novel, the twin themes of love and redemption are forgotten. Still, the film looked good and moved along at a nice pace.

The silent Greys were expensive "A" films full of great location shots and exciting action sequences. But when Paramount and Fox began to remake them in the 1930s, they became "B" films. During the early years of the Depression when studios were looking for ways to economize, Paramount recycled a great deal of silent footage and added synchronous sound. Thus the first remake of *Sunset Pass* (Paramount, 1933) contained innumerable long shots of Jack Holt spliced in with medium and closeup shots of Randolph Scott wearing the exact same clothes. As directed by Henry Hathaway, all this use of stock footage didn't hurt the film. Actually, the entire series of Paramount's adaptations of Zane Grey during the thirties are among the best "B" westerns ever made, despite their over reliance on stock footage. If anything, the stock footage gave the series a more expensive look far beyond what they really were. As with the other entries, *Sunset Pass* moved right along at a fast clip as Ash Preston (Randolph Scott), an undercover agent, is sent to break up a gang of rustlers. The story had little to do with the novel, but Grey admitted that Scott came closest to his own visualized ideal of the western hero.

The last remake of *Sunset Pass* (RKO, 1946) strayed even further from its source. Rocky (James Warren), a frontier lawman, tries to bring train robbers to justice, and in doing so, discovers that Ash, the brother of the girl he loves, is part of the gang. Although short on action, the film is a straightforward "B" without any pretensions, looking good but lacking the grandeur of the Paramount films.

A third novel, *Arizona Ames,* was serialized in 1929, this time in *McCall's.* In some respects, the novel bears striking resemblance to both *Wanderer of the Wasteland* and *Nevada.* Rich Ames of the Tonto Country is forced to kill three men, one of whom despoiled his sister. Fleeing Arizona, he is doomed to wander like Wenfell and Jim Lacy, and he takes to calling himself Arizona Ames. As he roams from place to place, he gives help to needy people. He shoots one man for beating his wife and for being a rotten human being in general. Later, he protects a Mormon from some bad men. When he finally wanders into Colorado, he meets and falls in love with Ester Halstead, with whom he plans to marry and settle down.

The only film of *Arizona Ames* became *Thunder Trail* (Paramount, 1937). With the exception of the lead character, Arizona Dick Ames (Gilbert Roland), the film had little to do with Grey's novel. The film opens with a prologue showing how Lee Tate (Charles Bickford) kills Jon Ames (William Duncan) and then steals the youngest son, Bob (James Craig). Years later, Arizona Ames wanders the West with the man who raised him, Rafael Lopez (J. Carroll Naish), searching for his father's killer. They come across farmer Jim Morgan (Monte Blue) and his daughter Amy (Marsha Hunt) who are being driven off their land by Lee Tate. Eventually, Arizona Ames wreaks vengeance on Tate and his gang and wins back his brother, who, in the meantime, has fallen in love with Amy. While Grey seems forgotten in all of this, the film itself proved to be an outstanding "B" western, full of intelligent acting. It also included a first rate musical score, the same one that had been used in *The Plainsman* a year before. The fact that the episodic novel had been dropped in favor of a tighter, more focused story certainly helped as did the solid direction of Charles Barton.

A fourth novel of 1929, *The Drift Fence,* serialized in *American Magazine,* helped Grey to regain some of the popularity he had been steadily losing. The book gave readers excellent glimpses into the life of the cowboy. A tenderfoot, Jim Taft, is suddenly thrust into running a ranch in Arizona. When he decides to build a drift fence a hundred miles long, he is faced with many obstacles, including some of the cowboys on his own ranch who Jim must often subdue with his fists. Molly Dunn, a local rancher isolated by the fence, is also hostile at first. So is her brother, a gunman called "Slinger," but Jim wins the respect of Molly's brother, who agrees to help Jim finish the fence. By story's end, Jim and Molly have fallen in love, and sixty of the planned one hundred miles have been completed.

The only film of *Drift Fence* (Paramount, 1936) is superior mainly because of the production values, which are impressive for a low budget actioner, rather than the story, which is routine. It looks better than it plays. Essentially, the story is a simple one. While Texas Ranger Jim Travis (Tom Keene) searches for the killer of his buddy, he runs across cattle rustlers harassing Molly Dunn (Katharine DeMille) and her brother Slinger (Larry "Buster" Crabbe). Also involved is Easterner Jim Taft (Benny Baker) who is having trouble with cattle baron Clay Jackson (Stanley Andrews), the head of the rustlers. Ranger Travis joins Taft to help him run his ranch and fight off the outlaws. At first hostile to Travis and Taft, Slinger finally joins them in the showdown that destroys the power of the cattle baron. The film is highlighted by good location photography and nice camera work. Good performances also help. However, in direct contrast to *Arizona Ames* where the novel is weaker than the film, *Drift Fence* is weaker than the novel. Episodic as the novel was, it was more original and far more interesting.

Similar in plot to *The Drift Fence* is *The Dude Ranger* (1930), also serialized in *McCall's.* Since some of Grey's popularity had returned with the former novel, it was only natural that he would try to duplicate the success. Once again, an Easterner, Ernest Selby, must hurriedly learn the ways of the West. This time there are rustlers operating on his range, and he sets out to stop them. It was rehashed Grey and one of the author's weaker efforts.

The one film of *The Dude Ranger* (Fox, 1934) was surprisingly sedate, especially for a George O'Brien vehicle. Still, the film followed the Grey novel very closely with Ernest Selby (O'Brien) inheriting a ranch. When he discovers rustlers operating on his land, he suspects the father of his girlfriend (Irene Hervey). Eventually he discovers the real culprit to be Dale Hyslip (Leroy Mason), the ranch foreman. The conclusion is exciting as hero and villain confront each other on the edge of a sheer precipice. With sixgun in hand, the villain slowly moves in on Selby until the hero's heels hang over the rim. But the gun is empty, and Selby wins the ensuing struggle. Actually, the main strength of this film is the same strength as the novel. The details of ranch life are exceedingly well done, realistically so. In addition, the leisurely pace allows the viewer to concentrate on some outstanding location photography. Even the reviewer for the *New York Times* pointed out, "When the Dude and the Red Rock foreman have it out on the dizzy edge of the precipice, you have more concern for the view than for the Dude's fate." After all, the Dude was George O'Brien, who could take care of himself.

Originally serialized in *American Magazine* in 1931, *West of the Pecos* did not see book publication until 1937. It was the third time that Grey used a black cowboy as a major character. Sambo Jackson becomes the protector of Terrill Lambeth, whose father, Colonel Templeton Lambeth, had wanted a boy so badly that he gave his daugther a boy's name, dressed her like a boy and taught her to act like a boy. The main white character, Pecos Smith, soon comes to respect and like Sambo, and together the two men break a cattle rustling ring. Thereafter, Pecos discovers that Terrill is a girl, they marry, and Pecos becomes a well respected rancher. While the characters are a bit wooden, the story moves along at a far better pace than much of Grey's other novels, mainly because the editors at *American Magazine* did some judicious cutting, especially at the beginning where Grey included a couple of unrelated incidents that slowed the action.

The first film of *West of the Pecos* (RKO, 1935) came between the time the novel appeared in *American Magazine* and its publication as a hardback. It included a black character, Jonah (Sleep 'n' Eat, aka Willie Best), but he was no heroic cowboy, only a clown for the white folk to laugh at. The plot suffered changes, also. Terrill Lambeth (Martha Sleeper) dons boys' clothes to facilitate her passage on a trail drive through rough country. At first, Pecos Smith (Richard Arlen) makes fun of her, and a feud develops that lasts clear across Texas. Along the way, the cowboys repel a Comanche attack, Pecos proves he is innocent of rustling, and he defeats the villain, Breen Sawtell (Fred Kohler). Despite the presence of so many clichés, *West of the Pecos* proved to be an enjoyable, unpretentious western, mainly due to the strength of the lead performers. However, the character of Jonah, so far removed from Grey's Sambo Jackson, is quite offensive. In presenting such a stereotypical view of a black man, the film violated not only the plot structure but also the moral integrity of the novel.

The remake of *West of the Pecos* (RKO, 1945) offered no such offense. In place of a black cowboy, it substituted an Irish-Mexican sidekick, Chito Rafferty (Richard Martin). The story had Terrill (Barbara Hale) travelling west with her father for his health. Convinced that she will have trouble fending off advances of cowboys, she dons the disguise of a boy. Along the way, they hire Pecos (Robert Mitchum) and Chito, who are on the run from corrupt vigilantes who control that part of Texas. Once Pecos discovers that Terrill is a girl, he falls instantly in love with her, which raises some interesting psychological questions that were never addressed in the novel or either versions of the film. In the end, he wipes out the vigilantes and settles down with Terrill. This is a well made "B," a model of its type — concise, fast paced, yet possessing a good, sound story and fine production values. Even though less ambitious than the first adaptation, this is the better film, if for no other reason than it did away with the racial stereotype of Jonah.

Somewhat similar to *The Border Legion* is *Robbers' Roost* (1932), which tells the story of a beautiful young woman, Helen Herrick, the sister of a rich English rancher, who is kidnapped by outlaws and held for ransom. Jim Walls, who works for her brother, goes after Helen, rescuing her from the bandits. The interesting part of this novel lies neither in the plot nor the characters but in the early manuscript versions of the novel wherein the motive of rape is suggested as the reason for the kidnapping. When this was pointed out to Grey, he immediately revised the manuscript, removing all such passages. While Grey admitted that rape — and far worse — was used extensively in the literature of the day, he felt it out of place in his novel. The Puritanical western morality that had been so prevalently displayed in such novels as *The Desert of Wheat* and *Code of the West* extended even to excluding offensive material from his own works.

Robbers' Roost (Fox, 1933) first reached the screen as a George O'Brien vehicle. Dudley Nichols in his first script assignment simplified Grey's story by removing several subplots, including all references to Mormons. Jim Wall (O'Brien) is suspected of rustling Herrick's cattle and must prove himself innocent, while at the same time, rescue Herrick's sister, Helen (Maureen O'Sullivan), from the clutches of the rustlers. As the O'Brien series went, this was one of the weaker entries, somewhat hampered by the overly sentimental Grey novel, but as usual, the film was graced by good photography and camera work as well as a fine cast.

When *Robbers' Roost* (United Artists, 1955) next reached the screen, it had undergone further changes. This time the hero's name is Tex

(George Montgomery); he gets a job on the ranch owned by wheelchair-bound Herrick (Bruce Bennett). Herrick hires rival outlaw gangs to look out for his cattle, believing that they will be so busy watching each other that they will be too busy to rustle his cattle. Tex joins the gang led by Heesman (Peter Graves) because he is seeking revenge against Hays (Richard Boone), the rival gang leader who killed his wife. But the two gangs join together and kidnap Helen (Sidney Findley), Herrick's sister. As Tex rides to the rescue, the two gang leaders kill off each other, making his job easier. Although made twenty years after the previous version, this film looks far cheaper plus it never captures the spirit of Grey. For that matter, it has little spirit of any kind, existing as routine horse opera at a time when westerns were on the decline. Perhaps that is why it appears so lifeless.

The lust for gold and what it did to men was examined in *Thunder Mountain*, serialized in 1932. The story takes place in Idaho where Kal Emerson and his two brothers discover gold on Thunder Mountain, but before they can act, the country is overrun with a gold-hungry population. One of the brothers is killed, and the Emersons' own claim is jumped. Kal finds himself infatuated with Sydney Blair, who proves unworthy, and he discovers his real love to be Ruth, a dance hall girl whom he marries. He also uncovers a gold thief who is the murderer.

The only film version (RKO, 1935) remained remarkably faithful to the novel. After Kal Emerson (George O'Brien) discovers the motherload, he and his partner Steve (Dean Benton) are tricked out of their mine by Rand Leavitt (Morgan Wallace), who kills Steve. A get-rich-quick girl, Sydney Blair (Barbara Fritchie) sets her sights on Emerson until she believes that he will lose his mine, and then she transfers her attention to Rand Leavitt. All this time the good-girl dance hall queen is pining away for the hero, but she is rewarded when Emerson sees who is really loyal. In the end, Emerson and Leavitt struggle hand to hand high atop a cliff, and as fate and the scriptwriters would have it, the villain slips and plunges to his death. Emerson gets his mine back and Ruth to boot. Not only is this film highlighted by the usual fine location photography, but the story is especially strong as are the performances. The usual Grey sentimentality adds to the proceedings rather than detracts, and even the lack of action gives the film time to develop character. Certainly this ranks among the finest of all the "B" westerns based on the works of Zane Grey, which is to say among the finest "B" westerns of all.

By now, Grey's popularity had declined so much that he had trouble finding good markets in which to serialize his novels. When he wrote

Knights of the Range, it was turned down by *Colliers* because they felt it was too much panorama and too little story and by *Cosmopolitan* because they said they could not work it into their schedule. It was finally serialized in 1935 in the *Chicago Tribune.* The problem with the novel is that it is routine, a true formula western of a good-bad man, Renn Frayne, who sides with Holly Ripple in her struggle against cattle rustlers. The film *Knights of the Range* (Paramount, 1940) certainly reflected the novel, emerging as a standard but well crafted "B." Frayne (Russell Hayden) almost goes to the bad before turning against the outlaws and winning Holly (Jean Parker). The main villain (Victor Jory) is a crooked lawyer exposed by the hero, and a climactic shootout wherein Fayne does in the villains closes out the action. The film offered nothing new, but it was competently done.

Like William Colt Macdonald (see Chapter Nine), Zane Grey created a western Three Musketeers in a magazine serial, *The Three Range Riders,* published in hardcover as *Raiders of the Spanish Peaks* (1938). It is the standard story of three cowboys — Laramie Nelson, Trace Williams and Lonesome Mulhall — helping an easterner, John Lindsay, and his three daughters to fight off rustlers. Only one feature raises this novel above the hoards of other western novels churned out by writers of that period. One of the outlaw gang is a black cowboy, Sam Johnson, who eventually turns against the rustlers and gives testimony that breaks the gang.

The only film version of this rather standard horse opera changed the title to *Arizona Raiders* (Paramount, 1936). Since the film was released two years before the hardcover edition, the old title was the one by which the public knew the story, but had the studio used *The Three Range Riders,* it would have seemed too similar to the Three Mesquiteers series over at Republic. In addition to the title change, the story line also came in for some alterations. Laramie Nelson (Larry "Buster" Crabbe) saves himself from being hanged and picks up two partners in the process: Tracks Williams (Raymond Hatton), a horse thief and bigamist, and Lone Alonzo Mulhall (Johnny Downs), a naive and lovesick dude. Together, the three manage to break up a rustling ring that has plagued Harriet Lindsay (Marsha Hunt). The involvement with the black cowboy has been dropped. However, the film did manage to avoid being a typical "B" western by turning the whole thing into a comedy, especially in scenes between Laramie and Tracks. This film has more laughs than most straight comedies made during this period, laughs that are as funny today as they were then. The only weakness of the film is the climactic horse stampede that uses too much stock footage flashing on a rear projection screen, an annoying and poorly done process that ruins an otherwise excellent "B" film.

The last of Grey's novels published during his lifetime was *Western Union* (1939), a historical novel that chronicled the building of the transcontinental telegraph. Narrated by the hero, Wayne Cameron, an idealistic young Easterner, the story opens in 1861 and tells of the problems the construction crews encounter. Even though plagued by Indians—Cheyenne, Arapaho and Utes—the novel makes a strong statement for the negative side of progress. It was the Indian's country first, and the white man has come along to despoil the redman and push him until he has only the waste places of the West left to him. While the novel contained the usual amount of familiar melodrama, the important ingredient here was the sweep of the events and the epic narrative. The story ends on a patriotic note as the first message is transmitted, to President Lincoln from the chief justice of California, pledging that state's loyalty to the United States in the Civil War.

The film *Western Union* (20th Century–Fox, 1941) is a beautiful western. Although it drops the episodic plot and substitutes its own story, and while it omits any ambivalent attitude toward the Indians— they are drunken, mischievous, dangerous children—it captures the sweep and pageantry of the Grey novel. It tells of the construction of the Western Union telegraph from Omaha, Nebraska, to Salt Lake City, Utah. The narrator of the novel, Wayne Cameron, has disappeared, replaced by Richard Blake (Robert Young), an arrogant Easterner who comes to the scene long after the film has begun and shares the hero's spotlight with Vance Shaw (Randolph Scott), a former outlaw who works for the telegraph. Even though Vance Shaw is a character invented for the film, he is closely allied with other Grey characters such as Lassiter and Nevada, the strong, silent gunman with a checkered past who uses his guns for good. The only characters remaining from the novel are Edward Creighton (Dean Jagger), the engineer in charge of building the telegraph, and his sister, Sue (Virginia Gilmore). A love triangle builds between Sue, Vance Shaw and Blake. It soon becomes obvious that Sue is falling in love with Vance Shaw, but when his own brother, Jack Slade (Barton MacLane), with whom he once rode, attacks Western Union, Vance rides off for a showdown. He tells Sue that, had he met her a few years before, his life would have been different. In the end, he guns down all of his brother's gang but is killed by his brother. On the scene steps Richard Blake to finish the job. Although wounded by Slade, Blake kills the outlaw, thus assuring the completion of the telegraph.

Of all the Grey adaptations, *Western Union* must rank as the very best, the top of the line. While scriptwriter Robert Carson threw out most of the Grey novel, he captured the spirit of Grey as well as any other adaptor. Also, the film was marvelously directed by Fritz Lang, his personal favorite, and Lang's own feelings about the American West, which he loved, are beautifully captured on celluloid. This is a superior genre work and a superior American film.

Just before he died, Zane Grey wrote a sequel to *Knights of the Range* titled *Twin Sombreros,* serialized by the New York News Syndicate (1940) and published as a hardback the following year. The novel opens five years after Brazos Keene had left Holly Ripple, but he is a young cowboy and full of life, so finds solace in the arms of other women. This time, Brazos is framed for the murder of Allen Neece. Once exonerated, Brazos investigates the murder, and discovers that Abe Neece, the murdered man's brother, once owned the ranch called "Twin Sombreros," which is now in the hands of a shady character known as Raines Surface. Neece has twin daughters, June and Janis, with whom Brazos becomes involved, although he has trouble making up his mind between the two. By book's end, Brazos has exposed Surface as the killer, and he restores the ranch to Neece. Although Brazos runs away, Janis follows him, and the two are married.

The lighter tone of *Twin Sombreros* disappeared in *The Gunfighters* (Columbia, 1947). Instead, screenwriter Alan LeMay opted for a darker mood, one in which Brazos Keene (Randolph Scott) is a gunman who retires after killing a friend. When another friend is killed by an unscrupulous cattle baron, Brazos again straps on his guns to settle matters. The cattle baron has two daughters, one good (Dorothy Hart) and one bad (Barbara Britton), whom Brazos must choose between. *The Gunfighters* is a routine western with a muddled script and sloppy editing, but it proved successful enough to convince star Scott and producer Harry Joe Brown to form their own production company. As an adaptation of *Twin Sombreros,* it is simply of another example of the novel being tossed out and another story substituted. The film character of Brazos Keene, brooding and morose, has more in common with Lassiter and Nevada than the Brazos Keene of the novel, who is more lighthearted and outgoing.

Although unfinished at the time of Zane Grey's death and later completed by his son Romer, *The Maverick Queen* (1950) is among the author's faster moving novels. The setting is Wyoming's Wind River Mountains where Kit Bandon buys mavericks from rustlers, which lays the foundation for a range war. Into the midst of the struggle comes

Lincoln Bradway, investigating the death of his friend, Jimmy Weston. Before the novel ends, Bradway uncovers the fact that his friend was hanged by cattlemen for rustling. Bradway falls in love with Kit's niece, Lucy, infuriating Kit who wants Bradway for herself. However, things work out when, even though Bradway tries to prevent it, Kit is hanged by the cattlemen, thus showing that, while westerners respected womanhood, there were certain codes that had to be observed.

The Maverick Queen (Republic, 1956) was the first of Republic's productions shot in "Naturama," the studio's own wide screen process. To date, it is also the last adaptation of a Zane Grey novel to reach the American screen, and as often happened, only a bare outline of Grey's novel remains. Kit Banion (Barbara Stanwyck) owns a hotel/saloon called "The Maverick Queen," and her partners include Sundance (Scott Brady) and Butch Cassidy (Howard Petrie). In rides Jeff (Barry Sullivan), an undercover Pinkerton agent who pretends to be Cole Younger. Of course, Kit falls in love with Jeff who is in love with Lucy Lee (Mary Murphy), a local rancher. When the real Cole Younger (Jim Davis) arrives on the scene, Kit winds up taking a bullet meant for Jeff, enabling the hero to settle down with his true love. As usual with Republic and director Joe Kane, who helmed many of the Roy Rogers vehicles, the film is fast moving, and the location photography showed up well in the new process. In addition, *The Maverick Queen* provides an interesting contrast of the outlaws portrayed by Newman and Redford in *Butch Cassidy and the Sundance Kid* (Paramount, 1969).

Despite the great number of Zane Grey adaptations, there are very few enduring classics — perhaps only *Western Union*. Some of the fault lies with the author's works, which were usually entertaining but never great. Some of the fault lies with the studios and what they chose to do with the material. However, much of the fault lies with the fact that the studios resigned Grey to the "B" units, thereby sealing the movies' fates. Today, with a few rare exceptions, these "B" films are almost forgotten except by a handful of western film buffs, which is too bad because many of these were well crafted models of their type, and a few, such as the *To the Last Man* (1933) and the *Heritage of the Desert* (1939), are among the very best "B's" ever made. They were also good adaptations. If they were not always strictly faithful in translating the novels, at least they captured the spirit of Grey.

Still, considering the influence that Grey had on the genre, it is surprising that so few important pictures emerged from his immense body of work. It may be that by the time the silent era ended, Grey was already passe, his work having been overexposed and overworked. The sentimental melodrama that worked so well in so many silents, especially in the Paramount Jack Holt series, appeared too overblown and unrealistic in sound. Whatever the reasons, Grey remains far better known for his novels than the films made from them. For many authors, the reverse proved true.

9. Other Writers of the Purple Sage

At the same time that Grey began writing or soon thereafter, other writers of westerns sprang up across the country, most of whom proved far less successful than he. Among these was Bertha Muzzy (B.M. Bower), whose early novels owe more to Owen Wister than Grey. Although born in Minnesota, she and her family moved to Montana when she was still a child, and the values of the West became her values and influenced all of her writings. Her first novel, *Chip of the Flying U,* which first appeared in *Popular Magazine* in 1904, is a ranch romance with little plot and little action, but it immediately found an eager and appreciative audience. Bower used Charles M. Russell, the famous western artist, as a prototype of Chip, a ranch hand who likes to draw and who hates women. Eventually he falls in love with a woman from the East who is called the Little Doctor. Chip himself is very literate and able to quote long passages from literary classics. Eventually, Chip and the Little Doctor marry, opening up all sorts of possibilities for sequels, which Bower was quick to write.

Chip of the Flying U was filmed four times. The first (Selig, 1914) was an early Tom Mix vehicle, and as scripted by fellow novelist Peter B. Kyne, contained plenty of action and adventure, none of which is found in the novel. It was remade as *The Galloping Devil* (Canyon Pictures, 1930) and then returned to its original title for a Hoot Gibson vehicle (Universal, 1926), one of a series of films that the star produced for Universal. The final version was also called *Chip of the Flying U* (Universal, 1939) with Johnny Mack Brown as Chip. As with the other versions, it had little to do with Bower's story other than the title. Chip is a ranch foreman suspected of a series of holdups, and he uncovers the real culprits who are working for foreign gun smugglers. Bower herself would never have recognized — or likely approved — of the various incarnations of Chip.

With the exception of the final version of *Chip of the Flying U,* all the films based on Bower's fiction were made as silents. Some of them such as *When the Cook Fell Ill* (Selig, 1914) are oriented more toward comedy, often making fun of ignorant Easterners just as Bower did in her novels and short stories. Others such as *The Wolverine* (Spenser Associated Photoplays, 1921) and *Points West* (Universal, 1929), the latter another Hoot Gibson vehicle, are straight action stories, although the Gibson films often included humor to accommodate the personality of the star. However, most of these films rest in obscurity, as does Bower herself. Her fiction has dated badly. Although she was probably a better writer than Wister, none of her books broke any new ground. Most were formulary westerns, many of which followed the adventures of Chip and his friends, collectively called the Happy Family. Clarence E. Mulford was to do much the same with his far more influential Hopalong Cassidy series. The films made from Bower's fiction are the same formula material, and not a one rose above the "B" category.

What O. Henry did for south of the border, Rex Beach did for the north country. Born in Michigan and dubbed the "Victor Hugo of the North," Beach spent three years mining in Alaska, and from his experiences, wrote his first novel, *The Spoilers* (1905). Film versions soon followed. The success of the 1914 *The Spoilers* inspired Rex Beach to start his own film company in 1917, and his first production was based on his novel *The Auction Block: A Novel of New York.* During his lifetime, fourteen of his novels, including *The Spoilers,* were brought to the screen either by himself or others. Several were made more than once.

However, his most famous novel remains *The Spoilers.* The story deals with greedy land speculators led by the crooked McNamara and Judge Chester. On the opposite side are Glenister and the honest miners. Love interest is provided by Cherry Malotte, a dance hall girl based on the famous courtesan of Virginia City, Julia Bulette, and Helen, the daughter of Judge Chester. The climax of the novel occurs when McNamara and Glenister fight it out hand to hand. In the end, Glenister wins the fight, his gold mine and the love of Helen. Cherry falls in love with the Bronco Kid, so everything turns out all right. The best qualities of the novel rest in the atmosphere and authenticity of the frontier setting, but in reality it is only romanticized adventure, filled with too much sentimentality and too many cardboard characters.

The same year Rex Beach wrote *The Spoilers,* he also collaborated

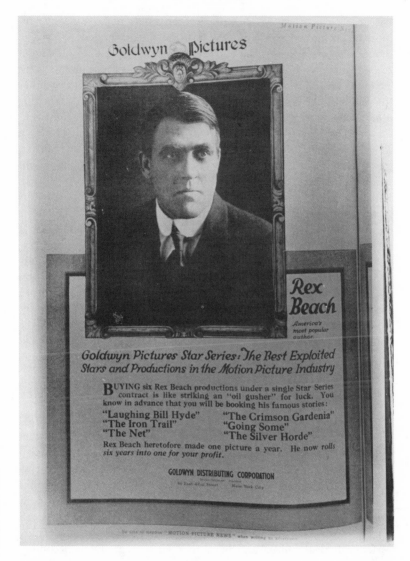

Ad in *Motion Picture News* of July 27, 1918, for series of features based on the fiction of Rex Beach with a picture of the author.

with another author for a stage version of his novel. Coming eight years later, the first film (Selig, 1914) is notable for several reasons. When the literary buyer for Selig approached Beach for the rights to the story, the author demanded $2,500, an enormous sum at the time. Instead of a flat fee, Beach agreed to a percentage of the profits, and in the long run, received far more than the amount he originally demanded. Also, even though five- and six-reel films had been made since 1912, this was a nine-reel production, almost 90 minutes long, a grand epic for the time. This is not to say *The Spoilers* was a great film. Actually, it didn't have either the polish or the knowhow of the Thomas Ince productions. Yet, the film vividly recreated life in the Alaskan gold field at the turn of the century, and its very lack of polish helped to enhance the realism. The town where a good deal of the action takes place is unglamorous and realistic, the streets filled with dingy false fronts and mud. Even the famous fight sequence in which McNamara (Tom Santschi) and Glenister (William Farnum) punch and claw at each other, praised at the time for its realism, remains oddly realistic because it is so forced and clumsy. After the fight, Glenister stands over the defeated McNamara and says, "I broke him — with my hands." Only on one major point did this first version deviate from the novel, but it was a key change that substantially altered the conclusion of the story. After the fighting has ended and Glenister has his mine back, Cherry Malotte discovers that Glenister was never in love with Helen. She and Glennister are united at fade out.

The film attempted to stay close to the Beach story, even to the point of title cards with dialogue straight from the novel. Occasionally awkward, the title cards sometimes show two and three characters speaking at once, which took attention away from the film. However, occasional descriptive passages from the novel did add color and vividness.

A second silent version (Goldwyn, 1923) followed the original novel and stage play. Again, it captured the atmosphere of turn-of-the-century boom town with its ugly shacks and muddy streets crisscrossed with deep, water-filled hollows. The action comes swift and early as Glenister (Milton Sills) and his sidekick battle eight or nine sailors after one of them pesters Helen (Barbara Bedford). Also, the climactic fight between McNamara (Noah Beery) and Glenister was extremely well staged, a panting, bloody bout in which the participants must periodically rest in order to fight more, their faces gradually becoming more marred and blackened, their mouths agape trying to suck in the air. Only in one area did this film vary from the novel. The producers decided that a melodrama of this sort needed comic relief, and they threw in Ford Sterling, who is totally out of place. The end finds Glenister and Helen united just as in the novel.

Minor changes appeared in the first sound version of *The Spoilers* (Paramount, 1930). Glenister (Gary Cooper) and his partner befriend

Helen (Kay Johnson) on the voyage to Nome, and Glenister becomes infatuated with her. Unscrupulous government officials arrive in Nome, headed by McNamara (William "Stage" Boyd), who is also in love with Helen, and Judge Stillman, her father. When these crooks start despoiling the mines, Cherry Malotte (Betty Compson), a faro dealer in love with Glenister, tells him that Helen is also involved in the conspiracy. When McNamara and the Judge try to gain entrance to Glenister's mine, a terrific fight breaks out. After Glenister is victorious, Cherry admits she lied about Helen, and Glennister and Helen are reunited.

The *New York Times* decried "the general lack of intelligence" of the film and pointed out that much of the goings on were muddled and absurd. Dialogue only emphasized the melodramatic aspects of the story, although director Edward Carewe attempted to give movement to the production by taking advantage of a mobile camera. Once again, the highlight of the film was the fight, and everything else, including the romantic relationships, tended to be subordinate to the action. Once again, the producers saw fit to throw in comic relief, a character called Herman (Harry Green).

When Universal purchased the rights to *The Spoilers* (Universal, 1942), they planned it as a vehicle for Marlene Dietrich who, three years previously, received accolades for her performance as the saloon hostess in *Destry Rides Again.* In previous versions, Cherry Malotte had been a relatively minor character, and here her role was considerably reworked and enhanced, almost to the point where it overshadowed McNamara (Randolph Scott) and Glenister (John Wayne). The writers also emphasized the romance between Cherry and Glenister. When Helen falls in love with Glenister, he responds with only a small flirtation, and she knows the romance is doomed from the start because she is working with her crooked uncle and McNamara. Unlike the earlier versions, McNamara also pursues Cherry. The Bronco Kid (Richard Barthelmess) works for Cherry and tries to win her for himself, but he is not related to Helen. When Glenister tries to recover his safe from McNamara, the Kid tries to kill him; the bullet strikes the sheriff, and Glenister is blamed. While Glenister is breaking jail, Cherry has McNamara up to her room so that he will not suspect what her lover is up to. The fight, the best and slickest of any of the versions, starts upstairs in her room, spills over to the saloon below and finally winds up out in the street.

This is the best of all the versions of *The Spoilers,* and while it may not reach the stature of such westerns as *Stagecoach* or *Shane,* it remains a minor classic. The changes in plot, especially elevating Cherry Malotte to a pivotal role, helped rid the story of its artificial sentimentality. However, in a sentimental gesture, the producers cast William Farnum, the first Glenister, as Glenister's lawyer.

The last version of *The Spoilers* (Universal, 1955) enlarged the role of Cherry (Anne Baxter) even further, making her more understanding and less hard-bitten. It is a glossy film without heart and without substance. In comparison to the previous versions, even the fight sequence seems subdued.

After *The Spoilers, The Silver Horde* (1909) is the best of Beach's novels. The first film version (Goldwyn, 1920) is without merit, and the only sound version (RKO, 1930) is simply a reworking of *The Spoilers.* It is an action tale set against the background of Alaskan salmon fishing. Boyd Emerson (Joel McCrea) is fighting for control of the fishery against Fred Marsh (Gavin Gordon) and is helped by dance hall girl Cherry Malotte (Evelyn Brent), whose character, not present in the novel, is a direct link to *The Spoilers.* In the end there is the customary fisticuffs, and Cherry wins the heart of the hero over the more ladylike Mildred Wayland (Jean Arthur). The other addition is a comic sidekick (Raymond Hatton). Overall, the film has a few good action sequences, and the documentary shots of a salmon cannery give an authentic feel to the proceedings. If nothing else, the film often captured the feel of Beach's novel. The fact that the story was rather shallow only reflected the source.

In some ways, Beach's most fascinating novel is *The Iron Trail* (1913), mainly because of its subject matter, building the first railroad in Alaska. The film adaptation was an early entry (1921) in the United Artists stable of films. The hero (Wyndham Standing) battles the villain (Thurston Hall) to complete the railroad. A climax has the hero and his men complete a bridge just as an ice floe comes rushing down the river to threaten the structure. The film tried hard to be an early *The Iron Horse,* but while it had a subject befitting the big screen, it lacked a director of the stature of John Ford and settled for adventure and little else. The film simply mirrored the weak Beach story.

Somewhat faithful to Beach were the three versions of *The Barrier* (1915). The first version was produced in 1917 by Beach himself, but it is the second (MGM, 1926) which proved the superior product. The film opens with a terrific sea storm in which Stark Bennett (Lionel Barrymore) allows his halfbreed wife to die. In the meantime, Bennett's daughter, Necia, has been raised in the Northwoods unaware of her heritage, and now she is engaged to an aristocratic Southerner, Meade

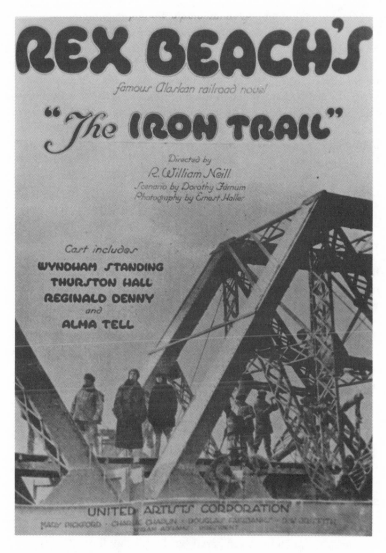

Poster for *The Iron Trail* (1921), based on the Beach novel. Notice that the author's name is larger than the title.

Burrell (Norman Kerry). Bennett shows up and delights in telling his daughter the truth. The climax of the film happens on an ice floe in which the hero saves Necia, and the two are reunited. It was a highly polished affair that, while it lacked any depth, did have some well staged action sequences. The last version of *The Barrier* (Paramount, 1937) changed the plot considerably. Gone are the great action set pieces, replaced by a flat story without much movement. Here the villainous father, John Gale (Robert Barrat), kidnaps the daughter of a woman he once loved, raising the child as his own. She is led to believe that she is a halfbreed Indian. When Necia matures, she is frustrated when she falls in love with a young army lieutenant and realizes that the army would never allow one of its officers to marry an Indian, even a halfbreed. Needless to say, she learns the truth and everything turns out happily in the end.

Another Beach novel, *Flowing Gold* (1922), a novel of the discovery of oil in Texas, also made it to the screen twice. The first version (First National, 1924) proved to be a fast moving but hokey melodrama in which a soldier of fortune, Calvin Gray (Milton Sills), is hired by a family to work the oil fields. A dastardly villain (Henry Nelson), a former army officer who once persecuted Gray, is out to steal the land, but Gray manages to thwart his schemes, save the son from the arms of a vamp and rescue the sister from a fire. The hero is amply rewarded with the hand of the heroine. The second version (Warner Bros., 1940) was a John Garfield vehicle, but it, too, was pretty routine stuff. After killing a man in self-defense, the hero is on the run from the law. He alights in a western oil field where he becomes involved with a woman drilling for oil (Frances Farmer) and a oilfield foreman (Pat O'Brien). The climax of the movie is an avalanche. Most of these ingredients were created for the film, and the whole thing seemed to miss the flavor of Beach's northern adventures. Perhaps the problem was that neither John Garfield nor Frances Farmer were happy with these types of roles, and combined with turgid direction and a weak script, the film failed to ignite any sparks.

One other Beach short story, "Rope's End," became *A Sainted Devil,* a vehicle for Rudolph Valentino, a melodrama without any connection to the North country where Beach's story takes place. Like most of Beach's fiction, with the exception of *The Spoilers,* it is stuck in time, dated not so much by his material but by his handling of it. None of his novels and short stories proved especially durable, and had it not been for the various film versions of *The Spoilers,* Rex Beach would be virtually forgotten today. Only these films keep alive his memory as an artist. The influence of Rex Beach proved as limited as his writings, and only a few authors, such as James B. Hendryx and James Oliver Curwood (discussed later in this chapter), attempted to imitate him, none very successfully.

 CLARENCE E.
MULFORD'S

BAR 20

WILLIAM BOYD
Hopalong Cassidy   ANDY CLYDE · GEORGE REEVES · DUSTINE FARNUM · VICTOR JORY · DOUGLAS FOWLEY · BETTY BLYTHE · FRANCIS McDONALD

Lobby card for *Bar 20,* one of the many Clarence E. Mulford novels adapted for a Hopalong Cassidy series entry.

Other formula writers quickly jumped on the Hollywood bandwagon. One was Frank Spearman, whose *Whispering Smith* (1906) was adapted three times, the last (Paramount, 1948) a good film but related to the novel only by title and the fact that the main character is a railroad detective. One of the few authors of the period whose books are still occasionally reprinted is William MacLeod Raine, but again his books and the films produced from them never rise above "B" status, although his writing is lively enough to account for the occasional reprint. Penning his first novel in 1920, W.C. Tuttle wrote for almost 50 years, yet never turned out one important western, although Buck Jones used two, *The Red Head from Sun Dog* (1930), which became the fifteen-chapter serial *The Red Rider* (Universal, 1934), and *Rocky Rhodes* (1934), the first feature Jones made at Universal (1934). Charles Seltzer and H.H. Knibbs also followed Wister, but their work and the films adapted from them have, for the most part, fallen into obscurity. All these writers share one thing in common — they were second rate writers who seldom rose above the cliché, and the film adaptations reflect their positions in the literary hierarchy.

Owen Wister created the first formulary western, and Zane Grey became the most popular western writer, but the man who created the most beloved western character was Clarence E. Mulford. He entered a western short story contest sponsored by *Metropolitan Magazine* and shared first prize. Soon after, he was writing a series of connected stories for *Outing Magazine,* which were published as *Bar 20* (1907). He followed with his first legitimate novel, *The Orphan* (1908), very much an imitation of *Virginian* in style and spirit.

It was after this that Mulford conceived of a series of novels and stories with a group of characters played off against a background of historical events in the Southwest. One of the central characters of this saga was to be Bill Cassidy, who had first appeared in *Bar 20,* a red-haired, hard-drinking, smoking, cursing, rough yet ethical cowhand. The first of the series, *Hopalong Cassidy* (1910), told of Hoppy's love affair with Mary Meeker and their marriage. Mixed up with the love affair is a group of outlaws high atop a mesa that the boys of the Bar 20 eventually smoke out. Other books quickly followed. *Bar 20 Days* (1911) was another collection of loosely connected stories about Hoppy and the gang, then a novel *Buck Peters, Ranchman,* in which the foreman of the Bar 20 goes to Montana to start his own spread. But it was not until *The Coming of Cassidy* (1913) that Mulford described the incident that created the permanent limp that led to Cassidy's nickname. *Hopalong Cassidy Returns* opens with the death of his wife and child, then goes on to a series of adventures with his sidekick Red Connors and Mesquite Jenkins.

Only one silent film was made from Mulford's work. Tom Mix filmed *The Orphan* as *The Deadwood Coach* (Fox, 1924), and while it didn't conform closely to the novel, it was given a solid promotion and was successful. In 1935 came Mulford's big film break. Producer Harry Sherman reached an agreement with the author to produce a series of films based on the Bar 20 saga. Sherman approached James Gleason and then David Niven to play the pivotal role of Cassidy but finally settled on William Boyd, and the first picture, *Hop-A-Long Cassidy* (Paramount, 1935) was supposedly based on the 1910 novel, although few of the events carried over. Even Cassidy's limp was incorporated by accident. Boyd was afraid of horses, and during the first week of production, he fell off the big white horse that Sherman had acquired for the film and broke his leg. Boyd's leg was put in a cast, but he couldn't disguise the limp, so Sherman came up with the idea of incorporating an early scene where Cassidy is shot in the leg, and is out of the picture for a while, then returns with a limp.

The real break with Mulford's Hopalong was in the character Boyd chose to play. Even though Sherman wanted to make a series of realistic westerns, Boyd adopted a black outfit modeled after the one Tim McCoy was wearing in his series at Puritan. This Hopalong drinks sarsaparilla, doesn't smoke and doesn't curse. As the series progressed, Boyd's interpretation became increasingly mild, engaging in less fights and less shootouts. It is Boyd's interpretation that is indelibly printed in the minds of moviegoers of the thirties and forties and the television audiences of the fifties, and Mulford's creation is almost forgotten.

Some of the series used the titles of Mulford's novels: *The Eagle's Brood* (Paramount, 1935), *The Bar 20 Rides Again* (Paramount, 1935), *Hopalong Cassidy Returns* (Paramount, 1936), *Trail Dust* (Paramount, 1936), *Bar 20* (United Artists, 1943) and *Hoppy Serves a Writ* (UA, 1943), yet the stories were not Mulford's work but that of scriptwriters at the studios. Sometimes they were even other writers' novels adapted to the Hoppy format. Both *Secrets of the Wasteland* (Paramount, 1941) and *The Leatherburners* (United Artists, 1943) were based on novels by Harry Sinclair Drago writing under the pseudonym of Bliss Lomax. In retrospect, Hopalong Cassidy is an outstanding "B" series in its own right, but it owes little to Mulford or to the characters he created.

One writer of stature did emerge from this early period, Eugene Manlove Rhodes, one of the giants of the western genre. Beginning with his first novel, *Good Men and True* (1910), through to his last, *The Proud Sheriff* (1935), he wrote only ten western books, five of which may well be ranked with the very best. Many of these were made into silent productions, eight all told, although none was especially important except *The Wallop* (Universal, 1921), one of the John Ford–Harry Carey westerns, which claimed to be based on a Rhodes short story, "The Girl He Left Behind Him."

However, Rhodes' most enduring work, arguably the finest novelette ever written of the American West, *Pasó por Aquí* (1927), did make a fine film. The story tells of Ross McEwen, who robs a store and flees into the desert with a posse led by Pat Garrett hot on his trail. At one point, with the posse closing in, McEwen throws the money away, and while the sheriff's men are grasping at the dollars in the blowing wind, McEwen makes his escape. The posse knows that the outlaw is going to make a break for the border, so they block all the water holes, but McEwen stumbles upon a ranch inhabited by a Mexican family stricken with diphtheria. Though McEwen could escape, he stays and nurses the family back to health. When Pat Garrett, who McEwen does not know by sight, happens upon the scene and realizes what the outlaw has done, he allows McEwen to get safely away.

This is a complex story in which the question of justice outside the law is raised. Garrett is convinced that McEwen has changed, and rather than turn him over to the conventional New Mexican authorities, turns him loose. Garrett can justify this to himself since no harm has been done to anybody and the money has been recovered. On another level, this story, somewhat akin to Crane's "The Bride Comes to Yellow Sky," is about the passing of the Old West. Garrett is the last of the old time sheriffs, McEwen the last of the old time outlaws. What McEwen once saw as open country and freedom is now filled with windmills and new people and permanence.

The film *Four Faces West* (United Artists, 1948) turned out to be surprisingly nonviolent, low key and very sensitive, capturing much of the flavor of Rhodes' short novel. Ross McEwen (Joel McCrea) robs a bank to get enough money to save his father's ranch, and a posse, led by Pat Garrett (Charles Bickford) gives chase. Along the way McEwen is helped by a pretty railroad nurse (Francis Dee) who pleads with McEwen to give the money back. McEwen is caught because he stops to give aid to a Mexican family stricken with illness. In the end, Garrett sends McEwen off to prison, but because of his good deed, he will not serve a long sentence.

The Hayes Office would not allow an outlaw to go unpunished for his deeds as Rhodes had done in the novel. It insisted upon capture and imprisonment, but even so, the scriptwriters managed to give the film an upbeat ending. Where the film really misses the mark is in the deeper levels, the symbolic ending of the Old West that enriches the novel and gives it texture. The film also softens Rhodes' material, making it far more sentimental than it should have been. However, it is still a good film, especially when it deals with its characters. The scenes between McEwen and the railroad nurse are especially touching and believable, and Garrett is a tough yet surprisingly sensitive lawman who first admires and then comes respect the outlaw whom he chases. All in all, this may not be a great adaptation but it is a loving one.

The same year, 1910, that Zane Grey published *Heritage of the Desert* and Rhodes published his first novel also saw the publication in the *Saturday Evening Post* of the short story "Bronco Billy and the Baby" by Peter B. Kyne. G.M. Anderson, who had appeared in *The Great Train Robbery* (1903) and had since formed his own production company, liked the story and set about filming it with himself in the lead. Shooting the film in a day, Anderson didn't bother with the niceties of acquiring the screen rights and was soon visited by Kyne, who liked the film well enough to waive legal action but at the same time making it clear that he would have to be paid. The story concerned the reformation of a "good-badman" who gives up his freedom to aid a stricken child. The film was an instant success and convinced Anderson of the wisdom of using Bronco Billy as a continuing character. Over the next few years, he made close to 500 short one- and two-reelers about the character.

Three years later, Kyne revised the story and published it as a short novel, *Three Godfathers* (1913). Basically it's a symbolic parable, a variation on the "divine child" archtype that Bret Harte had employed in "The Luck of Roaring Camp," relating the story of three outlaws who are reformed by a baby that they happen across in the desert. The outlaws are given names like the Worst Bad Man, the Youngest Bad Man and the Oldest Bad Man. Only the Youngest Bad Man survives to bring the baby out of the wilderness; the other two sacrifice their lives in order to accomplish the mission. Most of Kyne's fiction is so full of sloppy sentimentality and lack of characterization that it can no longer be read with pleasure. Although terribly dated, this is probably his most readable work. Its short length is a definite asset.

Kyne's novel became *The Three Godfathers* (Universal, 1916), with Harry Carey playing one of the three outlaws running from the sheriff's posse. After a desert sandstorm, the trio comes across a dying woman who is in the process of having a baby. Just before she dies, she implores the men to become the child's godfathers and take care of it. The outlaws agree to do as she asks. As they try to cross the desert with the child, they begin to realize they are throwing away their chances of escaping the law. Although some film critics thought the six-reel film too long by a full reel, it was a well directed effort complete with some very realistic details. At one point, the posse comes across the body of one of the outlaws and discovers a vulture picking at the corpse.

The film was remade as *Marked Men* (Universal, 1920) and directed by John Ford. Harry Carey was once again given the lead. The plot followed the earlier version in most details, including the survival of Harry Carey. Photographed in the Mojave Desert, the film has a gritty realism and proved a winner with audiences. The film was also notable as the last film collaboration between John Ford and Harry Carey.

Also shot on location in Mojave Desert and Panamint Valley, the first sound version, *Hell's Heroes* (Universal, 1929), was directed by William Wyler and was the studio's first all sound outdoor film. Even though it ran only 65 minutes, a few changes were made from the previous versions. It opens with Bob Sangster (Charles Bickford) flirting with a dance hall girl while awaiting the arrival of his three cohorts: Wild Bill Kearney (Fred Kohler), Barbwire Gibbons (Raymond Hatton) and Jose (Jose de la Cruz). When they attempt a holdup, Jose is killed along with another man, and the three remaining outlaws flee into the desert during a fierce sandstorm. In the desert, the fugitives discover a woman about to give birth, and she convinces the men to become the godfathers of the child and return it to the father. Even though the woman dies in childbirth, the outlaws are determined to keep their pledge. As they struggle to escape the desert with the baby, Wild Bill and Barbwire die, leaving Bob to go it alone. When his water runs out just a few miles from the town of New Jerusalem, Bob deliberately drinks from a poisoned water hole in order to get him the rest of the way. Clutching the baby in his sun-scorched arms, he staggers into town on Christmas Day. He finds the townspeople in church where he collapses and dies.

Hell's Heroes proved to be a hit. Not only did the public like it but also the critics. *Variety* called it "gripping, real and convincingly out of the ordinary." The *New York Times* said it "happens to be an interesting and realistic bit of characterization" and went on to praise the acting, especially Charles Bickford as Bob. Less static than most early sound films, it was indeed a realistic film that remains impressive for adding so much depth to such a slight story. Also impressive was director Wyler's decision to deliver such a downbeat ending, which added to its realistic approach and put more of a bite into the Kyne story. In many ways, this is the best version of *Three Godfathers*.

When it came to remaking the film once more, the original title of *Three Godfathers* (MGM, 1936) returned along with the happy ending. This time the outlaws rob the bank of New Jerusalem of its Christmas savings before dashing off into the desert, leaving Pedro, the guitar strumming member of the gang, dead behind them. The remaining outlaws are: Bob (Chester Morris), a callous, black-hearted rascal and leader of the group; Doc (Lewis Stone), who reads Schopenhauer between holdups; and Gus (Walter Brennan), an unlettered desert rat. This time, they find the dying mother with the child already beside her. Over the protests of Bob, Gus and Doc insist on taking the child to safety and keeping the promise to the mother. During the night, their horses drink from a poisoned water hole and die, and the three men with the baby are forced to cross the desert back to New Jerusalem on foot. By the time the journey is complete, even Bob has been rehabilitated, and it is he alone who survives to bring the child safely into New Jerusalem.

In this version, the parable of the Three Wise Men is intensified by the fine camera work of Joseph Ruttenberg and the melodramatic direction of Richard Boleslawski, the Polish director better known for his romantic dramas such as *The Garden of Allah* (Selznick, 1936).

(While not strictly an adaptation of Kyne's *Three Godfathers,* the film *Navy Born* [Republic, 1936] does bear remarkable similarity, even if it claims to be from an original story. Three naval officers hide a dead comrade's baby in an effort to keep the child out of the hands of a supposedly scheming sister-in-law [Claire Dodd]. One of the men [William Gargan] falls in love with the young aunt, so they end by sharing custody.)

The final, official version of *Three Godfathers* (MGM, 1948) was again directed by John Ford, a remake of his own *Marked Men,* and in sense, Harry Carey had something to do with this version. It opens with a shot of a cowboy in silhouette that looks much like Carey. He rides to the top of a hill, pushes his hat back and looks off into the distance. Then a title comes on: "Dedicated to Harry Carey, a bright star in the early western sky." The man impersonating Carey was stuntman Cliff Lyons, and he rode Carey's own horse, Sonny.

A few changes were made in the story for this version. Robert Hightower (John Wayne), Pedro (Pedro Armendariz) and William Kearney (Harry Carey, Jr.), called the Abilene Kid, ride into Welcome, Arizona, where they rob the bank. After the robbery, they flee into the desert, pursued by sheriff Buck Sweet (Ward Bond). At Tarapin Tanks, they find a tenderfoot has inadvertently blown up the water hole, then left his pregnant wife alone in their wagon. As in the previous versions, the three outlaws promise the dying woman that they will look after the infant, born on Christmas Day. A Bible instructs them to take the child to New Jerusalem, and they set out at night, following a star. The Kid and Pedro die along the way, leaving Bob to finish the journey alone. When he, too, collapses, their spirits return to urge him on. When he at last reaches his limit and can go farther, he finds a donkey on which to take the little child into New Jerusalem. Bob is met there by the sheriff who takes him back for robbing the bank. He gets one year in prison. The sheriff and his wife will take care of his godson until he is free.

All versions of *Three Godfathers* based on the Kyne story share a common motif of outlaws being redeemed through the child, a Christian message that formed the basis of the original story. More importantly, each version expanded and deepened the slight story and gave flesh to the characters. This is a rare example of the films, the original

Lobby card for the last version of *Three Godfathers* (1948), based on the short novel by Peter Kyne.

as well as the remakes, being better than the novel on which they are based.

Other Peter B. Kyne stories and novels were also filmed, but none had the impact of *Three Godfathers*. *The Parson of Panamint* (Paramount, 1916 and 1941) was made twice as low budget affairs without distinction, as is the novel itself. Many films from the twenties and thirties credit Kyne as their source, but most of these simply use his name. Universal claimed two serials, *Heroes of the West* (Universal, 1932) and *Flaming Frontiers* (Universal, 1938), were based on something called *The Tie That Binds*, but no bibliographical reference lists such a work by Kyne. Columbia was especially fond of this practice, and they ballyhooed a whole series of Charles Starret "B" westerns using this tactic. Their ads read "Peter B. Kyne's *Code of the Range*" (Columbia, 1936) or "Peter B. Kyne's *Stampede*" (Columbia, 1936). Whatever title the studio decided upon, they simply stuck the author's name in front. However, Kyne's reputation as a writer must rest with *Three Godfathers,* and even this slight novel would be forgotten today if it were not for the films.

One of the hardest of all types of writing to sustain is the comic novel. *Ruggles of Red Gap* (1915) by Leon Henry Wilson, first serialized in *The Saturday Evening Post* in 1914 as "Ruggles, Bunker and Merton," was an early attempt to use the West as a humorous backdrop. The story concerns an English valet, Ruggles, who is lost in a poker game to a western family. At first, he is frightened that there is an Indian behind every bush, but the longer he resides in Red Gap, the more Americanized he becomes. Also, he comes to have a startling effect on the family that won him, going so far as to make them the social butterflies of their community. However, what was funny in 1914 seems forced and dated by today's standards, and the book is almost unreadable, slow and ponderous and much too long for such slight material.

Two early silent versions of *Ruggles of Red Gap* (Essanay, 1918 and Paramount, 1923) were made, neither of which proved very important. By the time the first sound version of *Ruggles of Red Gap* (Paramount, 1935) was filmed, it was already creaking with age, and must be valued more for its performances than its humor, although the film is both warm and affectionate. The plot follows the novel very closely. After Ruggles (Charles Laughton) is won in the poker game, he is transported to Red Gap, a frontier town full of miners and other such brash types. Ruggles gives the rancher (Charles Ruggles) and his wife (Mary Boland) the social status they desire, but later he leaves their service and opens up his own restaurant. He also facilitates the romance of an English lord, his former employer, with the daughter of the rancher. In the end, Ruggles himself settles down with a spinster (ZaSu Pitts) and becomes a family man. In the novel as well as the film, the high point is a stirring delivery of the Gettysburg Address by Ruggles, which demonstrates fully his Americanization and leads to his acceptance by the townspeople.

Wilson's novel reached the screen once more as *Fancy Pants* (Paramount, 1950). In this version, Ruggles (Bob Hope) is an out of work actor brought home from England to be the family butler by a newly rich rancher and his wife. He becomes romantically involved with the daughter (Lucille Ball), and complications follow when the boyfriend (Bruce Cabot) believes the butler is expendable. The film eschewed most of the novel, although it did provide a few laughs along the way, and in some areas, improved upon the story. Certainly things moved a good deal faster than in the previous version. While Bob Hope may not have threatened Laughton as the definitive Ruggles, the film remains one of the comic's best roles.

Although inferior to a writer like Eugene Manlove Rhodes or even

B.M. Bower, Jackson Gregory wrote over 35 well plotted traditional westerns noted for their variety of locales. *Wolf Breed* (1917) takes place in Canada, while *Sentinel of the Desert* (1929) takes place along the Mexican-American border. While Gregory showed superior strength in plotting, most of his novels are flawed by heavy sentimentality, a common fault among western writers of the time. As a consequence, his novels never rose above the mediocre, and the films based on them never rose above "B" status.

In all, Gregory had nine works adapted for the screen, none of which proved particularly outstanding. The first was a short story, "Silver Slippers," which appeared as *The Man from Painted Post* (Douglas Fairbanks/ART, 1917), a story of Fancy Jim Sherwood (Douglas Fairbanks) who foils a gang of rustlers and wins the prettiest girl in the West by posing as a dude. However, when the chips are down, he fights and shoots with the best of them. In 1917, the idea must have seemed fresh enough, and even in the late thirties and early forties, William Boyd played the same type of role in several of the Hopalong Cassidy films. A far more unusual novel is *Man to Man* (1920), in which the hero, Steve Packard, is a derelict on an island in the South Seas when he learns that his father has died and left him the family ranch. He returns home, defeats the bad guys, and wins the love of his pretty neighbor. This novel became the basis for Harry Carey's last starring role at Universal, *Man to Man* (Universal, 1922), which proved to be a good, off-beat little western, although, like Gregory's novel, it offered little in the way of depth or insights. Altogether, seven silent films were based on Jackson Gregory's fiction, and *Man to Man* was probably the best of the lot.

Two satisfactory sound adaptations were made from novels by Gregory. *Mystery at the Spanish Hacienda* (1929) is a western murder mystery, although the identity of the murderer is never much in doubt. As a film it became *The Laramie Trail* (Republic, 1944). The story was simple enough. A young Virginian (Robert Livingston) meets a man falsely accused of murder, exposes the real murderer, and all ends well. Predictable as the novel and film are, both contain some nice action sequences and move at a fast clip. In addition, director John English invested some brooding atmosphere, and the fine, low key photography complimented the story. Ordinarily Republic preferred original stories to adaptations, and in this case, they treated the property with special care, and the results showed on the screen. The only other Gregory novel adapted for the screen was *Sudden Bill Dorn* (1937), a standard story of a gold hungry town tamed by the hero. As a film (Universal, 1938), it became a vehicle for Charles "Buck" Jones, the star's last for

Univeral, and the story provided a nice atmosphere of lawlessness in which the hero must operate. There is plenty of action, but compared with some of Jones' previous work, especially *The Ivory-Handled Gun* (Universal, 1935), a classic "B," *Sudden Bill Dorn* is conspicuously weak.

Far more prolific was James Oliver Curwood, a writer so indelibly associated with stories of the Canadian Northwest that frequently films that had nothing more to do with his fiction other than they were set in Canada and involved the Mounties credited him as their source. Like Rex Beach to whom his work is most closely related, Curwood's romanticism and extreme sentimentality mark him as too much a product of his generation, and his work has dated badly. Also included in Curwood's work is a strain of racism, especially prevalent in novels such as *The River's End* (1919), where the hero says of the Chinese villain, "You've a streak down your back the same color as your skin."

Stereotypes abound in his work as do silly plot complications and ridiculous dialogue. In *The River's End,* the innocent hero on the run from the law assumes the identity of a dead Mountie to whom he bears a striking resemblance. Matters are complicated when the hero gets back to civilization and finds a young woman under the spell of an evil Chinese man, who was also the dead Mountie's arch enemy. To make matters even worse, the dead Mountie's sister, who has not seen him in ten years, shows up with the intention of living with her brother. Then the hero falls in love with the dead Mountie's sister, and she finds herself strangely drawn to him. In the hands of a great author, the incestuous theme might have given the story an added twist, but Curwood could not exploit such material.

The first production of *The River's Edge* (Vitagraph, 1920) was of little consequence. The second, however, entitled simply *River's Edge* (Warner Bros., 1930) proved considerably better. The hero, John Keith (Charles Bickford), switches identity with the dying Mountie Conniston (Charles Bickford). The evil Chinese was done away with as was Conniston's sister replaced as a love interest by the Colonel's daughter. Another Mountie knows Keith is innocent but is killed before he can prove it, and a romantic rival informs the Colonel that Conniston has a wife and child in England. Keith takes a frightful beating for the dead Mountie's sins, but in the end, good prevails, and he is united with his true love. Another remake (Warner Bros., 1940) contains only minor alterations from the previous version, and once again Keith (Dennis Morgan) emerges victorious. All these are only action-adventure films without distinction (but, all are better than the novel).

Altogether, more than 70 films claim Curwood as their source, and not one of them can be described as anything more than adequate. Most are far below that, made by Monogram or Ambassador or other Poverty Row studios. This holds true to his most famous novel, *Kazan* (1914), which was adapted twice, first under its original title (Selig, 1921) and then under the title of *Ferocious Pal* (Principal, 1934). "Back to God's Country" (1911), was made three times (First National, 1919 and Universal, 1927 and Universal, 1952), yet every one failed to rise above "B" status. Curwood did not write any great or near great novels or short stories, and the films based on his work reflect his lack of talent.

Another minor western novelist, Hal G. Everts, wrote his first novel, *The Cross Pull* (1920), along the same lines as Curwood in *Kazan,* using a dog as one of the central characters. It is interesting to note that Evarts and Curwood both were very popular in France during their lifetimes and had many of their works translated into French. Evarts went on to write other western novels, several of which were noted for their historical accuracy.

The Cross Pull reached the screen as *The Silent Call* (H.O. Davis/AFN, 1921), a programmer without distinction. The story involves Flash, a half dog, half wolf, who possesses enough human traits to save the heroine, clear her father's name and chase the villain to a watery grave. While it was marginally entertaining, its importance lies in the casting of the dog Strongheart, Rin Tin Tin's chief competitor.

Of course, Everts' most important novel, made so by the film adaptation, is *Tumbleweeds* (1923), which appeared initially in *The Saturday Evening Post.* It deals with the Cherokee Land Rush and the cowboys who worked on the ranches and leased grasslands from the Indians. When William S. Hart read the novel, he was so intrigued by it that he immediately purchased the rights. The story is a simple one of cowboy Don Carver (William S. Hart) deciding to get in on the land rush, mainly because of his romance with Molly Lassiter (Barbara Bedford). The villain is Molly's half brother who conspires with another man to be "Sooners." When Don is sent into the strip by his boss to look for strays, he is arrested as a Sooner and thrown into the stockade, but on race day, he escapes, rides in the stampede for land, defeats the Sooners and wins Molly. But the plot of the film, which resembles the novel in large part, is unimportant. What is important is the depth which director King Baggot and producer William S. Hart imbued the film. Certainly the land rush sequence is one of the great action sequences ever put on celluloid. Even more, the film is a testament to the passing of the Old West. At one point, as the cowboys make their final cattle drive, Don Carver removes his Stetson and says, "Boys, it's the last of the West." The land rush itself is the final death knell of the open range and of a way of life that vanishes forever. It is this aspect that Everts the writer missed and Hart the filmmaker saw.

Only one other Everts novel, *Spanish Acres* (1925), made it to the screen, his only sound adaptation. Entitled *The Santa Fe Trail* (Paramount, 1930), it is a minor effort about a sheep rancher (Richard Arlen) who stops a land grabber while at the same time winning the hand of his lady love (Rosita Moreno). The Mexican characters speak in Spanish without subtitles or translations, but this technique was ahead of its time, and Depression audiences didn't approve. Few films followed its example, even though the technique succeeded cinematically.

Although Everts wrote formulary romantic westerns, the main thrust of his work was great, sweeping events. No novel of his more aptly illustrates this trait than *Tumbleweeds*. However, if it were not for the film version of the novel, even this work would lie buried in obscurity. As it is, only the title remains alive. His work, so popular in his own time, has not worn well with age. Although better than Curwood, and in his own small way, more influential, Everts is nevertheless too much a product of his own time, his books too full of romantic nonsense. Even the titles of his other novels have long ago faded from memory, regulated now to the dusty shelves of second hand book stores, collector items to those few who remember.

The most prolific western novelist was undoubtedly Frederick Faust, who wrote over 300 hundred western novels under 19 different pseudonyms including his most famous, Max Brand. The large body of his work was done for the pulps, and he wrote quickly, sometimes churning out 12,000 words on a weekend and whole novels in three weeks. By the 1930s, his books were outselling even Zane Grey.

Faust wrote an excellent novel, *The Untamed,* which appeared as a serial in *All Story Weekly* in December 1918 and then as a hardback the following year. *The Untamed* tells the story of a larger-than-life hero, Whistling Dan Berry, torn between freedom and love, who tries to come to grips with these forces. With Dan are two companions, Satan, his stallion, and Black Bart, a wolf dog, and it is with these animals he has an almost mystical communication. When Dan falls in love, his inner conflicts begin to intensify.

The Untamed (Fox, 1920) failed to follow much of the book and the character Tom Mix played was not the Whistling Dan Berry of the novel. In addition, the film failed in any way to capture the strange mood and tone of the book, yet it proved a huge success and became the first western that Fox opened to first run theaters in New York, which ushered in the heyday of the western film. It was remade once as *Fair Warning* (Fox, 1930), a George O'Brien vehicle that concentrated on pursuit.

Tom Mix went on to star in several more silent films based on Faust's novels. *The Night Horseman* (Fox, 1921) was a sequel to *The Untamed,* and once again Whistling Dan Berry was the protagonist. *Trailin'* (Fox, 1921) was considered by reviewers to be Mix's best film to date and was remade as *A Holy Terror* (Fox, 1931) with George O'Brien. In an effort to describe how Tom Mix acquired Tony, his horse, the studio adapted the pulp serial *Alcatraz* into *Just Tony* (Fox, 1922). Other Mix vehicles based on Faust's writings included *Mile-a-Minute Romeo* (Fox, 1923) based on the short story "Gun Gentleman," and *The Best Bad Man* (Fox, 1925), based on *Señor Jingle Bells.*

Occasionally one of Brand's stories would appear in a slick magazine rather than the pulps. Such was the case with "Dark Rosaleen," which first saw light of day in *Country Gentleman* in 1926. The story tells of an escaped prisoner named Lupin who runs across a newborn colt, which, unbeknown to Lupin, was sired to run a local race called the Comanche Cup. The motherless colt instantly attaches herself to Lupin, but he is separated from her for four years when he is recaptured and sent back to prison. Once again Lupin escapes and returns to her, and he discovers that she still remembers him. At the expense of his own freedom, Lupin wins the Comanche Cup for the original owner, Colonel Savary. In the process, he also wins the love of the Colonel's daughter and is exonerated of all past crimes. The plot is typically Max Brand, and the characters are certainly stereotypical, but it moves at a nice pace and the relationship between Dark Rosaleen and Lupin is emotionally involving.

On the screen, the story became *The Flying Horseman* (Fox, 1926), a Buck Jones vehicle. A drifting cowboy (Jones) first takes a bunch of boys under his protective wing and later a girl (Gladys McConnel) whose father's ranch is coveted by the villain. The hero is framed for murder, escapes from jail and wins a race, which enables the heroine to pay off her mortgage. In thwarting the villain, the hero also proves himself innocent of the murder and winds up with the girl. While a few of the surface details remain from "Dark Rosaleen," the core of the story, the relationship between man and horse, has vanished, replaced by a standard horse opera without any of the Max Brand touches. Why then did the studio choose to purchase the property? It is easy enough to understand. Max Brand was a recognizable name, an important name, to the American reading public and especially to western fans. On the lobby card and posters advertising *The Flying Horseman,* the author's name was prominently featured in bold letters. His name drew the public just like Buck Jones or Tom Mix.

The most popular of Faust's novels also proved to be his most popular film adaptation. *Destry Rides Again* (1930) is interesting because it is as much a detective novel as a western. The local ne'er-do-well of the town of Wham, Harrison Destry, is convicted of a crime more on his reputation rather than any hard evidence and sent to prison. Once he gets out of prison, he is determined to hunt down the jury members and kill them, but the scope of his hunt widens to include finding the culprit responsible for his imprisonment, who turns out to be his best friend Chester Bent, the one man Destry trusted. The novel was weak in many areas, especially in the character of Destry, who discovers the villain only when he is told by a young boy he befriends, leaving the reader with the uncomfortable feeling that, had he not been hit in the face with the information, Destry might have kept going right along as the dupe of Chester. Destry is simply not insightful and generates little interest.

The first adaptation of *Destry Rides Again* (Universal, 1932) followed the novel in some areas, but for the most part, went its own way. Tom Destry (Tom Mix) owns a stagecoach line and is running for sheriff of the town. Framed on a murder charge, Destry is sent to prison where he vows revenge. Later pardoned, he returns to town where he feigns illness, but when the crooked sheriff's gang tries to terrorize him, he quickly dispatches them with blazing guns. In the finale, Destry saves his girl from the crooked sheriff, who then confesses to having framed the hero. Despite the changes in plot, the film worked well on a "B" level. The film was re-released in 1939 as *Justice Rides Again.*

The next version of *Destry Rides Again* (Universal, 1939) threw out the novel and kept the title, yet surprisingly enough, it became classic film. The town of Bottle Neck is ruled by Kent (Brian Donlevy), a ruthless gambler who cheats suckers out of their land and also owns the saloon where Frenchy (Marlene Dietrich) works. When the sheriff is murdered, the crooked town officials appoint town drunk Wash Dimsdale (Charles Winniger), but the scheme backfires in their collective faces when he takes the job seriously and sends for the son of his old pal. Tom Destry (James Stewart) arrives without guns, and he is mocked by all the evil denizens of the town. Only after Wash is killed does Destry strap on his guns and go calling on Kent and his henchmen. Frenchy, who has fallen for the charms of the gangling Destry, leads the women of the town to battle Kent. When Kent attempts to shoot Destry, Frenchy throws herself in the path of the bullet and dies. Destry then shoots Kent, and the town is made safe.

This is a comedy film that mocks many western conventions. Destry is a gunless, milk-drinking deputy sheriff who seems too laconic to tame a town. Early on, he stops a saloon fight between Frenchy and Lily (Una Merkle) by dumping a pail of soapy water on the pair. Frenchy is constantly wisecracking with Destry, and often it is their confrontations that take center stage rather than Destry's attempt to bring law and order to Bottle Neck. Within the framework of this film, Faust and his original story have vanished altogether.

The novel came to the screen once more as simply *Destry* (Universal, 1955) with Audie Murphy essaying the title role, but the film was a lackluster remake of the 1939 film, even though George Marshall, who had directed the earlier version, also directed this one. This time, he could not overcome vapid casting and a weakened script.

During the late thirties and early forties most of the films based on Faust's work were about young Dr. Kildare, although a few westerns were adapted. *The Valley of Vanishing Men* (Columbia, 1942) was a fifteen-chapter serial with no connection to the book except the title. Even the central character, Jim Silver, or Silvertip as he was often called, one of Faust's most famous creations, was dropped, replaced by Wild Bill Tolliver to conform with the moniker used by the star, "Wild" Bill Elliott. *Singing Guns* (Republic, 1950) was an interesting experiment using singer Vaughn Monroe as the lead. Less interesting was *My Outlaw Brother* (United Artists, 1951), based on *South of the Rio Grande* (1936), with Mickey Rooney searching for his brother who has disappeared below the border. As the *New York Times* pointed out, it was "slow going laced by sporadic but unsuccessful tries at humor."

The best of the later Faust films is *Branded* (Paramount, 1950), which owes much of its plot to O. Henry's "The Double-Dyed Deceiver" but which was concocted out of two novels Faust wrote under the pseudonym of Evan Evans. The first, *The Border Kid* (1928), tells the story of Ricardo, who attempts to steal the inheritance from Maud Ranger but with whom he falls in love. In order to win her love, he rides single-handedly into an outlaw town and faces a bunch of hired killers. In the other, *Montana Rides* (1933), the first of a series, the central character tries to square himself with a rancher who trusts him by riding across the Rio Grande to rescue the rancher's kidnapped son.

The motivating force behind *Branded* was the success of an earlier Alan Ladd vehicle, *Whispering Smith,* and the studio wanted to put the actor back in the saddle. The script called him Choya and had him an adventurer posing as the long lost son of a rancher (Charles Bickford) but falling in love with his "sister" (Mona Freeman). Conscience stricken, he rides off across the border to get the real son who has been raised by outlaws, and despite enormous odds, returns him safely to the ranch. The script is literate, and the icy performance by Ladd, even when he turns out to be the hero, is reminiscent of many of Faust's protagonists. Eschewing action for atmosphere, *Branded* comes closer than any other film to capturing Faust on film.

Emerson Hough, discussed in Chapter Six, tried his hand at a conventional western in *North of 36* (1923), which deals with the great cattle drives. The daughter of a murdered Texas rancher, Taisie Lockhart finds herself with a depleted stock due to rustlers and is on the verge of bankruptcy. As there is no market in Texas, she decides, with the aid of loyal ranch hands, to drive her cattle over the Chisholm Trail to Kansas. Although as in *The Covered Wagon,* a conventional romance interferes with the narrative, the details of the drive are realistically described.

The year after Hough died saw the release of *North of 36* (Paramount, 1924), and while it did not reach the splendor of *The Covered Wagon,* it proved to be an acceptable adaptation. The plot remains basically the same with Taisie (Lois Wilson) driving cattle to Kansas. She is aided by Ben MacMasters (Jack Holt) with whom she falls in love. Villainy comes in the guise of Sim Rudabaugh (Noah Beery), who is after land scrip held by the heroine. The plot twists sometime became dowright silly. When Rudabaugh steals the scrip, he does so with ridiculous ease and meets few challenges until the final few moments. However, the end takes a turn toward the brutal. An earlier scene showed Rudabaugh watching a young Comanche maiden swimming in a milk-white pool. When she is found dead, the Indians go wild. In order to appease them, MacMaster turns the villain over to the Indians to dispense justice.

Just as realistic detail was the strong point of the novel, so was it the strong point of the film. The massing of the herd with the cattle coming from all over Texas is especially effective as is a stampede with the cattle charging hell-bent for hell-knows-where with the cowboys trying to turn them. Also, the river crossing is beautifully done, the cattle seemingly strung out for miles in both directions and swimming a stream a half mile wide. The cattle themselves were true longhorns, the last such herd in existence, which had been located on a ranch in the exact vicinity where the novel opens. Often when the camera comes in close, the cattle are genuinely afraid and skittish. In the hands of a more imaginative director, the herd itself might have become a character as it did in *Red River*, but it never gets a chance. It is overshadowed by the infantile story.

A few critics liked the film. *Photoplay* claimed it a screen achievement and said, "What the perfect 36 is to a beauty chorus, *North of 36* is to the western movie." the *New York Times* came close to the general consensus. While admitting that it was an enjoyable film, the reviewer pointed out that it was not nearly as good as *The Covered Wagon*. "One of the chief failings in this production," said the *Times*, "is the lack of real suspense, which materially weakens the whole story."

Despite the story problems, the film was remade as *The Conquering Horde* (Paramount, 1931). This version was too talky with the characters always crouching close to the hidden microphone. Action disappears for long stretches. This time Dan MacMasters (Richard Arlen) comes to help Taisie (Fay Wray) because he is in reality an undercover agent for the government, adding one more asinine complication to the Hough story. Again, the film's strength lies in the details of the drive: the cowboys driving the cattle, the sandstorm, the deluge of rain, the cattle and horses struggling through the slime and mud.

Paramount just couldn't get the story out of its collective mind, so the studio tried once more to get it right with *The Texans* (Paramount, 1938). They didn't do it any better this time. Kirk Jordan (Randolph Scott) drives 10,000 cattle belonging to Granny (May Robson) and Ivy Preston (Joan Bennett) from Texas to Kansas and opens up the Chisholm Trail in the process, which makes one wonder why they called it the Chisholm Trail. Along the way they have trouble with both Indians and carpetbaggers. Mixed into the plot are the Ku Klux Klan and the building of the transcontinental railroad, which would have never been completed if the hero had not gotten the cattle to market. As before, the best scenes are those that depict the hardships of the trail. The *New York Times* put it succinctly when the reviewer said, "It is just another romance with unjustified pretensions to importance."

The twenties continued to see the imitators of Wister and Grey proliferate. Walt Coburn had several pulp stories made into films. "Triple Cross for Danger" became *Fighting Fury* (Universal, 1924), a Jack Hoxie western. Four sound westerns from Columbia listed Coburn as their source, but most likely they were only using his name, since films like *The Return of Wild Bill* (Columbia, 1940) was a "Wild" Bill Elliott vehicle based on a character that the actor had established as far back as 1936 in the serial *The Adventures of Wild Bill Hickok* (Columbia, 1936).

The Three Mesquiteers were created by William Colt MacDonald in a series of novels, but *Santa Fe Stampede* (1938) was strictly a studio creation.

Far more important than Walt Coburn was William Colt Mac-Donald, not because he was a better writer but because he created more enduring characters. Using Alexander Dumas as his model, he penned *Law of the Forty-Fives* (1933) and developed the concept of a sagebrush trio called "The Three Mesquiteers"—Tucson Smith, Lullaby Joslin and Stony Brooke. The first Three Mesquiteers film, *Law of the .45's* (First Division, 1935), starred Guinn Williams as Tucson and Al St. John as Lullaby. The story dropped Stony Brooke, and it was a low budget, dull affair. The next adaptation was *Powdersmoke Range* (RKO, 1935), an all-star production with Harry Carey, Hoot Gibson, Guinn Williams, Bob Steele, Tom Tyler and a host of stars from the silent era. The film followed the book closely enough, except that it kills off the character of Sundown Saunders (Tyler) where MacDonald not only allowed him to live but had him reappear from time to time in various sequels. After this, Republic Studios picked up the series and made 51 entries with various actors periodically taking over the leads. A few early entries such as *Roarin' Lead* (Republic, 1936) and *Riders of the Whistling Skull* (Republic, 1937) took their titles and some of their plots from MacDonald's novels, but soon the practice was dropped and only the characters were used with original stories provided by the script department. Although MacDonald wrote screenplays for some of the better Tim McCoy films at Columbia, he was never called upon to adapt his own works.

With the exception of Frederick Faust, these early imitators of Wister and Grey are seldom read today, although paperback reprints of individual titles of a few do appear from time to time. Faust was an innovative writer who created his own fantasy world, a world full of myth and mysticism, a world full of heroes who are far bigger than life. His fiction is far removed from most other writers, and his novels read as well today as when he first wrote them. For various reasons — lack of strong plotting, weak characters, overt sentimentality — most other writers of this early period have not fared so well. Even authors such as Clarence E. Mulford and William Colt MacDonald are remembered more for the characters the screen created than the ones they created in their novels. Even a seminal author and a true artist such as Eugene Manlove Rhodes is difficult to find except on a few library shelves or second hand book stores. Reprints of his fiction seldom appear. However, all these authors are important because they helped to establish the foundations and set patterns for the western that were to flourish in both literature and film for decades to come.

10. The Western Grows Up

A few writers who began in the twenties saw a serious side to the western, one not confined by formula, and attempted to expand the horizons of the burgeoning genre. The fact that they were not always successful is unimportant. What is important is that they added a sense of maturity and opened up new vistas in western literature.

Among these was Will James, a pseudonym for Joseph Dufault, whose *Smoky, the Cowhorse,* won the Newbery Medal in 1934, and certainly the charming prose is simple enough for a child yet engaging enough for an adult. This is an adventure story about a spirited gelding who relates only to Clint, a cowboy. The cow horse is stolen, sold to a rodeo, given to a livery stable and finally forced to pull a vegetable wagon. During this time when he is abused, he learns to hate human beings, but in the end, Clint finds him and restores the horse's health and spirit. The book reviewer on the *New York Times* wrote, "There have been many horse stories. . . . But not one of them can compare with this book by Will James." This, only his second novel, was to be the high water mark of Will James' career.

Smoky (Fox, 1933) came to the screen with Will James occasionally interrupting the narrative with little asides on the psychology of horses. The best part of the film is the genuine affection with which it shows the education of a horse. Smoky grows from a shy, awkward foal to the finest horse at the roundup, suffering first the humiliation of branding and then the gradual process of being broken to the saddle. Of course, Smoky submits only to Clint (Victor Jory), and there is a particularly fine scene where, frightened by a cottontail, Smoky throws his master, hurting him badly, then patiently drags him back to the line camp. As in the novel, the pair are separated. Smoky is captured by a rustler and eventually ends up with a junk dealer who signs him over to a glue factory. Clint arrives in the nick of time to rescue him. This is a touching and sentimental little film and a worthy adaptation of Will James' novel. Thirteen years after its release, Thomas Pryor, writing in the *New York Times* still called it "the finest film of its type ever made."

The remake of *Smoky* (TCF, 1946) had the advantage of Technicolor. After Clint (Fred MacMurray) gently breaks Smoky and the two become companions, another cowhand beats the horse, and infuriated, Smoky tramples and kills him, then runs off to the mountains. Eventually tracked down by hunters and put in a rodeo, he ends up the property of a junkman, his spirit completely broken. Clint finds him and nurses him back to health at the ranch. This version also included a romance between Clint and the pretty ranch owner (Anne Baxter) plus a few songs from a ranch hand (Burl Ives). Although this does not have the charm of the original, it is a pleasant film and better than most remakes. It also does a nice job capturing the spirit of the novel.

Smoky (TCF, 1966) was remade once again, but it was a mediocre affair that did not approach either of its predecessors. The only other Will James work to reach the screen was the somewhat fantasized autobiographical *The Lone Cowboy* (1930), the first time under its own title (Fox, 1933) and again as *The Shootout* (Universal, 1971), neither of which proved very important. After *Smoky, the Cowhorse,* Will James never again wrote anything as important. Where once he had been hailed as the authentic voice of the American cowboy, his reputation is now in decline, although *Smoky* remains a literate and sensitive novel, and the first two film adaptations deserve respect.

In contrast to Will James, one writer whose reputation has grown over the years is Ernest Haycox (discussed in chapters three and five) whose novels and short stories often originated in pulp magazines but whose writing is superior. While there is not much blood and thunder in his stories, they are full of characters who live and breathe, and his West seems authentic and real. Of his formulary western novels adapted for films, few changes—and no important ones—were made from printed page to screen because his stories were not only very visual but also moved at the proper pace, the pace of a natural-born storyteller.

Haycox often used the love triangle in his novels, and the films carried over this plot device in such works as *Bugles in the Afternoon* and *Canyon Passage,* both discussed previously. In *Man in the Saddle* (1938), he told the story of rancher Owen Merritt whose first love marries local land baron Will Isham. Jealous of Merritt, Isham proceeds to force him off his land and have him branded a coward and killer. With the support of Nan, who loves him, Owen fights back and eventually defeats the combined forces of Owen and his hired guns. As in much of Haycox's fiction, the antagonist is not so much villain as a man tragically flawed, possessed by envy, greed and power. The hero is complex and introspective, and unlike much formulary western fiction, capable of being aroused by a woman. *Man in the Saddle* is an excellent example of Haycox at his finest.

The film *Man in the Saddle* (Columbia, 1951) followed the plot and intricacies of character laid out by Haycox, and as a result, it was an "adult" western before the term became popular. As the story progresses, Owen Merritt (Randolph Scott) slowly grows in authority until he finally emerges as the commanding presence in the film. On the other hand, Will Isham (Alexander Knox) slowly deteriorates until the end finds him a shell of the man he was at the beginning. The taut direction of Andre de Toth admirably compliments Haycox's fine novel.

Another Haycox novel, *Trail Town* (1941), became *Abilene Town* (United Artists, 1946), and again the screenwriters stuck close to the original source. Essentially it tells of the struggle between the farmers and the cowboys for control of Abilene with sheriff Dan Mitchell (Randolph Scott) caught in the middle. Two women fight for the sheriff's attentions. The first is the lovely town girl Sherry (Rhonda Fleming), but she is ultimately appalled at the violence of his job and turns to a more dependable farm boy (Lloyd Bridges) for romantic comfort. The marshal wins the hand of Rita (Ann Dvorak), the saloon prima donna whose stage routines Dan always seems to interrupt. What this film ultimately lacks is the presence of strong adversary for Dan Mitchell. What it substitutes is a coalition of rowdy cowboys and crooked saloon owners, but it does not have anyone the size of Will Isham, and it needs this. A weaker novel and film than *Man in the Saddle, Abilene Town* is nevertheless a fine example of conventional material well handled.

Occasionally writers whose main outputs were in other genres ventured into westerns. Such was the case with W.R. Burnett (discussed in Chapter Four), who was noted more for his gangster novels such as *Little Caesar* and *The Asphalt Jungle* than his westerns. Yet, almost forgotten today, he wrote one of the most powerful westerns of the thirties, *Saint Johnson* (1929), a novel based on the exploits of Wyatt Earp and his feud with the Clantons in Tombstone, Arizona, in the 1880s.

Of the many novels of W.R. Burnett, none was filmed more than *Saint Johnson* (1930), which has had four screen adaptations. In many ways, the novel was ahead of its time, although it is in no way a psychological western of the type that became so popular in the late 1950s and early 1960s. The central character, Wyat Johnson, never doubts himself and never struggles with internal devils. Instead, Burnett treated his protagonists more like gangsters than lawmen, and the story seldom feels like a western, confined as it is to Alkali, Arizona. The novel is bleakly realistic, even to eschewing any love interest, which is especially remarkable since it was written during a period when most western novels were highly romantic.

Although Burnett disguised his characters by giving them different names, the events loosely follow a portion of *Tombstone* (1927) by Walter Noble Burns, a biography built on fantasy. Wyat Johnson, a law officer who has previously cleaned up Dodge City and other frontier cow towns, is in the process of doing the same to Alkali. Even though some good citizens stand behind Johnson, a lawless element headed by Poe Northrup and sheriff Fin Elder offers opposition. On Johnson's side are his two brothers, Luther and Jimmy, plus two friends, Deadwood and Brant, the latter based on the real-life character of Doc Holliday. When the lawless element pushes Wyat too far, he and his followers meet the Northrup's in a shootout. The Northrups are wiped out, but later Jimmy is ambushed and killed by a surviving gang member, El Guero. Turning his back on the law, Wyat faces the killer in the streets of Alkali and coldly and brutally kills him.

> El Guero turned swiftly and made a break for the dark alleyway between the Palace and the Transcontinental. Wyat took one step sideways to clear his range and fired. El Guero stopped and took hold of the corner of the dance hall with both hands. Then Wyat fired three more shots. El Guero slid slowly to the sidewalk and knelt there, supporting himself against the building. Brant fired a shot from close range and El Guero fell over backwards.

The next day, Wyat and the others calmly ride out of town.

The first film version of *Saint Johnson* became *Law and Order* (Universal, 1932), re-released in the late forties as *Guns a' Blazin'*, and changed Wyat Johnson to Frame Johnson (Walter Huston). In the novel, there was a "Frame"—Frame Tod, a despicable cowboy who sides with the Northrups—and on the surface, the change seems inexplicable. The real Wyatt Earp, however, had just died in 1929, and the studio thought it prudent to play down the similarity in names. Then, just as inexplicably, they drew attention to the connection with Earp by changing the setting to Tombstone where the real Earp had been a lawman. The character of Jimmy Johnson has been dropped, and only Luther Johnson (Russell Hopton), Deadwood (Raymond Hatton) and Brant (Harry Carey) accompany the hero into Tombstone. At first,

Frame is reluctant to accept the job of town marshal but is eventually goaded by the good citizens into pinning on the star. Immediately he comes into conflict with the town bosses, Poe Northrup and his two brothers.

Two crucial events remain from the novel. The first involves a dimwitted miner (Andy Devine) who shoots a cowboy in the back, and when a mob comes to lynch the prisoner, Frame faces them down and forces them to disperse. The second is when Frame forces through an ordinance that forbids carrying guns within the city limits. This action sets off a series of events that lead to the gunfight at the OK Corral.

In the novel, Wyat, Luther and Deadwood face Poe Northrup and his three companions. Although Luther and Deadwood are wounded, neither is hurt badly, but two of the Northrups are killed and another wounded. The film gives us a fullscale battle. Poe Northrup ambushes Brant, and as the gambler lies dying, he blames Frame's inaction as the cause. This spurs Frame into action. With Luther and Deadwood, he marches down the middle of the street, killing Northrups right and left. When they reach the OK Corral, they find a half dozen more men waiting. In a frantic gun battle during which the camera moves in and out of the action like one of the participants, the Northrups are wiped out, but at the cost of the lives of Deadwood and Luther.

The ending of *Law and Order* finds Frame, wounded and dispirited, surrendering his badge to the town judge. "Well, you wanted law and order and you got it," he says. "But this isn't the end. After we're gone, there'll be other bad men in other towns breaking the law and totin' guns unless somebody's got the guts to stop them. Tombstone's only one town." He then rides slowly out of town.

Women are conspicuously absent in both the novel and film. The few in either are hard prostitutes or saloon girls without hearts of gold. It is a man's world where men settle their affairs without the hindrance of romance. It is in the character of Wyat/Frame where the novel and film deviate the greatest. In the novel, Wyat not only owned part of a saloon but he also allowed his brother Jimmy to go free and covered up for him after the kid participated in a stage holdup. In this and the killing of El Guero, Johnson acts more like a gangster than a lawman. In the film, Frame is a stern man who lives by the strict code of the law, a man unable to bend. When the town passes the ordinance forbidding the carrying of guns, Frame insists that he and the others stop wearing theirs, also.

Saint Johnson was remade five years later as a thirteen-chapter serial, *Wild West Days* (Universal, 1937), and the novel disappears among the constant action and cliffhangers. Indians as well as outlaws after gold cavort around the countryside causing all sorts of problems for the hero and his friends, and not one event from the Burnett novel survives. Even the main character became someone called Kentucky Wade (Johnny Mack Brown), who more closely resembles Red Ryder than Wyatt Earp.

Universal resurrected *Saint Johnson* in *Law and Order* (Universal, 1940). Deadwood (Fuzzy Knight) and Brant (James Craig) resurfaced again, although Wyat/Frame became Bill Ralston (once again, Johnny Mack Brown). This time the hero has a girlfriend, Sally Dixon. Only one scene from the novel remains, and even that is greatly altered. When Sally's brother Jimmy kills a man in self defense, the outlaws attempt to rouse the town to lynch him. The hero then faces down the mob. When Brant meets his death at the hands of the villains, Poe Daggett and his three brothers, the hero is again spurred into action and cleans up the town. The story concludes with the hero telling his girl that he will return for her as soon as he finds that little ranch that he's been looking for. Neither this film nor *Wild West Days* rise above the level of a "B," and both violated the spirit of the novel.

In the final screen adaptation, *Law and Order* (Universal, 1953), Frame Johnson returned in the person of Ronald Reagan, who, when offered the role as Frame, jumped at the chance. Speaking about westerns in general, Reagan said, "They're recent enough to be real and old enough to be romantic. Mix that up with horses, action, a little love, and lots of money and you've found a rich strike." Unfortunately, this remake was no rich strike but a dry hole.

At best a conventional western, this *Law and Order* might have been a good Buck Jones film if it had been made twenty years before, but by the time it reached the screen, it creaked with clichés. Burnett's *Saint Johnson* had been a gritty, realistic enforcer of frontier law, but in this *Law and Order,* he became the reluctant lawman forced to take up his guns one last time. Little remains from the novel except the character of Jimmy Johnson. When Jimmy kills a villain in self-defense, he is tracked down and arrested by Frame. Even the climactic gunfight at the OK Corral has been avoided, and the ineffectual villain (Preston Foster) dies by being trampled under a team of horses. Frame isn't even allowed to do the job himself.

Another American author who dipped into the genre but was not considered a western writer was Edna Ferber with *Cimarron* (1930), probably her best and certainly her most overtly feminist novel. The story of Sabra and Yancey Cravat is set against the Oklahoma Land Rush of 1889 and continues through the discovery of oil. Yancy sees the frontier as symbolizing a new life with "no class distinctions, no snobbery, no high-falutin' notion." On the other hand, the virtuous women, including Sabra, are set upon making the new frontier community as much like the old as speedily as possible. Having just moved to Oklahoma Territory with his new bride, Yancy seems the dreamer, impractical and irresponsible, yet he manages to start the first newspaper in the territory. In addition to housework and raising her children, Sabra soon finds herself helping with the newspaper. On those occasions when Yancy, driven by his restlessness, abandons her, she runs it herself. Yancy is the dreamer, Sabra the doer, and it is she who becomes Oklahoma's first United States congresswoman.

Like so many novels of the thirties, this suffers from over sentimentalizing, which takes away from its strengths. The ending when Sabra finds Yancy dying in the oil field is sickly sweet and unbelievable. The best part of the novel is in its ironical use of the Osage Indians who have been dislocated to make room for the white settlers and the "useless" reservation land has been found rich in oil deposits. There is almost a sinister edge to their presence as they both acquire wealth and mock it at the same time. They wear their blankets to cover their beaded Parisian frocks. But as individuals, they are stage Indians just as Yancy is a stage hero, cardboard figures who strut across the pages, say their lines and strut off.

Cimarron (RKO, 1931) became the only western to win an Academy Award for best picture, and while it might not be the classic that it appeared to be at the time, it still retains some powerful moments. Certainly the opening sequence, the Oklahoma land rush, the same event that was used six years earlier as the climax of William S. Hart's final film, *Tumbleweeds,* is one of the most exciting action scenes ever put on celluloid. But how can a film that runs another two hours match such a beginning? The answer is simple: it can't.

The story remains much as Edna Ferber wrote it. Yancy (Richard Dix) opens the newspaper, becomes the leading citizen of the new town and he and Sabra (Irene Dunn) have two children. When the Kid and his gang attempt to rob the bank, it is Yancy who kills two of the outlaws. At an open town meeting, he kills Lon Yountis who was responsible for the previous editor's death. Over the protestations of Sabra, he defends Dixie Lee on charges of being a harlot. When wanderlust gets in his eyes and he quietly disappears, Sabra becomes a dominant force in civic and state activities. When her son is killed in a railroad accident, she finds the strength to persevere. As the years pass and Yancy becomes only a memory, she becomes a grandmother and matriarch of the town. On the day the town is to unveil a monument to Yancy, an old worker is fatally injured in an accident at a nearby oil field. Rushing to the scene, Sabra discovers it is Yancy, and kneeling in the dust she cradles him in her arms as he dies.

The action of the film covers forty years, and as such, the events are episodic. The best are the early scenes of the land rush and the bustling new town, and these remain in the mind long after the film has ended. After this, the pace slows considerably with only a few moments, such as the showdown with Yountis, to liven things up. The story is never quite convincing, especially Sabra's devotion to Yancy's memory long after he has departed, and even though the novel should justly be regarded as an early paean to feminism, it is nevertheless dated and fails as the historical drama it strives to be.

A remake of *Cimarron* (MGM, 1961) in color was a shambles. Sabra (Maria Shell) orders Yancy (Glenn Ford) to leave because he refuses an offer that would make him governor of the state. He says okay and doesn't return. It's no wonder. This Sabra is a deceitful and spiteful creature who becomes a simpering saint. Even more than its predecessor, this film goes nowhere after the opening land rush. It is a labored effort without much to recommend it.

Another Pulitzer Prize winner, Conrad Richter, molded the genre's conventions into an outstanding novel, *The Sea of Grass* (1937). What could easily have been just another novel of cattlemen versus nesters emerges as a complex tale of the end of the Old West as symbolized by the life of one man, cattle baron Jim Brewton, and his struggle against the nesters for ownership and use of the prairie—the sea of grass—on which to raise his cattle. When he tries to run the nesters off, a range war breaks out. Opposed to Brewton is new District Attorney Brice Chamberlain, who makes political capital by representing the nesters and proclaiming himself as the defender of the common man. He successfully strips Brewton of the sea of grass and opens it to colonization. Chamberlain claims that God is "clearly on the side of the settlers," and a heavy rain seems to bless the new settlers. Brewton knows better. The dry years come again, and the nesters are forced out, but in their wake, they have destroyed the sea of grass.

Within this plot is also intertwined the personal story of Jim Brewton. The same train that brings Chamberlain into town also brings Lutie, the woman Brewton is to marry. But theirs is not a happy marriage. She hates the sea of grass and wants to return to the East. Her renunciation of frontier life is exemplified by her choice of Chamberlain as a lover. She eventually leaves the ranch. Chamberlain does not have the courage to face Brewton in a gun battle, and he allows Lutie to leave alone. Selfish to the last, he never joins her.

Behind her, Lutie leaves her children, including Brock, who is Chamberlain's son. As he grows older, he grows restless and irresponsible. When he is caught cheating at cards, he runs away and becomes an outlaw. Trapped by a posse, Chamberlain is asked to talk the boy into surrendering, but he refuses. Brewton goes in Chamberlain's stead, only to have the wounded Brock die in his arms. The struggle between Brewton and Chamberlain for the sea of grass is symbolically represented in Brock, and only after his death is ownership made clear. On his tombstone, Brewton has the name Brock Brewton carved so "that all who ride may read."

In the film *The Sea of Grass* (MGM, 1947), much of the action remains the same but the motivations are not those Richter imparted to his characters. Brice Chamberlain (Melvyn Douglas) champions the cause of the homesteaders because he believes in it. He also loves Lutie (Katharine Hepburn), and waits the whole film in vain for her to come back once their affair is over. He is gloom personified, as if he is the wronged husband. Lutie herself is no capricious, willful woman as Richter drew her; rather, she is a woman overwhelmed by the sea of grass (in reality, a wheat field) and her husband's granite character. She always looks tense, but the chief interest in her character resides in her beautiful nineteenth century gowns, which she wears in strikingly good taste. When she leaves Brewton (Spencer Tracy) and runs off to Chamberlain, Brewton has driven her to it by his stoicism. Much of the film has Brewton gazing at the sea of grass to show his rugged individualistic nature, and one begins to wonder if she wasn't driven away by just plain boredom.

After Lutie returns and tells Brewton of her affair, he takes that stoically, too. A child, Brock, is born from the liaison, and Brewton cherishes the boy. Another child is born, a daughter this time, and after this, Brewton kicks Lutie off the ranch. Left without parental guidance, Brock (Robert Walker) grows into a wastrel. When he kills a man in a card game, he takes to the outlaw trail only to be hunted down and shot, finally dying in Brewton's arms. At the urging of the daughter (Phyllis Thaxter), Lutie returns to Brewton so that they are reunited at fade out.

The film is extremely slow, even though director Elia Kazan does everything in his power to speed things up. The problem lies in the limp script, which cannot bridge the years successfully and which bends and twists Richter's novel until it has lost all shape. Changes in Richter's novel also accounted for weak characterizations; Hepburn overacts, Tracy underacts and Melvyn Douglas doesn't quite know what to do. They all seem to be trying very hard to give their roles substance where none exists, and only the role of Brock adds excitement to the otherwise dreary film.

The formulary western returned with Frederick Glidden, who began writing in 1936 under the pseudonym of Luke Short, who became known as the "dean of living western writers." When Hollywood turned his novels into films, they made very few changes, mainly because his fiction was so tightly structured and his plot lines fit so neatly into cinematic adaptation, there was little need for change.

His first novel to reach the screen was *Gunman's Chance* (1941), one of his finest and most representative works, which became the very impressive *Blood on the Moon* (RKO, 1948). Trying to lose his past, Jim Garry (Robert Mitchum) comes to work for Tate Riling (Robert Preston), a former associate. Garry soon sees the kind of villainy that Riling plans, and he shifts his allegiance to Lufton and Lutfon's young daughter (Barbara Bel Geddes). By using many indoor locations and expressive lighting, dark shadows sometimes covering much of the screen, the film becomes as much a psychological drama as an action picture, a western *film noir,* and the blending of both make this a superior film. A fight sequence between Garry and Riling is especially realistic and brutal — at the end, both men lie exhausted on the floor, bloodied and battered — and it may be the best of its kind with the exception of the fight scene from *Shane.* If anything, the addition of the dark mood added a dimension that even the novel did not possess, deepening the story and characters, especially the standard Glidden ploy of having his hero wishing to atone for a shady past.

While other adaptations of Glidden's novels failed to match the quality and depth of *Blood on the Moon,* several of them were very good. *Ride the Man Down* (Republic, 1952), the 1942 novel, shows the influence of Ernest Haycox and is reminiscent of that author's *Man in the Saddle.* The story concerns a ranch foreman (Rod Cameron) who tries to keep a ranch together after his boss dies. Another classic Glidden novel, *Coroner Creek* (1946) became the first of the Harry Joe Brown–Randolph Scott productions (Producers-Actors Corp., 1948), a solid story of murder and revenge. Chris Danning (Randolph Scott) tracks the man who sold guns to the Indians who in turn killed his fiancée. The film includes a particularly violent fight where the villain's henchman stomps on Chris's trigger finger, and Chris repays him by doing the same

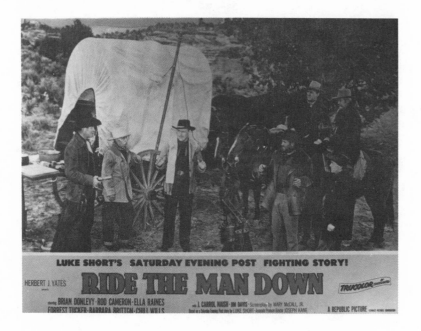

Lobby card for *Ride the Man Down* (1953), based on the Luke Short novel.

to the henchman. When he finally confronts the killer (George Macready), Chris forces him to fall on the same knife his fiancée died by. *Station West* (RKO, 1948) is unusual and intriguing in that it is really a humorous, hard-boiled murder mystery disguised as a western, and John Haven (Dick Powell) seems like Philip Marlowe out west. Directed too slackly, *Vengeance Valley* (MGM, 1951), the story of Owen Daybright (Burt Lancaster) who keeps covering up for the son of his adopted father, lacks tension and is far from satisfying.

The only Glidden film to come close to matching *Blood on the Moon* was *Ramrod* (Harry Sherman Productions, 1947), a superior western directed with a hard edge by Andre de Toth. The novel (1943) opens with Dave Nash, whose wife and child have just died, wandering into the town of Signal. When he hires on as foreman of the Circle 66 owned by the beautiful Connie Dickason, he immediately clashes with Frank Ivey, a local rancher greedy for more land. However, the film opens with Dave Nash (Joel McCrea) already working for Connie (Veronica Lake) and drops any mention of a former wife and child. Omitting the

Lobby card for *Ramrod* (1947), the best film adapted from a Luke Short novel.

self-regeneration theme helps the film to jump more quickly into the plot, but it misses an essential ingredient of the novel. What is exceptional about this film is the constant presence of evil that permeates the story. Also, there is the persistent feeling that the characters are not in control of themselves. This is especially evident in Dave's close friend, Bill Schell (Don Defore), who coldbloodedly kills a man yet sacrifices himself for Dave. The film is also surprisingly violent for its time. Bill Schell is nearly cut in half by a shotgun blast when Frank Ivey (Preston Foster) shoots him in the back. When Dave kills Ivey, he too uses a shotgun, cutting him down before Ivey can clear the holster.

The late thirties also saw the first published novel of Frank Gruber who, while not nearly as influential as Frederick Glidden, still made the transition from pulps to slicks. His odyssey is chronicled in his semiautobiographical *The Pulp Jungle* in which he listed and expounded upon the seven basic western plots: the ranch story, the empire story, the Union Pacific story, the revenge story, Custer's last stand, the outlaw story and the marshal story. As Gruber said of these, it wasn't plots that were important but what the author did with them. Gruber did just fine; the film adaptations of his works didn't do as well.

His first western novel, *Peace Marshal* (1939), serialized in *Adventure* magazine, floated around Hollywood for three years before Harry Sherman, the producer of the Hopalong Cassidy series, purchased the property and turned it into *The Kansan* (United Artists, 1943), a Wyatt Earp–type story of a roaming gunfighter (Richard Dix) who cleans up a Kansas cow town. While it missed the internal struggle of the lawman, the rousing action made for a superior "B" and probably the best adaptation of a Gruber novel. The moody, laconic *Tension at Table Rock* (RKO, 1956), based on the novel *Bitter Sage* (1956), added color and kept intact the character of the gunman who is reputed to be a "back-bitin' sidewinder who murdered his own best friend." While screenwriter Winston Miller amplified the novel and tried to give it plenty of psychological overtones, it is a plodding film with wooden characters. Much the same can be said for *The Big Land* (Warner Bros., 1957), based on *Buffalo Grass* (1956), Gruber's most ambitious western novel about the founding of a cow town and the feud that develops between the two founders. The film changed the plot, dropping the feud and adding some stock villains. The result was a lackluster effort that failed to do justice to the novel. *Town Tamer* (Paramount, 1965) was based on a Gruber short story that had appeared in *Short Stories* in 1957. The only connection between the short story and the novel is the central character who is a "town tamer." The film is notable for all the old timers who appeared in the subordinate roles such as Bob Steele, Sonny Tuffs and others. Their presence failed to lift the film above the atrocious.

The late thirties also saw Paul Wellman (discussed in several chapters in the present work) publish *Jubal Troop* (1939), an interesting novel in which the author attempted to show thirty years in the life of a roaming cowboy. The story begins during the terrible blizzard of 1886 as Jubal Troop flees from a posse looking for the killer of Shep Horgan. In the years that follow, Jubal finds adventures in Texas, Mexico, the Dakotas and Oklahoma, making a fortune, losing it and making another. He also follows a woman for ten years, finally marries her, loses his fortune once again and wins again. Stephen Vincent Benét thought the novel too weak in characters to be compelling, and while other critics agreed, most pointed out that the author's knowledge of his material and the sweep of the novel were enough to make it good entertainment.

On the screen, the novel became *Jubal* (Columbia, 1956) and managed to trivialize the book, compressing events of years into months. That is not to say it is a bad film; the sexual tensions and the depth of characters, especially that of Jubal (Glenn Ford) and Pinky (Rod Steiger), a western Iago, raise it above the standard horse opera, but the events do not conform to the novel. The *New York Times* critic went so far as to write a thirteen-stanza poem ending his review with:

> Howsoe'er, its drama drippeth
> Like the old familiar rain,
> Or—to put it more precisely—
> Like a plain, warmed-over "Shane."

Had the producers and writers been more visionary and attempted to adapt the novel, they might have produced an interesting film, but it was apparently too big a task. Today, a novel with such scope might be made as a miniseries for television, which could do it justice.

An offbeat western from the forties is *The Stranger* (1942) by Lillian Bos Ross, which has a few action sequences and is essentially a love story. In California of 1870, Zande Allan meets his mail order bride, Hannah Martin, and although disappointed that she has lied about her age—she said she was twenty-five but she is nearer thirty—he marries her anyway. Although an easterner, she soon proves her worth. Zande believes he wants a woman who will bend to his will, but what he gets is a woman who is stronger than he. They fight, they fume, they separate, but in the end, he comes back, a better and stronger man for the struggle. There are plenty of western elements present in the novel, although it never falls into formula. Also, the atmosphere is extremely well done, as are the characters. However, despite its strengths, the novel has rested in relative obscurity until the film version brought renewed interest.

Jan Troell, a Swede who previously directed *The Emigrants* (1970) and *The New Land* (1973), helmed *Zandy's Bride* (Warner Bros., 1974). As with his previous efforts, it proved to be a beautiful film but on the slow side. Much of the story follows the novel. Zandy (Gene Hackman) is a rancher in the Big Sur Mountains of California who sends for a mail order bride (Liv Ullmann). Once she arrives, he treats her savagely but expects her to treat him with love and devotion. Gene Hackman as Zandy looks good, but Liv Ullmann as Hannah is all wrong. In the novel, Hannah was a plain looking easterner, which Ullmann is not, and her thick accent seems decidedly out of place. The film attempts to be an early *Heartland,* and it looks amazingly authentic, but the mechanical script never allows the characters to grow properly, and the story lacks life.

Whatever drawbacks these novels and short stories may have had, they all had the distinction of furthering the development of the western. Frederick Glidden, Ernest Haycox and Frank Gruber showed that it was a genre that could deepen the formula and make it far more adult in theme and content. Others such as Will James, Paul Wellman, Conrad Richter and Edna Ferber showed that the genre could do away with formulary elements and make it a more viable form of literature. W.R. Burnett showed that the western could merge with other genres and be something quite different. Whatever their successes, they broadened the horizons of the American western and paved the way for other writers and films that would take the genre to even greater heights and explore many untouched areas. While the film adaptations may not have always equaled their fictional counterparts, they, too, played their part in the maturation of the western.

11. The New Traditionalists

After World War II, the face of the traditional western changed. One reason can be traced directly to the influence of a rapidly maturing genre and the writers who reached beyond the boundaries of formula, discussed in the previous chapter. However, the war had also brought a new demand for realism to literature and films in general, and these changing values found their way even into the formula western. No longer would the stereotypical hero be molded in the image of the Virginian or the screen's Hopalong Cassidy. For a few more years the pulps and "B" westerns continued to churn out such fluff for the undiscriminating, but both were dying breeds. The general public had become too mature and demanded realism and depth.

The first of the new traditionalists was an author who created another archetypical — although not stereotypical — hero just as Wister had done with the Virginian. In 1946 "Rider to Nowhere" by Jack Schaefer appeared in *Argosy*. The author expanded the short story, turning it into a short novel, *Shane* (1949), his most famous work. It tells the now classic story of the disillusioned gunfighter who rides into a Wyoming valley in the midst of a struggle between homesteaders and cattlemen. The struggle can only be solved by Shane's controlled violence, after which he must ride out of the valley. On the surface, it is a deceptively simple story that had been told in countless pulp novels and "B" films, but what made Schaefer's novel so effective and original were the mythic qualities he gave the story. The novel is almost an allegory: Shane is God's instrument sent into the valley to help the forces of good — the homesteaders — against the forces of evil — the cattle baron. At one point, after he has knocked out Joe Starrett, he says to Marian, Joe's wife, "Tell him no man need be ashamed of being beaten by Shane." In a world where no one else can win, Shane can.

Alan Ladd in *Shane* (Paramount, 1953). Notice that for Shane's gunfighter outfit the film substituted buckskin rather than the more symbolic black in the novel.

When he came to direct *Shane* (Paramount, 1953), George Stevens wanted to capture the lyricism that Jack Schaefer had infused into the novel. That he succeeded is found in the film's enduring popularity; many critics point to *Shane* as the greatest western film, certainly with some justification. Not only does it follow the events of the novel with fidelity but it also captured the feeling and spirit, and this above all remains with the viewer long after the film is over.

The first scene opens with Shane (Alan Ladd) riding down out the high Tetons into a fertile valley where he meets Joe Starrett (Van Heflin), his wife Marian (Jean Arthur) and their son Joey (Brandon

James Cagney as Jeremy Rodock in *Tribute to a Bad Man* **(MGM, 1956).**

deWilde). The valley is torn with strife as Ryker (Emile Meyer), a cattleman, is attempting to push the homesteaders off the free range. Starrett hires Shane, not as a gunman but as a farmhand. On a trip into
town, Shane is drawn into an argument with Chris Calloway (Ben
Johnson), but Shane walks away without fighting. On a return trip,
Shane goads Calloway into a fight, whips him and then all of Ryker's
men gang up on Shane. Joe Starrett jumps into the fray, and together
the two men thoroughly whip the cowboys.

After this, Ryker sends for Wilson (Jack Palance), a notorious
gunman, who immediately pushes one of the farmers, Tory (Elisha
Cook, Jr.) into a fight and kills him. In order to hold the farmers
together, Starrett decides to face Wilson and Ryker, but Shane intervenes, and in a terrific fight, finally subdues Joe by using his pistol
to knock the farmer unconscious. Joey, who has come to worship
Shane, cries out that he hates him for having used a gun on his father.
As Shane rides into town to face Wilson and Ryker, Joey runs after him
to apologize. He arrives just as the showdown comes, and he sees it all.
Afterward, as Shane prepares to ride away, Joey pleads with him to

stay. In words taken straight from the novel, Shane says, "There's no going back from a killing, Joey. Right or wrong. The brand sticks and there's no going back." He rides off up into the mountains from where he came, Joey's voice trailing after him. "Come back, Shane. Pa needs you. Ma wants you, too. Shane!" The words echo against the cold mountains.

The film is so full of images, sounds and dialogue that a viewer can constantly find new rewards on repeated viewings. The unspoken relationship between Marian and Shane is clear to all, including Joe, who says as he is about to go out and face Wilson, "I know if anything happens to me, you'll be taken care of. Probably better than I could." After Shane has knocked Joe unconscious and is about to ride off to face Wilson, Marian asks, "Are you doing this for me, Shane?" Shane answers, "For you Marian. And Joe. And Little Joe." Yet the only physical contact between the two is limited to a sturdy handshake as Shane is about to ride off.

There are minor differences between the novel and film. The novel is narrated by the young boy, which adds to the story's mystical quality. While the film has no narrator, it tries hard to show the action through Joey's eyes, but the viewpoint is a multiple one. Some of the events of the novel, such as the killing of Ernie Wright, not Torrey, happen off stage and are related to the boy who in turn narrates the story. In the film, we see these events directly without Joey being there. Also, a few of the events are different. In the novel, the big fight happens in two separate sequences. First, Shane whips Chris badly. The cattleman and his men retaliate a month or so later when Shane returns to town with the farmers. The film gives us both fights as one continuous encounter, broken only by Ryker's offer to Shane to join him after he had beaten Chris. When Shane refuses, Ryker and his men jump him. In the novel, Ernie Wright is murdered by Wilson when the gunman pushes the farmer into a fight by accusing him of having Indian blood. In the film, it is the hotheaded Torrey (Elisha Cook, Jr.) who is goaded into a foolish fight when Wilson makes slurring remarks about Southerners. The novel concludes after Shane has ridden off and Chris Calloway, his arm still in the sling, comes to Starett's farm and says, "I'm a poor substitute, Starrett. But as soon as this arm's healed, I'm asking you to let me work for you." Of course, the film simply ends with Shane riding off to the mountains and Joey calling after him. The viewer already knows of Calloway's reformation; earlier he warned Shane of the trap set by Ryker.

None of these changes are substantial or in any way change the in-

Lobby card for *Monte Walsh* (Cinema Center, 1970), which calls itself "A Real Western."

tent or spirit of the novel. So much of the novel has been captured on celluloid that the changes seem minor indeed. Even the casting of Alan Ladd as Shane approaches Schaefer's description of the character. "He was not much above medium height, almost slight in build. He would have looked frail alongside father's square, solid bulk." Like the novel, this film is an outstanding example of the nostalgic vision of the Old West, not a vision as it was, but as we wish it had been.

A short novel, *First Blood* (1953), by Schaefer was an interesting follow up to *Shane*, a novel again told in first person, this time by a young boy at the threshold of manhood who becomes a deputy sheriff, then is confronted by a mob, led by the man he idolizes. In the process of standing up to the mob, he kills his hero. Made into *The Silver Whip* (TCF, 1953), it was an offbeat story, although not exactly the one Schaefer wrote. The young stage coach driver (Robert Wagner) loses his first job when he is held up by bandits. The stagecoach guard (Dale Robinson), the boy's idol, is wounded and vows vengeance. In the meantime, the sheriff (Rory Calhoun) makes the young man a deputy. Once the bandits have been captured, the sheriff is called out of town, and the guard organizes a mob. When they come to take the prisoners, the young boy shoots his idol, wounding him but not seriously, and turns back the mob. Although not a great film, it manages to tell its story reasonably well.

Many of Jack Schaefer's western short stories are among the best of their kind. "Jeremy Rodock" (1951) certainly must number among these. Narrated by a young ranch hand, it tells of rancher Rodock who is known as a hanging man. When rustlers strike, he follows them, discovering the stolen horses cloistered in a valley, their hooves damaged so that they can not get away. Rodock sets a trap and captures the thieves, but rather than hang the three men, he forces them to walk fifty miles on their bare feet. Rodock pushes them on, trying to break their spirits, and he manages to do so with two of the men. The third is too proud and too strong. Just before they reach town, Rodock puts the thieves on their horses and sets them free. Even though the young narrator has found himself upset over the treatment of the rustlers, in the end he admits of Rodock, "They don't make men like that around here any more."

Tribute to a Bad Man (MGM, 1956) used a few ideas from "Jeremy Rodock," but for the most part, the original story disappeared under typical Hollywood treatment. Into the lawless frontier of the 1870s rides a Pennsylvania grocery clerk, Steve Miller (Don Dubbins), who befriends Rodock (James Cagney). As Steve stays to grow under Rodock's tutelage, a father-son relationship develops. Steve seeks the affection of Jocasta (Irene Papas), but she loves the older Rodock, and it is through her love that Rodock learns to temper justice with mercy. Other than the fine photography and the fine performance by Cagney, the film offers little but a weak domestic drama that plays like warmed over Oedipus.

Jack Schaefer's most ambitious novel is *Monte Walsh* (1963), which strips the myth from the cowboy and shows him plausibly and authentically. Opening in 1876 when Monte is sixteen, the story carries through to his death in 1913. It is a realistic novel stripped of romanticism. The film *Monte Walsh* (National General, 1970) opens in the later years of Monte's life, and with a few exceptions, tells its own story, not Schaefer's. In the novel, Monte dies an old cowhand, buried by his best friend Chet Rollins, but the film has Chet (Jack Palance) as cowboy turned shopkeeper and murdered in a robbery. Falling back on the mythic western for its source, the climax comes with a showdown

Lobby card for *High Noon* **(Stanley Kramer, 1952), but there is no reference to Cunningham's "The Tin Star" on which the film is based.**

between Monte (Lee Marvin) and the killer. The final scene finds Monte on the range as he spots a coyote, bears down on the creature with his rifle, then does not fire. Somewhere in all of this was supposedly an ecological message which gets lost in the story's retrenching into a more traditional formula. The result is not a very good movie, although some of the parts are better than the whole.

Like *Shane,* the classic *High Noon* also came from western fiction. Originally published in *Collier's,* "The Tin Star" (1947) by John M. Cunningham was a formulary story of a sheriff in a Montana town and his young deputy. Sheriff Doane is an older man, his hands already arthritic, who is at the end of a long career. He and his deputy Toby are awaiting Jordon and his men who plan to kill the old sheriff. Toby tells the sheriff that he will stick by him until this mess is over, but after that, he is quitting. Once the fight starts, Toby is wounded, and Doane is left to fight it out alone. He, too, is wounded, but he manages to throw himself in front of a bullet meant for Toby, and Toby in turn kills the last of the gang. As Doane lies dying, he asks if Toby is still going to quit, but the youngster shakes his head.

"The Tin Star" became *High Noon* (Stanley Kramer, 1952), a classic for which Gary Cooper won an Academy Award as best actor. In the story, Marshal Will Kane (Cooper) is warned that the killer just released from prison and returning to town has promised to kill the lawman. Except for the killers coming to town and the lawman forced by his own code to face them, little else remains from Cunningham's story.

The marshal asks many people for help, including a judge (Otto Kruger) and the sheriff's former mistress (Katy Jurado), all who are characters invented for the film. An old lawman (Lon Chaney, Jr.) from whom Kane seeks advice seems closer to the character of Doane created by Cunningham than does Kane, who is neither arthritic nor old. Kane does not receive any help from his deputy (Lloyd Bridges), who actually turns against him and tries to run him out of town. In the story, the sheriff's wife is long dead, and at one point, he stops by her grave and plucks away the weeds. In the film, Sheriff Kane has just married, and this adds to his problems, seeing that his wife is a Quaker and opposed to all violence. This also presents an ironic twist when she is the only person to come to Kane's aid when she shoots one of the villains. In the story, the sheriff dies protecting his young deputy, but the film ends with Kane tossing his badge in the dust and riding out of town with his wife.

Cunningham's story is easily forgettable, but *High Noon* is an outstanding film. When the writer, Carl Foreman, and director Fred Zimmermann threw out most of the original story and substituted their own, they made the right choice, using many of the formulary conventions of the genre but adding so much more depth.

A second Cunningham story, "Yankee Gold" (1947), which first appeared in the now defunct slick magazine *Pic,* proved to be a more enjoyable short story, although the film did not reach the heights of *High Noon.* The story concerns Hull, a Southerner framed out of a government job, who drifts to Colorado where he joins crooks led by Mourret, an unreconstructed rebel, who plan to rob a local mine owner. Hull falls in love with the mine owner's daughter and betrays his former associates. He not only wins the girl but wins a job in the process. While the bare-bones outline sounds overworked and cliché ridden, Cunningham invested his character with enough individuality to make the story entertaining.

The story became *The Stranger Wore a Gun* (Scott-Brown/Columbia, 1953), one of the multitude of 3-D films spawned during the early fifties. The hero, Jeff Travis (Randolph Scott), a former member of Quantrill's Raiders, heads for Arizona at the close of the war where he takes up with Mourret (George Macready) and his men who are planning to rob a gold shipment from a local miner. Travis comes to his senses in time,

The Stranger Wore a Gun (1953) based on "Yankee Gold" by John Cunningham who is uncredited on the lobby card.

tricks the crooks into fighting among themselves and then polishes off Mourret in a glorious finale that has the two men blazing away at each other in a saloon going down in flames. The main ingredients of the short story remain intact with only one major change. Travis gets the girl all right, but she is not the mine owner's daughter, and together the two ride off to Texas to start a new life. By remaining faithful to its source, *The Stranger Wore a Gun* failed to rise above the merely adequate, but overall, it is a pleasant enough oater, despite the fists and guns shoved in the audience's faces to accommodate the 3-D process.

Another John Cunningham story, "Raiders Die Hard" (1952), which appeared in *Dime Western,* also made its way to the screen. Although the plotting reflects its pulp origins, it retains a measure of originality in having a handicapped hero. Judge Scott Ogilvie has a withered left arm as a souvenir of the Civil War. When he presides over the trial of a young tough accused of murder, the man's three brothers warn the judge that they will kill him if he sentences their brother to hang. In the meantime, a devious sheriff tries to steal the affections of the judge's girl, and just about succeeds when the final showdown comes. The sheriff proves a coward and runs away, and the judge stays to defeat the outlaws. The girl sees the error of her ways and rushes into the judge's arm to ask forgiveness.

The screen version became *Day of the Badman* (Universal, 1958), and by now the story of a town cowed by bandits was old hat. As Judge Jim Scott (Fred MacMurray) is confronted with the problem of sentencing the young killer, four members of his gang ride into town and begin to threaten everyone in sight. The judge is both afraid and yet determined to do his duty. However, the townsfolk cower before the bandits, and even the cowardly sheriff (John Ericson) asks the judge to release the prisoner. The judge remains firm. Finally, violence erupts, and the judge and his friend Sam Wyckoff (Edgar Buchannan) wipe out the gang and deliver the killer for hanging. In the process, the judge wins back his girl who had also turned against him. Very few changes were made from the Cunningham story, except the judge was given four men to face with rather than three, which invites comparison to *High Noon*. Despite its familiarity, *Day of the Badman* emerges as a good, taut little thriller.

Another formulary writer, Frank Bonham, said of his first novel, *Lost Stage Valley* (1948), that it "celebrates the courage and determination of the men who drove the stages and the passengers who rode them." Bonham had written extensively for pulps before this, and his writing, especially his plotting, showed his origins. He wrote swift, lean action stories with romantic heroes. Set in Arizona during the Civil War, *Lost Stage Valley* concerns the Apache Pass Stage Line, which has been losing coaches over a period of time. Butterfield sends two investigators, Grif Holbrook and Barney Broderick, to handle the situation. For most of the novel, Grif fights getting close to his young companion, but during the climactic battle, he comes to realize that Barney has the makings of a superior man. *Lost Stage Valley* is an enjoyable first novel, and it is the relationship between the two undercover agents that makes it so.

Lost Stage Valley was the only film adaptation of a Frank Bonham work, reaching the screen as *Stage to Tucson* (Columbia, 1950). In many respects, the film stayed close to the novel. When several stolen stagecoaches in Arizona wind up in Atlanta, Grif Holbrook (Rod Cameron) and Barney Broderick (Wayne Morris) are sent to investigate. They discover that Senator Jim Maroon (Roy Roberts) is behind the troubles. He claims he is helping the South but in reality he is lining his own pockets. While the film changed the older-younger relationship between the main characters, it provided a spark by having them quarrel over Kate Crocker (Kay Buckley), even coming to blows. A sense of humor

Bend of the River (1952) was based on *Bend of the Snake* by Bill Gulick, who is uncredited on the lobby card.

also added to the proceedings. *Stage to Tucson* proves to be a likable "B" and a good adaptation. The plot may be a bit farfetched, but both novel and film have enough action to keep things moving right along.

While Frank Bonham had a faithful film adaptation of his novel, Bill Gulick's first western, *Bend of the Snake* (1950), disappeared on the screen. The novel was very much a conventional action story of a gunman who joins up with settlers in Oregon. It was well written, but when it became *Bend of the River* (Universal, 1952), most of the events and characters had been changed until little resemblance to the novel remained. Amazingly, this film became director Anthony Mann's most satisfying western. The hero, Glyn McLyntock (James Stewart), not only leads the settlers into Oregon but also fights to settle with them and, in doing so, wipe out his past as a border raider. McLyntock's alter ego is Emerson Cole (Arthur Kennedy), a likable gunman with no intention of reforming. When the two meet in a last, desperate struggle in the middle of the Snake River, McLyntock is symbolically washed clean as Cole's body is carried away by the rushing water. None of these events are part of the novel.

Another formulary western writer, who writes under the pseudo-nyms of Matt Kinkaid and Clay Randall as well as his own name, is Clifton Adams. His best novels are those he wrote in the late sixties, such as *The Last Days of Wolf Garnett* (1970), which won the Spur Award from the Western Writers of America as best western novel of the year. To this novel and others like it, he brought a fine sensitivity to his depiction of the harsh realities of frontier life. He displayed a rare ability to create vivid and realistic women characters. Unfortunately his only two novels to reach the screen were from his earlier period and are formulary westerns minus the strengths that he was later to exhibit.

His first novel, *The Desperado* (1950), was filmed under the same title (Allied Artists, 1954) and was part of the last series of "B" westerns ever made. It tells the story of two young Texans, Tall Cameron (James J. Lydon) and Ray Novack (Rayford Barnes), who flee carpetbaggers. They meet a fugitive gunfighter, Sam Garrett (Wayne Morris), who trails along with the boys. When the boys have a falling out, Novack kills a sheriff and his deputy. Tall Cameron is arrested, and Garrett helps to prove the boy innocent and to capture Novack. While the film follows the novel closely, it is tired looking and without much life. The novel *Gambling Man* (1956), another formulary western, fared no better on the screen. Called *Outlaw's Son* (United Artists, 1957), it told of Nate Blaine (Dane Clark), an outlaw who returns from prison to keep his son from a life of crime. The film is notable for being Ellen Drew's last film appearance. Although directed by Lesley Selander, who ably helmed so many of the Paramount "B" westerns, he had a poor script based on a so-so novel. Although Selander tries to inject some life into the proceedings, the film never rises above the level of the second half of a double bill.

One writer of the fifties who tried to invest some depth into his formulary westerns was Norman A. Fox, who had several of his novels made into films. *Roughshod* (1951) told the story of a gunfighter who longs to find something solid around which to build a life. During the course of the novel, gunman Reb Kittredge is hired by Matt Telford to drive Dan Saxon and his daughter Rita off their ranch. When Saxon purposely loses his ranch to Kittredge in a poker game, it pits the hero against Telford. The novel became *Gunsmoke* (Universal, 1953) an Audie Murphy vehicle that drops a few characters and adds a few but, on the whole, is faithful to its source. After Kittredge (Audie Murphy) is tricked into a card game and wins the ranch, the story becomes all too predictable, and throughout, the characters never seem especially fresh. Yet, *Gunsmoke* is an entertaining little film with some nice performances.

Tall Man Riding (1951) became an adequate oater (Warner Bros., 1955) starring Randolph Scott and again directed efficiently by Lesley Selander. Larry Madden (Randolph Scott) returns to his hometown to wreak vengeance on Tuck Ordway (Robert Barrat), the cattle baron who had him run off and his ranch burned to keep Madden from marrying his daughter, Corinna (Dorothy Malone). Added to the plot is an evil saloon owner, a crooked lawyer and a gunman, the Pecos Kid, who try to muscle in on Ordway. At the showdown, Madden discovers that Ordway is blind, and he saves him from being killed by the Pecos Kid. Understanding that she still loves Madden, Corinna goes back to him with her father's blessing. If there is a problem with the film, it lies in the talky script which often drags between the action. Still, like the novel, it invests some depth in the characters, especially Madden and Ordway. In addition, both the novel and film are enjoyable examples of the genre.

A western coming-of-age novel, *The Rawhide Years* (1953), tells the story of Ben Mathews, an orphan who needs to discover the truth about his past. Unlike Fox's other novels, this one covered a number of years and a vast amount of territory from Mississippi to Montana. However, the film (Universal, 1956) dropped the novel's plot, substituting an inferior one of its own. Gambler Ben Mathews (Tony Curtis) is falsely accused of a murder, and after hiding out for three yars, returns to clear himself and to find Zoe (Colleen Miller), the girl he left behind. With the aid of Rick Harper (Arthur Kennedy), he wipes out the gang headed by Andre Boucher (Peter Van Eyck) and wins back Zoe. With the exception of its sense of humor, this is a standard oater in which the characters seldom come alive. Only Arthur Kennedy gives a good performance, playing the same type of character, although far less malevolent, that he had played in *Bend of the River* four years earlier.

The best of the films adapted from a Norman Fox novel is *Night Passage* (Universal, 1957), a slick, polished affair about two brothers, one good (James Stewart), one bad (Audie Murphy), who get mixed up in a train robbery. The script by Borden Chase followed the events of Fox's novel (1956) but was all too familiar, so much so that Anthony Mann, set to direct, walked out because he objected to the weak script. Certainly it holds no surprises, and the central character has no devils driving him as in Mann's *Winchester 73* or *The Naked Spur,* both James Stewart vehicles. Grant McLaine (James Stewart) is hired by the railroad to safeguard the delivery of a $10,000 payroll. The train is robbed by the Utica Kid (Audie Murphy) and his gang, and Grant takes after them. It turns out that the Utica Kid is also McLaine's brother, and although Mclaine tries to get his brother to go straight, the Kid refuses until the very end when, as McLaine is surrounded by the gang and appears doomed, the Kid jumps sides and saves his brother at the cost of his own life. If the story is a little too predictable, the fine performances, good photography and rip-roaring direction help to smooth the rough spots.

In many respects, Norman A. Fox is reminiscent of Ernest Haycox. Certainly, both authors attempted to deepen and enrich the formulary western, specifically by creating complex characters whose motivations are key to the plots. Often these men are caught up in a quest for vengeance like Reb Kittredge of *Tall Man Riding* or for self knowledge like Ben Mathews of *The Rawhide Years*. It is the characters who are also are the core of the films. While none of the adaptations proved especially notable, all were enjoyable and reflected the author's care in creating believable and well rounded characters.

Although Todhunter Ballard wrote extensively for motion pictures and television, only one novel of his reached the screen. His first western, *Two Edged Vengeance* (1952), was a standard revenge story of son seeking the man who murdered his father. While a skillful writer, he was hardly original, and it is only fitting that Republic, a studio noted for its "B" product, should have adapted this novel. The film, *The Outcast* (Republic, 1954), was given color and a better than average cast, and like the novel, it was nothing new, although as directed by William Witney, a master of "B" westerns and serials, it proved to be an entertaining minor "A" without pretensions. Jed Cosgrave (John Derek) returns to the range where his uncle, Major Cosgrave (Jim Davis), has killed his father and forged a will to gain possession to a vast ranch. Jet has two love interests to keep him busy during his fight with his uncle, and he is constantly playing with his gun as a way of reinforcing the image of his manhood. This film, which premiered a year after the sexually symbolic *Johnny Guitar,* is also full of sexual overtones, and certainly the hero's gun becomes a low-keyed phallic symbol. However, the film lacks the continuously overt symbolism of *Johnny Guitar,* although the sexual drive of Jed Cosgrave does add a measure of originality not found in the novel.

Another formulary western writer, Wayne D. Overholster, wrote under his own name as well as a variety of pseudonyms. Under the moniker of "Lee Leighton" he penned *Law Man* (1953), which appeared on the screen as *Star in the Dust* (Universal, 1956), a programmer concerning a small Western town awaiting the hanging of a killer (Richard Boone), the cattlemen who want to save him, the farmers who want to hang him, the banker (Leif Erickson) who hired him and the sheriff (John Agar) who has to straighten it all out. Although the novel *Cast a Long Shadow* (1955), written under the Overholster name, was a fine, offbeat novel narrated in first person by the hero, the film (United Artists, 1959) was just another programmer starring Audie Murphy. It is too bad that Overholster's work was not treated better by Hollywood because he was a first rate writer of formulary westerns who was adept at creating characters and setting.

Beginning in 1950 with the publication of *No Survivors,* Henry Wilson Allen wrote a number of good westerns under the pseudonyms of Will Henry and Clay Fisher. Several of these, including the much underrated *Yellowstone Kelly* (discussed in Chapter Four), were made into films of varying quality. His first novel, *Santa Fe Passage* (1952), adapted for the screen (Republic, 1955) is an action packed story of a scout (John Payne) who agrees to get a wagon train loaded with guns through hostile Indian country. Only a skeleton of the original plot remained, which really didn't matter since neither the book nor the film were anything other than forgettable entertainment. A better novel was *The Tall Men* (1954) if for no other reason than Allen created a more complex central character in Ben Allison. Like *Blazing Guns on the Chisholm Trail* by Bordon Chase, this is a novel of a trail drive from Texas to Montana. The film (TCF, 1955) slanted the script as a star vehicle, miscasting Ben Allison (Clark Gable) as well as his love interest, Nella (Jane Russell). Only the character of Nathan Stark (Robert Ryan) emerges as the novel meant him to be, a "tall" man with strength to win his dreams.

Both *Santa Fe Passage* and *The Tall Men* were written under the Clay Fisher pseudonym, and it is interesting to note how the pen name came about. When Random House fiction editor Harry Maul rejected Allen's second novel because it was too grim, Allen decided that he must be writing two separate kinds of fiction. From that point, every time Maul rejected one of Allen's novels, it became a "Clay Fisher" book. Allen himself admitted that the only real difference between his two pseudonyms was that he used Clay Fisher when the novel tended to have a bit more historical base.

Even though they both had an historical base, *To Follow a Flag* (1952) and *Journey to Shiloh* (1960) were published under the Will Henry pseudonym. As a film, *Pillars of the Sky* (Universal, 1956) is a dreary cavalry versus Indians story enlivened only by the fact that the hero officer (Jeff Chandler) doesn't get the girl in the end because she goes back to her husband. *Journey to Shiloh* (Universal, 1968), was a dull, pretentious and talky story of seven friends known as the Concho

County Comanches who go off to join the Confederate Army and are killed off in reverse order of their billing. Neither of these films does justice to the novels on which they are based.

Two other novels published under the moniker of Will Henry were excellent entertainment, but like all the films based on his work, the adaptations were terrible. The first, *MacKenna's Gold* (1963), is an examination of greed much along the lines of B. Traven's *The Treasure of Sierra Madre,* only it is presented in formulary western conventions. As a film (Columbia, 1969), it was a star vehicle for Gregory Peck as MacKenna, with an all-star cast backing him up. In reality, the film bore little resemblance to the novel, emerging as a poorly directed, pretentious attempt at a grand statement about greed, and it was a failure on all counts. The last filmed Allen novel was *Who Rides with Wyatt* (1954), a retelling of the Tombstone years and the gunfight at the O.K. Corral in a much more romantic tone than W.R. Burnett's earlier *Saint Johnson.* Changing the title to *Young Billy Young* (United Artists, 1969), the film dropped all mention of Wyatt Earp and substituted a story of a town lawman who reforms a tough kid. The bleak relationship between Wyatt Earp and the Ringo Kid, the heart of the novel, has been so emasculated that there is no real connection between novel and film.

Louis L'Amour was a prolific writer, and it is only natural that many of his formulary western novels and short stories have been adapted for the films, although the most important has remained his first, *Hondo* (discussed in Chapter 4). Most other adaptations have fared less well. A minor short story, "Rider of the Ruby Hills," was turned into *Treasure of the Ruby Hills* (United Artists, 1955) wherein a rancher (Zachary Scott) gets mixed up in a range war with hidden treasure on the side. It is a routine effort at best. *Killkenny* (1954) became *Blackjack Ketchum, Desperado* (Columbia, 1956), a standard tale of a gunman (Howard Duff) who tries to live down his reputation but is forced to strap on his six-shooters one last time when an evil cattle baron (Victor Jory) attempts to take over a peaceful valley. Though it has overtones of *Shane,* the film went in another direction by having the hero pursue romance rather vigorously. *Utah Blaine* (Columbia, 1957), based on the novel (1954) written under the pseudonym of Jim Mayo, looks better than it plays due to imaginative camera angles, but the plot is all too predictable. Utah Blaine (Rory Calhoun) is given half a ranch when he saves a man from hanging, then finds the ranch is under siege by a local cattle baron. By story's end, he has taken the measure of the villain. *Guns of the Timberland* (Warner Bros., 1960) is offbeat in that it concerns partners in a logging business who conflict with local ranchers. Overall, it is a dreary affair, and even the novel (1955) was not up to L'Amour's usual standards.

With the possible exception of *Hondo,* Louis L'Amour has written competent and exciting westerns but no great ones. *Heller with a Gun* (1955) is a good example. It is the story of King Marby, a typical L'Amour hero, who gets involved with a traveling threatrical troupe. Filmed as *Heller in Pink Tights* (Paramount, 1960), the film shifts the emphasis from the gunfighter (Steve Forrest) to the troupe itself, the manager (Anthony Quinn) and the leading lady, Angel (Sophia Loren). Director George Cukor, helming his only western, produced a wonderful film, deepening the characters and situations and tuning the whole thing into a romantic comedy mixed with slices of Americana, but in the process, most of the L'Amour novel disappeared. Even the character of King Marby has been radically changed.

Several important differences exist between book and film. A subplot in the novel involving a ruthless killer who is hired by the troupe to guide them across the prairies is dropped. The film has Marby tag along because he is interested in Angela. In the novel, Angela turns against Marby because she cannot understand the western code, just as Molly rebels in *The Virginian,* and Marby understands that their values will always be in conflict. He voluntarily rides out of her life, leaving her to Tom Healy, the manager. In the film, Healy proves himself an equal of Marby, not with a gun but with his spirit and determination, and Angela realizes that it is Healy she loves. There is also the emphasis on secondary characters. L'Amour spent little time developing them, consigning most of his efforts to the story of King Marby. On the other hand, Cukor gives us some wonderful supporting characters. There's Doc Montague (Edmund Lowe), a broken-down, hypochondriacal Shakespearean ham; Loran Hathaway (Eileen Heckart), the second leading lady dressed in a red fright wig constantly chuckling wildly over her daughter; the daughter, Della Southby (Margaret O'Brien), the pretty and guarded ingenue; and finally, De Leon (Raymond Novarro), the villainous employer of Marby. The novel is fluff, entertaining fluff to be sure, but fluff. The film has many wonderful Cukor touches that enrich it far beyond what the novel accomplished.

Two other adaptations of L'Amour's novels rate mention. *Kid Rodelo* (Trident Films, 1966) was in reality a Spanish film based on L'Amour's novel (1966). This was typical L'Amour, but American director Richard Carlson, who also appeared in the film with a cast principally of Americans, turned the story of an ex-convict (Don Murray) wreaking vengeance on the men who bilked him and sent him to prison into a blood-splattered spaghetti-like western amazingly aimed at the juvenile audience. *Catlow* (MGM, 1971), although distributed by MGM, was another European western with an American director (Sam Wanamaker) and American cast; it misses all the humor in the L'Amour novel (1963) and butchers the book.

Much western literature that was made into films often originated in slick magazines, foremost among which was *The Saturday Evening Post.* The works of many authors previously discussed appeared among its pages, but the magazine did not harken strictly with big name writers. Occasionally a lesser writer was serialized in *Post,* and once that happened, that writer's chances of having his work adapted for the screen rose considerably. Such was the case with T.T. Flynn, whose *The Man from Laramie* was serialized in the *Post* in 1954, and later appeared as an original paperback novel from Pocket Books. Flynn never again wrote an important work.

As with most of *Post's* serializations of westerns, *The Man from Laramie* was formula all the way. Will Lockhart travels from Wyoming to New Mexico in search of the man who sold repeating rifles to the Indians, which indirectly caused the death of Will's brother. Once in New Mexico, Lockhart encounters trouble with a ranch called Barb, owned by Alec Waggonman and run by Vic Hansbro. Along the way, Lockhart falls in love with the rancher's daughter and is accused of killing her brother. Lockhart proves his innocence and exposes foreman Vic Hansbro as the gunrunner as well as the murderer. While the novel reads easily in the slick style associated with the *Post,* it seldom rises above adequate, a weak imitation of Luke Short.

When *The Man from Laramie* (Columbia, 1954) came to the screen, it was part of the Anthony Mann series with James Stewart that was to help revitalize the western film in the 1950s. While the film retains most of the plot, Mann and his scriptwriters concentrated on the obsessiveness of Lockhart (James Stewart). However, Lockhart is not the only one who is obsessed. His mirror image is the almost blind, megalomaniacal Alec Waggonman (Donald Crisp). The old man is in the process of choosing a successor to his empire. When he picks his son, Dave (Alex Nicol), who is weak and ineffectual, ranch foreman Vic Hansbro (Arthur Kennedy) is outraged since he feels that it is he who has held the empire together for years.

Occasionally, the film turns very brutal, and some of these scene are drawn directly from the novel. An early incident has Dave Waggonman slaughter a whole herd of mules owned by Lockhart because he claims that Lockhart is trespassing on. While this is strong stuff, it wasn't enough for Mann who had his writers add and change other scenes to bring them more in line with the hero's obsessiveness. At one point, Dave has his men hold Lockhart while he shoots him in the hand at point blank range. When Dave is murdered by Hansbro, the blame easily falls on Lockhart. When old man Waggonman discovers the truth about his foreman, Hansbro pushes him from the cliff. In the end, Lockhart has Hansbro in his clutches, but he doesn't kill him. Instead, he sets him free with full knowledge that the Indians will kill Hansbro because they believe he has betrayed them. This ending is far more satisfying and far more in keeping with the screen character of Lockhart than the novel's ending where villain and hero have the more traditional gunfight.

Just before he died in 1957, director Anthony Mann announced his intention to film *King Lear* as a western. In a sense, the character of Alec Waggonman can be seen as a dress rehearsal. As the character created by T.T. Flynn, Waggonman was only an old man who comes to understand that he's been wrong in his judgments, and he is alive at the end to make amends. Not so in the film. His tragedy here is far deeper. Only at the moment of his death does he come to realize how wasted his life and that of his son have been. In that way, he mirrors Lear.

A far better writer than T.T. Flynn was Donald Hamilton, the author of only five western novels who, once he turned to writing the superspy Matt Helm series, abandoned the genre. His first western appeared as a serial in *Collier's,* and he later expanded it into *Smoky Valley* (1954), a well-done albeit conventional story of small ranchers beset upon by a larger one. However, the novel features Hamilton's quintessential hero, John Parrish, a self-contained, quiet man with a clear understanding of his own strengths and weaknesses. Parrish tries to avoid trouble, but when he is pushed too far, he responds in kind. Matters are complicated when he falls in love with Judith, the cattle baron's daughter.

On the screen, the novel became *The Violent Men* (Columbia, 1955), a satisfying action film. The script made several changes, all based around a character that did not exist in the novel, adding a sense of maturity even if it did not improve anything. In the novel, the heroine, Judith, has a sister, Martha. However, in the film, Martha (Barbara Stanwyck) is Judith's mother who Judith (Dianne Foster) bitterly resents because she knows that Martha is having an affair with Cole (Brian Keith), the ranch foreman. It is Martha who manipulates events until they backfire in an all out range war ultimately won by Parrish (Glenn Ford).

Parrish is the same character on the screen as Hamilton created him, and this is important to the overall concept of the story. Parrish tries to avoid trouble, and just when everyone, including Anchor, believes him to be a spineless weakling, he turns on them with vicious and logical force. Even when he kills Cole, he does so with cool precision, calmly shooting him from a distance where the fast draw becomes ineffective. In the last analysis, if the film and novel seem overly familiar, it's because the basic story has been done so many times before. However, the familiarity doesn't interfere with the entertainment value of either the novel or film.

The Big Country (1958), also by Hamilton, is an updating of Zane Grey's *To the Last Man,* telling the story of a feud between two warring families. James McKay, a Maryland sea captain, comes to Texas in 1886 to marry the daughter of a local cattleman, who is one part of the feud. As in *Smokey Valley/The Violent Men,* the hero attempts to stay out of the conflict, even though his bride to be is the daughter of one of the participants. What is interesting about this novel is the reversal of East-West values. Here, the Easterner is more than the equal of any man on the ranch, capable of riding and subduing bucking broncos, of riding off unescorted across the Texas plains, of fending for himself and of facing up to the villains.

As a film, *The Big Country* (United Artists, 1958) became a star-studded epic running almost three hours. Four writers were employed, and William Wyler, a very talented director, was given control. Somehow, most of the original story and most of the relationships show up intact. McKay (Gregory Peck) goes west to marry Patricia Terrill (Caroll Baker), only to discover that her father (Charles Bickford) and Rufus Hennassey (Burl Ives), two patriarchs of the feuding families, are at war over Big Muddy, a ranch owned by Julie Maragon (Jean Simmons). At first, everyone on the ranch, including foreman Steve Leach (Charlton Heston), believe McKay to be a coward because he refuses to go along with their hazing and to join in the feud. When McKay realizes that even Patricia does not understand him, he turns to Julie from whom he purchases Big Muddy and thus jumps into the center of the hurricane, hoping to calm the storm himself. But when Julie is kidnapped by Rufus' son, Buck (Chuck Connors), McKay goes into the Hennassey lair to rescue her, and by the time it is all over, no one doubts the hero's courage.

There is surprisingly little difference between the novel and film.

In the novel, the relationship between Steve Leach, the ranch foreman, and Patricia is more overt. It is clear that they have made love long before she became engaged to McKay. The film is less clear on the issue, although Leach's smoldering looks in her direction and her responses to his advances seem to hint at such a liaison. If there is an important difference, it lies in pace. The novel moves quickly, the way formulary western fiction should, but the film saunters along, content to build characters at the expense of action.

More noted for his mystery and crime fiction, Elmore Leonard began his career writing a number of highly polished westerns. His first to reach the screen was a short story, "The Captives" (1955), which appeared in *Argosy*. It tells the story of Pat Brennan, who hitches a ride on a stageocach that has been chartered by Willard Mims and his new bride, Doretta, the daughter of stagecoach magnate Gateway. The stage is held up by three of the worst bandits in the West. After they kill the driver, they take Brennan and the married couple as prisoners. Mims is weak and tells the outlaws who Doretta is. For his betrayal, the outlaws kill him and then try to ransom the girl for $50,000. When two of the outlaws are out of camp, Doretta distracts the remaining one, allowing Brennan to jump him and kill him. Before the other two can recover, Brennan and Doretta have killed them, too.

While Leonard's story relies on action as did most of his western fiction, he also explored character. Brennan is a stereotypical hero, but in Doretta he created a full character. When the story opens, she is a mousey little woman who keeps saying, "I can't help it." By the end, she has become a strong woman, fully capable of helping Brennan. Without her change of character, neither she nor Brennan would have survived.

On screen, the story became *The Tall T* (Columbia, 1957), one of the films in the Budd Boetticher–Randolph Scott cannon. However, Burt Kennedy's script must also come in for its share of praise. Despite the forced comedy at the beginning, once the plot takes over and Brennan (Randolph Scott) and the others are captured, the suspense builds steadily to a satisfying climax. Kennedy did an excellent job translating Leonard's story, keeping all the plot complications intact. However, the director did shift the emphasis just slightly, and in doing so, created a classic confrontation between good and evil, a confrontation that is often clouded in shades of gray rather than the traditional black and white. The main struggle is between Brennan, the hero, and Usher (Richard Boone), the villain, who are mirror images of one another. Both are laconic loners. Brennan is a slightly world-weary, puritanical hero who finds himself at the mercy of the more flamboyant yet desperately lonely Usher. Both try to avoid the inevitable showdown, yet both know that, if it comes, they must face it. The existentialist end where Brennan outduels Usher is a hollow victory for Brennan who has failed to prove that he is either stronger or wiser. He has simply proven more devious by using the wiles of a woman to gain his own freedom. If anything, his is a Pyrrhic victory since he has come to understand that life is built upon chance. It could just have easily been Usher who walked away leaving Brennan lying in the dust. In many ways, this is the bleakest of Boetticher's films. It is also an extremely faithful adaptation that is even better than the good short story on which it is based.

Leonard's *Hombre* (1961) was voted among the twenty-five best western novels of all time by the Western Writers of America, and it is a fine novel. Molded in formulary terms, it goes far beyond such rigid categorizing to explore the character of a man who exists on his own terms. Like *Shane,* this novel is told from the viewpoint of a young person, Carl Allen, 21, who works for a stageline. While he seems much younger than John Russell, called Hombre, the fact is that they are both about the same age. From the first, Carl is fascinated by Russell. Russell has lived with the Apaches, and while he is white, he is Apache in soul and spirit. In an early encounter in a bar, Russell calmly smashes his rifle butt into the face of a man harassing an Apache friend. Later, when Russell is stranded with the other stagecoach passengers, it is he who saves them and ultimately sacrifices his life for them in an almost Christlike gesture. The events carry the reader along, but it is in the character of Russell where this novel comes alive, remaining with the reader long after the book has been put aside. In addition, the lean prose and sharp dialogue add to the effectiveness of the novel.

In *Hombre* (20th Century–Fox, 1967), an important change occurs in the character of Russell (Paul Newman). In the novel, the narrator describes him as having some Mexican blood, but as played by Paul Newman, his blue eyes brilliant the first time he walks on the screen dressed as an Apache, it is easy to see that this character is all white. However, like the novel, he speaks very little, and his character seems cold and unsympathetic. At first ostracized by the stagecoach passengers, much as Ringo was ostracized in *Stagecoach,* Russell reluctantly comes to their aid, due mainly to the taunts of Jesse (Diane Cilento), a tough but sympathetic working woman. Like the novel, the film is also a pessimistic variant on *Stagecoach.* A divergent group of passengers is thrown together under adverse circumstances. In this case, the hero, Russell, is killed by Grimes (Richard Boone) and his men just as he kills them.

The novel is one of the really great formulary westerns — a revisionist view, but nevertheless, within the formulary mold — that is part *Stagecoach*, part *Treasure of Sierra Madre*. In addition, both the photography and the direction are excellent. All the performances are also of the highest caliber, especially those of Newman as Russell and March as the banker. Although the script invents the characters of Jesse and Grimes, it is a literate adaptation that sticks very closely to the novel. But too often, the film fails to involve us, especially in the character of Russell who is at the center of the film. In the novel, the narrator made us care by caring himself, but we have no such help in the film. We must take Russell just as the others take him — on his own terms — and his basic coldness distances the film. Finally, the characters themselves have no real depth; they are personalities and types. There is the crooked banker who blusters and fusses; his long suffering wife who hates Indians so much that she refuses to sit beside an Indian-lover; the Mexican stage driver; the Mexican bandit; a young couple whose marriage is on the rocks; the cruel outlaw leader; and finally, the stoic hero. In the final analysis, *Hombre* remains a fine motion picture, one in which the diverse elements blend together very successfully, yet it is a film that fails to be the great classic it sought to be.

Far more conventional than *Hombre* is Elmore Leonard's *Valdez Is Coming* (1970). When a rich rancher, Tanner, forces Bob Valdez to kill a black man, Valdez tries to extract money from Tanner for the widow. Tanner has his men humiliate Valdez and throw him off his land, but in his past, the soft-talking, easy-going Valdez was both a scout for the army and a marshal. He begins to hound Tanner, killing his men and finally kidnapping his wife. In the end, Valdez wins, turning both Tanner's men and Tanner's wife against him; it is Tanner who is humiliated. *Valdez Is Coming* is an enjoyable book, although it is a formulary western, revisionist only in the sense that the hero is of Mexican descent.

Like the novel, the film *Valdez Is Coming* (Norlan/Ira Steiner Productions, 1970) stresses the sterling character of Mexican-American Valdez (Burt Lancaster), a man who persists in pursuing a just compensation for the pregnant Apache wife of the black man Valdez is forced to kill. But while the story follows the novel very closely, the casting of Lancaster as Valdez is all wrong. He is too much associated with all-American roles — or at least with roles that do not require him to play ethnic characters. The part cries out for a Latino, and no matter how hard Lancaster tries, he cannot convince us that he is one.

On the other hand, the film is an excellent action piece, ably directed by Edwin Sherrin in his first-time effort. There is one particularly exciting scene where Valdez ambushes his pursuers. He sits high atop a ridge, and with his Sharps rifle he once used on buffalo, shoots half a dozen of the horsemen from extremely long range. Still, a scene like this is far more exciting if we have come to care about the characters, and the well written script has allowed us to do exactly that. Valdez is a warm, caring man who has been pushed too far. He is far warmer than John Russell in *Hombre.* Even so, this film is a lesser achievement than *Hombre* for two reasons. First, the original story is too much in the formula mold, exciting and enjoyable, but nothing new. Second, and more importantly, the casting of Lancaster greatly weakens the integrity of the film.

Elmore Leonard turned to writing far more lucrative crime thrillers like *Stick, The Switch,* and *52 Pick Up.* Although the crime thrillers have brought him far more fame and fortune than his westerns, he has never come close to matching the power of *Hombre.* On the whole, his westerns seem better plotted and better written. It is also interesting to note that the western films based on his novels are far superior to the film adaptations of *Mr. Majestyk, The Big Bounce, The Moonshine War, Stick* and *52 Pick Up.*

A popular paperback series featuring a character named Buchanan appeared in 1956 with *The Name's Buchanan* by Jonas Ward, a pseudonym for William Ard, who went on to write five more titles in the series. After Ard's death, the series continued with other writers. All entries, including the first, were formulary westerns filled with cardboard characters and stereotypical situations. Buchanan is a loner and soldier of fortune who rides through the West encountering many adventures. In his first novel, he finds himself no longer in the employment of a Mexican revolutionary bandit and heads back for the United States. Just across the border into Texas, he encounters a Mexican girl who has been raped by Roy Agry, one of the crooked clan that runs Agrytown. Buchanan becomes involved in the fight against the dastardly family, which ends with the apocalyptic destruction of the evil town. Of his whole family, only Simon Agry survives, his mind gone, roaming the burned out street looking for his money.

Director Budd Boetticher and scenarist Charles Lang saw the weaknesses in the novel and opted for a lighter approach, turning *Buchanan Rides Alone* (Scott, Brown Productions, 1958) into a tongue-in-cheek farce. Buchanan shuffles from one situation to another without ever quite understanding why the other characters act as they do. When he rides into Agrytown, a place so corrupt that the ruling family is trying to double-cross each other, he is thrown into jail with Juan (Manuel Rojas), who has killed one of the Agrys for molesting his sister. While the Agrys try to cheat each other out of the ransom money, Buchanan is saved from hanging by Pecos, a fellow Texan. In the escape Pecos is killed, which is the only scene which goes against the farcical tone. The climax has Buchanan in possession of the ransom money and holding off the Agrys. In their greed, the villains turn on one another.

Beside the crucial changes in tone and mood, there is one key difference between novel and film. In the novel, Buchanan kills Abe Carbo, a vicious henchman of the Agrys, driving a knife deep into his belly. However, in the film, Carbo (Craig Stevens) survives, the one man who has amidst all the betrayals and backstabbings remained loyal to Simon Agry (Tol Avery). In fact Carbo, who will inherit Agrytown now that his boss is dead, has the last line of the film. As he glances around at the bodies scattered across the landscape, he turns to the townspeople and says, "Well, don't just stand there. Go and get the spades." It may be that this film had some influence on Akira Kurosawa when he came to make *Yojimbo* (1961), which later became the model for the Italian western *A Fistful of Dollars* (1964). The plots of both bear striking similarities to *Buchanan Rides Alone*.

Revenge is often a plot device in formulary western fiction, a device that Al Dewlen used in *The Night of the Tiger* (1956). The central character, Julius Rupp, is returning home to his wife he foolishly left eleven years before, his saddlebags full of money. One night, three men accuse him of cattle rustling, jump him, brand his chest and steal his money. He finally does return home and takes his vengeance on those responsible. The book is over-written and pretentious. It tries to invest some sort of mythological, legendary aura to the plot, and includes an introduction in which a census taker in 1950 hears the story and is entranced by it — but it is flat and uninvolving.

The book became *Ride Beyond Vengeance* (Tiger Co./Sentinel Films/Fenady Associates, 1966). On so many levels, this film proves disappointing. First, it had the appearance of a made-for-television film, which is not surprising since it was made by the same production team responsible for Chuck Connor's television series *Branded*. Connor also played Julius Rupp. Second, a double flashback is used to tell the story that, with the exception of the introduction, novelist Dewlen told chronologically; this complex structure slowed the film considerably. What scriptwriter Andrew Fenady did to improve the story was drop several characters who cluttered the story, and he also dropped the introduction. The only notable feature is the violence, which many critics condemned, but in retrospect, can be seen as a response to the Italian westerns that were at the time flooding the domestic market.

Like Norman Fox and Donald Hamilton, Frank O'Rourke tried to fill his novels with characters that avoided the stereotypical. Such a novel was *The Bravados* (1957). This story opens as three prisoners escape, killing a jail guard, kidnapping the daughter of the town's richest merchant and making their getaway on stolen thoroughbred horses. The dead guard proves to be the sheriff's cousin; the girl is the fiancée of Jim Douglas, the novel's hero; and the horses belong to Josefa, a lady rancher. These three form a posse and pursue the fugitives. When the kidnapped girl, Emma, is rescued, she lies to Jim Douglas that she was not raped. When he discovers the truth — that she was raped by all four men — he dumps her, not for being raped but for lying. The end finds Douglas paired with Josefa.

The film *The Bravados* (TCF, 1958) throws out most of the novel and substitutes a story of Jim Douglas (Gregory Peck), who arrives in town seeking four outlaws who he believes raped and killed his wife. The four men escape, and Douglas takes after them, killing them one by one as each protests his innocence. When Douglas faces the lone survivor, he learns that the four outlaws were guiltless and that a neighbor was the actual culprit. When he returns to town, the citizens acclaim Douglas a hero, but he knows his is a hollow victory. He is a murderer himself.

At rare moments, there is power in this film, especially in the scene where Douglas realizes that he has killed in vain. However, most of the film is a lackluster affair, and too often Peck seems to be sleepwalking through his part. In addition, Josefa (Joan Collins) is wasted, her character having nothing to do but wait around for Douglas to return. In the novel, she is an integral part of the action, refusing to sit back and let the men take care of things. Despite objections from Douglas and the other men, she joins in the hunt. In addition, the film is full of one-dimensional characters, including Douglas himself, whose obsessive revenge is the cornerstone of the plot. The only really consistently outstanding feature is the photography, which often highlights the gorges and mountains of Yucatan and Jalisco where the film was shot.

A far more interesting novel by Frank O'Rourke is *A Mule for the Marquesa* (1965), which tries hard to be something more than a formulistic western and for the most part succeeds. When a wealthy miner's wife is kidnapped by Raza and taken into Mexico, the miner, Grant, hires Fardan to get her back. Fardan in turn hires three other men, and these mercenaries cross the border and penetrate deep into rebel country, finally rescuing Mrs. Grant. Grant is an old man, and it turns out that his young wife has rigged the kidnapping to gain control of several mines of Grant. Even though Fardan knows this, he carries out his part of the deal and takes Mrs. Grant back to her husband. The rebel forces of Raza pursue, there are pitched battles, one of the mercenaries dies; and, in the end, Raza is killed and Mrs. Grant returned safely to her husband. Certainly, *A Mule for the Marquesa* is not a great novel. It is, however, an entertaining one with an unusual setting — Mexico during the revolution. Also, the complete absence of a romantic interest for the hero is refreshing. The only woman character, Mrs. Grant, is certainly less than admirable, although she grows and changes as the story progresses.

The novel became *The Professionals* (Columbia, 1966), one of the most successful westerns of the sixties. On the surface, it appears to be a simple adventure story, but it is really much more. In many respects, the story remains the same. Fardan (Lee Marvin) is hired by Grant (Ralph Bellamy) to steal his wife, Maria (Claudia Cardinale), from her kidnapper, Raza (Jack Palance). In his journey into the Mexican desert — a descent into hell — Fardan is accompanied by Dolworth (Burt Lancaster), Ehrengard (Robert Ryan) and Sharp (Woody Strode). After they first overcome the elements — at one point, Ehrengard is struck down by heat prostration — and an encounter with ten of Raza's men, whom they kill, they finally arrive at Raza's camp. In a daring night raid, they rescue Maria, only to discover that she prefers Raza, whom she has known since childhood, to Grant who "owns" her. With Raza on their trail and with the captive Maria, the four men flee back north. By the time they reach the border, most of Raza's men have been wiped out and Raza is a captive of the mercenaries. But when Grant shows up and orders his men to kill Raza, Fardan prevents them. Disgusted with Grant and his need to possess his wife, Fardan and the others turn Raza and Maria free and send them back across the border. When Grant calls Fardan a bastard, Fardan replies, "Yessir. In my case, an accident of birth. But you, Mr. Grant, are a self-made man."

Several things deepen this film and make it a work of art. For one, the characters, all of them, are complete and fully realized. While the four mercenaries could easily have been stereotypical heroes, they emerge as men with ghosts and demons. For instance, after the four men have wiped out the advance band of Raza's men, Ehrengard is told to shoot the horses, but he argues against the cruel act. With a cynical grin, Dolworth points out that they have just killed ten men and no one "batted an eye," but that Ehrengard has trouble killing a few horses. A second area in which writer/director Richard Brooks added depth was in the struggle of conflicting loyalties. Both Fardan and Dolworth fought with Raza and the Revolution, but now they have taken a job to fight against him because of the ten thousand dollars each is offered by Grant. The loyalties get so skewed that Dolworth finally ends up killing a woman, one of the rebels, whom he had not only fought beside but whom he had also loved. The third area was the script, a literate adaptation of an enjoyable novel. Often the dialogue is eloquent and revealing, deepening the characters and expounding on the conflicts. Finally, Brooks meshed all the elements into a classic western, one in which the parts fit together to make an integrated whole. The dialogue and introspective scenes easily flow right into the action sequences and back again, and the end where Grant is exposed for the villain that he is, remains satisfying even after repeated viewings. This must rank as one of the truly excellent adaptations.

One of the most prolific of western writers to appear after World War II has been Ray Hogan, who is the author of more than 110 novels. Most of his characters are rather uncomplicated, but his books are fast paced, as exemplified by an early work, *Outlaw Marshal* (1958). It is the story of Marshal Decket who uses his badge as a means to bully and push people around. When Decket loses his prisoner, Shotgun Travers, he tries to cover his error by accusing a young cowboy, Clay Santell, of being his escaped prisoner. Santell also escapes, but this time with Decket and a posse hot on his trail. Along the way, Santell forces a young girl, Melissa, to join him. In the end, Santell manages to bring the real Travers to justice, and Decket is killed. It is all very predictable and lacks any of the insight or fire of such authors as Ernest Haycox or Luke Short.

Outlaw Marshal became *Hell Bent for Leather* (Universal, 1960). The film made very few changes, and most of these were in names, for instance, the character of Melissa became Janet (Felica Farr), but just as in the novel all the characters were one dimensional. Only Deckett (Stephen McNally) as the evil marshal brings any life to the story, and since the screenplay concentrated too much on the character of Clay Santell (Audie Murphy), it weakened the film even more. In many ways, however, the film adequately mirrored the novel, capturing the "B" structure of the plot and characters. If the film has a redeeming factor, it lies in some of the humor between Clay Santell and Janet after he has kidnapped her. But there is too little of that humor in this uninspired film.

Of all the formulary western writers who began after World War II, one of the best story tellers is Cliff Huffaker. Not only does he have a fine sense of plotting, but his characters are also well rounded and individual. Even in a novel like *Posse from Hell* (1958), the villains are so cold-blooded that they kill off several townspeople and threaten to kill off many more if their demands are not met, yet they are believable psychopaths. When the posse pursues them with a determined viciousness, the reader easily understands why. However, the main thrust of the novel lies in the character of Banner Cole, a young man who has been a deputy a scant eight days when outlaws invade his town of Paradise, kill five people, including the town marshal, kidnap a girl and ride off. During the ensuing pursuit, Banner Cole becomes a man.

The screenplay for *Posse from Hell* (Universal, 1961) was also written by Huffaker, and he transferred the events of his novel intact. Actually, his writing style, extremely visual, was made for such translation. Only the internal dialogue of Banner Cole (Audie Murphy) is missing. After the raid on the town, seven men set out in pursuit of the outlaws, all escapees from prison. Slowly the posse dwindles until only two are left, Cole and Easterner Seymour Kern (John Saxon). Along the way, they pick up Helen Caldwell (Zohra Lampert), whom the outlaws have raped and left to die in the desert. The trio ultimately catch up with the villains and dispatch them. While the bare outline sounds rather mundane, the film is full of good performances. Especially notable are Vic Morrow and Lee Van Cleef as two of the villains. Also, the novel and script by Huffaker are strong enough to give the characters some depth. In addition, the film was shot around Mt. Whitney where many of the Hopalong Cassidys were made, and the location photography gives the film a ruggedly authentic look. This must rank as one of the better Audie Murphy vehicles.

Posse from Hell was under 160 pages. A later novel, *Seven Ways to Sundown* (1960), was less than 130 pages. While Huffaker often gave the reader good, believable characters, they seldom had much depth because he simply did not take time to explore their psyches. The novels read quickly and easily and provide an enjoyable couple of hours, but beyond that, they offer very little. *Seven Ways to Sundown* falls into this category. It is an entertaining novel, but like Chinese food, it doesn't stick with you very long.

Seven Ways to Sundown (Universal, 1960), although written after *Posse from Hell,* actually reached the screen first. Again an Audie Murphy vehicle, it tells the story of a young Texas Ranger, Seven Jones (Audie Murphy), called Sundown Smith in the novel, who is assigned to bring in outlaw Jim Flood (Barry Sullivan). But the two become friends, making Jones' job that much harder. Jones finally accomplishes his task after Flood kills his mentor, Sgt. Hennessey (John McIntire). But Flood has been so caught in by the friendship with the ranger that, in the climactic gunfight, he purposely misses, allowing Jones to kill him. Once again Cliff Huffaker wrote the screenplay.

Both this film and *Posse from Hell* share a sense of humor amidst the formulistic plot, more so than existed in either novel. Perhaps this can be laid to the efforts of its star, Audie Murphy, who possessed a wry sense of humor on camera. At one point, Jim Flood asks the name of the hero. Playing the straight man, Jones replies that his name is Seven Ways to Sundown Jones. "We all have our crosses to bear," says Flood. However, *Seven Ways to Sundown* is inferior to *Posse from Hell,* mainly because the characters are not nearly so well drawn and the story possesses far less intensity and immediacy. Still, Audie Murphy as Jones projects a certain amount of charm, and his relationship with Barry Sullivan as Jim Flood provides enough spark to make the film interesting.

Cliff Huffaker was fortunate in that on every film adapted from his novels, he wrote the screenplay. He also adapted his novel *The War Wagon* (1962), which became a film (Universal, 1967) starring John Wayne and Kirk Douglas. Once again, the author simply transferred his own novel to the screen, and if there is a difference between book and movie, it lies in a more overt sense of humor. Similar to the film *Seven Ways to Sundown,* the humor lies in the interplay between Taw Jackson (John Wayne) and Lomax (Kirk Douglas), two antagonists who join forces. At one point after Jackson and Lomax gun down two villains, they argue over who was faster on the draw. Lomax claims that he was. "Mine hit the ground first," replies Jackson.

The story has the two joining forces to rob an armor-plated stagecoach carrying $100,000 in gold. The gold belongs to Pierce (Bruce Cabot), who years ago defrauded Taw Jackson of his gold mine. Joining Taw and Lomax in the enterprise are several other misfits: Levi Walking Bear (Howard Keel), a devious Indian; Billy Hyatt (Robert Walker, Jr.), a youthful drunk and a genius at handling explosives; and Wes Catlin (Keenan Wynn), a wagon driver who travels with his 18-year-old wife. Most of the action is lethargic, far more so than the novel, which is a fast read. It is only in the comic moments that the film comes alive and the characters are their most individual and believable.

The War Wagon boasts the biggest budget of any of the adaptations of Huffaker's novels, although both *Posse from Hell* and *Rio Conchos* (discussed in Chapter 4) are superior films. While John Wayne was a little long in the tooth to play the part of Taw Jackson, he is fine in the role, and his interplay with Kirk Douglas is the highlight of the film. The problem with this adaptation may well be that the original novel is weak, lacking the intensity and drive of Huffaker's earlier works.

Although *The Appaloosa* (1963), by Robert MacLeod, opens at the battle of Adobe Walls in Texas, it is really a formula western about a cowboy in search of his horse, an Appaloosa, that has been stolen from him by Mexican bandit Chuy Medina. Matt Fletcher pursues Chuy into Mexico where he meets Trini, a former girlfriend of Chuy. After an arduous ordeal, the hero kills Chuy and regains his Appaloosa, but only at the cost of Trini's life. The novel is a swift-paced affair peopled by some interesting characters without much depth.

When *The Appaloosa* (aka *Southwest to Sonora,* Universal, 1966) came to the screen, it retained many of the formulistic qualities, but as directed by Sidney Furie and with Marlon Brando interpreting the role of Matt Fletcher, the film attempted to be far more than a formula western. Even though elements of the plot are retained, the changes proved quite severe. Matt Fletcher (Marlon Brando) is a buffalo hunter whose wife has been killed. While he is in church promising God that he is through with sinning, Trini (Anjanette Comer) steals his Appaloosa and rides off. She is on the run from Chuy Medina (John Saxon), to whom she was sold as a child. Fletcher returns Trini to Chuy, who immediately falls in love with the Appaloosa and offers to buy it. When Fletcher refuses, the bandit leader and his men jump Fletcher, beat him up and leave him in the desert to die. Fletcher recovers and goes into Mexico after Chuy and the Appaloosa. At Chuy's hideout, he arm wrestles the bandit for possession of the horse, but Fletcher loses, the back of his hand ground into a deadly scorpion. Once again he survives, and once again he enters the outlaw's compound, killing several of the bandits, rescuing Trini and getting his horse back. Fletcher and Trini flee, and Chuy pursues. In a confrontation in the mountains, Fletcher comes to realize that he loves Trini more than the horse, and using the Appaloosa as a decoy, he manages to draw the fire of Chuy, which exposes the bandit's position, and Fletcher kills him. Together, Fletcher and Trini ride off toward Texas on the Appaloosa.

With all the closeups of wrinkled brows, gleaming teeth and sweating faces, the film looks and feels like a spaghetti western. In addition, most of the performances are either overblown or underplayed. John Saxon is a stereotypical Mexican villain, Anjanette Comer seems half dead and Brando chews up the scenery. Also, Brando is draped in serapes to disguise his bulging belly, which only emphasizes his miscasting. In the novel, Fletcher was a lean, mean buffalo hunter, who, while not a gunfighter, was a dangerous man. An early confrontation with a marshal, a confrontation left out of the film, exposes this part of his character. As a result, it is very hard to accept Brando as Matt Fletcher. Still, the film has a few things to recommend it. It has a brooding atmosphere throughout. Also, the photography, when the camera isn't locked into closeups, is often stunningly beautiful. However, while Brando's previous western, *One-Eyed Jacks,* remains a minor classic, this one, while occasionally interesting, is an inferior work.

Although Charles Portis had a previous novel to his credit, he could hardly have anticipated the success of *True Grit* (1968). Critics were enthusiastic, calling it "an epic and a legend" and claimed it was a book "that speaks to every American who can read." Many critics even compared the novel to *Shane.* Although Mattie Ross, the narrator, is a teenage girl, she is the equivalent of the young boy who narrates *Shane. True Grit*'s central character, scruffy, one-eyed old Rooster Cogburn, might be Shane thirty years later. In addition, Portis constructed his dialogue so that it sounded antiquated, as if it were spoken in the 1880s. Combined with the swift action scenes, the novel moves right along at a fast clip. In retrospect, while *True Grit* may be a very fine western, it does not match the power and strength of *Shane. True Grit* is simply a good tale filled with some memorable characters. *Shane* is the essence of the mythical Old West distilled into is purest form and told as an allegory.

When Marguerite Roberts wrote the screenplay, she wisely did not tamper with the plot, which remains intact. In fact, not only is it an extremely faithful adaptation, but Roberts even went so far as to lift whole passages of dialogue straight out of the novel. When Mattie Ross (Kim Darby) goes hunting for her father's killer, Tom Chaney (Jeff Corey), she seeks the help of a man with "true grit." She hires Rooster Cogburn (John Wayne), a hard-drinking, one-eyed U.S. marshal, and they are joined by Texas Ranger La Boeuf (Glenn Campbell), who is after the big reward money. Cogburn rightfully guesses that Chaney has joined Ned Pepper (Robert Duvall) and his gang, but it is Mattie who accidentally stumbles upon the murderer and is taken prisoner. In an attempt to rescue her, Cogburn faces a shootout with Ned Pepper and three of his men. In the meantime, La Boeuf is attacked and mortally wounded by Chaney, and in trying to defend herself, Mattie tumbles into a deep pit, breaking her arm and stirring up a nest of rattlesnakes. Cogburn arrives just in time to finish off Chaney and, although he himself is wounded, pulls Mattie from the pit just as she is bitten by a rattler. In a race for Mattie's life, Cogburn runs horses into the ground and steals others as he carries the stricken girl to town and a doctor. After Mattie recovers, they meet for one last time at the graveside of Mattie's father to say goodbye.

So much of this novel and film avoid the clichés inherent in the story. All love interest, even between the young Texas Ranger and Mattie, is strictly avoided. However, it is the character of Cogburn that sets this novel apart from other formulary western fiction; he is like a crusty sidekick out of some "B" western, the kind of role that Gabby Hayes might have played in the forties, yet he is the hero. For all his crotchetiness, Cogburn is the complete character, an individual. Kim Darby as Mattie is also excellent. She is determined yet vulnerable, shrewd yet naive, brave yet frightened. She and Wayne make the relationship between Mattie and Cogburn totally believable. Only the character of La Boeuf seems weak, and this is due to Glenn Campbell's amateurish performance. Chosen for his name rather than his acting talents, Campbell proved that he was no actor. Next to John Wayne in a part that seemed made to order for him and for which he won an Academy Award, Campbell appeared pathetically weak. Often the interplay and jibes between the two, which were good comic touches in the novel, fail to work on the screen because Campbell seems no match for Wayne. Despite the miscasting of Glenn Campbell, director Henry Hathaway, who had been at the helm for so many of the early Zane Grey adaptations at Paramount, blended all the elements together into an excellent western, capturing the tone and feeling of Portis' novel.

Like Elmore Leonard, Brian Garfield has made a reputation in the crime genre far exceeding that which he achieved in writing westerns. His most famous novel, mainly because of the film starring Charles Bronson, is *Death Wish,* a novel of vigilante justice in modern New York. Garfield was, however, also a fine writer of formulary westerns of which *Gun Down* (1971) must be regarded as one of his best. Like *Death Wish,* it is a story of revenge. In 1913, Zach Provo breaks out of Yuma prison intent upon killing Sam Burgade who sent him to jail 28 years before. Burgade is a retired lawman who has witnessed the passing of the Old West and now shares his world with automobiles. When Provo kidnaps Burgade's daughter, the ex-lawman uses the old ways to track down the killer, save his daughter and wipe out Provo and his gang.

This is a well-written novel from a man who loves the West and western movies. Not only has Garfield written western novels but he is also the author of *Western Films,* a short critical history of the genre that includes capsule reviews of individual films. In fact, the novel shows the influence of films in its use of violence, which is often reminiscent of a spaghetti western, yet, despite being set in 1913, it shows little revisionist tendencies. *Gun Down* is a good formulary novel that merges the Old West with the New, much in the same way as *The Professions* and *The Shootist.*

Gun Down became *The Last Hard Men* (20th Century–Fox, 1976), and the script followed the book with little variance. Although directed rather slackly by Andrew McLaglen, the film maintained a somber mood and made no attempt to glamorize the period or events. Actually, the violence of the novel is carried over to the film, and while it fails to have the stylized appearance of a spaghetti western, it captures the book's harshness. As Burgade (Charlton Heston) pursues Provo (James Coburn), he systematically kills off most of the gang. However, at one point, he must sit helpless in the night as he listens to his daughter being raped by Provo's men. The final confrontation between outlaw and former lawman is bloody and brutal. Provo shoots Burgade several times, and just as he bends over his arch enemy to finish the job, Burgade pulls out a hidden pistol and blows Provo over the edge of a cliff.

Given a stronger director, this might well have been an excellent film. As it is, *The Last Hard Men* is a satisfying action piece. Although it aspires to be a commentary on the passing of the Old West — automobiles make occasional appearances and the ineffective young sheriff (Michael Parks) is an apostle of modernization — the main thrust of the story is revenge, and it is this aspect that remains with the viewer long after the film is over.

The traditional western hero reemerged in *Gone to Texas* (1973) by Forrest Carter, a novel that takes place directly after the close of the American Civil War. Josey Wales, whose family is rubbed out by Redlegs, chooses to ride the guerrilla trail, and when hostilities cease, he refuses to surrender. He robs a bank with his young companion, Jamie, who becomes a substitute for Josey's dead son. Jamie is wounded in the escape, and Josey and Jamie are pursued by Federal troops and bounty hunters as they try to reach Texas and safety. Jamie dies, and soon after, Josey picks up an Indian, Lone Watie, who rides with him as they head for Mexico and the Confederate forces that are fighting there. They are joined by an Indian girl, Little Moonlight, who Josey rescues. Later, he also rescues Laura Lee and her Grandma Sarah from white renegades who trade with the Comanches. Together they all go to a ranch near the border owned by Laura and her grandmother. Here they are confronted by a band of Comanches led by the great warrior Ten Bears. He and Josey strike up a friendship based on mutual respect. Local townspeople — Ten Spot, Rose and Kelly — know Josey's real identity, but when Texas Rangers show up to arrest him, they lie and tell the Rangers that Josey was killed across the border in Mexico.

Despite its episodic structure, *Gone to Texas* is an excellent traditional western. The action is fast and furious as Josey goes from one scrape to another. Although in many ways a stereotypical western hero, Josey Wales is a well drawn character. He often does things that other such heroes would never contemplate. On the night that Jamie dies, Josey finds himself surrounded by Federal troops. Tying Jamie's body to a horse, he stampedes the animal through the camp, and while the soldiers chase the dead boy, Josey makes his escape. Subordinate characters such as Lone Watie and Laura Lee are also especially well drawn, individual and believable. If there is a weakness in the novel, it lies in the absence of a single villain to pit against Josey.

In *The Outlaw Josey Wales* (Warner/Malpaso, 1976) scriptwriters Phil Kaufman and Sonia Chernus corrected the problem. Most of the major events of the novel make their way into the film. However, there are a few changes. Jamie is wounded when he tries to surrender to the Redlegs who orchestrate a particularly vile ambush. There is no bank robbery as there was in the novel, and a central villain has been added. Josey (Clint Eastwood, who also directed) is chased all the way into Texas by the leader of the Redlegs (Bill McKinney), the same man who commanded the raid on Josey's farm that resulted in the death of Josey's wife and young son. The final confrontation between the two allows Josey to extract his full measure of revenge and adds a most satisfying conclusion to the story. Dialogue is often lifted right from the novel. Most of the humor also made it from the book, especially the various scenes involving Josey and Lone Watie (Chief Dan George). The poetic quality of Josey's meeting with Ten Bears (Will Sampson) is also retained. Like the novel, the film creates some memorable characters, and Josey's relationship with first Jamie (Sam Bottoms) and later Lone Watie brings added freshness to the story. Even the embryonic love affair between Josey and Laura Lee (Sondra Locke) is handled with restraint and sensitivity.

Both novel and film succeed as action entertainment. In addition, since both are about the need for relationships, even in the most self-sufficient of us, both also succeed admirably on this level, also. *The Outlaw Josey Wales* is a fine western film and a fine adaptation.

Forrest Carter scripted his own novel *The Vengeance Trail of Josey Wales* (1976) which became *The Return of Josey Wales* (Multi/Tacar Productions, 1986), a film that was never released theatrically in the United States but which found its way to the video market. Although the story picks up where *Gone to Texas* left off, this novel and film seem a cheap imitation of *The Magnificent Seven* or *The Professionals*. Josey (Michael Parks, who also directed) goes into Mexico to find the killers of Kelly and Rose, setting off a mini-war during which he extracts vengeance for the death of his friends. At times, the dialogue, because it is written by Carter, sounds authentic, but the film is so poorly done as to be without much merit.

It would seem that the traditional, formula western, while still being written, is now dead as a theatrical film. Throughout the 1970s and 1980s, the only real success has been *Gone to Texas/The Outlaw Josey Wales* and *Pale Rider* (Warner Bros., 1985), but these films owe their successes to the popularity of director/star Clint Eastwood. In the late eighties a few adaptations of Louis L'Amour have made it to television as movie of the week or a made-for-cable special, but that is all. The special-effects science fiction or the urban crime drama, both genres for a high tech society, have replaced the formula western. Most of the formula elements of the western have shifted to these other genres, which seem more suited to the quickly changing world in which we now find ourselves.

The traditional western remains a product of a time when relationships and values seemed less complex, when the line between right and wrong seemed easier to distinguish. That time is gone. The traditional screen western is also gone. It may never return. If it does, we can be assured of one thing: it will undergo more changes, just as it did after World War II. The problem may well be that the traditional western may have explored all it is capable of exploring. Frank Gruber's seven basic story lines may have reached their inevitable dead ends, overused and overabused. Their assimilation into other genres may be the final death knell.

III : The New West

12. The Revisionists

The 1940s saw the first western novel accepted as a classic among mainstream literature with Walter Van Tilburg Clark's *The Ox-Bow Incident* (1940), a novel which stands as a direct counterpoint to *The Virginian*. In the earlier novel, the hero and his followers capture the rustlers, including his friend Steve, and hang them. They feel justified because the men are guilty. In *The Ox-Bow Incident*, the issues and answers are far more complex. This is true of most revisionist westerns that attempted to broaden and redefine the genre.

In 1885, rustlers are active around the town of Bridger's Wells, Nevada, and the community has suspicions that the law is not doing everything in its power to stop them. When word is brought that a cattleman has been killed and his cattle rustled, people of the town raise a posse and set out to right wrongs. They capture three men who are driving the missing cattle and have no bill of sale. One of them even has a revolver of the slain man. Though it has no legal sanction, the posse determines the men are guilty and execute them. On the way back to town, the posse is met by another posse headed by the sheriff. Among the riders is the man supposedly murdered and who sold the cattle to the accused rustlers.

What begins as a standard horse opera ends as a study of human misery. There are no heroes in this story, and the one man, Davies, the old storekeeper who first tries to keep the mob from going out and later attempts to defend the rustler, is ineffectual and fails to take action when he should. When Martin, the leader of the accused rustlers, writes a letter to his wife, Davies reads it to the mob, but he finds no sympathetic ear. When the Mexican riding for Martin shows great courage in removing a bullet from his leg, it also fails to move the posse. The mob is without sentimentality and respect for courage. The three men are executed. After the posse learns the truth, two of the men, father and son, commit suicide. Davies is racked by guilt over his inaction. Within these events are two separate themes. The first is that a group of generally decent men can be turned into a bloodthirsty mob. The second is that appearances can be deceiving, even to those who think they know and understand the truth. On another level, the book is an indictment of vigilante justice and of the individual's acquiescence in it.

The film version of *The Ox-Bow Incident* (TCF, 1943), while also a radical contribution to the western, did compromise in one area. The book opens with two cowboys riding into town and joining the posse when it's formed. They are not heroes, just ordinary men who assist in taking the law into their own hands. Unlike some of the posse, the experience sobers them. In the film, these cowboys, Gil Carter (Henry Fonda) and Art Croft (Henry Morgan), are the titular protagonists, and once the posse captures the accused outlaws, Gil and Davies take the lead in trying to stop the hanging. They prove ineffectual, and the film remains as bleak and uncompromising as the novel. The story and theme are intact, cataloguing a wide range of human faults — revenge, cruelty, ambivalence, moral weakness, irrationality, demagoguery. The forces of good, reason and justice prove powerless and ineffectual.

Even though this film, like the novel, is very talky, especially in the second half, director William Wellman sustained the atmosphere throughout. As the events draw closer and closer to their conclusion, the camera moves closer and closer to the faces, laying bare the emotions of the characters. As a result, we can see contrast between individuals with clarity and immediacy and are drawn deeper and deeper into the tragedy. As always, the emphasis is never on action but on the characters and their states of mind.

It was this atmosphere that led to the film's failure at the box office. During the war years, the country wanted more escapist fare, not a brooding, pessimistic western. More importantly, the uncomfortable message was at odds with accepted western mythology. However, critics admired it, and the film won several awards for outstanding film of the year. Undoubtedly, it began a new trend whereby the old mythology of the West was presented in new and more critical terms. Today, it remains as important and original as the day it was released, a milestone in the development of the western and a timeless study of man's inhumanity to man.

More optimistic is Van Tilburg Clark's *The Track of the Cat* (1949). It is the story of one Nevada family, the Bridges, whose fate is all tied up with a black mountain cat. The family is composed of a father who constantly drinks, a mother, a spinster sister and three brothers. Of the brothers, Arthur is the dreamer, Curt is the boss of the family and Harold is the one in whom reality and compassion form the strongest, most durable of the Bridges. The story opens on a morning when Gwen, Harold's girl, has come to visit. During the night, a mountain cat has been prowling around the cabin, its cries penetrating the October storm. A mystical element is introduced in the character of the Indian hired man, Joe Sam, who each year carves a figure of a cat to keep the mountain lion away. But this year, he has not finished on time. Curt and Arthur go hunting the cat, and when Curt returns alone for tracking gear, he dawdles awhile with Gwen, trying to impress her. While he is doing so, the cat attacks and kills Arthur. When he finally returns to the hunt, Curt discovers his brother's body. Curt takes the dead Arthur back to the family and then goes hunting for the cat. When he fails to return in two days, Harold and Joe Sam go after him. The pair manage to kill a mountain lion which may or may not be the killer they seek. No matter, for with the killing, Harold has proven his manhood. Later, Harold finds the body of Curt, who has fallen from a cliff. There are no paw prints to indicate the presence of a cat or that a cat had anything to do with Curt's death.

The mountain lion against which each brother is pitted comes to reflect the character of each. Arthur, the dreamer, fails to take elementary precautions and dies because of his dreaming. Curt relies too much on his own physical powers and forsakes the interior strengths which make up the whole man. Only Harold is the complete man, and he defeats the animal; its pelt, which will cover his marriage bed, symbolizes his victory over the wilderness. Like *The Ox-Bow Incident*, *The Track of the Cat* is multilayered, and as such, ranks with its predecessor as a truly important novel of the American West.

As a film, *The Track of the Cat* (Wayne-Fellows/Warner Bros., 1954) is a slow, ponderous affair. The problem is that the book is talky, a good deal of the action taking place in the kitchen of the house, and the film followed suit. Too much of it is static. To further emphasize the bleak nature of the story, director William Wellman chose to film the story in color, but almost everything—the sets, the house, the horses, the clothes—is in black and white. Only the flesh tones of the characters, an occasional glimpse of blue sky, a yellow scarf worn by Gwen (Diana Lynn), and the brilliant red mackinaw worn by Curt (Robert Mitchum) possess color.

The film follows the book to the letter, including the symbolic overtones that the author so clearly intended. If anything, it even clarifies

Curt's feelings. Since he has sacrificed most for the family, he is going to control it, including possessing Gwen. When the cat begins to kill the cattle, he sees it as a threat to his authority and becomes possessed with tracking it down and killing it, even at the expense of the life of his brother Arthur (William Hopper). In a sense, the cat has become a mirror image of the evil within Curt, and as Curt chases the beast, it is almost as if he is chasing himself. After Curt is killed, Harold (Tab Hunter) takes up the challenge and proves his manhood, killing the beast that has haunted the family. Throughout this film, including the climax, the cat is never seen. It is a dark, mysterious force that prowls outside waiting to kill and destroy the family. In the end, Harold has purged the evil. Perhaps he has even purged the devil itself.

While this film attempted to break new ground and contained several interesting sequences, it proved to be both a financial and artistic flop. Certainly Wellman's choice to make a black and white film in color adds the requisite bleakness. In addition, Mitchum's brooding Curt is one of the actor's most underrated performances. Beulah Bondi was also highly effective as Ma Bridges, whose cold dominating personality drove her husband to drink and her daughter to spinsterhood. However, the rest of the cast fails to measure up. Tab Hunter is wooden as Harold. The character of Arthur needed a more sensitive actor than William Hopper, who found his niche in life playing Paul Drake on the *Perry Mason* television show. Diana Lynn as Gwen was simply too weak for the part of the strong willed neighbor girl who wants Harold to assert himself. In addition, the film contains one of the strangest bits of casting ever put on film. Carl "Alfalfa" Switzer of Our Gang fame plays the part of Joe Sam, a 100-year-old Indian. While Wellman's experiment must be admired, *The Track of the Cat* is just too weak in too many areas to be the classic it aspired to be. On the other hand, it is a curiosity worth viewing.

Sex, except in its clean and sanctified state, had never been part of the western until Nevin Busch wrote *Duel in the Sun* (1944). In constructing the plot, he said, "I thought the only way to succeed was to build a western around a woman and use a sexual idea instead of an action idea." The story takes place in Texas of the 1880s. The chief character is Pearl Chavez, an orphan with Indian blood who becomes the protégé of cattle baron McCanles. When she is fourteen, the elder son Lewt rapes her. They become lovers for several years, until Pearl realizes that he will never marry her because of her Indian heritage, yet he will not give her up. In the duel of the title, she kills Lewt and sets herself free to marry the bookish brother Jesse, who loves her in spite of her past. While an entertaining novel, *Duel in the Sun* is neither particularly authentic — the author got most of his information and slant on western history while writing screen plays like *The Westerner* (Goldwyn, 1940) — nor does it put much strain on the intelligence. Even though it was the author's most successful novel, Busch admitted that it was due in large part to the film.

When David O. Selznick purchased the rights, he did so for purely monetary reasons. He disliked westerns in general, but he said, "Seeing how profitable westerns always were, I decided that if I could create one that had more spectacle than had ever been seen in a western and combine it with a violent love story, than the two elements would give me a great success." Also, he was reacting to the boom in movie audiences; attendance had been building steadily during the war years and would peak in 1946. More importantly, the same year *Duel* was published also saw the publication of *Forever Amber,* and Selznick guessed that movie audiences were ready for something sensational. He gave it to them.

Director King Vidor and producer Selznick did not always agree on what should be included in the film. At a special preview after the film had been edited, Vidor objected to the scene where Lewt blew up a train, then rode away whistling "I've Been Working on the Railroad," feeling it destroyed all sympathy for the character. Selznick responded, "I want to make Lewt the worst son of a bitch that's ever been on the motion picture screen, and I believe the train wreck scene will help me prove my point." Lewt turns out to be exactly the son of a bitch Selznick hoped for.

One of Selznick's first orders was for his scriptwriter, Oliver Garrett, to change the ending which saw Pearl (Jennifer Jones) and Jesse (Joseph Cotton) ride off happily into the sunset. Selznick wondered "what kind of bedmates she and Jesse will be after this wanton murder of his brother . . . especially since the audience and Jesse both know that she has loved the man she killed unceasingly throughout the entire picture." Instead, the ending became one where Pearl shoots Lewt (Gregory Peck), Lewt shoots her, then still drawn to him, she crawls up the mountain and they speak their last words of love as they die in each other's arms. Selznick thought this ending "a lot less unpleasant than the original."

Selznick thought one scene important enough to keep intact. This was the rape where Pearl eventually surrenders, then enjoys the act. However, Selznick did change the setting from an oppressively hot day to a muggy, overcast evening. Just as Pearl gives in, there is a tremendous burst of thunder, and forked lightning flashes across the horizon.

This emphasis on sex is carried through all the scenes between Pearl and Lewt, and it is clear that they enjoy what they are doing. This emphasis also led to the scene where Pearl, locking her arms around Lewt's legs, is dragged across the floor screaming for Lewt to take her to Mexico with him. One scene, later cut from the film, showed Pearl attempting to seduce Lewt by dancing for him as her mother had danced at the beginning of the film.

Overall, Selznick's version throws away almost all the novel except for the relationship between Pearl and Lewt, although it even added and subtracted until the psychological foundations that Busch so carefully built in the novel disappear, replaced by creatures who are motivated only by sex. Defending his truncating of the book, Selznick said, "If the book fails to achieve outstanding distinction in its own medium, there is no reason to believe that a faithful transcription would achieve distinction in another medium; with *Duel in the Sun,* I was enormously attracted by the characters and relationships but felt that the story and characters got lost in a maze of wild west exploits . . . and that the story needed to be expanded in scope."

Nevin Busch's second attempt at a western was *The Furies* (1948), which stresses psychological rather than sexual obsession and relates the love-hate relationship between a father and his daughter. Set in New Mexico in the 1880s, it tells of T.C. Jeffords who writes off his two sons as worthless successors to his empire because they take after their dead mother and lack his vitality and ruthlessness. Not so his daughter Vance, who matches his own strong will with hers. But when he marries his mistress, he makes an implacable enemy of Vance, and the two clash in all-out war. While the novel moves at an acceptable pace, which disguises much of the illogical plot and lack of subtle characterization, it nevertheless is an exciting and enjoyable book.

As a film, *The Furies* (Paramount, 1950) is an ambitious work by director Anthony Mann. The story has Greek tragedy overtones of dynastic struggles all mixed up with Freudian psychology. One of the sons is dropped from the story, but the one who remains is weak and out of favor with his father, T.C. Jeffords (Walter Huston). When Jeffords gets too close to his long-time mistress (Judith Anderson), Vance (Barbara Stanwyck) stabs her in the eye, disfiguring her. In retaliation, Jeffords hangs Herrera (Gilbert Roland), whom he believes his daughter loves. Actually she is in love with gambler Rip Darrow (Wendell Cory), changed from Curley Darragh in the novel, who wants to reclaim the Furies, a strip of land originally owned by his father but now in the hands of Jeffords. Once the feud between Jeffords and his daughter erupts, Rip sides with Vance, and they both go after the cattle baron.

While neither of Busch's two western novels can be considered classics, the books helped to pave the way for the adult western that was to become so popular in the late 1950s and 60s. The films are a different matter. *Duel in the Sun,* despite the fact that it threw away most of Busch's story, is a kitsch classic, a compendium of sleazy sexual innuendos and outright bad taste. The scenery and costumes are gaudy; the acting is overblown; the story is plain silly. Yet it remains a fascinating movie because of the very excesses that make it look as if it had been directed by Maxfield Parrish rather than King Vidor. *The Furies,* a noir western, is fascinating because it reaches so high and never quite gets there.

An author with serious pretensions, MacKinlay Kantor, had an early novel of the West, *Happy Land and Gentle Annie* (1944), adapted unsuccessfuly to the screen as *Gentle Annie* (MGM, 1944), a story of a marshal (James Craig) coping with two ranchers and their mother (Marjorie Main) who see no problem with an occasional bank robbery to augment their income. Offbeat it may have been, but the title kept action addicts away and the limp direction turned off the critics as well as most paying customers.

However, with *Wicked Water* (1948), MacKinlay Kantor tried his hand at a more serious western. This time his central character is Bus Crow, a character based on the real Tom Horn. Crow is a killer hired by big ranchers to drive off the little ranchers who, they believe, are stealing their cattle. In Pearl City, Crow becomes involved with Mattie MacLaird, a dance hall girl who is drawn to him; but when he kills a little boy, she turns against him and informs Marshal Rochelle, who had fought with Crow in Cuba. He arrests Crow, who is tried and hanged.

Wicked Water is neither a formulistic western nor a romanticized version of an outlaw's life. Instead, it is gritty and realistic, a hard look at the life of a killer. Even Crow's relationship with Mattie is never romanticized. At one point, he hits her in the face with a full bottle of whiskey, scarring her. Later, as Crow awaits the hangman, he asks to see Mattie, who comes to visit him for the last time. He tells her that he knows she informed on him, and he spits in her face. Therefore, when Crow meets his death, the reader feels no sympathy for him. Even though Crow may stand symbolically for the passing of the West, it is a part of the West that we are better off without, part that allowed unbridled killers to roam the country without hindrance from the law.

By the time Bus Crow dies, the Old West is dead, and the New West, the West that destroys the killer, has taken its place.

Wicked Water became *Hanna Lee* (aka *Outlaw Territory*, Border, 1953), an entry in the 3-D process, which proved to be more trouble than it was worth. In fact, the shoddy direction only calls attention to the process, as if first time codirectors John Ireland and Leo Grimes never had time to concentrate on much else. A better script would have helped. The dark, brooding story of Kantor is replaced by a bland one in which Hallie (Joanne Dru), Bus Crow's dance hall girlfriend, saves the life of Rochelle (John Ireland) by shooting Crow (MacDonald Carey). The whole scene in the jail where Bus confronts Mattie and spits in her face has been omitted. Also, while the character of Bus Crow is deromanticized and the whole film has an unromantic feel, it is a routine affair, far weaker than it should have been, given the source. The later *Tom Horn* (United Artists, 1980) covered the same material much better.

Unfortunately, Hollywood never bothered to film any other western fiction by Kantor, although his short story collection *The Gun-Toter and Other Stories of the Missouri Hills* (1963) is among the better examples of homespun western fiction. He is a writer who deserved far better treatment on the screen than he received.

Attempting a major novel, Gwen Bristow wrote *Jubilee Trail* (1950), a sweeping western about early California. The title refers to the trail that led from Santa Fe to Los Angeles in the 1840s, and the story tells of traversing the trail and the early American population in the City of Angels before the discovery of gold. Bristow worked on the book for five years, doing extensive research, and the final result was a romantic novel full of strong female characters; it was also exciting and suspenseful. Republic Studios, headed by Herbert J. Yates, purchased the property for $100,000, ostensibly as a vehicle for Vera Hruba Ralston, Yates's wife, but surprisingly she became a peripheral character, playing a heart-of-gold saloon girl who takes an innocent young Eastern girl (Joan Leslie) under her protective wing. The story then becomes a tug of war betweeen the girl's brother-in-law (John Russell) and a frontier trader (Forrest Tucker) for the girl's affections. Except for the costumes and sets, which were elaborate for a Republic production, the enormous research that went into the novel seldom shows up on the screen, and the whole proceedings are disappointingly slow for a studio that concentrated on action films.

One of the great western novels out of the 1950s was *The Wonderful Country* (1952) by Tom Lea. The story is about Martin Brady, who, as a youth, must flee to Mexico where he becomes a hired gunman for the Castro Brothers, two Mexican landlords who rule like bandits. From the first, Brady's double allegiance is emphasized, even by name. In the states he is known as Martin Brady, in Mexico as Martin Bredi. He is constantly sent back and forth across the Texas-Mexico border on missions for the Castros, and he is never certain which place is his home. Of himself, Brady says, "I wish I was plain one thing. I wish in my own mind, I was not the stranger everywhere, like nothing was my own."

Brady slowly comes to realize that he cannot live on both sides of the border because each stands for a different set of values. Mexico, where Brady spent his youth, is a symbol of wild freedom and irresponsibility. Brady's horse, Lagrimas, "Tears" in English, is a symbol of this life. In contrast, Texas stands for stability and progress, all wrapped up in the character of Louisa Rucker, with whom Brady falls in love. Brady must make a choice himself, and in making it, renounce something important to him.

Even though this novel is full of commonplace themes and situations found in formulary western fiction, it rises above such limitations by Lea's adroit handling of his material. The contrast between Louisa Rucker, Brady's love interest, and the horse Lagrimas, was a potentially hackneyed symbol, but it is so sensitively presented that it becomes a profound statement of the attractiveness of opposing ideals. Brady himself emerges as a completely realized human being who must make a choice between two things that are dear to him. It is not a woman or a horse he must give up; it is a way of life.

Remarkably faithful to the novel, *The Wonderful Country* (United Artists, 1959) is a superior, intelligent film. Brady (Robert Mitchum) crosses the border on a gun-running mission for the Castros when his horse shies and throws him, breaking his leg. As he recuperates in the small town of Puerto, Texas, he becomes involved with another gunrunner's wife (Julie London). Asked to join the Texas Rangers, he is about to stay in Texas, when he is forced to kill a man and flee back to Mexico.

It is Brady's inner struggle as he seeks to find redemption that is the main focus in the film, much as in Lea's novel. The author's evocative prose is mirrored in the wonderful images that cross the screen. Brady's interrelationship with the land is magnified by the superb photography. Even though occasional events are different from the novel, it doesn't matter; Lea's story is captured on celluloid under Robert Parrish's inspired direction. Like *Shane, The Wonderful Country* is a classic western novel that became a classic film.

A modest success compared to Lea's novel, Noel Loomis's *Johnny Concho* (1956) first appeared as a paperback original, and today would barely be remembered if it were not for the film. Loomis himself is remembered more for his work as a writer on such television shows as *Bonanza* and *Have Gun, Will Travel*. *Johnny Concho* was the story of a town bully who exists on the reputation of his brother, a feared gunman. When his brother is killed, he must come to terms with his own cowardice. As a film, *Johnny Concho* (United Artists, 1956) suffers from miscasting in the title role (Frank Sinatra), an unpleasant script and generally lackluster direction. Only the appearance of a gun-toting preacher (Keenan Wynn) adds originality and livens up the story, but he is around for a very short time. Before and after his appearance, there may be images moving around and talking, but the screen is dead.

Another author who attempted to write a great western novel was Oakley Hall with *Warlock* (1958). Like *The Wonderful Country,* this novel is also full of formulary western conventions and, like the earlier novel, rises above hackneyed situations. It is a complex work full of shifting narrative viewpoints and conflicting values that, if it fails to satisfy, does so because it fails to deliver the emotional punch of *The Wonderful Country.* The novel's basic theme, like that of so many conventional westerns, is the coming of the law. *Warlock* is a lawless frontier community that gradually becomes a respectable city. Within the city, there are four groups vying for control of the law: the respectable townspeople, a group of well-meaning citizens who hire a notorious gunman, Clay Blaisedell, as town marshal; miners who wish to make the mine owners bow to their wishes and are not above using violence to get their way; the mine owners who want to break the power of the workers by hiring "regulators" to enforce their will; and a group of cowboys, led by Abe McQuown, who terrorize the town. Each group sees justice only in the terms of its own interests; only John Gannon, a one-time cowboy who becomes a deputy sheriff, comes to realize that the problems of the town stem from the fact that none of the factions really believes in justice. The triumph of law is made clear when John Gannon is murdered by one of the cowboys, and the town legally tries, convicts and hangs the killer. At the start of the book, no town jury would have convicted a cowboy murderer.

The film *Warlock* (TCF, 1959) dropped all reference to miners and mine owners. There is only the town of Warlock threatened by Abe McQuown's cowboys. The citizens hire Clay Blaisedell (Henry Fonda) as town marshal to restore order to the beleaguered streets, and he arrives escorted by his friend Morgan (Anthony Quinn) who acts as his backup gun. Added to the film were hints at latent homosexuality between these two men. When Clay takes up with a local woman, it drives Morgan to distraction and ultimately ends in a confrontation and Morgan's death.

The novel concludes with a discussion of Gannon's death, but the film ends far more romantically. After Blaisedell kills Morgan and uses a saloon as his funeral pyre, almost igniting the whole of Warlock in the process, he realizes that the town no longer needs or wants him, that his time as a gunman is over. As he is about to ride out, Gannon (Richard Widmark) as deputy sheriff faces him, even though he knows he is no match for Blaisedell. As Gannon reaches for his gun, Blaisedell easily outdraws him. Then, the gunman tosses his gun into the dirt. Quickly, he draws his other pistol, then does the same. Unmolested, he mounts his horse and rides out of town. Gannon is still alive as the credits begin to roll.

The film jumps from one subplot to another. As Bosley Crowther said in his review for the *New York Times,* "It's pretty exciting, once it gets all the plots staked out and its several important characters distributed to their proper sides." Yet, like the novel, the film is emotionally distant and uninvolving, and as such, misses being the great western it might have been and sought to be.

A.B. Guthrie, whose *The Big Sky* and *The Way West* were important novels, completed his trilogy with *These Thousand Hills* (1956), which follows the fortunes of Lat Evans, the grandson of Lije Evans from *The Way West.* Lat arrives in Montana at the end of a trail drive, where he decides to settle and start a ranch of his own. He develops a friendship with a beautiful prostitute named Callie from whom he borrows $1000, her life savings, to risk on a horse race, which he wins. Taking his new fortune, he abandons Callie, starts his ranch and marries a respectable girl. When Lat's close friend, Tom Ping, marries a prostitute, Lat turns his back on his friend, even refusing to attend the wedding. Lat is finally humbled when he discovers that he is an illegitimate child fathered by a man whom he hates. He also loses his reputation in the community when it is discovered that he was at one time a vigilante. He returns to his wife secure in the knowledge that she still loves him and that his cattle roam his "thousand hills."

Avoiding many of the genre's conventions, *These Thousand Hills* unfortunately falls short of its goal of being a great western novel. The problem lies in the complexities of characters and their involvement in the historical process. *The Big Sky* was a tragic vision but here the author settles for a facile and unconvincing optimism.

When it came to writing the script for *These Thousand Hills* (TCF, 1959), Alfred Hayes made extensive changes in the plot. First, a character named Jehu (Richard Egan), probably based on Hector in the novel, shows up as a local cad who, after Lat (Don Murray) abandons Callie (Lee Remick) to marry the banker's daughter (Patricia Owens), moves in and takes his place. He mistreats her something awful, finally forcing Lat to ride into town to take care of the situation. A fight ensues, and Lat proceeds to get the stuffings beaten out of him. Just as Jehu pulls his rifle from his saddle intent upon finishing off Lat, Callie shoots the villain and saves her former lover. Second, in a scene straight out of *The Virginian,* Tom Ping goes bad and begins to rustle cattle. Joining the posse, Lat helps to hunt down his old friend, and when he is caught, the posse strings him up. Only at the last minute, Lat has a change of heart and tries to stop the hanging, but it is too late.

The curious code of honor and social values implicit in the novel are even more confusing in the film. After Callie stakes Lat to $2000 to start his ranch and he falls in love with the banker's daughter, his old friends begin to sneer and frown. Their sympathies, as well as the script's, turn against him and seem to favor the no-account Tom Pink as the more honorable of the two. Lat's burden of shame forces him to march right out in the middle of the street and fight Jehu in defense of his old girlfriend.

None of this material stems from Guthrie's novel, and the script staggers off in its own direction. The character of Jehu and the events surrounding him are added to give the film tension, but little is generated. With the exception of Callie, the characters are bland and seem to drift without purpose. The dialogue often sounds like a sermon. Even though *These Thousand Hills* was not the best Guthrie, it was better than most formulary western fiction; this is not true of the film, a flat, dull failure.

Dorothy Johnson is an outstanding writer whose output is relatively small. Her reputation rests mainly on two collections, *Indian Country* (1953) and *The Hanging Tree* (1958), both of which contain some of the finest short stories of the American West. "The Man Who Shot Liberty Valance," which originally appeared in *Cosmopolitan,* became an important John Ford film. Told as a flashback, it opens in 1910 at the funeral of Bert Barricune. In attendance are Senator Ranse Foster and his wife, who are recognized by a young reporter who asks them what they are doing there. Tempted to tell the truth, Ranse says only, "Bert Barricune was my friend for over thirty years." Ranse then reminisces about Bert.

As a young Easterner, Ranse is left stranded in the Arizona desert by outlaw Liberty Valance. Half dead, Ranse is rescued by Barricune, and the rough Westerner nurses him back to health. When Ranse goes into town to press changes against Valance, the marshal refuses to act, although he does mention that there is a reward offered for the outlaw. In town, Ranse meets Hallie, whom Bert is also interested in, and gets a job as a saloon swamper, all the time waiting for Liberty Valance to come back to town. When Liberty does show up, Ranse goes out to meet him with a pistol he bought off a drunk cowboy. In the shootout, Ranse is wounded in the arm, crippling him for life, but Liberty is killed. As Ranse is recovering from the wound, Bert admits that it was he who killed the outlaw and not Ranse. When Ranse asks why, Bert says, "Hallie likes you. I'm a friend of Hallie's. That's all I ever will be, long as you're around."

Years later, after Ranse and Hallie are married, Bert spurs him into running for governor. The irony, of course, is that Ranse has become a hero for shooting Libery Valance, which leads to his political career. Since it was Bert who killed Liberty, Ranse's whole political life is built upon a lie. Like all Dorothy Johnson's fiction, the story, even though sporting a complicated plot, showed a verbal economy, accomplishing in a few pages what might take other authors a whole book.

There are many disparities between the short story and John Ford's *The Man Who Shot Liberty Valance* (Paramount, 1962). The film added characters, such as the newspaper editor, Dutton Peabody (Edmund O'Brien), and the faithful servant, Pompey (Woody Strode). It also changed the name of Bert Barricune to Tom Doniphon (John Wayne). Told as a flashback, it opens as Ranse (James Stewart) and Hallie (Vera Miles) return to the town of Shinbone for the funeral of Doniphon. When a reporter notices him and asks why the Senator has come, Ranse tells him the true story of the man who shot Liberty Valance. When Ranse concludes his story, the reporter tosses his notes in the fire. "You're not going to print it?" asks Ranse. "No sir," says the reporter. "This is the West. When the legend becomes fact, print the legend."

In the short story, Ranse is left out in the desert to die because Liberty takes pleasure in cruelty. In the film, Liberty and his two men rob a stage, and in the process, he rips up Ranse's law books and says, "I'll teach you law — Western law." Using his quirt, he beats Ranse senseless and leaves him to die in the desert. The story shows only one more meeting between Ranse and Liberty, the final showdown, and none between Bert and Liberty. The film adds considerably more con-frontations between the heroes and Liberty Valance, thus strengthen-ing the conflict and filling the final showdown with far more tension. In Johnson's story, Ranse waits around to gain personal vengeance on Liberty; it becomes his primary motivating force. In the film, Liberty (Lee Marvin) is pushed by the large cattle interests to run for the ter-ritorial convention, and the small farmers pick Ranse. When the local newspaper editor runs an editorial criticizing Liberty, the outlaw beats the editor and then lets it be known that he is out gunning for Ranse.

The changes the film made do not suggest that Johnson's story failed in any aspect. On the contrary, "The Man Who Shot Liberty Valance" is a nearly perfect short story. But film is a different medium and the additions by Ford and scenarists Willis Goldbeck and James Warner Bellah accommodate the medium. Even the extensive use of sets rather than the open vistas usually employed by Ford help to capture the closed-in feeling of the story.

However, the film does fall short of capturing the short story in cer-tain areas. John Wayne and James Stewart were too old for their parts. In the story, both Ranse and Bert were much younger — Johnson even refers to "young Barricune" — but in the film, Stewart shows gray around the temples and Wayne sports a bulging belly that was to grow even larger as the years went by. Also, the scene where Tom realizes that he has lost Hallie and burns down the house that he was building for her weakens the character. If *The Man Who Shot Liberty Valance* is not great John Ford, it is important John Ford in which the director takes a revisionist look at the western; despite certain drawbacks, it is a good adaptation of Dorothy Johnson's story.

The title story of Johnson's second collection, "The Hanging Tree," was about a mining camp and some of the people in it, principally Doc Frail, the prospector-doctor, and Elizabeth Armistead, the young girl whose father is murdered on the way to the diggings. The longest story in either collection, actually a novelette, "The Hanging Tree" suffers from its length. The author seems most at home with the short story. Still, it stands head and shoulders above most other western fiction. Like most of the author's stories, the central female character, if not strong at the start, grows in strength, and by the end, only she has the power to stop a lynch mob from hanging Doc.

The film *The Hanging Tree* (Warner Bros., 1959) weakens the character of Elizabeth (Maria Schell) by concentrating on Doc Frail (Gary Cooper). Also, Elizabeth is an immigrant, not a factor in the Dorothy Johnson story. In addition to these changes, the film has Doc

Frail kill Frenchy (Karl Malden) after Frenchy has raped Elizabeth, whereas in the novelette it is the mad preacher Grubb whom he shoots down. Despite these changes, the film captures the flavor of the frontier mining camps and even manages to convey some of the power of the Dorothy Johnson story.

The bleakest of all revisionist western novels must be *Welcome to Hard Times* (1960) by E.L. Doctorow. The observer-recorder of the narrative, Blue, a man in his late forties, begins the narrative as an optimist, but by the time the story has reached its end, he is a man without hope and without a future. The first two thirds of the novel relate the events in more or less chronological order, but during the last third, the very act of recording the events sets Blue's mind whirling, and he grows ever more fatalistic.

The story opens with Clay Turner, the Bad Man from Bodie, entering the town of Hard Times. Immediately, he begins to wreak havoc, brutally killing two men and also killing Flo, one of the town's two bar girls. After setting fire to the town, Turner departs, and most of the town wanders away from the ashes. Only Blue, the mayor of Hard Times; Jimmy, the son of a slain carpenter; Molly, the other bar girl who has been badly burned; and John Bear, a stoical Indian, remain.

Blue takes care of Molly and Jimmy, and during a terrible winter, the three become almost like a family. However, Molly is haunted by the fear that the Bad Man will return, and she transfers her fears to Jimmy. Blue tries to calm their fears, claiming that the community will be able to stand up to Turner if he again shows. However, Molly cannot forget that Blue turned coward and did nothing when Turner destroyed the town.

The town begins to rebuild itself as other souls wander in and miners come down from the hills looking for a good time. But the mine plays out, and a planned road is never built into Hard Times. Then, the Bad Man reappears, bringing destruction once again. This time, Blue sets a trap, stringing barbed wire across the front of the saloon door and luring Turner out. With the Bad Man entangled in the barbed wire, Blue carries him to Molly. Enraged, she takes a knife to him and extracts her revenge. Horrified, Jimmy pulls out a gun and shoots both Molly and the Bad Man and then flees.

Bodies litter the deserted streets. The first time, Blue buried the dead, but this time, wounded and weak, he does not have the strength. He thinks of burning the town to cremate the dead and keep the buzzards at bay, but he doesn't. "I keep thinking someone will come by sometime who will want to use the wood." From the dead town will rise another town.

Doctorow once said in an interview that he had no affinity or feeling for the western genre, but in his job at the studios, he read a countless number of western screenplays. From these readings, he was forced to think about the use of the western myth. One day he came to the conclusion: "I can lie better than these people." However, *Welcome to Hard Times* is not a lie, but it is not strictly a western and has little historical validity. However, it is a symbolic exploration into the cyclic theory of history with the town of Hard Times representing the rise and fall of civilizations, all done in the guise of a western. It is also an outstanding first novel that is a deep and rewarding reading experience.

The film *Welcome to Hard Times* (MGM, 1967) was scripted by director Burt Kennedy, and even though the events strayed a bit, he managed to retain the violent and harsh nature of the novel. Originally made for television, it proved to be too bleak and cold for the networks and was released to the theaters first. The Man from Bodie (Aldo Ray) destroys the town of Hard Times, and through the winter, Blue (Henry Fonda) must live with his cowardice. When the Bad Man returns, a crazed Molly (Janice Rule) forces Blue to face up to the Bad Man, and in a desperate confrontation, the town burning around them, Blue shoots and kills his adversary.

Several things conspired to make this film a failure at the box office. First, it was too far out of the norm; the characters — the evil gunman, the prostitute with a heart of gold, the frightened townspeople — were more symbols than flesh and blood. Added to this, Blue is stoic and almost an antihero until the last few minutes when he finally grows enough backbone to carry the fight to the Bad Man. Rather than a Westerner with a code of ethics, Blue is simply a man trying to survive. Second, the deromanticized environment, so bleak and harsh, was difficult to accept for purists of the genre. Finally, the violence was not the violence of spaghetti westerns, but a grimmer, more realistic violence and esthetically unglamorous.

While it may not reach the heights of the novel, the film *Welcome to Hard Times* is an attempt by writer/director Kennedy to stretch the limits of the genre. It may be an imperfect film, but only in the areas where it deviated from the novel and substituted its own plot. For instance, the end of the film with a shootout between hero and villain is far too traditional. Doctorow's ending is far more satisfying and far more in keeping with the tone and mood of the story. However, despite its imperfections, this is a film worthy of attention.

Death of a Gunfighter (1968) by Lewis Patten is another of the end of the West novels. In this case, Frank Patch, the marshal of Cottonwood Springs, Kansas, is asked to resign his position that he has held for twenty years. When he took the job, the town promised him he could have it for as long as he wanted, provided he brought law and order to the community. He did just that, killing five men in his first week. Now, however, the town believes he has outlived his usefulness, and they want a regular police force with uniformed men. Patch refuses to resign, and various resentments begin to build. He kills two townspeople when they try to ambush him. Later, when his arch enemy, Locke, also tries to ambush him, he kills Locke and his two henchmen. But by now, the town has banded together, and they ambush Patch. The young boy, Dan, who has been Patch's friend from the outset, is the only one who tries to warn the marshal, but Patch is killed, mourned only by Dan and the whore Claire.

Death of a Gunfighter tries to be a cross between the more ambitious *Warlock* and the classic *Shane,* but is far less of an achievement than either of these two novels. Certainly, it fails to probe the depths of characters as Oakley Hall did, and the vast, panoramic scale of *Warlock* is missing. Because all the action except a brief flashback takes place in the town, there is a claustrophobic feel to the book. In addition, the relationship between the boy and the marshal is diffused by the use of multiple viewpoints, and the book thus misses the intimacy of *Shane.* Still, it is a readable book, and the complex character of Patch is often quite fascinating.

The film *Death of a Gunfighter* (Universal, 1969) ran into problems when star Richard Widmark forced the firing of director Robert Totten halfway through shooting. The studio brought in Don Siegel, and the finished product, shot completely out of sequence, has its separate work woven together. Totten was a meticulous director, taking his time with every shot, but Siegel rushed through his part, completing the last half in only nine days. The constant change of pace is all too evident. Still, it is interesting on one point. It anticipates Siegel's own adaptation of *The Shootist* by Glendon Swarthout, a book related thematically to *Death of a Gunfighter.*

Although the script sticks very close to the novel, the film fails on most counts. Widmark looks so tired as the gunslinger-marshal that one has to wonder if he wasn't just disgusted with the film. The relationship between Patch and the young boy is curtailed so badly that it becomes only a very minor part of the film. One important character, Trinidad, the county sheriff, is dropped altogether. Many others are added. A story already cluttered with too many marginal characters simply becomes more cluttered. The film attempted to be daring in casting Lena Horne as Claire, the long suffering mistress of Patch, but she is wasted in a poorly conceived script. The downbeat ending doesn't help either, failing to leave the audience with even the same ray of hope as the novel where the boy Dan comes to the realization that Patch will remain alive in his memory. The film simply ends with Patch's murder by the town. Of course, the film failed at the box office.

It is difficult to categorize Marilyn Durham's *The Man Who Loved Cat Dancing* (1972) as a revisionist western. Rather, it is a mainstream novel that happens to be set in the West, and as such, evokes no feeling of the West or of the 1880s. It's heroine, Catherine Crocker, is essentially a twentieth century character who espouses contemporary views about women rather than those of her own century. Her brutalizing at the hands of the outlaw leader and her eventual falling for him give her ample opportunity to spout her views. While the novel may not be a classic or even important western, it is a well plotted story.

The film *The Man Who Loved Cat Dancing* (MGM, 1973) is a curiously inept effort that is remembered more for the stories involving the two stars, Burt Reynolds and Sarah Miles, than any inherent qualities that it might possess. While the script by Eleanor Perry remains close to the novel — and it was rumored that Robert Bolt, Miles' husband, reworked part of it — it never comes alive but instead is a vapid story filled with uninteresting characters. Reynolds is the outlaw on the run after he has killed the man who raped his Indian wife, Cat Dancing, and he kidnaps the unhappily married Catherine Crocker (Miles), who, despite rough treatment, slowly falls for him. The film makes one important concession. The novel ends with the death of the outlaw; the film has him wounded but a survivor, and he and Catherine are together at fade out. The change probably didn't damage the film any more than it already had been. If anything, this film was directed with less feeling for the West than the book, which is quite a negative accomplishment, and it is certainly far less enjoyable than the book.

Of all the revisionist westerns, few are as good as *The Shootist* (1975) by Glendon Swarthout. It is a marvelous piece of writing with fine, well rounded, believable characters who remain alive far after the reader has finished the book. It is also realistic and antiromantic, yet it uses many formulary elements.

The story is a simple one of a gunman, John Book, dying of prostate cancer. He comes to El Paso seeking help, but all the doctor can do is give him six weeks to live. He takes a room at the lodgings of widow

Bond Rogers, whose son, Gillom, immediately recognizes Book. At first both Mrs. Rogers and the marshal try to get Book out of town, but when he tells them he is dying of cancer, he is allowed to stay. Slowly, he comes to care for Mrs. Rogers and her son, not in some romantic way but, as Book himself says, he has no one else to care about. One night violence erupts when two men try to sneak in to kill him, but Book, even though he is dying, refuses to be killed. He also refuses to let fate decree how he shall die, and he calls out five city toughs and tells them to meet him in the saloon. In a shootout, he kills all five, but he is wounded so badly that when Gillom enters the saloon, Book can speak just enough to ask the youngster to kill him.

Despite the fact that *The Shootist* is relatively short, a simple summary cannot do it justice. The novel is filled with too many important incidents that further the action and build characters, and there is not one wasted word in the entire work. In many ways, it is the perfect western novel. *Shane* was perfect, too, but these two novels, opposite sides of the same coin, are completely different in treatment and outlook. *Shane* is a very romantic treatment of the subject, *The Shootist* a very realistic one. Yet, so many plot devices connect the two — a young boy who becomes attracted to the gunman, the boy's mother who is also drawn to him, the town that turns against the gunman, and finally the gunman shooting it out with the villains and the boy a party to it all.

The Shootist (Dino de Laurentiis Corp., 1976) became John Wayne's last film, and it is among the star's very best. It opens with tinted clips from some of Wayne's other films, including *Red River,* in which we see him supposedly as Book gunning down man after man. Therefore, later when we see him riding down a street filled with trolley cars and milk wagons, it is jarring, as if he is totally out of place in the modern world. After all, here is a giant of the West, a true primitive, surrounded by civilization. Then when we learn that Book has cancer, which Wayne had and was later to die of, we are again jolted. In the novel, Book was a character who had no history outside of the novel. Not so with Wayne. As the audience, we have seen John Wayne in countless westerns — he is, after all, almost an icon — and to have him reduced to dying on screen of prostate cancer is shocking.

The film is obviously intended as an elegy for the western, but director Don Siegel saw in Wayne and the character of Book his consummate hero who stoically faces up to death and meets it on his own terms. It is in Book's relationship with Mrs. Rogers (Lauren Bacall) and especially with Gillom (Ron Howard) around which the films grows and takes on added meaning. Since the death of his father, Gillom has been falling in with the wrong people, and he needs direction. In a way, when Book challenges the three toughs—cut down from five in the novel—to meet him in the saloon, he is not only choosing his own way to go out but he is also choosing the path that Gillom will take in life. Book kills the three toughs, but he is shot down by the bartender. Gillom snatches up one of Book's pistols and downs the bartender. Although the ending has been changed, the result is the same. Book is dead, and Gillom has chosen to be like Book, a loner, an outsider. Realistic yet touching, harsh yet moving, this is a magnificent film, and like the novel, one that works within formalistic conventions to present a deep, resonant story full of wisdom.

Ever deepening and more complex characters, more meaningful thematic content, a hard edge of realism, an upward spiraling of violence—all these became part of the new western that began to appear in the early 1940s and has continued right up until today. It may well be that the revisionist *The Ox-Bow Incident* signalled the beginning of the death of the formulary western exemplified by Zane Grey and Clarence E. Mulford by indicating these new directons and a new maturity. This trend seems to have reached its logical conclusion with *The Shootist* in which a traditional western hero is reduced to dying of cancer, a "modern" disease that destroys the primitive. Between these two landmark novels, other revisionist works also brought a new look and changed forever the structure and content of the western. Just as these works influenced whole generations of writers, they also influenced whole generations of films adapted from them. Films that were influential—*The Ox-Bow Incident, The Man Who Shot Liberty Valance, The Shootist*—undoubtedly changed the nature of the motion picture western by doing for film what the novels and short stories did for literature.

13. The Modern West

There are a number of novels that while not strictly westerns—
they might be called "country westerns"—are derivative in their settings
and plots. This type of fiction was particularly popular around the turn
of the century through the early 1920s, but after that, it quietly and
gratefully died, remembered now more as a curiosity rather than any
significant contribution to literature. This subgenre is best typified by
Harold Bell Wright and John Fox, Jr.

One of the most popular novelists of the first quarter of the twentieth century was Harold Bell Wright. The success Wright found can
be traced to the growing demand in America for wholesome, domestic
fiction. Within his novels he included both sermons and sentimentality,
love interest and conflict. Most of his novels had outdoor settings and
included a great deal of patriotism. He also attempted to inject morally
uplifting Christian messages, and the titles often indicated the
message— *That Printer of Udells: A Story of Practical Christianity; A Vigorous
Story,* or *The Calling of Dan Matthews: The Ministry of Daily Life; A Vital
Story.*

The Shepherd of the Hills marks the beginning of "country westerns."
It tells of Daniel Howitt, a former minister of a large church in Chicago
who travels to the Ozark Mountains in order to escape the civilization
that has disillusioned and broken him by its artificial and shallow ways.
If the city has betrayed him, the country restores him. The hill
folk recognize immediately that this is a special man, a man of God.
But if the hills transform Howitt, he, in turn, becomes a shepherd
and teacher to those who know him, bringing together Young Matt,
Wright's ideal man, and Sammy, Wright's ideal woman. Sammy is a
motherless girl whose father is involved with crooks, and Howitt
reshapes her from a rough, primitive girl to a fully developed woman

271

ready for the responsibilities of the home. Even after her reformation, she is still untainted and pure, a true child of nature. Only at the end does a cloud appear on the horizon. Word comes that the railroad is headed into Howitt's beloved Ozarks, and just before the former minister dies, he utters his fears: "Before many years, the railroad will find its way yonder. Then many will come, and the beautiful hills that have been my strength and peace will become the haunt of careless idlers and a place of revelry." Not long after Howitt is gone, Matt and Sammy hear a distant explosion. Workers are blasting to make a path for the railroad. Underlying this optimistic tale is a strain of pessimism and fear. The city will soon destroy the country.

The first time *The Shepherd of the Hills* (Wright, 1919) reached the screen proved to be the most faithful adaptation, mainly because Harold Bell Wright produced, wrote and directed the film, but it was a crude effort by a man who little understood the cinema. A second silent version (First National, 1928) was also made, and once again, the basic plot of the Wright novel was followed. However, the most famous version of *The Shepherd of the Hills* (Paramount, 1941), and the best of the three, is actually an early John Wayne vehicle. Wright was still alive at the time but the scriptwriting chores were turned over to Grover Jones and Stuart Anthony. This time little of the original novel made it to the screen.

Young Matt (John Wayne) is a hotheaded mountain boy who has vowed to kill his father, who he believes deserted him and his mother years before and wrecked her life. Matt's all consuming desire for revenge has kept his sweetheart, Sammy Lane (Betty Field), from marrying him. Into the hills comes the Shepherd (Harry Carey), called so by the mountain folk for all the kindnesses that he does for them. The climax comes when Matt discovers the Shepherd is also his father, who has been in jail for years. Before Matt can carry out his revenge, the Shepherd, his own father, shoots Matt to keep him from becoming a murderer and suffering the same fate as he. Matt recovers from his wound and is reconciled with his father. Now he and Sammy can look forward to a bright, unspoiled future.

While most of the plot of Wright's novel is missing, many of the other ingredients are here. It is an overly sentimentalized, corny drama that extols the virtues of the mountain folk. Where the scriptwriters made an important change is in the darkness of Matt's character, his incessant need for revenge to clear the cloud of uncertainty that hovers over him. In the end, the cloud vanishes and optimism reigns. There is no threat of the railroad or of onrushing civilization to darken the horizon. It looks as if the idyllic mountain life will go on forever, untouched and unspoiled, now that the Shepherd has returned to set things right.

Wright's one true western, *The Winning of Barbara Worth* [1911]: *The Ministry of Capital: A Clean Story,* is perhaps Wright's best novel. The book jacket further elaborated the novel as "a clean a story as man ever wrote — a story with big incidents, strong people, high ideals and the Spirit of the West."

When Samuel Goldwyn decided to produce *The Winning of Barbara Worth* (United Artists, 1926), he wasn't interested in the "clean story" but rather the big incidents, the kind that make for entertaining films along the lines of *The Covered Wagon* or *The Iron Horse.* In writing the scenario, Francis Marion followed the novel closely but omitted Wright's philosophical musings on capitalism, the result of which seems the opposite of the author's intention to show "the ministry of capital." Instead, villain James Greenfield (E.J. Ratcliffe), is an unscrupulous builder who uses cheap material to build a dam in the Imperial Valley of California. To the West comes engineer William Holmes (Ronald Colman) to work on a rival dam. At first, Holmes is out of place in this new environment, but he soon proves his mettle. In the meantime, he falls in love with Barbara Worth (Vilma Banky), an orphan who has been raised by Jefferson Worth, Holmes' employer. Also in love with Barbara is shy Abe Lee (Gary Cooper in his first role), another employee of Worth. When Holmes discovers that Greenfield's dam is about to collapse, he and Abe Lee rush to warn the threatened settlers. They are attacked by Greenfield's men, and in the ensuing shootout, Lee is killed but Holmes gets away. Greenfield's dam collapses, and Greenfield is washed away in his own flood. Without further trouble, Holmes completes his dam and marries Barbara Worth.

While a simple summary sounds as if the film is an action packed adventure, the reverse is actually true. With the exception of the final shootout and the flood, most of the film is a love triangle which mirrors the title, *The Winning of Barbara Worth,* not the epic that Goldwyn had imagined. Some critics pointed out that casting was also a problem, that Vilma Banky, an Hungarian, and Colman, an Englishman, were not right for their parts. However, the public loved them together, and Goldwyn paired Banky and Colman in three more films, turning them into one of the hottest love duos of silent films. Both the public and the critics also loved Gary Cooper, and this film launched his career. In addition, cameraman Greg Toland beautifully captured all the desert drama of howling sandstorms as well as the climactic flood that wipes the land free of the capitalistic blight of Greenfield, certainly the single most impressive scene in the film.

While *The Winning of Barbara Worth* lacks the ingredients to make it a truly great silent film, it is an enjoyable one. Although not exactly what Goldwyn had in mind, the film is a pleasant diversion with some good acting and outstanding location photography. If the film misses being what Harold Bell Wright intended, it is stronger for it.

Harold Bell Wright had several other novels made into films. *When a Man's a Man* (1916) grew out of the author's battle with tuberculosis which plagued him most of his life. He recuperated in Arizona, and like Zane Grey, came to feel that the West held powers to restore both physically and spiritually. It was made first as a silent (First National, 1924) and then as a sound feature (Fox, 1935). *The Mine with the Iron Door* (1923), which gave a very sympathetic portrait of an Apache Indian, was also made twice (United Artists, 1924, and Columbia, 1936). In addition, two novels with nonwestern settings were made into westerns. *The Recreation of Brian Kent* (1919) became *Wild Brian Kent* (20th Fox, 1936) in which a polo playing socialite from the East (Ralph Bellamy) comes west and helps save a ranch for an old woman and her daughter. *Helen of the Old House* (1921) became *Western Gold* (Principal, 1937), a below average "B" starring Smith Bellew, a singing cowboy who never made it big.

Like Harold Bell Wright, John Fox, Jr., wrote one of the most popular of all "country westerns" with *The Trail of the Lonesome Pine* (1913), which had an advance sale of more than 100,000 copies in the first edition. In all, the novel has sold well past the two million mark. In many ways, it is superior to *The Shepherd of the Hills* or any of Wright's other novels with the exception of *The Winning of Barbara Worth*.

The novel is set in Big Stone Gap, Kentucky, an area where Fox grew up. Incidentally, he was a member of the Home Guard, which, in the novel, struggles against the lawless elements of the countryside. When the region became the focus of industrialists who promised to make it the Pittsburgh of the South, Fox invested a great deal of money which he lost when the project collapsed, and the town never recovered.

The Trail of the Lonesome Pine opens with Jack Hale, an engineer from the outside world entering the area of Big Stone Gap where he meets and falls in love with June Tolliver, a highly intelligent but ignorant mountain girl. Recognizing her basic ability, Jack persuades her to attend school in Big Stone Gap and later to go to Louisville to live with his sister. As June becomes more educated and worldly, Jack, still back in Big Stone Gap, drifts into a shiftless and meaningless life. June returns, straightens him out and the two eventually marry.

The central love story is weak and sentimental and far too similar to other such romances. What distinguishes this novel is the abundance of local color that the author injects into the narrative: mountain entertainment such as corn shuckings and quilting parties; women who smoke their pipes and eat after their men; stills built and used by the men to raise money. Of far more interest than Jack and June are the minor characters, such as: Devil Judd Tolliver, June's father, who is suspicious of all outsiders and of the outside world; Bad Rufe Tolliver who kills a man during a mountain feud and is sentenced to hang; Red Fox, a preacher who is also a murderer and suffers the same fate as Rufe. By any standards, *The Trail of the Lonesome Pine* is not a great novel, but it does have its strengths, which probably makes it the best this subgenre has to offer.

In 1912 *The Trail of the Lonesome Pine* became a Broadway play written by Eugene Walter. The first film version (Paramount, 1916) was directed by Cecil B. DeMille, who hired Walter to write the scenario, and as a result, most of Fox's plot disappeared and the plot of the play was substituted. A district revenue officer, Jack Hale (Thomas Meighan), is sent into the Virginia mountains to locate a whiskey still. There he falls in love with June Tolliver (Charlotte Walker), daughter of moonshiners, who use June as a decoy. The end finds old Judd Tolliver (Theodore Roberts) destroying his own still and killing the relative who betrayed him, and then allowing June and Jack to marry. The film opened to generally good reviews with Theodore Roberts as Judd singled out as the highlight of the film. *The Trail of the Lonesome Pine* was remade again as a silent (Paramount, 1923) with Antonio Moreno as Jack and Mary Miles Minter as June. This lackluster version was directed by Charles Maigne and followed the plot of the previous version.

The only sound version of *The Trail of the Lonesome Pine* (Paramount, 1936) was Paramount's first venture into color, and the process added much to the story and to the box office receipts. With a strong screenplay from Grover Jones, who later worked on *The Shepherd of the Hills,* and Horace McCoy, it also proved to be the best of the three versions. The story was completely changed. Jack (Fred MacMurray) is an engineer who comes to the mountains where he becomes involved with a feud between neighboring clans. He first tries to educate June Tolliver (Sylvia Sidney), then he falls in love with her, much to the consternation of her brother Dave (Henry Fonda). When Dave is killed in the feud, his mother Melissa (Beulah Bondi) cries out against violence and bloodshed, helping to bring peace to the region. June and Jack are united at fade out.

Considering the popularity of the novel and of the two previous films, this version could easily have been only a poor imitation, but rather than looking the part of a throwback, it appeared modern and updated. With the strong screenplay, vigorous direction from Henry Hathaway, and fine acting, it proved that a remake could actually be better than its predecessors, a rare triumph indeed. Like the novel on which it is based, *The Trail of the Lonesome Pine* is the best of the "country westerns."

This sub-genre passed away long ago, seemingly for good, until it suddenly resurfaced almost forty years later, minus the heavy sentimentalizing and sermonizing. The new breed of country westerns were to probe far deeper into the psyches of the American hinterland. Such films as *Badlands* (Columbia, 1973), *Sugarland Express* (Universal, 1974) and *Thieves Like Us* (United Artists, 1974) took the country western into a far darker and more pessimistic world than that envisioned by Harold Bell Wright and John Fox, Jr.

One of the strangest of all fiction writers is B. Traven, a recluse who emigrated to Mexico where he wrote a number of novels and short stories, the most notable of which is *The Treasure of Sierra Madre* (1935), a searing indictment of capitalistic greed. Few people ever met B. Traven. When John Huston was in the process of filming the movie in Mexico, a man showed up on the set one day and offered him a business card with the name H. Croves and a letter from Traven explaining that "H. Croves" was his representative. Huston soon deduced that Croves was Traven, although he was never able to confirm it.

The strangeness of Traven's character carried over to his novel, *The Treasure of Sierra Madre,* a western only in its inclusion of many formalistic ingredients — American prospectors searching for gold; a wild, primitive landscape through with the men must pass; bandits who attack the prospectors; Indians who rescue them. Yet, this is a nightmarish and revisionist picture of gold mining, an antiromantic view that is more interesting in examining greed and its effects on men than in presenting a tale of adventure.

The story opens in Tampico and much of the early action takes place in the Hotel Oso Negro, a dirty, dingy flophouse where a form of communism has evolved. Men who steal are severely dealt with by the other lodgers, and women are never molested. Here lives old man Howard, who looks too old to walk, and here Howard meets first Dobbs and later Curtin with whom he forms a partnership to search for gold. When Dobbs and Curtin are exploited by capitalist Pat McCormick, they find him in a bar and beat him up, rolling him for money that he owes them. Later, when Dobbs wins the lottery, he throws that money into the pot, and the men have enough to join Howard in a trek into the Sierra Madre Mountains. At one point, they are attacked by bandits led by Gold Hat. They are also joined by Lacaud, a half-mad prospector from Arizona. When Howard, Dobbs and Curtin finally leave the mountain, the gold exhausted, Lacaud remains behind still working the gutted mine.

Their life on the mountain has not been an idyllic existence. On the contrary, greed has slowly eaten away at their insides, and Dobbs turns on Curtin after Howard has been swept off to the Indian village to help cure a stricken native child. Alone with only the burros and gold, Dobbs runs into three bandits who murder him for the burros and his boots. In the meantime, Howard and the Indians have found Curtin still alive, and they ride after Dobbs. Of course, all they find is his body. Howard has been offered a permanent position as medicine man with the Indians, and he invites Curtin to join him as his assistant. As the book ends, Curtin is considering staying with Howard.

When John Huston came to adapt *The Treasure of Sierra Madre* (Warner Bros., 1948), he made a decision change several important episodes. He completely dropped an early one where Dobbs (Humphrey Bogart), another American and a cowardly Indian travel through the jungles to an oil camp in hope of finding jobs. During the night, they are spooked by what they believe to be a tiger and spend the night in a tree, but morning light shows it only to be a burro. At another point, Howard tells a parable of a doctor who cures an Indian chief's son of blindness and is rewarded with a silver mine. But the doctor gets too greedy, and exploits the Indians by forcing them to dig the mine. The doctor is murdered by the Indians, and the doctor's wife takes over the mine; she disappears, and the regional viceroy steals her money. This parable anticipates Howard's later action when he leaves the village to search for Curtin (Tim Holt). He takes no riches, only a very good horse. In Huston's script, Howard (Walter Huston) needed no parable to motivate his goodness.

Another story from the novel involves Lacaud. As the bandits are moving up the mountain to attack the camp, he tells a long story of bandits robbing a train and killing countless women and children. In the film, the character of Lacaud becomes Cody (Bruce Bennett), and while he tells no such story, Huston makes use of it by having Howard, Dobbs and Curtin on a train that is attacked by Gold Hat and his bandits. The incident is far less violent than Lacaud's story. Only four people on the train are killed, all off screen.

In the novel, Lacaud introduces himself and offers little other information. He is still alive and working the mine as the others leave.
However, in the film Lacaud/Cody is seen by Dobbs and Curtin as
threat to their position, and they persuade Howard that the three must
kill him. Just as they are about to do it, Gold Hat (Alfonso Bedoya) and
his bandits attack, and in the ensuing fight, Cody is killed. In Cody's
pocket, they find a letter and discover that he has left behind a wife, a
child and a fruit orchard in Texas. This particular scene is far too sentimental and nostalgic for such a tough minded film and seems decidedly
out of place.

Another change involves Gold Hat. In the novel, he appears only
once when the bandits attack the mine. It is in this scene that he utters,
"Badges? I don't have to show you any stinkin' badges." However,
Huston has him appear three times — at the train holdup, at the mine
and later at the water hole as one of the three bandits who kills Dobbs.
It is at the water hole that Huston has Gold Hat recall the phrase just
before he and his men kill Dobbs.

With the exception of the latter sequence, none of the changes hurt
the film. On the contrary, each change strengthened it cinematically,
adding continuity and tightening the story. Despite their few
differences, both the novel and the film deal with the overpowering cor-
ruption of greed. Slowly, the desire for gold comes between the partners. At first, when their diggings produce only moderate dust, they
treat the stuff with relative nonchalance, but as it grows, so does their
fear of one another. Basically a good man — he has fought beside Curtin
and loaned his friend money to finance his part in the expedition —
Dobbs crumbles before the lust for gold. His ragged clothes fall from
his body, dirt clings to him as if part of his skin and he slouches like an
animal as he mumbles to himself of the deceptions he falsely believes
Howard and Curtin are planning. In this microscopic examination of
one of man's basic weaknesses, Traven's novel and Huston's film are
one and the same.

Fred Gipson wrote a number of interesting novels that are also on
the fringes of western literature and somewhat akin to Harold Bell
Wright and John Fox, Jr. *Hound Dog Man* (1949) was the story of a
young boy's entrance into the hardships and wonders of the frontier.
The adaptation, which became *The Return of the Texan* (TCF, 1952) was
an interesting film that shifted the emphasis to the father (Dale Robinson) and the time to present. It was an unassuming and quiet little film
that, in tone, caught the flavor of Gipson's novel even though most of
the events came from the scriptwriters. Another novel, *Old Yeller* (1956),

is an excellent book for teens, telling the story of fourteen-year-old Travis and his love for his dog, Old Yeller. The stray dog hunts for game, guards the crops and protects the family. After rescuing Travis' mother from a diseased wolf, Old Yeller gets hydrophobia. Travis says, "It was going to kill something inside of me to do it, but I knew then that I had to shoot my big yeller dog. I stuck the muzzle of the gun against his head and pulled the trigger."

Travis is forced to kill Old Yeller for the good of the household, and this painful act symbolizes the responsibility of approaching manhood. Like the novel, the film (Buena Vista, 1958) uses understatement to achieve its purpose. The ending has been changed, but not much is damaged in the process. Instead of a rabid wolf, Travis (Tommy Kirk) is attacked by a pack of wild boars, and even though he and Old Yeller fight them off, both are injured. From this battle, the dog contracts rabies, and Travis is forced to shoot him. In the novel, the fight with the boars took place much earlier, and Old Yeller's stomach is ripped open. Travis sews Old Yeller together, and the dog survives until the fatal encounter with the wolf.

A later novel, *Savage Sam* (1962), was also filmed by Disney (Buena Vista, 1963), and while it was officially a sequel to *Old Yeller,* it had little in common other than the character names of the principals. Where in the previous film, the dog had been the central figure, here he is only a character who influences the action. It also misses the depth of characterization and warmth of the earlier entry. However, this and the other two adaptations of Fred Gipson's novels are enjoyable films, and it must be said that this minor author was well served by Hollywood.

With *Cimarron,* Edna Ferber wrote a novel that began with the death of the Old West amidst the birth of the New. But it was the New West itself that is her subject in *Giant* (1952), a big, sprawling novel of modern Texas. Although the reviews were mixed, the novel proved her best since *Cimarron* and showed a tightness of style and content, but many Texans were upset at her portrayal of their native state.

Giant is the story of the Benedict family, whose ranch is a symbol of Texas itself. Most of the conflict in the early part of the novel, which opens in the 1930s, centers on the struggle between Bick Benedict and his wife, Leslie, the outsider, who is able to think for herself. While this relationship is often forced—Leslie's feelings for Bick and for Texas are interchangeable, as if one is the other—later, when the children come along, the novel deepens considerably. When his son marries a woman of Mexican descent, Bick is forced to come to terms with his own prejudices. The Benedict family becomes a symbol of all families that must develop and grow in order to preserve their love for one another, and this is both a moving and deeply felt portion of the novel.

The film *Giant* (Warner Bros., 1956) made more of the prejudice issue than the novel. About half way through the three hour and seventeen minute running time, Leslie (Elizabeth Taylor) is helping the Mexican peons, and Bick (Rock Hudson) becomes very upset. They argue, and she flees back to Maryland from where she came. Bick goes after her, and they reconcile. Years later, when Bick's son (Dennis Hopper) marries a Mexican girl, Bick is distressed, but when his son and wife are kept from attending Jett Rink's party and his son beaten up, Bick threatens to give Jett (James Dean) the beating of his life. Another incident further illuminates Bick's changing attitudes. When his daughter-in-law and grandchild are insulted by a cafe owner, Bick takes exception, and a fight breaks out, a grand, glorious fight in which Bick, now in his fifties, is badly beaten.

In light of later civil rights movements, the stand of *Giant* seems small and feeble. However, it is not here that the film shows it strengths. Actually, the fight at the cafe seems overdone, a bludgeon to pound in the point in case anyone has missed it. Nor does the film show strength in the characters of Bick and Leslie, rather stiffly acted by Rock Hudson and Elizabeth Taylor. Actually the strong point of *Giant* is in the very area that many Texans objected to the novel — the absurdity of the Texas nouveaux riches which had so much money that they had no idea how to spend their wealth except by bigness. Explaining the ranch to Leslie, Bick says, "My papa built it to show the cotton crowd he was just as big as they were." Jett builds a hotel in Waco to show just how important he has become, and the final ballroom scene of the party is a massive event. Only in the end does Bick halfheartedly admit that bigness isn't worth pursuing.

Another strong point is the character of Jett Rink, who seems more alive on the screen than in the novel. Perhaps this is because of James Dean's outstanding performance as the sullen, arrogant Texan who is an outsider himself and who becomes one of the richest men in Texas and changes the lives of the Benedict family forever. However, where both the novel and the film miss a point is in the character of Bick's sister (Mercedes McCambridge) who resents the prim and proper Eastern woman that Bick has taken for a wife. What might have developed as a smoldering and fiery conflict between East and West ends abruptly when the sister is thrown from a horse and dies.

Giant is full of vivid and lasting images — the Benedict house standing tall and alone on the empty plain; the gusher that drenches Jett in oil; Jett drunkenly struggling to deliver his triumphant speech; the vast wine cellar that topples like dominoes. Here lies the film's major strength. In its various images, director George Stevens, a perfectionist behind the camera, makes the Texas of *Giant* come alive far better than Edna Ferber did in her novel. George Stevens had a feeling for the country and its people, a feeling that Ferber failed to display in her novel.

Occasionally an action writer would turn away from the past and write a contemporary story of the West, which is exactly what Steve Frazee did in "My Brother Down There," which first appeared in *Ellery Queen's Mystery Magazine* and was later anthologized in *Best American Short Stories: 1953*. It is the story of a manhunt for four escaped convicts in the Colorado wilderness and its long range effects on both the hunted and the hunters. As the manhunt progresses, the main character, deputy sheriff Bill Melvin, begins to understand that we are all brothers in one way or another. When he finally has the last convict sighted in his rifle, he cannot pull the trigger and another deputy, one who enjoys killing, finishes the job. Made as a "B" to fill the second half of double features, Frazee's story became *Running Target* (United Artists, 1956). In this version, it is the sheriff (Arthur Frantz) who leads the posse after the four dangerous fugitives. Of course, a love interest is thrown in. Surprisingly, the script delivers solidly drawn characters, and the acting and direction are also quite good. For a low budget effort, this is a remarkably satisfying film, and in many ways, very faithful to its source.

Another Frazee story, "The Singing Sands" (1954), has echoes of *Treasure of Sierra Madre*. The story opens with a young man, Anderson, and his older, wiser companion, Jasper Lamb, carrying a mule load of gold out of the Rocky Mountains. Pursued by a gang of men who want the gold, Jasper persuades Anderson to hide the gold near some sand dunes. But when they return several months later, they discover sand ten feet deep has shifted over the gold. Anderson wants to dig the gold out, but the older Lamb, recognizing the impossibility of the task, says that Anderson can have his share of the gold and rides off. For months, Anderson fights the shifting sand, trying to get to the gold. All the time, Hollister, one of the men who chased them, is watching. At last, Anderson also sees the impossibility of the job. When confronted by Hollister, Anderson sells him the secret of the gold and rides off himself. Years later, Hollister dies, a crazed old man muttering of lost gold.

There is no way that a plot summary can adequately set the tone and mood of this excellent story, and unfortunately, neither the plot not the tone made it to the film *Gold of the Seven Saints* (Warner Bros., 1961), a cheaply made and poorly written adventure film without distinction. Shaun Garrett (Roger Moore), an Irish cowboy, and his strong, silent partner Rainbolt (Clint Walker) must transport a cache of gold through the desert and across the mountains, and they are pursued by men who want the gold. A girl (Leticia Roman) shows up, and the partners briefly argue over her before the final showdown with the pursuers. Black and white stock footage, routine direction and a weak script turn a really excellent story into an extremely weak film.

The clash of the Old West and the New West is again delineated clearly in Edward Abbey's *The Brave Cowboy* (1956), subtitled *An Old Tale in a New Time*. It laments the sad fate of Jack Burns, a cowboy whose values are those of the nineteenth century. In that time he would have been perceived as heroic, but he lives in the twentieth century and his actions turn him into a hunted man. When Burns returns to New Mexico from Montana, he learns that his friend Bondi is in jail. He purposely gets himself thrown in jail in order to help Bondi break out, but Bondi wants no part of the scheme. He is willing to wait out his time. Burns breaks out, and with his horse, he heads into the mountains pursued by the law that uses automobiles, helicopters and all the technology possible to capture him. Just as he seems to have made good his escape, technology delivers a deadly and ironic blow. He is trying to get himself and his horse across a busy, rain-slick highway when they are struck down and killed by a truck carrying toilet seats.

In his various nonfiction books, particularly the wonderful *Desert Solitaire,* Abbey has attacked the developers and exploiters of the modern west. He often has a three-fold message contained within: 1) preserve the wilderness, 2) limit commercial growth along with the population, and 3) resist governmental intrusion. All three of these ideas are embodied in *The Brave Cowboy*. In fact, all three are wrapped up in the conclusion. The highway across which Burns is trying to escape cuts right through the wilderness of New Mexico. It is crowded with cars and commercial vehicles that threaten and finally destroy the protagonist and his horse. And, finally, it is the law that drives the cowboy to his death.

The Brave Cowboy is an important and satisfying work of fiction. Its style is vivid and moving, its tone consistent and its characters three dimensional. If it has a weakness, it lies in the irony of the denouement, which may be a little heavy handed. However, Abbey has foreshadowed the event so well that it is far less jarring than it would otherwise have been. *The Brave Cowboy* ranks among the best of contemporary westerns.

The novel became *Lonely Are the Brave* (Universal, 1962), a self-consciously serious commentary on the contemporary West. Script-writer Dalton Trumbo attempted to invest mythic qualities in the Abbey story, and while it may fall short of this lofty goal, Jack Burns (Kirk Douglas) does emerge as the last real cowboy who is in conflict with and ultimately defeated by technology. As the film opens, Burns is alone on the desert when overhead passes a screaming jet, a symbol of all that the cowboy hates. Soon after, he rides up to a barbed wire fence and contemptuously cuts the wires in order to ride through. Modern boundaries and modern laws have little meaning to him. He is a man of the open range, a hundred years out of date.

When Burns breaks jail, he is tracked by a determined by sympathetic sheriff (Walter Matthau) who half hopes the cowboy will escape. Burns can escape if he will only release his horse, but the horse is a symbol, too, a symbol of the freedom and of outmoded ideals that Burns loves. He cannot let go. So together, the pair climb the mountains in an effort to escape. The law brings to bear all its modern resources, but even these don't appear to be enough. At one point, Burns shoots a helicopter out of the sky. Occasionally, just as in the novel, the action pulls away from Burns and his pursuers to concentrate on a driver and truck full of toilet seats travelling across the country. At last, the two stories come crashing together, and Burns is still alive to hear a lawman shoot his horse.

The ending of the film is more ambiguous than the novel. The films ends with Burns still alive, busted up inside, dying perhaps, but alive. In the novel, immediately after his horse is shot, Burns dies in the trucker's arms. Along the highway, people encased in their machines rush by, unfeeling, uncaring. It is a powerful end, more powerful than the film's. Although the direction is a bit strident, *Lonely Are the Brave* is a fine film and a good adaptation of the novel, but the novel, a wonderful piece of fiction, carries far more power and impact.

The comic western began with Henry Leon Wilson's *Ruggles of Red Gap* in 1915, and various writers have attempted to master the sub-genre right up to the present. Among those who have practiced this difficult form of storytelling, Max Evans must be considered one of the most gifted with the publication of his novel *The Rounders* (1960). It tells the story of two cowboys, Ben Jones and Howdy Lewis, who are perpetual losers. They cannot win at anything, yet they manage constantly to engage the readers' sympathies because they represent Everyman. Each is an average guy who just never seems to get out of life what he wants, just as the average American seldom gets what he wants. But what sets this novel apart from most mainstream American literature is that the land rather than society influences the cowboys, influences them in a way that heroes from Cooper to Steinbeck have been influenced by the land.

The film *The Rounders* (MGM, 1965) is one of those curious items that the studio had no idea how to handle. As a result, it was released on the second half of double bills with *Get Yourself a College Girl,* a disaster that almost ruined the careers of several budding stars. However, *The Rounders* was a charming film full of good humor and good performances. Also, it was wonderfully scripted by Burt Kennedy, who also directed. Realizing that the slight novel was rich in incident and character, he stuck close to the source.

Ben Jones (Glenn Ford) and Howdy Lewis (Henry Fonda) are a couple of Arizona cowhands who hope to make enough money busting broncos so they can retire and open a bar. Their scheme backfires. They enter a drunk horse in a rodeo and clean up on the bets, but as usual, they lose all their money when the horse destroys a stable. In the midst of all of this, they become involved with twin sisters, Agatha and Meg Moore, and later two strippers from Las Vegas (Sue Ann Langdon and Hope Holiday), with whom they go skinny dipping. Perhaps the studio believed the film to be a downer since the two cowboys end up exactly where they began — broke and not much wiser for their efforts. If so, the studio missed the point of the movie, a funny, fast moving little film that provided plenty of good entertainment in its 85 minutes. It caught the tone and the mood of the novel from which it was adapted, in large part due to the wonderful leadership of writer-director Burt Kennedy, who understood the gem he had. It's too bad the studio didn't understand.

Descended from two generations of cattle ranchers, Larry McMurtry is a native Texan whose novels, while mostly contemporary, reflect values and influences from the historical American West and the conflict of these values with the modern world. He often focuses on the rootless character of the new American West, a West in which technology in the form of cars and moving pictures are part of the terrain. In the area of relationships, he often focuses on the instability of modern marriage. Women emerge as strong characters who are often liberated but unsettled. It is McMurtry's keen social observation of this new American West that has gained him the reputation as the creator of the "urban western."

Of McMurtry's earlier novels, the best known is probably his first, *Horseman, Pass By* (1961), mainly because it became the basis of the film

Hud, a title which is both misleading and inappropriate since the novel is really about other characters more than about Hud. Actually the story is told from the perspective of seventeen-year-old Lonnie Bannon, but the theme is the passing of a way of ranching that had begun in the nineteenth century, a period that was still vaguely visible at the time the action occurs. Homer Bannon, a relic from the past, represents the values of courage and endurance that assured the survival of the Old West, but he also resists change, including allowing drilling for oil on his ranch. His antagonist is Hud Bannon, Homer's stepson, whose only values are those that involve profit. Caught between these two forces, Lonnie tries to forge his own values based on the concepts of right and wrong.

The death of a single cow early in the narrative sets the stage for all that is to follow. The cow has died of hoof and mouth disease, and the entire herd must be destroyed. Hud insists that Homer sell the cows to whoever will buy them before the final tests are known. When Homer refuses, Hud sets in motion legal maneuvers to have the old man declared incompetent and have himself made executor of the estate. Too old to start anew, Homer retreats into the past. Thus is set in motion the conflict between the old and the new. The herd is destroyed by government agents, and Homer observes, "Don't take very long to kill things. Not like it takes to grow." Homer personally shoots two longhorns he raised and kept for sentimental reasons. Lonnie understands the symbolic meaning of the act, and he has a premonition of his grandfather's death, which occurs soon thereafter when Hud finds the old man critically injured. After Homer's death, Lonnie feels that he can no longer stay on the ranch, and he sets out to find himself, becoming one of the rootless, wandering Westerners that McMurtry is so fond of.

Hud (Paramount, 1963) was advertised as a character with a "barbed-wire soul," and even before he appears, the audience is alerted to his reputation. Early one dawn, Lonnie (Brandon de Wilde) wanders through a Texas town and past a bar with a broken window. Out rushes the angry owner who screams that Hud (Paul Newman) did it the night before. When Lonnie finally locates Hud's Cadillac outside a married woman's house, he honks the horn and Hud comes out buttoning his shirt, a smirk on his face. About this time, up drives the husband in his station wagon—obviously a salesman just returning from a long business trip—who is understandably upset to find two men outside his wife's door. Hud shifts the blame to his nephew before whisking them both off in his Cadillac.

Hud drinks too much, drives too fast and plays around with any woman in skirts. He even tries to seduce Alma (Patricia Neal), his housekeeper, who is drawn to him but who lashes out at him for being a "cold-blooded bastard." When he attempts to rape her, he drives her away. She is not the only one who thinks badly of Hud. His own aging father, Homer (Melvyn Douglas), claims that he has always hated Hud for "not giving a damn." It is even hinted that Hud was responsible for his own brother's death, and this may be the cause of his father's hatred. Of those who might have loved him, Hud can only say, "My mama loved me, but she died."

When the diseased cattle are discovered, Hud tries to sell the herd before it becomes known, but his father prevents him and complies with the government's regulations. As in the novel, Homer shoots his longhorns, although the action happens off screen. Through all of this, Hud remains cynical. Homer dies of a stroke, and Lonnie, disillusioned, decides to leave the ranch. As he walks away, Hud shouts after him, "You'll find out the world is full of crap!" But the only one full of crap is Hud. Everyone else in the film is basically good. Hud can't even make out a case for himself as a man warped by a corrupt world for the world in which he lives doesn't seem all that corrupt.

Hud is a superior contemporary western. The black and white photography of James Wong Howe adds a dimension to the novel by capturing the bleak, barren Texas landscape and using it as a symbol of the spiritual desolation inherent in the script. Martin Ritt directed superbly, allowing the action to flow naturally out of the characters, and the greased pig contest and the shooting of the cattle are first rate sequences. Only the fight in the bar that brings a momentary sense of camaraderie between Hud and Lonnie seems forced and reminiscent of too many old westerns.

The film makes one basic but important change of emphasis. Hud becomes the central character. It is essentially his story, and though we may condemn his actions, we cannot help but admire the son-of-a-bitch. After all, he is played by Paul Newman, and even at his most cruel moments, he somehow has us rooting for him rather than Homer. In the novel the perspective is that of Lonnie, but the focus is upon Homer and his struggle against Hud's New West values. While all the characters are well rounded, there is never a time when the reader's sympathies lie with Hud. Even the fact that Hud is a stepson in the novel rather than a son as he is in the film adds a bit of distancing between the two antagonists and allows the reader to side more easily with Homer.

McMurtry's second novel, *Leaving Cheyenne* (1963), proved to be far less successful than *Horseman, Pass By*. One of the central characters of this novel is Johnny, another of McMurtry's wandering cowboys, who is content always to be a hired hand. His life intertwines with Gid, a bronc buster of unusual talent who wants the money that dealing in land and cattle can offer. Together these two men become involved with the spontaneous, liberated Molly. Johnny enjoys the casual joy she brings, but Gid feels guilt. It is their love for her that is a reflection of their places in the new West. Johnny is the complete individualist, a wanderer, but he is misplaced in the modern West where his profession is no longer essential. On the other hand, Gid loves the land, but in the modern capitalistic society, he eventually succumbs to big business ranching. The structure of *Leaving Cheyenne* allows each of its three main protagonists to narrate a section. Gid tells his story first, then Molly, and finally, Johnny, this last section concluding after Gid's death, some forty years after the story has opened. Although both Gid and Johnny love Molly, she marries a third fellow, Eddie. Instead of having his children, she has one by Gid and one by Johnny, and both her sons by her lovers are killed in World War II.

In some ways, this is a richer novel than *Horseman, Pass By*. The characters seem more natural, more real, probably because we are allowed into the thoughts of each of the three main characters. Because Gid and Johnny and Molly seem so alive, the end is particularly touching, and when we put the book aside, it is like saying goodbye to old friends. But, like so many second novels, it fails to carry the same impact as *Horseman, Pass By*, perhaps because it does not have a central antagonist as strong as Hud. Also, the long passage of some forty years between the opening when the trio are kids until the end when they are past middle age dilutes the intensity of the narrative.

Columbia first titled the film *Molly, Gid and Johnny*, then retitled it *The Wild and the Sweet* before settling on *Lovin' Molly* (Columbia, 1973), a title with a supposedly double meaning. Regardless of the title, it proved to be a disaster. The first problem lay with the script that tried to explain the story of Molly (Blythe Danner) who marries someone else but for the next forty years beds Gid (Anthony Perkins) and Johnny (Beau Bridges). The story opens in 1925, and through the use of voice over, propels us into 1945 and then to 1964 when Gid falls to a heart attack. Even more than in the novel, the years got in the way of the story, turning it into shambles, and with the exception of an excellent performance by Blythe Danner, the characters never come alive. Even worse, director Sidney Lumet, whose previous films included such wonderful classics as *12 Angry Men* (1957), *The Pawnbroker* (1965) and *The Hill* (1965), missed the wistfulness of the novel so badly that Larry McMurtry castigated the director in print, accusing Lumet of having absolutely no feeling for the West. The Texas of Sidney Lumet might well have been Maine for all the importance and individuality its given. McMurtry was right; *Lovin' Molly* is a disaster.

McMurtry's third novel, *The Last Picture Show* (1966), is considerably more accomplished and ambitious than either *Horseman, Pass By* or *Leaving Cheyenne* and reveals more clearly the author's talent for social observation. In *The Last Picture Show*, McMurtry examines the narrow viewpoints and limited ambitions that plague the town of Thalia, Texas, patterned after Archer City where the author was born. Thalia is also a symbol of all small towns across America. If this is typical of life in a small town, then it is no wonder that so many of McMurtry's characters go off seeking a better life.

Narrated in third person, *The Last Picture Show* tells the story of Sonny Crawford, a high school football player, whose father, Frank, is a former principal who killed Sonny's mother. Disabled by a car wreck, Frank works in a domino parlor where he earns just enough money to keep himself in drugs. Soon after the novel opens, Sonny and his dull girlfriend Charlene break up because she refuses to let him touch her in her private parts for fear that she will get pregnant. This leads to a trip to Fort Worth with Duane, Sonny's best friend, as the two go to a whorehouse. Back in Thalia, the pair divide their time between the pool hall, the movie theater and the all-night cafe, all owned by Sam the Lion, whom Sonny likes because Sam takes care of the boys. Sam had three sons, all who died before they were eighteen.

Sonny develops a relationship with forty-year-old Ruth Popper, the neglected wife of the football coach, and under her guidance, he begins to learn the rules of mature love. But his head is turned by the fickle and callow Jacy Farrow, who has been dating both Duane and a rich kid named Lester Marlow. She cares little for Lester but uses him to get in with the rich kids of Wichita Falls. Once she is also finished with Duane, she discards him and turns her attention to Sonny, who finds her more alluring that the middle aged Ruth, and this puts a strain on the relationship between Sonny and Duane. By this time, Sam has died, and his steadying influence is gone. Duane's anger erupts, and in a barroom brawl, he hits Sonny with a beer bottle, permanently blinding him in one eye. Now his physical blindness mirrors his intuitive blindness. When Jacy suggests that she and Sonny elope, she makes sure her parents know about it in time to stop them. Sonny never realizes that he is just a pawn in her games. At the end, Duane is in uniform and headed for Korea; Billy, their mentally retarded friend, is dead, killed by a speeding truck; and the picture show is closed. Sonny returns to Ruth Popper and asks to resume their relationship, to which she reluctantly agrees. His childhood has ended; he is growing up.

If there is a problem with *The Last Picture Show*, is lies in the third person viewpoint, which attempts to explain too much about the characters, a technique the author was still using in *Lonesome Dove* (1984); but this is a minor complaint because this is a wonderful novel of small town life, a sort of *King's Row* or *Peyton Place* of Texas, full of the same type of sensational events that made the earlier novels best sellers. However, McMurtry downplays the sensational aspects of the sexual shenanigans, showing instead that sex is the only thing that breaks the monotony of small town life.

In planning *The Last Picture Show* (BBS/Columbia, 1971), director Peter Bogdanovich made several important decisions prior to shooting. First, although he considered casting James Stewart as Sam the Lion, he opted to go with a cast of no names. While many of the actors and actresses went on to very successful film careers, they were relatively unknown at the time, and the introduction of fresh faces and the lack of stars added to the evocative feeling of small town life. Second, to emphasize the bleakness, Bogdanovich chose to photograph the film in high contrast black and white, which also helped to give the film a classic feel. Bogdanovich has stated that in making *The Last Picture Show* he was inspired by John Ford and Orson Welles. Certainly the composition of some scenes is reminiscent of *Grapes of Wrath* and the isolation within the Texas town with its dingy, ugly streets reminds one of the sleazy border city in *Touch of Evil*. Finally, Bogdanovich chose Larry McMurtry to write the screenplay from his own novel, and the author wisely made very few changes.

The film suggests that all the adolescent sexual encounters bring with them pain and disappointment, but it also implies that the passing years may well turn them into treasured memories. In the only monologue in the film, Sam the Lion (Ben Johnson) reminisces nostalgically to Sonny (Timothy Bottoms) about a moment from his youth when he and a woman went swimming in the nude. The woman turns out to be Lois Farrow (Ellen Burstyn), the mother of Jacy (Cybill Shepherd), who is capable of pushing her daughter into a marriage for money, yet she, too, clings to that moment with Sam. "I guess if it wasn't for Sam, I'd just about missed it, whatever it is," she tells Sonny.

This clinging to the past, this longing for something better, is also evident in the fantasy world of the motion pictures themselves. Sitting in the old theater, Spencer Tracy tries to cope with Elizabeth Taylor in the fantasy world of *Father of the Bride* while out in the audience Sonny and Charlene (Sharon Taggert) grope in the dark. When Sonny and Duane (Jeff Bridges) attend the theater just before it closes for good, they watch *Red River.* The great herd that crosses the Texas prairies is a far cry from the few pitiful head of cattle that pass through town crowded on the backs of trucks, and the West of the imagination is a far cry from the dying town where tumbleweeds drift down the street full of boarded up windows.

The need for something better also pushes Sonny into a relationship with Ruth Popper (Cloris Leachman), the wife of Sonny's football coach. It seems perfectly natural that Ruth should invite Sonny in for a cool drink after he has done her a kindness and that she should want him to stay just a while longer. The adolescent Sonny first feels unrest, then sympathy, then he, too, is caught up in the same sexual passion born of frustration. When she turns on Sonny with shrill virulence after she learns that Jacy has stolen his affections, it is completely understandable because it is so completely natural. All the relationships within both the novel and the film bear the same stamp of honesty and truth.

The Last Picture Show is an extremely powerful and touching examination of life in small town America. Many critics hailed Bogdanovich's film as the most impressive debut by a young director since Orson Welles with *Citizen Kane,* although in reality it was the director's second film. He had previously directed the low budget *Targets* (1969) for Roger Corman's American International. Certainly the visual style that helped to enrich the story and the insight into the material itself must be credited to Bogdanovich, but it is Larry McMurtry's novel and his film script that captured and delineated character so perfectly. *The Last Picture Show* is a fine novel and a great adaptation.

Among modern western novelists, J.S.P. Brown has found favorable critical attention, especially with his novel *Jim Kane* (1970). The central character is a modern cowboy caught up in a world where the old values no longer exist, where a man's word is no longer the bond it once was. In this respect, the novel works as a testament to the dying West, but on other levels, it is a difficult and unrewarding book. Episodic in structure, the story has Kane going back and forth between the United States and Mexico in pursuit of horses and money. While the centerpiece of the plot has Kane betrayed by those Americans he thought he could trust and befriended by Mexicans he mistrusted, the story lacks a central focus, and as such, seems to drift from incident to incident without cohesion. The strong point is the characters, all of whom, including Kane, seem as real as the Arizona desert.

Jim Kane became *Pocket Money* (Coleytown/First Artists, 1972), the first from a new studio formed by Paul Newman, Sidney Poitier, Barbra Streisand and others, much along the lines that United Artists had been formed in the 1920s. Considering the talent behind the creative strings, the expectations from critics and public alike were quite high. Unfortunately, *Jim Kane* was weak for adaptation, and the screenplay by Terry Malick and John Gay tried to turn the whole thing into a comedy along the lines of a modern day *Butch Cassidy and the Sundance Kid.*

The script followed the novel. Jim Kane (Paul Newman) is an easygoing Arizona cowboy whose bad luck hovers over him like a black cloud. The current herd of horses he has brought in from Mexico has been quarantined, he owes money to his ex-wife and to the bank, and he's broke. In a bar, he runs into Stretch Russell (Wayne Rogers), who tells him that his boss, Garrett (Strother Martin), needs 200 head of steers brought up from Mexico for the rodeo circuit. Despite warnings that Garrett is crooked, Kane accepts the job and seeks out his friend Leonard (Lee Marvin) to help him. In Mexico, the pair is double-crossed and left stranded by Garrett. Kane winds up in jail, forcing Leonard to sell Kane's truck for bail money. When the two men finally face Garrett in his hotel room, they are so impotent, they can only throw a television out of the window in disgust. The film ends with Kane and Leonard about to hop a freight back to the States, hoping they can escape more trouble.

Pocket Money attempts to be a comedy, and while it has a couple of good jokes, it lacks the genius of *Butch Cassidy and the Sundance Kid.* Paul Newman mugs his way through his part, and Lee Marvin underplays so badly as to appear lethargic. Only Strother Martin's superior performance stands out. In addition, Stuart Rosenberg's direction, like Marvin's acting, is lethargic. Film reviewers castigated the film when it was first released, and age hasn't helped it any. Even though faithful to its source, it remains a disjointed, failed comedy.

Like most facets of western literature, even the modern western seems to be hibernating. It has been many years since an adaptation has reached the screen, but it may well be that this subgenre offers the best hope of future adaptations. Because of the fewer restrictions of formula, it probably has the best possibility for growth and change, unlike the traditional western which seems to have reached a dead end. It also offers the best chance to produce real works of literature. Certainly *The Treasure of Sierra Madre* and *The Brave Cowboy* fall into this category. So, too, do the rich and varied novels of Larry McMurtry. Even flawed novels like *Giant* and *Jim Kane* have moments of greatness. Few other subgenres can offer so many classics and so much hope.

14. They Went Thataway: Closing Thoughts on the Western

By the 1980s, few westerns were reaching American theaters. The two most important were *Pale Rider* and *Silverado,* neither of which was based on fiction. However, *Pale Rider* does owe a large debt to *Shane,* which it resembles in structure and plot, although its success is due more to the popularity of star/director Clint Eastwood than the film's inspirational source or even the fact that it is a western. *Silverado* was based on an original script by director Lawrence Kasdan, but unlike his earlier homage to *film noir, Body Heat,* the film seemed formless and overblown, and while it was enjoyable, it certainly wasn't the classic the director intended. Perhaps he should have looked to a source outside himself for his script.

The western continues to be a viable form of literature. Larry McMurty continues to turn out his urban westerns, including *Texasville,* a sequel to *The Last Picture Show.* He has even written a more traditional western with the magnificent *Lonesome Dove.* James Michener has written *Centennial* and *Texas,* both blockbuster best sellers. Louis L'Amour novels continue to sell at an unprecedented rate. A number of firms publish hardback formula westerns as well as paperback originals each year, and prolific series such as *Longarm* and *Stagecoach* fill the racks of newsstands.

Yet, except for an occasional film such as *Pale Rider* or *Silverado,* the movie western seems a thing of the past. Where adaptations of western literature were once an important consideration of Hollywood, today studios and filmmakers look elsewhere for their material. The reasons are many. First, the conventions of the formula western have been assimilated into urban crime and science fiction films, both fast moving, high tech dramas suited for a computerized, mechanized age. Urban crime dramas such as *Lethal Weapon* owe much to *Riders of the Purple Sage* and other formula westerns that created the laconic gunman who is a law unto himself. In its own way, *Star Wars* is as much a formula western as *Shane*. In addition, the traditional western cannot compete with the high concentration of violence in urban crime and science fiction films, a violence that has escalated over the years, becoming ever more anarchic. With the exception of the spaghetti westerns and their imitators, the formula western relies on a controlled violence that is aesthetically satisfying but basically unrealistic.

The gradual death of the formula western film affected all other adaptations of the genre. Even revisionist westerns were doomed, although in the 1970s an occasional adaptation like *Little Big Man* and *The Shootist* proved successful. However, *Little Big Man* commented indirectly upon our involvement in Vietnam and struck a responsive chord in the American psyche. Its success was partially due to reasons outside the novel and outside the film. This is not to denigrate *Little Big Man*. On the contrary, it was an excellent novel, and also a good film. Even more blatant in comparing the government's actions against the Indians with our actions in Vietnam was *Soldier Blue,* adapted from *Arrow in the Sun,* but it was a bad movie and died. On the other hand, *The Shootist* was a vehicle for John Wayne, and although a wonderful film, its success did not lie with the brilliant novel but with the star. People went to see an action film starring the Duke, not because of the reputation of the novel.

The question arises: Would *Shane, Little Big Man* or *The Shootist*— or, for that matter, any other novel which reached the screen—be remembered quite as well without the successful adaptation? There is no doubt that fiction that has reached the screen has been given added impact and emphasis because of these adaptations. *Shane* has constantly been in print since it was first published. *Little Big Man* is constantly being reprinted. Only *The Shootist* has failed to grow in reputation over the years, and that may be due to the depressing nature of the material. But, if it were not for the film, would it be remembered at all? Probably not, yet it is a terrific novel, the equal of *Shane* or *Little Big Man*. If people occasionally turn to the novel today, it is probably because of the film's reputation.

Fiction less successfully adapted to the screen sometimes falls further and further into obscurity. An excellent example is *A Distant*

Trumpet, whose reputation had to be damaged by the film, a disaster on all counts. If one had seen the film without reading the novel, would he or she seek out the book? I think not. It would be easy to assume that the novel was like the film, vapid and sterile and unworthy of consideration. Yet *A Distant Trumpet* is marvelously rich in characterization and incident, and deserves to be ranked among the top half dozen or so novels of the American West, which makes the film all that much more of a travesty.

Obviously not all western fiction adapted to the screen is dependant on films for its reputation. Howard Fast's excellent "Rachel" has appeared only in an obscure collection of the author's short stories and is seldom reprinted, and the film *Rachel and the Stranger,* a good and faithful adaptation, could not lift the story from obscurity. On the other hand, many of Zane Grey's novels and short stories are still in print and Grey himself is still popular to some degree, yet few people associate his name with any particular film, despite the fact that he is the most filmed author in the history of American motion pictures. Much the same can be said for Max Brand and Louis L'Amour, both of whose western novels crowd paperback racks. Their names are far more important than most of the films adapted from their works. Each has had only one work which became an important motion picture, Brand with *Destry Rides Again* and L'Amour with *Hondo.* The popularity of these two novels has undoubtedly been enhanced by the film adaptations, but the popularity of the authors themselves reaches far beyond these two films.

While we have looked at one genre in detail, the lessons we have learned can apply to all literature adapted for the screen. Some authors have had their reputations enhanced by films, others have been damaged, others have benefited little either way, and a few—a very few—have remained more important than the films adapted from their work. Beyond this are the adaptations themselves. David O. Selznick said, "If the book fails to achieve distinction in its own medium, there is no reason to believe that a faithful transcription would achieve distinction in another medium." In other words, rotten novels do not make good movies unless changes are made. For the most part, bad novels became bad films, and studios usually failed to improve on the product no matter if it were bad or good. More often than not, they took good material and made it bad. Only in a few, wonderful instances did the literature and film come together as important equals— *The Ox-Bow Incident, Shane, Little Big Man, The Shootist, The Last Picture Show, Welcome to Hard Times,* to name a few. When this happened, the magic of the book became magic on the screen.

Someone once said to Theodore Sturgeon, a noted science fiction author, that 95 percent of science fiction was crap; he replied that 95 percent of everything was crap. This point could just as easily apply to film adaptations of fiction. It doesn't matter that 95 percent of it is crap. There is still that 5 percent that isn't, and that makes the whole process worthwhile.

Appendix I
Biography, History and
the Western Film

On a few occasions, Hollywood purchased the rights to works of western biography or history and turned them into fictional films. In most cases, the studios just wanted the titles, and once in their possession, the books were dropped and fictional stories substituted. Often the historical facts themselves disappeared under a barrage of fanciful concoctions that whitewashed or distorted events by romanticizing them beyond all recognition.

Walter Noble Burns' *The Saga of Billy the Kid* (1926), which claimed to be a "biography" of the famed outlaw, was the first such biography to be sought by Hollywood. The book is long on imagination and short on historical validity and predates the "nonfiction novel," *In Cold Blood,* that Truman Capote wrote in the 1960s. The author interviewed some old timers who remembered the Kid and the Lincoln County War, but much of his research has been discounted by later historians. Burns' Billy the Kid turned out to be a Robin Hood, an innocent boy forced into the role of outlaw by villainous law and order advocates. In addition, many of the book's conversations sound as if they have jumped straight from a novel. What seems apparent is that the author became enamored with his subject, and this destroyed all his objectivity and resulted in an entertaining but highly inaccurate "biography."

MGM purchased the rights to the book and turned it into *Billy the Kid* (MGM, 1930), which had the advantage of being shot on location in Lincoln County, New Mexico. To add more authenticity, star Johnny Mack Brown used William Bonney's actual six-guns, supplied by William S. Hart who acted as technical advisor. But when it came to the story, scriptwriters Laurence Stallings and Charles MacArthur followed the book by making Billy the Kid a good/badman, more rebel than outlaw, who fought and killed only because he was forced by circumstances beyond his control. He is a knight errant who dispenses justice that is often very direct and very violent. When Billy confronts two of the villains responsible for murdering his friend and mentor, he shoots them down without giving them a chance and watches as their bodies roll down the stairs.

A later sequence partially drawn from the book is one of the great action scenes in western films. Billy and his followers are trapped by the villainous posse in a burning house, and as each of the men dash out the front door, he is shot down by the lawmen hidden safely behind an adobe wall. Billy is the last. Calmly he rolls a cigarette, but when he searches his pockets, he can find no match. A burning timber drops beside him, and he lights his smoke. Drawing both guns, he walks out the door and begins to pick off the men behind the wall, their bodies spinning away with the impact of the bullets. Leaping over the wall, he mounts his horse and rides off. His six shooters empty, he spins around in the saddle, sitting backward on the horse, and drawing the rifle, he continues his murderous fire.

Except for a few incidental facts concerning Billy and the Lincoln County War, the film is highly inaccurate and has little to do with history. A romantic interest (Kay Johnson) is added, and although MGM had two endings filmed, one where Billy is killed by Pat Garrett (Wallace Beery) and one where Garrett allows Billy to escape, American audiences saw only the latter. This is not to say *Billy the Kid* is a bad film. On the contrary, it is very important and enjoyable western, but it has little to do with reality or history. It is, however, faithful to the spirit of Burns' *The Saga of Billy the Kid*.

MGM remade *Billy the Kid* (MGM, 1941) as a prestige production, and while it has the advantage of color and fine outdoor photography, it has little else. A miscast and too old Robert Taylor plays Billy, who is ultimately tracked down and dispatched by Pat Garrett (Brian Donlevy). Although only 95 minutes long, it is slow and ponderous. Once again the studio sought to whitewash William Bonney, making him the Robin Hood–like figure invented by Walter Noble Burns, and once again both reality and history are left behind in this inferior remake.

Another whitewash was *Wyatt Earp, Frontier Marshal* (1931) by Stuart N. Lake. Earp was still alive as the author compiled his material, and most of the story is based on interviews with the former lawman.

Obviously Earp slanted the material to show himself in a good light. Like Burns with Billy the Kid, Lake saw Earp as some knight who brought justice to the West. Since the publication of this book, other historical works beginning with *The Earp Brothers of Tombstone* (1960) by Frank Waters and *Wyatt Earp: The Untold Story* (1963) by Ed Bartholomen have painted a revisionist picture of Wyatt Earp.

While only a third of Lake's biography is devoted to the Tombstone days, the two films based on the book concentrate on these years and culminate in the gunfight at the O.K. Corral. The first of these was *Frontier Marshal* (20th Century–Fox, 1939). As directed by Allan Dwan, the film follows Lake's view of Wyatt Earp (Randolph Scott) as a romantic hero, but it throws out much of the biography and substitutes a story of all its own about the hero cleaning up Tombstone. All mention of his brothers is dropped. In addition, Doc Holliday (Cesar Romero) loses his girl (Nancy Kelly) to Earp, and it is Holliday's death that ignites the final showdown at the O.K. Corral. In the end, the lawman vanquishes the villains and brings law and order to Tombstone.

If one can overlook the inaccuracies, *Frontier Marshal* is an entertaining western, but its main interest lies in its influence on *My Darling Clementine* (20th Century–Fox, 1946). Director John Ford lifted several sequences almost intact from the earlier film, the most noteworthy of which is the scene where Wyatt Earp (Henry Fonda) subdues a drunken Indian (Charles Stevens in both films). Like *Frontier Marshal*, the Ford film views Wyatt Earp as a romantic hero, but Ford saw a deeper meaning to Earp's role as lawman; Wyatt Earp is a harbinger not only of law and order but also of civilization.

My Darling Clementine is no more accurate than its predecessor. Although Earp's brothers have been restored to him, two of them, James and Virgil, are murdered prior to the O.K. Corral, leaving only Wyatt, Morgan Earp (Ward Bond) and Doc Holliday to face the Clantons led by Old Man Clanton (Walter Brennan). Holliday (Victor Mature) is shot and killed in the encounter, but in the end, Wyatt and Morgan stand victorious with all the Clantons dead around them. The actual events of the Earps in Tombstone — even according to Lake's biography — get lost in the scriptwriters' imaginations, which changes characters and incidents until little historical reality remains. Even the relationship between Wyatt and Doc has been altered to fit the dictates of the script.

Romantic and inaccurate as it is, *My Darling Clementine* remains a classic western film, one of the half dozen greatest ever made. John

Ford invested enough mythical qualities in the characters of Earp and Holliday to make them human and larger than life at the same time. In addition, while some of the plot is based on historical events, the fabrications strengthen the story cinematically. Ford himself knew that his story was inaccurate, but he didn't care. He knew the difference between sticking to the facts and telling a good story.

A far more historically valid approach than that used by Walter Noble Burns and Stuart N. Lake was taken by Walter Prescott Webb, a noted historian whose monumental *The Great Plains* (1931) is the definitive work on the subject. In *The Texas Rangers* (1935), Webb chronicled a hundred years in the history of the Texas Rangers from their creation in 1835 until their virtual demise in 1935. It was a history book rich in incident and stirring in its narrative, and for its time, was also a book extremely nonprejudicial in its treatment of the American Indian. Today it still stands as a classic of regional history.

The first film version of *The Texas Rangers* (Paramount, 1936) claimed to be based on "data" in Walter Prescott Webb's book, but in reality, the story was fabricated by scriptwriter Louis Stevens from an idea suggested by King Vidor and Elizabeth Hill. It told of three bandits who get separated and go their opposite ways. Jim Hawkins (Fred MacMurray) and Wahoo Jones (Jack Oakie) become Texas Rangers while their ex-partner Sam Magee (Lloyd Nolan) continues on the outlaw trail. When Jim and Wahoo are ordered to bring in Magee, Jim refuses and is jailed by the Rangers. Wahoo goes it alone, and Magee kills him. Jim finally realizes that his duty lies in tracking down Magee, which he does. Romantic interest is provided by Amanda Bailey (Jean Parker), who falls in love with Magee, but she finally comes to see what kind of man Magee is, and she shifts her allegiance to Jim Hawkins.

The film has nothing to do with Webb's book except the title — not one of the characters is mentioned anywhere in Webb's text — although a prologue that extols the exploits of the Texas Rangers tries to inject a measure of reality. Despite this, *The Texas Rangers* is an entertaining "A" western. It includes some outstanding action sequences, notable among which are a fight with Indians and the final showdown between hero and villain. Also, for the time it was made, the relationship between Magee and Amanda is quite surprising. It is evident that they are living together without benefit of clergy, yet her fallen status does not prevent her at fade out from looking forward to a happy future with the hero. Most importantly, the film allows the characters to emerge as individuals rather than caricatures.

The Texas Rangers was remade as *The Streets of Laredo* (Paramount, 1948). A few names were changed — Jim Hawkins became Jim Dawkins (William Holden), Sam Magee became Lorn Reming (MacDonald Carey) — but the story remained basically the same. The addition of color looks nice but adds little to the story. The new version makes the hero less competent, and in the end, he is incapable of dispatching the villain; in order to save the Dawkins, the girl (Mona Freeman) is forced to shoot him. Still, if one is unfamiliar with the earlier version, it is an entertaining film.

Somewhat between the popular histories of Walter Noble Burns and Stuart N. Lake and the academic histories of Walter Prescott Webb lies the work of Mari Sandoz. Sandoz's *Cheyenne Autumn* retells the story of the great Cheyenne migration in 1878 from their reservation in desert country to the Yellowstone, an impossible journey through hostile country with the forces of the U.S. Army pursuing the Cheyenne all the way. The narrative has a real momentum, reading more like fiction than history, yet it remains the definitive account of this little known heroic and tragic moment in American history.

Cheyenne Autumn (Warner Bros., 1964) is often considered Ford's apology to the Indians for the one dimensional treatments in his previous films, but as discussed in Chapter 3 above, Ford showed great compassion for the Indian in times when other filmmakers were afraid to do so. However, the fact remains that this is the only Ford film in which Indians are the central characters. Unfortunately, it is not very good Ford, and it pays scant attention to historical reality.

The basic story of the Cheyenne's attempt to reach the Yellowstone remains the centerpiece of the film, but there are too many subplots cluttering the landscape. A captain in the army (Richard Widmark) is in love with a Quaker school teacher (Carroll Baker) who accompanies the Indians in their flight. Along the way, Wyatt Earp (James Stewart) and Doc Holliday (Arthur Kennedy) saunter onto the scene, but their connection to the story is tenuous at best. None of these characters or incidents is to be found in Sandoz's book. In addition, the Indian characters who exist in her book as well as on the screen — Little Wolf (Ricardo Montalban) and Dull Knife (Gilbert Roland) — are burdened with a story involving Dull Knife's son and Little Wolf's wife. The result is that these extraneous stories tend to divert the viewer's attention from the real story, the Cheyenne's struggle to reach their homeland. The film needed a better script and more judicious editing — it originally ran 159 minutes. As it is, it is overblown and pretentious. It also has one other glaring weakness. It uses ethnic actors to portray the

Cheyenne, and like so many other westerns, it cries out for real Indians in the lead roles.

These biographies and histories were certainly misused by Hollywood. That is not to say that the films made from them were bad. On the contrary, *My Darling Clementine* (1946) is a classic, and *Billy the Kid* (1930) and *The Texas Rangers* (1936) are both very good and entertaining films. However, they are not in any meaningful way related to their sources; they are concoctions of their studios and scriptwriters. As history, to paraphrase Henry Ford, they are "bunk."

Appendix II
Western Authors and
Their Film Adaptations

Below are listed authors of western fiction and various film adaptations of their works. Often an author is given credit for an adaptation but the source is unknown. For instance, Columbia claimed Peter B. Kyne as their source for a series of "B" westerns. *Gallant Defender* (1935), *Stampede* (1936), and *Code of the Range* (1936), all Charles Starrett vehicles, were credited to Peter B. Kyne, but in reality the studio simply used the author's name for prestige and not one of the films was based on any work. Therefore, in the following list I have designated where the source is unknown. In addition, I have also listed original western stories written directly for the screen and western screenplays by authors who were involved in the Hollywood system. In at least two cases, the authors also directed films based on their own works. Adaptations that I feel are especially noteworthy, I have marked with an *. Film titles (where these differed from the published version) are in *bold italics*.

Abbey, Edward (1927-)
    The Brave Cowboy (1956)
                     Lonely Are the Brave,
                     Universal, 1962

Adams, Clifton (1919-)
    The Desperado (1950)
                     Allied Artists, 1954
                     Cole Younger, Gunfighter
                     Allied Artists, 1958
    Gambling Man (1956)
                     Outlaw's Son, UA, 1957

Albert, Marvin H.
    Apache Rising (1957)   **Duel at Diablo,** UA, 1966
    The Bounty Killers   **The Ugly Ones,** UA, 1968
    The Law and Jake Wade   MGM, 1958
     (1956)
    The Man in Black   **Rough Night in Jericho,**
                                 Universal, 1967
    Renegade Posse (1958)   **Bullet for a Badman,**
                                 Universal, 1964

Note: Albert received either all or partial credit for the following western screenplays: **Duel at Diablo** (UA, 1966); **Rough Night in Jericho** (Universal, 1967)

Allen, Henry Wilson (1912–)
    Journey to Shiloh (1960)   Universal, 1968
    MacKenna's Gold (1963)   Columbia, 1969
    Santa Fe Passage (1952)   Republic, 1955
    The Tall Men (1954)   20th Fox, 1955
    To Follow a Flag (1952)   **Pillars in the Sky,** Universal,
                                 1956
    Who Rides With Wyatt   **Young Billy Young,** UA, 1969
     (1954)
    Yellowstone Kelly (1957)   Warner Bros., 1959

Andrews, Robert Hardy
    Great Day in the Morning (1950)   RKO, 1956
    Notes: Original story for the screen: *Best of the Badmen* (RKO, 1951); *The Kid from Texas* (Universal, 1950); *Wyoming Mail* (Universal, 1950)
    Andrews received either partial or complete credit for the following western screenplays: **The Kid from Texas** (Universal, 1950); **Best of the Badmen** (RKO, 1951); **Mark of the Renegade** (Universal, 1951)

Appel, David
    Comanche   **Tonka,** Buena Vista, 1958

Arnold, Elliot (1912–1980)
    Blood Brother (1947)   ***Broken Arrow** 20th Fox, 1950

Athanas, William Verne (1917–1962)
    The Proud Ones (1952)   20th Fox, 1956

Ballard, Todhunter (1903–1980)
    Two Edged Vengeance   **The Outcast,** Republic, 1954
     (1951)

Barnes, Margaret Ayer (1886–1967)
 Westward Passage (1931)   RKO Pathé, 1932

Barrett, Michael
 The Reward   20th Fox, 1956

Baxter, George Owen **see** Faust, Frederick

Beach, Rex (1877–1949)
 The Barrier (1920)   MGM, 1926
           Paramount, 1937
 Don Careless and the   ***The Avengers,*** Republic, 1950
  Birds of Prey (1928)
 Flowing Gold (1922)   First National, 1924
           Warner Bros., 1940
 The Iron Trail (1913)   UA, 1921
 "The Michigan Kid"   ***The Michigan Kid,*** Universal,
           1947
 Pardners (1905)   Mutual, 1917
 "Rope's End"   ***A Sainted Devil,*** Paramount,
           1924
 The Silver Horde (1909)   Goldwyn, 1920
           RKO, 1930
 The Spoilers (1905)   *Selig, 1914
           Goldwyn, 1923
           Paramount, 1930
           *Universal, 1942
           Universal, 1955
 The Winds of Chance   First National, 1925
  (1918)
 Note: Source unknown: ***The Brand*** (1919); ***Lightning Bill Hyde*** (Fox,
1918); ***North Wind's Malice*** (Goldwyn, 1920)

Bechdolt, Frederick Ritchie (1874–1950)
 "Back to the Right Trail"   ***Thieves' Gold,*** Universal, 1918

Bellah, James (1899–1976)
 "Big Hunt" (1947)   **She Wore a Yellow Ribbon,*
 "Command" (1946)   RKO, 1948
 "Command" alone was also
  used for   ***The Command,*** Warner Bros.,
           1955
           A Thunder of Drums, MGM,
           1961

"Massacre" (1947)   *Fort Apache, RKO, 1948
"Mission with No Record"   *Rio Grande, Republic, 1950
(1948)
"The White Invaders"   A Thunder of Drums,
(1954)   MGM, 1961

Note: Bellah also received all or partial credit for the following western screenplays: Fort Apache (RKO, 1949); The Legend of Nigger Charlie (Paramount, 1972); The Man Who Shot Liberty Valance (Paramount, 1962); Rio Grande (Republic, 1950); Sergeant Rutledge (Warner Bros., 1960); She Wore a Yellow Ribbon (RKO, 1949); A Thunder of Drums (MGM, 1961)

Berger, Thomas (1924–   )
    Little Big Man (1964)   *National General, 1970

Bickham, Jack Miles (1930–   )
    Apple Dumpling Gang   Buena Vista, 1975
    (1971)
    Baker's Hawk (1974)   Doty-Dayton, 1976

Birney, Hoffman (1891–   )
    The Dice of God   The Glory Guys, UA, 1965

Bishop, Curtis (1912–1967)
    Bugle's Wake [as Brandon, Curt] Seminole Uprising, Columbia
    Shadow Range   Cow Country, AA, 1953

Blackburn, Thomas
    Raton Pass (1950)   Warner Bros., 1951
    Range War (1949)   Short Grass, AA, 1957
    Sierra Baron (1955)   20th Fox, 1958

Notes: Original story for screen Cattle Queen of Montana, 1955

Blackburn received either all or partial credit on the following western screenplays: Cattle Town (Warner Bros., 1952); Cavalry Scout (Monogram, 1951); Colt .45 (Warner Bros., 1950); Cow Country (Allied Artists, 1953); Davy Crockett, King of the Wild Frontier (Buena Vista, 1955); Johnny Tremain (Buena Vista, 1957); Raton Pass (Warner Bros., 1951); Riding Shotgun (Warner Bros., 1954); Short Grass (Allied Artists, 1951); Sierra Passage (Monogram, 1951); Westward Ho, the Wagons (Buena Vista, 1957); Wild Dakotas (Associated, 1956)

Bond, Lee
    "Homesteads of Hate"   Land of the Open Range,
                                     RKO, 1942

Bonham, Frank (1914–   )
    Lost Stage Valley (1948)   **Stage to Tucson,** Columbia,
                                        1951

Borland, Hal
    When the Legends Die (1963)   Sagoponack, 1972

Bower, Bertha Muzzy (1871–1940)
    Chip of the Flying U   Selig, 1914
      (1906)   **The Galloping Devil,** Canyon
                                Pictures, 1920
                                Universal, 1926
                                Universal, 1939
    Flying U Ranch (1914)   Robertson-Cole, 1927
    Jean of the Lazy A   **Ridin' Thunder,** Universal,
      (1915)   1925
    "Lonesome Trail"   **Lonesome Trail,** Selig, 1914
    Points West (1928)   Universal, 1929
    The Ranch of the   **The Wolverine,** Associated,
      Wolverine (1914)   1921
    The Range Dwellers (1907)   **Taming of the West,** Universal,
                                1925
    "The Reveler"   **The Reveler,** Selig, 1914
    The Uphill Climb (1913)   Selig, 1914
    "When the Cook Fell Ill"   **When the Cook Fell Ill,** Selig,
                                  1914
    Note: Sources Unknown: **How the Weary Went Wooing** (Selig, 1915);
King of the Rodeo (Universal, 1929); **North of 53** (Fox, 1917); **Shotgun Jones**
(Selig, 1914)

Bowman, Earl W.
    Ramblin' Kid (1930)   **Long, Long Trail,** Universal,
                                    1929

Boyles, C. Scott (1905–   )
    The Border Jumpers   ***Man of the West,** UA, 1958
      (1955)
      [as Brown, Will C.]

Brand, Max **see** Faust, Frederick

Brandon, Curt **see** Bishop, Curtis

Breslin, Howard
    "Bad Day at Honda"   **Bad Day at Black Rock**
    [In *American Magazine*,   MGM, 1965
    1946]

Bristow, Gwen (1903–1980)
    Jubilee Trail (1950)   Republic, 1955

Brown, Forest
    Boss of Lonely Valley (1939)   Universal, 1937

Brown, Harry
    Stand at Spanish Boot   **Apache Drums,** Universal, 1951
    The Stars in Their Crowns   **El Dorado,** Paramount, 1967
    Note: Brown is credited with either all or partial credit on the follow-
ing western screenplays: **Bugles in the Afternoon** (William Cagney, 1952);
The Fiend Who Walked the West (20th Fox, 1958); **Many Rivers to Cross**
(MGM, 1955); **Only the Valiant** (William Cagney, 1951)

Brown, Joseph Paul Summers (1930–   )
    Jim Kane (1970)   **Pocket Money,** National
                                      General, 1972

Brown, Will C.   **see**   Boyles, C. Scott

Burnett, William Riley (1899–1982)
    Adobe Walls (1953)   **Arrowhead,** Paramount, 1953
    The Asphalt Jungle (1949)   **The Badlanders,** MGM, 1958
    The Dark Command (1938)   *Republic, 1940
    High Sierra   ***Colorado Territory,** Warner
                                      Bros., 1949
    Saint Johnson (1930)   ***Law and Order,** Universal,
                                      1932
                                      Wild West Days, Universal,
                                      1937 [12 chapter serial]
                                      Law and Order, Universal,
                                      1940
                                      Law and Order, Universal,
                                      1953
    Notes: Source unknown: **Yellow Sky** (20th Century Fox, 1948)
    Burnett received either all or partial credit for the following western
screenplays: **Belle Starr's Daughter** (20th Fox, 1949); **San Antonio** (Warner
Bros., 1945); **Sergeants Three** (UA, 1962)

Burns, Walter Noble
    The Robinhood of El Dorado   MGM, 1934
    (1932)
    The Saga of Billy the Kid   ***Billy the Kid,*** MGM, 1930
    (1926)   **Billy the Kid,** MGM, 1941

Burtis, Thomson
    "War of the Wildcats"   **In Old Oklahoma,** Republic,
                        1943

Busch, Niven (1903–)
    Duel in the Sun (1944)   *Selznick, 1946
    The Furies (1948)   Paramount, 1950
    Notes: Original story for screen **Belle Starr** (1941); **The Capture** (RKO, 1950); **Distant Drums** (Warner Bros., 1951); **The Man from the Alamo** (Universal, 1953); **The Moonlighter** (Warner Bros., 1953)
    Busch received all or partial credit for the following western screenplays: **Belle Starr** (20th Century-Fox, 1941); **Distant Drums** (Warner Bros., 1951); **The Man from the Alamo** (Universal, 1953); **The Moonlighter** (Warner Bros., 1953); **Pursued** (Warner Bros., 1947); **The Treasure of Pancho Villa** (RKO, 1955); **The Westerner** (Goldwyn, 1940)

Carder, Michael
    Decision at Sundown (1955)   Columbia, 1957

Carpenter, John Jo   **see**   Reese, John Henry

Carr, Mary J.
    Children of the Covered Wagon   **Westward Ho, the Wagons,**
                        Buena Vista, 1956

Carter, Forrest (1925–)
    Gone to Texas (1975)   ***The Outlaw Josey Wales,***
                        Warner Bros., 1976
    The Vengeance Trail of   **The Return of Josey Wales,**
    Josey Wales (1976)   Multi/Tacar Prod., 1986

Chadwick, Joseph
    "Phantom 45's Talk Loud"   **Rim of the Canyon,** Columbia,
                        1949

Chanslor, Roy
    The Ballad of Cat Ballou   **Cat Ballou,** Columbia, 1965
    Johnny Concho   Republic, 1954

Note: Chanslor received either all or partial credit on the following western screenplays: *The California Mail* (Warner Bros., 1936); *The Daltons Ride Again* (Universal, 1945); *Idaho* (Republic, 1943); *The Michigan Kid* (Universal, 1947); *The Vigilantes Return* (Universal, 1947)

Chase, Bordon **see** Fowler, Frank

Clark, Walter Van Tilburg (1909-1971)
    The Ox-Bow Incident (1940)   *20th Fox, 1943
    The Track of the Cat (1949)   Warner Bros., 1954

Coburn, Walter (1889-1971)
    "Black K Rides Tonight"   *The Return of Wild Bill,*
                              Columbia, 1940

    "Burnt Ranch" [in *Western*   *The Westerner,* Columbia, 1934
      Story, April, 1, 1923]
    "Ride 'Em Cowboy"   *Between Dangers,* Pathé, 1927
    "The Sun Dance Kid"   *The Fighting Comeback,* Pathé,
                              1927

    "The Survival of Slim" [in   *The Desert of the Lost,* Pathé,
      Western Story, May 3, 1924] 1927
    "Triple Cross to Danger" [in *Fighting Fury,* Universal,
      Western Story, August 11, 1923] 1924
    Note: Sources unknown: *Rusty Rides Alone* (Columbia, 1933); *Silent Men* (Columbia, 1933)

Cook, William Everett (1922-1964)
    Comanche Captives (1960)   *Two Rode Together,* Columbia,
                              1961

    Frontier Feud (1954)   *Quincannon, Frontier Scout,*
                              UA, 1956

    Guns of North Texas (1958)   *The Tramplers,* Embassy, 1968

Cooper, James Fenimore (1789-1851)
    The Deerslayer (1841)   Vitagraph, 1913
                              Leatherstocking, Pathé, 1924,
                              [ten chapter serial]
                              Republic, 1943
                              20th Fox, 1957

    The Last of the Mohicans   *Leatherstocking,* Biograph, 1909
      (1826)   Pat Powers, 1911
                              *Associated Exhibitors, 1920
                              Mascot, 1932 [12 chapter serial]
                              UA, 1936

Last of the Redmen, Columbia,
1947

The Pathfinder; or the
Inland Sea (1840)

The Pathfinder, Columbia,
1953

The Pioneers (1823)

Monogram, 1941

Corcoran, William
Golden Horizon (1937)

Trail Street, RKO, 1947

Crane, Stephen (1871–1900)
"The Bride Comes to
Yellow Sky"

*Face to Face, RKO, 1952

Croy, Homer (1883–1965)
Jesse James Was My Neighbor,
1949

I Shot Jesse James, Lippert,
1949

West of the Water Tower,
1923

Paramount, 1924

Cullum, Ridgwell (1867–1943)
The One Way Trail (1911)

The Yosemite Trail, Fox, 1922

The Twins of Suffering Creek
(1912)

The Man Who Won, Fox, 1923

Cunningham, John M.
"Raiders Die Hard" (1952)

Day of the Badman, Universal,
1957

"The Tin Star" (1947)

*High Noon, UA, 1952

"Yankee Gold" (1947)

The Stranger Wore a Gun,
Columbia, 1953

Curwood, James Oliver (1879–1927)
The Alaskan (1923)

Paramount, 1924

The Ancient Highway (1925)

Paramount, 1925

Back to God's Country (1911)

First National, 1919

Universal, 1927

Universal, 1953

Baree, Son of Kazan (1916)

Vitagraph, 1918

Vitagraph, 1925

"Caryl of the Mountains"

Trails of the Wild,
Ambassador, 1935

The Country Beyond (1922)

Fox, 1926

The Courage of Marge O'Doone
(1918)

Vitagraph, 1920

The Danger Trail (1910)	Selig, 1917
"Dawn Rider"	**Galloping Dynamite,** Ambassador, 1937
"Fatal Note"	**Phantom Patrol,** Ambassador, 1936
The Flaming Forest (1921)	MGM, 1926
Flower of the North (1912)	Vitagraph, 1921
"Footprints"	**Fighting Trooper,** Ambassador, 1934
"Four Minutes Late"	**Northern Frontier,** Ambassador, 1935
"Getting a Start in Life"	**Rough Riding Rhythm,** Ambassador, 1937
"God of Her People"	**The Man from Hell's River,** Western, 1922
God's Country and the Woman (1915)	**God's Country and the Law,** Arrow, 1921
	Warner Bros., 1937
The Gold Hunters (1909)	Davis, 1925
	Trail of the Yukon, Monogram, 1949
The Golden Snare (1921)	First National, 1921
"Hell's Gulch"	**Timber War,** Ambassador, 1935
The Honor of the Big Snows (1911)	**Jan of the Big Snows** American, 1922
The Hunted Woman (1916)	Vitagraph, 1916
	Fox, 1925
"In the Tentacles of the North"	**Tentacles of the North,** Rayart, 1926
	Snow Dog, Monogram, 1950
Isobel (1913)	**In Defiance of the Law,** Selig, 1914
"Jacqueline"	**Jacqueline, or Blazing Barriers** Arrow, 1923
Kazan (1914)	Selig, 1921
	Ferocious Pal, Principal, 1934
"The Man from Ten Strike"	**Gold Madness,** Principal, 1923
"The Midnight Call"	**Wildcat Trooper,** Ambassador, 1936
Nomads of the North (1918)	First National, 1920
"The Other Man's Wife"	**My Neighbor's Wife,** Davis, 1925

Philip Steele of the Royal Mounted (1911)	**Steele of the Royal Mounted,** Vitagraph, 1925
"Playing with Fire"	**Song of the Trail,** AMB, 1936
"The Poetic Justice of Uko San"	*I Am the Law,* Affiliated, 1922
"The Quest of Joan"	**Prisoners of the Storm,** Universal, 1926
"Retribution"	**Timber Fury,** Eagle Lion, 1950
The River's End (1919)	First National, 1920
	Warner Bros., 1930
	Warner Bros., 1940
"Song of the Trail"	**Song of the Trail,** Ambassador, 1936
"Speck on the Wall"	**Law of the Timber,** PRC, 1941
Swift Lightning (1926)	**Call of the Yukon,** Republic, 1938
The Valley of the Silent Men (1920)	Paramount, 1922
"Wheels of Fate"	**Code of the Mounted,** Ambassador, 1935
	Dawn on the Great Divide, Monogram, 1942
"When the Door Opened"	**When the Door Opened,** Fox, 1925
The Wolf Hunters (1908)	Rayart, 1926
	The Trail Beyond Lone Star, Monogram, 1934
	Monogram, 1949

Note: Sources unknown: **Battle of Frenchman's Run** (Vitagraph, 1915); **The Broken Silence** (Arrow, 1922); **Call of the Klondike** (Monogram, 1950); **Fangs of the Arctic** (Monogram, 1953); **The Fifth Man** (Selig, 1914); **The Fighting Texan** (Ambassador, 1937); **God's Country** (Screen Guild, 1946); **Hearts of Men** (Anchor, 1928); **His Fighting Blood** (Ambassador, 1935); **The Last Man** (Vitagraph, 1916); **'Neath Canadian Skies** (Screen Guild, 1946); **North of the Border** (Screen Guild, 1946); **Northwest Territory** (Monogram, 1951); **The Red Blood of Courage** (Ambassador, 1935); **Roaring Six Guns** (Ambassador, 1937); **The Silver Trail** (Reliable, 1937); **Skull and Crown** (Reliable, 1935); **Thundergod** (Anchor, 1928); **Valley of Terror** (Ambassador, 1937); **Vengeance of Rannah** (Reliable, 1936); **Whistling Bullets** (Ambassador, 1937); **The White Mouse** (Selig, 1914); **Wilderness Mail** (Selig, 1914); **Yukon Gold** (Monogram, 1952); **Yukon Mail** (Monogram, 1952)

Cushman, Dan (1909-   )
　　Stay Away, Joe (1953)　　　　　　MGM, 1968
　　Note: Original story for screen: ***Timberjack*** (Republic, 1954)

Davis, Norbert
　　"A Gunsmoke Case for　　　　***Hands Across the Rockies,***
　　　Major Cain"　　　　　　　　Columbia, 1941

Dawson, Peter　**see**　Glidden, Jonathan Huff

Dewlen, Al (1921-   )
　　The Night of the Tiger　　　　***Ride Beyond Vengeance,***
　　　(1956)　　　　　　　　　　　Columbia, 1966

Doctorow, E.L. (1931-   )
　　Welcome to Hard Times (1960)　　MGM, 1967

Drago, Harry Sinclair (1888-1980)
　　Buckskin Empire (1942)　　　　***Buckskin Frontier,*** UA, 1943
　　Colt Comrades　　　　　　　　UA, 1943
　　　[as Bliss Lomax — 1939]
　　The Leatherburners　　　　　　UA, 1943
　　　[as Bliss Lomax — 1940]
　　Out of the Silent North　　　　Universal, 1922
　　　(1923)
　　Secrets of the Wasteland　　　　Paramount, 1941
　　　[as Bliss Lomax — 1940]
　　Whispering Sage (1922)　　　　Fox, 1927
　　Note: Drago receive all or partial credit for the following western
screenplays: ***The Cowboy Kid*** (Fox, 1928); ***The Desert Rider*** (MGM, 1929);
Hello Cheyenne (Fox, 1928); ***A Horseman of the Plains*** (Fox, 1928); ***The
Overland Telegraph*** (MGM, 1929); ***Painted Post*** (Fox, 1928); ***Silver Valley***
(Fox, 1927); ***Sioux Blood*** (MGM, 1929); ***Where East Is East*** (MGM, 1929)

Dufault, Joseph Ernest Nephtali (1892-1942) [as Will James]
　　Lone Cowboy (1930)　　　　　Paramount, 1933
　　　　　　　　　　　　　　　Shoot Out, Universal, 1971
　　Sand (1929)　　　　　　　　20th Fox, 1949
　　Smoky the Cowhorse (1926)　　***Smoky,*** Fox, 1933
　　　　　　　　　　　　　　　*20th Fox, 1946
　　　　　　　　　　　　　　　Smoky, 20th Fox, 1966

Durham, Marilyn (1930-   )
　　The Man Who Loved Cat Dancing　　MGM, 1973
　　　(1972)

Emmons, Della Gould (1890–1983)
  Sacajawea of the Shoshones   **The Far Horizons,** Paramount,
  (1955)   1955

Erskine, Lauri York (1894?–1976)
  Renfrew of the Royal Mounted   Monogram, 1937
  (1922)
  Renfrew Rides Again   **Fighting Mad,** Monogram,
  (1927)   1939
  Renfrew Rides North   **Yukon Flight,** Monogram,
  (1931)   1940
  Renfrew Rides the Range   **Crashing Thru,** Monogram,
  (1935)   1939
  Renfrew Rides the Sky   **Sky Bandits,** Monogram, 1940
  Renfrew's Long Trail   **Danger Ahead,** Monogram,
  (1942)   1940

Evans, Max (1926–   )
  The Rounders (1960)   *MGM, 1965

Evarts, Hal George (1887–1934)
  The Cross Pull (1920)   **The Silent Call,** First National,
                                        1921
  Spanish Acres (1925)   **The Santa Fe Trail,**
                                        Paramount, 1930
  Tumbleweeds (1923)   *UA, 1925
  Note: Source unknown: **The Big Trail** (Fox, 1930)

Fast, Howard (1914–   )
  "Rachel" (1945)   * **Rachel and the Stranger,**
                                        RKO, 1946

Faust, Frederick (1892–1944) [as Max Brand except where noted]
  The Adopted Son (1917)   Metro, 1917
  Alcatraz (1923)   **Just Tony,** Fox, 1922
  "The Black Rider" [in   **The Cavalier,** Tiffany, 1928
  Western Story, Jan. 3, 1925]
  The Border Bandit (1947)   * **Branded,** Paramount, 1951
  Montana Rides Again (1934)
  [both as Evan Evans]
  "Cuttle's Hired Man [in   **Against All Odds,** Fox, 1924
  Western Story, March 1, 1924]
  "Dark Rosaleen" [in *Country*   **The Flying Horseman,** Fox,
  Gentleman, Dec. 1924–Jan.   1926
  1925]

Destry Rides Again (1930)	Universal, 1932
	*Universal, 1939
	Destry, Universal, 1955
Free Range Lanning	**The Fighting Streak,** Fox, 1922
[as George Owen Baxter, 1921]	
Gun Gentleman	**Mile-a-Minute Romeo,** Fox, 1923
Hired Guns (1948)	**The Gun Fighter,** Fox, 1923
The Night Horseman (1920)	Fox, 1921
Señor Jingle Bells (1928)	**The Best Bad Man,** Fox, 1925
Singing Guns (1938)	Republic, 1950
South of the Rio Grande (1936)	**My Outlaw Brother,** UA, 1951
"Three Who Paid" [in *Western Story,* April 8, 1922, as George Owen Baxter]	**Three Who Paid,** Fox, 1923
Trailin' (1920)	Fox, 1921
	A Holy Terror, Fox, 1931
The Untamed (1919)	Fox, 1920
	Fair Warning, Fox, 1930
The Valley of Vanishing Men (1947)	Columbia, 1942 [15 chapter serial]

Notes: Source unknown: **Lawless Love** (Fox, 1918)

Original story for screen: **The Desperadoes** (Columbia, 1943)

Faust was given partial credit for the screenplay of: **The Deerslayer** (Republic, 1943)

Felson, Henry Gregor (1916–   )

Why Rustlers Never Win	**Once Upon a Horse,** Universal, 1958

Ferber, Edna (1885–1968)

Cimarron (1930)	*RKO, 1931
	MGM, 1961
Giant (1952)	*Warner Bros., 1956

Fergusson, Harvey (1890–1971)

Wolf Song (1927)	Paramount, 1929

Fessier, Michael

"The Woman They Almost Lynched" [published in *Saturday Evening Post,* June 1, 1951]	**The Woman They Almost Lynched,** Republic, 1953

Note: Fessier received either all or partial screen credit for the following western screenplays: *Frontier Gal* (Universal, 1945); *Red Garters* (Paramount, 1954); *Valley of the Giants* (20th Fox, 1938)

Fisher, Vardis (1895–1968)
    Mountain Man (1965)   **Jeremiah Johnson,* Warner
                                 Bros., 1972

Fleischman, Albert Sidney (1920–   )
    Yellowleg (1960)   *The Deadly Companions,*
                                 Pathé-American, 1961
    By the Great Horn Spoon (1963)   *The Adventures of Bullwhip*
                                 Griffin, Buena Vista, 1967
Note: Fleischman received partial credit for the screenplay of: *The Deadly Companions* (Pathé-American, 1961)

Fluharty, Vernon L.   **see**   Carder, Michael

Flynn, Thomas Theodore (1902–   )
    The Man from Laramie (1954)   Universal, 1955

Foreman, Leonard London (1901–   )
    "Adios, My Texas"   *The Lone Gun,* UA, 1953
    The Renegade (1942)   *The Savage,* Paramount, 1952
    The Road to San Jacinto   *Arrow in the Dust,* Allied
     (1943)   Artists, 1954
    Note: Source unknown: *The Storm Rider* (20th Century–Fox, 1957)

Foster, Bennett
    "Trail Town Fever"   *Flame of the West,* Monogram,
                                 1945

Fowler, Frank (1900–1971) [all work written as Bordon, Chase]
    Blazing Guns on the Chisholm   **Red River,* UA, 1948
     Trail (1948)
    Lone Star (1952)   MGM, 1952
    Notes: Original story for screen: *Gunfighters of Casa Grande* (MGM, 1965); *Man from Colorado* (Columbia, 1949); *Vera Cruz* (UA, 1954)
    Fowler received either all or partial credit for the following western screenplays: *Backlash* (Universal, 1956); *Bend of the River* (Universal, 1952); *The Far Country* (Universal, 1955); *Flame of the Barbary Coast* (Republic, 1945); *Gunfighters of Casa Grande* (MGM, 1965); *Lone Star* (MGM, 1952); *Man Without a Star* (Universal, 1955); *Montana* (Warner Bros., 1950); *Night Passage* (Universal, 1957); *Red River* (UA, 1948); *Ride a Crooked Trail* (Universal, 1958); *Winchester 73* (Universal, 1950)

Fox, John, Jr. (1862–1919)
 Trail of the Lonesome Pine (1913) Paramount, 1916
              Paramount, 1923
              Paramount, 1936

Fox, Norman (1911–1960)
 Night Passage (1956)   Universal, 1957
 The Rawhide Years (1953) Universal, 1956
 Roughshod (1951)   ***Gunsmoke,*** Universal, 1953
 Tall Man Riding (1951)   Warner Bros., 1955

Franklin, George Cory
 "Into the Crimson West"   ***Prairie Schooners,*** Columbia,
              1940

Frazee, Steve (1909–)
 "Death Rides This Trail"   ***Wild Heritage,*** Universal, 1958
 Many Rivers to Cross (1955) MGM, 1955
 "Running Target" (1953)   ****Running Target,*** UA, 1956
 "The Singing Sands" (1954) ***Gold of the Seven Saints,***
              Warner Bros., 1961

Garfield, Brian (1939–)
 Gundown (1971)   ****The Last Hard Man,*** 20th
              Fox, 1976

Garth, David
 Four Men and a Prayer   ***Fury at Furnace Creek,*** 20th
              Fox, 1948

Gerould, Katherine
 Conquistador (1927)   ***Romance of the Rio Grande,***
              Fox, 1929
              Romance of the Rio Grande,
              20th Fox, 1941

Gill, Tom
 Gay Bandit of the Border (1931) ***The Gay Caballero,*** Fox, 1932

Gilroy, Frank D. (1925–)
 "The Last Notch"   ***The Fastest Gun Alive,*** MGM,
              1956
   Note: Gilroy received credit for the screenplay of: ***The Fastest Gun
Alive*** (MGM, 1956)

Gipson, Fred (1908-1973)
    Hound-Dog Man (1949)   ***Return of the Texan,*** 20th Fox, 1952
                                        20th Fox, 1959
    Old Yeller (1956)   *Buena Vista, 1958
    Savage Sam (1962)   Buena Vista, 1963
    Note: Gipson received either all or partial credit for the following screenplays based on his novels: **Hound Dog Man** (20th Fox, 1959); **Old Yeller** (Buena Vista, 1958)

Glidden, Frederick Dilley (1908-1975) [all novels written as Luke Short]
    Ambush (1950)   MGM, 1949
    Coroner Creek (1946)   Columbia, 1948
    Dead Freight for Piute (1940)   ***Albuquerque,*** Paramount, 1948
    Gunman's Chance (1941)   ****Blood on the Moon,*** RKO, 1948
    High Vermillion (1948)   ***Silver City,*** Paramount, 1951
    Ramrod (1943)   *UA, 1947
    Ride the Man Down (1942)   *Republic, 1953
    Station West (1947)   *RKO, 1948
    Vengeance Valley (1950)   MGM, 1951
    Notes: Source unknown: **Hurry, Charlie, Hurry** (RKO, 1941)
    Glidden received partial credit for the screenplay of: **Blood on the Moon** (RKO, 1948)

Glidden, Jonathan Huff (1907-1957) [written as Peter Dawson]
    "Lone Gone" (1950)   ***Face of a Fugitive,*** Columbia, 1959
    Renegade Canyon (1949)   Columbia, 1949

Goulden, Ray
    Glory Gulch   ***Five Card Stud,*** Paramount, 1968

Granger, George, and Roberts, K.
    Ten Against Caesar   ***Gun Fury,*** Columbia, 1953

Gregory, Jackson (1882-1943)
    The Bells of San Juan (1919)   Fox, 1922
    Desert Valley (1921)   Fox, 1926
    The Everlasting Whisper (1922) Fox, 1925
    Judith of Blue Lake Ranch (1919) ***Two Kinds of Women,*** Robertson-Cole, 1922
    Man to Man (1920)   Universal, 1922

Mystery at Spanish Hacienda
   (1929)
The Outlaw (1916)
"Silver Slippers"

Sudden Bill Dorn (1937)
Timber Wolf (1923)

Grey, Zane (1872–1939)
   Arizona Ames (1932)

   "Avalanche"
   The Border Legion (1916)

   Call of the Canyon (1924)

   "Canyon Walls"
   Captives of the Desert
      (1952)
   Code of the West (1934)

   Desert Gold (1913)

   The Desert of Wheat
      (1920)
   The Drift Fence (1933)
   The Dude Ranger (1951)
   Fighting Caravans (1929)

   Forlorn River (1927)

   The Heritage of the Desert
      (1910)

   Knights of the Range (1939)
   The Last Trail (1909)

The Laramie Trail, Republic,
   1944
Hearts and Spurs (Fox, 1925)
The Man from Painted Post,
   Douglas Fairbanks/ART, 1917
Universal, 1937
Fox, 1925

*** Thunder Trail,** Paramount,
   1937
Avalanche, Paramount, 1928
Goldwyn, 1918
Paramount, 1924
Paramount, 1930
Republic, 1940
Paramount, 1925
Republic, 1942
Smoke Lightning, Fox, 1933
Drums of the Desert, Para-
   mount, 1927
Paramount, 1925
Home on the Range, Para-
   mount, 1935
RKO, 1947
Kaybee, 1914
Paramount, 1921
Paramount, 1926
Paramount, 1936
Riders of the Dawn, Hodkin-
   son, 1920
Paramount, 1936
Fox, 1934
Paramount, 1931
Wagon Wheels, Paramount,
   1934
Paramount, 1926
Paramount, 1937
Paramount, 1924
*Paramount, 1932
*Paramount, 1939
Paramount, 1940
Fox, 1918
Fox, 1921

	Fox, 1927
	Fox, 1933
The Light of the Western Stars (1914)	Sherman-United, 1918
	Paramount, 1925
	Paramount, 1930
	Paramount, 1940
"Lightning"	*Lightning,* Tiffany, 1927
The Lone Ranger (1915)	*The Last of the Duanes,* Fox, 1919
	Fox, 1923
	The Last of the Duanes, Fox, 1924
	Fox, 1930
	The Last of the Duanes, Fox, 1930
	The Last of the Duanes, 20th Fox, 1941
	20th Fox, 1942
Lost Pueblo (1954)	*The Water Hole,* Paramount, 1928
Man of the Forest (1920)	Paramount, 1921
	Paramount, 1926
	*Paramount, 1933
The Maverick Queen (1950)	Republic, 1956
The Mysterious Rider (1921)	Paramount, 1921
	Paramount, 1927
	Paramount, 1933
	*Paramount, 1938
Nevada (1928)	Paramount, 1927
	Paramount, 1935
	RKO, 1944
"The Outlaws of Palouse"	*End of the Trail,* Columbia, 1936
Raiders of Spanish Peaks (1938)	*The Arizona Raiders,* Paramount, 1936
The Rainbow Trail (1915)	Fox, 1918
	Fox, 1925
	Fox, 1932
Riders of the Purple Sage (1912)	Fox, 1918
	Fox, 1925
	*Fox, 1931
	*Fox, 1941
Robbers Roost (1932)	Fox, 1933
	UA, 1955

(Grey, Zane, *cont.*)

Stairs of Sand (1943)	Paramount, 1929
	Arizona Mahoney, Paramount, 1936
Sunset Pass (1931)	Paramount, 1929
	Paramount, 1933
	RKO, 1946
Thunder Mountain (1935)	Fox, 1935
The Thundering Herd (1925)	*Paramount, 1925
	Paramount, 1933
To the Last Man (1922)	Paramount, 1923
	*Paramount, 1933
	Thunder Mountain, RKO, 1947
Twin Sombreroes (1941)	***Gunfighters,*** Columbia, 1947
The U.P. Trail (1918)	Hodkinson, 1919
Under the Tonto Rim (1926)	Paramount, 1928
	Paramount, 1933
	RKO, 1947
The Vanishing American (1925)	Paramount, 1925
	Republic, 1955
Wanderer of the Wasteland (1923)	*Paramount, 1924
	Paramount, 1935
	RKO, 1935
West of the Pecos (1937)	RKO, 1937
	RKO, 1945
Western Union (1939)	*20th Fox, 1941
Wild Horse Mesa (1928)	Paramount, 1925
	Paramount, 1932
	RKO, 1947
Wildfire (1917)	***When Romance Rides,*** Goldwyn, 1922
	Red Canyon, Universal, 1949

Notes: Sources unknown: ***Born to the West*** (Parmaount, 1926); ***Golden West*** (Fox, 1932); ***Life in the Raw*** (Fox, 1933); ***Roll Along Cowboy*** (20th Century-Fox, 1937); ***The Vanishing Pioneers*** (Paramount, 1928)

Original story for screen: ***Golden Dreams*** (Goldwyn, 1922); remade as: ***Rocky Mountain Mystery*** (Paramount, 1935)

The following films were based on a comic strip, ***King of the Royal Mounted,*** credited to Zane Grey: ***King of the Mounties*** (Republic, 1942, a 12 chapter serial); ***King of the Royal Mounted*** (20th Century-Fox, 1936); ***King of the Royal Mounted*** (Republic, 1940, a 12 chapter serial); ***Yukon Patrol*** (Republic, 1942, a feature version of the 1940 serial)

Gruber, Frank (1904–1969)

Bitter Sage (1954)	***Tension at Table Rock,*** RKO, 1956
Broken Lance (1949)	***Warpath,*** Paramount, 1951
Buffalo Grass (1956)	***The Big Land*** (1957)
Fighting Man (1948)	***Fighting Man of the Plains,*** 20th Fox, 1949
Peace Marshal (1939)	***The Kansan,*** UA, 1943
Town Tamer (1957)	Paramount, 1965

Notes: Original story for screen: ***The Cariboo Trail*** (20th Century-Fox, 1950); ***Denver and Rio Grande*** (Paramount, 1952); ***Oregon Trail*** (20th Fox, 1959)

Gruber received either all or partial credit for the following western screenplays: ***Arizona Raiders*** (Columbia, 1965); ***Dakota Lil*** (20th Century-Fox, 1950); ***Denver and Rio Grande*** (Paramount, 1952); ***Fighting Man of the Plains*** (20th Century-Fox, 1949); ***Flaming Feather*** (Paramount, 1952); ***The Great Missouri Raid*** (Paramount, 1951); ***In Old Sacramento*** (Republic, 1946); ***Pony Express*** (Paramount, 1953); ***Rage at Dawn*** (RKO, 1955); ***Silver City*** (Paramount, 1951); ***The Texas Rangers*** (Columbia, 1951); ***Warpath*** (Paramount, 1951)

Gulick, Grover Cleveland "Bill" (1916–)

Bend of the Snake (1950)	* ***Bend of the River,*** Universal, 1952
The Hallelujah Train (1963)	***The Hallelujah Trail,*** UA, 1965
Man from Texas [serialized in *Saturday Evening Post,* 1950]	***The Road to Denver,*** Republic, 1955

Guthrie, Alfred Bertram (1901–)

The Big Sky (1947)	*RKO, 1952
These Thousand Hills (1956)	20th Fox, 1958
The Way West (1949)	UA, 1967

Notes: Guthrie received either all or partial credit for the following western screenplays: ***The Kentuckian*** (UA, 1955); ***Shane*** (Paramount, 1953)

Hall, Oakley (1920–)

Warlock (1958)	*20th Fox, 1959

Hamilton, Donald (1916–)

The Big Country (1958)	*UA, 1958
Smokey Valley (1954)	* ***The Violent Men,*** Columbia, 1955

Hardy, Stuart   **see**   Schisgall, Oscar

Harrison, C. William
   "Petticoat Brigade"   *The Guns of Fort Petticoat,*
                                                Columbia, 1957

Harte, Francis Bret (1836–1902)
   "Cressy"   *Fighting Cressy,* Pathé, 1919
   "The Golden Princess"   *The Golden Princess,* Para-
                                              mount, 1925
   "In the Carquinez Woods"   *The Half Breed,* Triangle, 1916
   "The Luck of Roaring Camp"   *The Luck of Roaring Camp,*
     (1868)   Monogram, 1937
   M'liss: An Idyll of the Red   *The Girl Who Ran Wild,*
     Mountain (1863)   Universal, 1922
                                                The Man from Red Gulch,
                                              PDC, 1925
                                              RKO, 1936
   "The Outcasts of Poker Flat"   *The Outcasts of Poker Flat,*
                                              Universal, 1919
                                              Man Hunt, Pictures Co., 1931
                                              RKO, 1937
                                              20th Fox, 1952
   "The Saint of Calamity Gulch"   *Taking a Chance,* Fox, 1928
   "Salomy Jane's Kiss"   *Salomy Jane,* Alco Films, 1914
                                              Paramount, 1923
   "Tennessee's Partner"   *The Flaming Forties,* PDC,
                                              1924
                                              Tennessee's Partner, RKO,
                                              1955

Haycox, Ernest (1899–1950)
   Bugles in the Afternoon (1944)   Warner Bros., 1952
   Canyon Passage (1945)   *Universal, 1946
   Man in the Saddle (1938)   *Columbia, 1951
   "Stage to Lordsburg"   **Stagecoach,* UA, 1939
                                              Stagecoach, 20th Fox, 1966
   "Stage Station"   *Apache Trail,* MGM, 1942
                                              Apache War Smoke, MGM,
                                              1952
   Sundown Jim (1938)   20th Fox, 1942
   Trail Town (1941)   **Abilene Town,* UA, 1946
   Trouble Shooter (1937)   *Union Pacific,* Paramount,
                                              1939

Note: Original story for screen: ***Montana*** (Warner Bros., 1950).
Haycox received credit for the screen treatment of the western comedy: ***Heaven Only Knows*** (UA, 1947)

Hecklemann, Charles (1913–   )
   Deputy Marshal (1947)   Lippert, 1949
     Note: Original story for screen: ***Frontier Feud*** (Monogram, 1945);
Stranger from Santa Fe (Monogram, 1945)

Hendryx, James Beardsley (1880–1963)
   Snowdrift: A Story of the Land   ***Snowdrift,*** Fox, 1923
     of Strong Cold (1922)

Henry, O.   **see**   Porter, William Sidney

Hoffman, Lee (1932–   )
   The Valdez Horses (1967)   ***Chino,*** Intercontinental Releasing Corp., 1976

Hogan, Robert Ray (1908–   )
   Apache Landing   ***The Stand at Apache River,***
                        Universal, 1953
   Outlaw Marshal (1958)   ***Hell Bent for Leather,*** Universal, 1960

Holt, Felix
   The Gabriel Horn   ***The Kentuckian,*** UA, 1954

Horgan, Paul (1903–   )
   A Distant Trumpet (1960)   Warner Bros., 1964

Hough, Emerson (1857–1923)
   The Broken Gate (1917)   ***One Hour of Love,*** Tiffany,
                        1927
   The Covered Wagon (1922) *Paramount, 1923
   The Man Next Door (1917) Vitagraph, 1923
   North of 36 (1923)   Paramount, 1924
                        The Conquering the Horde,
                        Paramount, 1931
                        The Texans, Paramount, 1938
   The Sagebrusher (1919)   Hodkinson, 1920
   The Ship of Souls (1925)   Associated Exhibitors, 1925

Huffaker, Cliff (1928–   )
   Flaming Lance (1958)   ***Flaming Star,*** 20th Fox, 1960

Guns of the Rio Conchos	*__Rio Conchos,__ 20th Fox, 1964
Nobody Loves a Drunken Indian (1967)	__Flap,__ Warner Bros., 1970
Posse from Hell	*Universal, 1961
Seven Ways from Sundown	Universal, 1960

Notes: Huffaker received either all or partial credit for the following western screenplays: __The Comancheros__ (20th Fox, 1961); __Flaming Star__ (20th Fox, 1960); __Flap__ (Warner Bros., 1970); __Posse from Hell__ (Universal, 1961); __Rio Conchos__ (20th Fox, 1964); __Seven Ways from Sundown__ (Universal, 1960)

Jackson, Helen Hunt (1830–1885)
    Ramona (1885)

Biograph, 1910
Clune, 1916
UA, 1928
Fox, 1936

James, Will   **see**   Dufault, Joseph Ernest Naphtali

Jennings, William Dale (1917–)
    The Cowboys   Warner Bros., 1972

Jessup, Richard
    Chuka   Paramount, 1967

Note: Jessup received credit for the screenplay of: __Chuka__ (Paramount, 1967)

Johnson, Dorothy Marie (1905–)
    "The Hanging Tree" (1958)   *__The Hanging Tree,__ Warner Bros., 1959

    "A Man Called Horse" (1953)   __A Man Called Horse,__ National Gen., 1970

    "The Man Who Shot Liberty Valance" (1953)   *__The Man Who Shot Liberty Valance,__ Paramount, 1962

Kantor, MacKinlay (1904–1977)
    Arouse and Beware   __The Man from Dakota,__ MGM, 1940

    Happy Land and Gentle Annie (1944)   __Gentle Annie,__ MGM, 1944
    Wicked Water (1947)   __Outlaw Territory__ [aka __Hanna Lee__], Border/Realart, 1953

Kelland, Clarence Buddington (1881–1964)
    Arizona   Columbia, 1940
    Sugarfoot (1942)   Warner Bros., 1951

Note: Kelland received either all or partial credit on following western screenplays: *Arizona* (Columbia, 1940); *Sugarfoot* (Warner Bros., 1951); *Valley of the Sun* (RKO, 1942)

Ketchum, Philip (1902–1969)
"The Town in Hell's Back Yard" [in *Ten Story Western Magazine*]

The Devil's Trail, Columbia, 1942

Knibbs, Henry Herbert (1874–1945)
Overland Red (1914)

Universal, 1920
The Sunset Trail, Universal, 1924

The Ridin' Kid from Powder River (1919)

Universal, 1924
The Mounted Stranger, Universal, 1930

Kyne, Peter Bernard (1880–1957)
"All for Love"

Valley of Wanted Men, Conn, 1935

"Bread Upon the Waters"

A Hero on Horseback, Universal, 1927

"Oh, Promise Me"

The Bukaroo Kid, Universal, 1926
Gordon of Ghost City, Universal, 1933

"The Parson of Panamint

The Parson of Panamint, Paramount, 1916
The Parson of Panamint, Paramount, 1941

"Renunciation"

Judge Not, or the Woman of Mona Diggings, Universal, 1915

"The Sheriff of Cinnabar"
The Three Godfathers (1913)

Red Courage, Universal, 1921
Bronco Billy and the Baby, Essanay, 1908
Universal, 1916
Marked Men, Universal, 1919
*Hell's Heroes, Universal, 1929
MGM, 1936
*MGM, 1948

"The Tie That Binds"

Heroes of the West, Universal, 1932
Flaming Frontiers, Universal, 1938

Tide of Empire (1927)	MGM, 1929
"Tidy Toreador"	*A Hero on Horseback,* Universal, 1927
Valley of the Giants	Warner Bros., 1927
	Warner Bros., 1938

Note: Sources unknown: *Code of the Range* (Columbia, 1935); *Flaming Guns* (Universal, 1932); *Gallant Defender* (Columbia, 1935); *Local Bad Man* (Allied, 1933); *The Mysterious Avenger* (Columbia, 1936); *Rio Grande Romance* (Victory, 1936); *Secret Patrol* (Columbia, 1936); *Wild Horse* (Allied, 1931)

Lake, Stuart
Wyatt Earp, Frontier Marshal	*Frontier Marshal,* Fox, 1934
	Frontier Marshal, 20th Fox, 1939
	My Darling Clementine, 20th Fox, 1946

Note: Original story for screen: *Wells Fargo* (1937); *The Westerner* (Goldwyn, 1940); *Winchester 73* (Universal, 1950)

L'Amour, Louis (1908–1988)
The Burning Hills (1956)	Warner Bros., 1956
Catlow (1963)	MGM, 1971
"The Gift of the Apaches"	*Hondo and the Apaches,* MGM, 1967
Guns of the Timberland (1955)	Warner Bros., 1960
Heller with a Gun (1955)	**Heller in Pink Tights,* Paramount, 1960
Hondo (1953)	*Warner Bros., 1955
Kid Rodelo (1966)	Paramount, 1966
Kilkinny (1954)	*Blackjack Ketchum, Desperado* Columbia, 1956
Last Stand at Papago Wells (1957)	*Apache Territory,* Columbia, 1956
"Rider of the Ruby Hills"	*Treasure of the Ruby Hills,* AA, 1955
Shalako (1962)	Cinerama, 1968
"Showdown Trail"	*The Tall Stranger,* AA, 1957
Utah Blaine (1954)	Columbia, 1957

Note: Sources unknown: *Four Guns to the Border* (Universal, 1954); *Stranger on Horseback* (UA, 1955)

Landis, James
The Lone Texan	20th Fox, 1959

Lawton, Harry (1927–   )
    Willie Boy: A Desert Manhunt   **Tell Them Willie Boy Is Here,**
    (1960)   Universal, 1969

Lea, Tom, Jr. (1907–   )
    The Wonderful Country (1952)   *UA, 1959

Leighton, Lee   **see**   Overholster, Wayne

LeMay, Alan (1899–1964)
    The Searchers (1954)   *Warner Bros., 1956
    The Unforgiven (1957)   UA, 1960
    Thunder in the Dust (1934)   **The Sundowners,** Eagle-Lion,
                                    1950
    Useless Cowboy (1943)   **Along Came Jones,** RKO, 1945
    Note: Original story for screen: **Rocky Mountain** (Warner Bros., 1950); **Trailin' West** (Warner Bros., 1949); **The Walking Hills** (Columbia, 1949)

    LeMay received either all or partial credit for the following western screenplays: **Cheyenne** (Warner Bros., 1947); **Gunfighters** (Columbia, 1947); **High Lonesome** (Eagle-Lion, 1950 [LeMay also directed **High Lonesome**]); **North West Mounted Police** (Paramount, 1940); **Rocky Mountain** (Warner Bros., 1950); **San Antonio** (Warner Bros., 1945); **The Sundowners** (Eagle-Lion, 1950); **Trailin' West** (Warner Bros., 1949); **The Vanishing American** (Republic, 1955)

Leonard, Elmore (1925–   )
    Hombre (1961)   *20th Fox, 1967
    "The Hostage"   * **The Tall T,** Columbia, 1957
    "3:10 to Yuma"   **3:10 to Yuma,** Columbia, 1957
    Valdez Is Coming (1970)   *UA, 1971

Lewis, Alfred Henry (1858–1914)
    Faro Nell and Her Friends (1913)   **Faro Nell, or in Old Californy**
                                  Paramount, 1929
    Wolfville: Episodes of Cowboy   **Dead Shot Baker,** Vitagraph,
       Life, et.al. (1897–1913)   1917
                                  The Tenderfoot, Vitagraph,
                                  1917

Linford, Dee
    Man Without a Star   Universal, 1955

Lockhart, Caroline
    The Dude Wrangler (1921)   Sono Art–World Wide, 1930

Lomax, Bliss **see** Drago, Harry Sinclair

Longstreet, Stephen (1907–)
    Stallion Road   Warner Bros., 1947
    Notes: Original story for screen: *Silver River* (Warner Bros., 1948)
    Longstreet received either all or partial credit for the following western
screenplays: *Silver River* (Warner Bros., 1948); *Stallion Road* (Warner
Bros., 1947)

Loomis, Noel Miller (1905–1979)
    Johnny Concho (1956)   UA, 1956

Lott, Milton (1919–)
    The Last Hunt (1954)   *MGM, 1956

McCulley, Johnson (1883–1958)
    "The Broken Dollar" [in *Far*   **Black Jack,** Fox, 1927
      West, Jan., 1927]
    "The Brute Breaker" [in *All*   **The Ice Flood,** Universal, 1926
      Story, August 10, 1918]
    Captain Fly-by-Night (1926)   Robertson-Cole, 1922
    The Curse of Capistrano   **The Bold Caballero,** Republic,
                             1936
                             Don Q, Son of Zorro, UA, 1925
                             Ghost of Zorro, Republic, 1949
                             *** The Mark of Zorro,** UA, 1920
                             *** The Mark of Zorro,** 20th Fox,
                             1940
                             Son of Zorro, Republic, 1947
                             Zorro Rides Again, Republic,
                             1937
                             Zorro's Black Whip, Republic,
                             1944
                             Zorro's Fighting Legion,
                             Republic, 1939
    "King of Cactusville" [in   **Outlaw Deputy,** Puritan, 1935
      Western Story, August, 1923]
    "Little Erolinda" [in *Adventure,* **The Kiss,** Universal, 1921
      Feb., 1916]
    Saddle Mates (1924) [in *Western* Pathé, 1928
      Story, Jan. 1924, by Strong,
      Harrington)
    The Trusted Outlaw (1934)   Republic, 1937
    Note: Sources unknown: *Ride for Your Life* (Universal, 1924)

Original story for screen: **Doomed Caravan** (Paramount, 1941); **Mark of the Renegade** (Universal, 1951); **Outlaws of Stampede Pass** (Monogram, 1943); **Overland Mail** (Universal, 1942); **Riders of the Border** (Monogram, 1944); **Rootin' Tootin' Rhythm** (Republic, 1937); **Rose of the Rio Grande** (Monogram, 1938); **South of the Rio Grande** (Monogram, 1945)

McCulley is given partial credit for the following screenplay: **Doomed Caravan** (Paramount, 1941)

MacDonald, William Colt (1891–1968) [There were 53 films in all based on the Three Mesquiteers created by MacDonald, although only the few that follow were based on actual novels]

Gold Town Gold (1935)	Republic, 1936
Law of the Forty-Fives (1933)	**Law of the .45's,** First Division, 1935
Powdersmoke Range (1934)	*RKO, 1935
The Riders of Whistling Skull (1934)	Republic, 1937
Roarin' Lead (1935)	Republic, 1936

The following list represents the remainder of the Three Mesquiteers' films based on the characters created by MacDonald but not based on any novel or short story. All were made by Republic. **Blocked Trail** (1943); **Call the Mesquiteers** (1938); **Code of the Outlaw** (1942); **Come on Cowboys** (1937); **Covered Wagon Days** (1940); **Cowboys from Texas** (1939); **Gangs of Sonora** (1941); **Gauchos of El Dorado** (1941); **Gunsmoke Ranch** (1937); **Heart of the Rockies** (1937); **Heroes of the Hills** (1938); **Heroes of the Saddle** (1940); **Hit the Saddle** (1937); **The Kansas Terrors** (1939); **Lone Star Raiders** (1940); **New Frontier** (1939); **The Night Riders** (1939); **Oklahoma Renegades** (1940); **Outlaws of Sonora** (1938); **Outlaws of the Cherokee Trail** (1941); **Overland Stage Raiders** (1938); **Pals of the Pecos** (1941); **Pals of the Saddle** (1938); **The Phantom Plainsmen** (1942); **Pioneers of the West** (1940); **Prairie Pioneers** (1941); **The Purple Vigilantes** (1938); **Raiders of the Range** (1942); **Range Defenders** (1937); **Red River Range** (1938); **Riders of the Black Hills** (1938); **Riders of the Rio Grande** (1943); **Rocky Mountain Rangers** (1940); **Saddlemates** (1941); **Santa Fe Scouts** (1943); **Santa Fe Stampede** (1938); **Shadows on the Sage** (1942); **The Three Mesquiteers** (1936); **Three Texas Steers** (1939); **Thundering Trails** (1943); **The Trail Busters** (1940); **The Trigger Trio** (1937); **Under Texas Skies** (1940); **Valley of Hunted Men** (1942); **West of Cimarron** (1941); **Westward Ho** (1942); **Wild Horse Rodeo** (1937); **Wyoming Outlaw** (1939)

Note: Original story for screen: **Along the Navajo Trail** (Republic, 1945); **Daring Danger** (Columbia, 1932); **Man of Action** (Columbia, 1933); **One Man Justice** (Columbia, 1937); **The Riding Tornado** (Columbia, 1932); **Texas Cyclone** (Columbia, 1932); **Too Much Beef** (Colony, 1936); **Two Fisted Law** (Columbia, 1932); **Two Fisted Sheriff** (Columbia, 1937); **The Western Code** (Columbia, 1932)

McLeod, Robert (1917–)
    The Appaloosa   Universal, 1966
    100 Rifles   20th Fox, 1969

McMurtry, Larry (1936–)
    Horseman, Pass By (1961)   ***Hud,*** Paramount, 1963
    The Last Picture Show (1966)   *Columbia, 1971
    Leaving Cheyenne (1963)   ***Lovin' Molly,*** Columbia, 1974

Maddow, Ben **see** Yordan, Phillip

Mann, Edward Beverly (1902–)
    The Boss of Lazy 9 (1936)   ***Boss Rider of Gun Creek,***
                                        Universal, 1936
    Stampede (1934)   ***Stormy Trails,*** Colony, 1936
                                        Stampede, Allied Artists, 1949
    Notes: Source unknown: ***Guns for Hire*** (Kent, 1932)
    Original story for screen: ***Desert Phantom*** (Supreme, 1936); ***Guns in the Dark*** (Republic, 1937); ***Lightning Crandall*** (Republic, 1937); ***Ridin' the Lone Trail*** (Republic, 1937); ***Trail of Vengeance*** (Republic, 1937)

Marshall, James
    Santa Fe   Columbia, 1951

Martin, Charles
    Left Handed Law (1936)   Universal, 1937

Monaghan, Jay (1891–1981)
    Last of the Badmen   AA, 1957

Morrow, Honore Willsie (1880–1940)
    On to Oregon (1926)   ***Seven Alone,*** Doty-Dayton,
                                        1974

Mulford, Clarence Edward (1883–1956)
    The Orphan (1908)   ***The Deadwood Coach,*** Fox,
                                        1924
    [There were 66 Hopalong Cassidy films, most of which were original stories. The few based on novels are listed below. For additional Hopalong Cassidy entries, see Drago, Harry Sinclair]
    Bar 20 (1907)   ***Bar 20,*** UA, 1943
    Bar 20 Days (1911)   ***Partners of the Plains,*** Para-
                                        mount, 1938
    The Bar 20 Rides Again (1926)   Paramount, 1935

Bar Twenty Three (1921)	*** Three Men from Texas,** Paramount
Black Buttes (1923)	**Hopalong Rides Again,** Paramount, 1937
Cottonwood Gulch (1925)	**North of the Rio Grande,** Paramount, 1937
Hopalong Cassidy (1910)	*Paramount, 1935
Hopalong Casidy and the Eagle's Brood (1931)	**The Eagle's Brood,** Paramount, 1935
Hopalong Cassidy Returns (1924)	Paramount, 1936
Hopalong Cassidy Serves a Writ (1941)	**Hoppy Serves a Writ,** UA, 1943
Hopalong Cassidy's Protege (1926)	**Call of the Prairie,** Paramount, 1936
Me and Shorty (1929)	**Cassidy of the Bar 20,** Paramount, 1938
The Round Up (1933)	**Hills of Old Wyoming,** Paramount, 1937
Rustler's Valley (1924)	Paramount, 1937
Tex (1922)	**Texas Trail,** Paramount, 1937
Trail Dust (1934)	Paramount, 1936

[The following Hopalong Cassidy films are based on the characters created by Mulford but are not based on any novel or short story.] **Bar 20 Justice** (Paramount, 1938); **Border Patrol** (UA, 1943); **Border Vigilantes** (Paramount, 1941); **Borderland** (Paramount, 1937); **Borrowed Trouble** (UA, 1948); **Dangerous Venture** (UA, 1947); **The Dead Don't Dream** (UA, 1948); **Devil's Playground** (UA, 1946); **Doomed Caravan** (Paramount, 1941); **False Colors** (UA, 1943); **False Paradise** (UA, 1948); **Fool's Gold** (UA, 1946); **Forty Thieves** (UA, 1944); **The Frontiersman** (Paramount, 1938); **Heart of Arizona** (Paramount, 1938); **Heart of the West** (Paramount, 1936); **Hidden Gold** (Paramount, 1940); **Hoppy's Holiday** (UA, 1947); **In Old Colorado** (Paramount, 1941); **In Old Mexico** (Paramount, 1938); **Law of the Pampas** (Paramount, 1939); **Lost Canyon** (UA, 1942); **Lumberjack** (UA, 1944); **The Marauders** (UA, 1947); **Mystery Man** (UA, 1944); **Outlaws of the Desert** (Paramount, 1941); **Pirates on Horseback** (Paramount, 1941); **Pride of the West** (Paramount, 1938); **Range War** (Paramount, 1939); **The Renegade Trail** (Paramount, 1939); **Riders of the Deadline** (UA, 1943); **Riders of the Timberline** (Paramount, 1941); **Santa Fe Marshal** (Paramount, 1940); **The Showdown** (Paramount, 1940); **Silent Conflict** (UA, 1948); **Silver on the Sage** (Paramount, 1939); **Sinister Journey** (UA, 1948); **Stagecoach War** (Paramount, 1940); **Stick to Your Guns** (Paramount, 1941); **Strange Gamble** (UA, 1948); **Sunset Trail** (Paramount, 1938); **Texas Masquerade** (UA, 1944); **Three on the Trail** (Paramount, 1936); **Twilight on the Trail** (Paramount, 1941); **Undercover Man** (UA, 1942); **Unexpected Guest** (UA, 1947); **Wide Open Town** (Paramount, 1941)

Naughton, Edmund
    McCabe   **McCabe and Mrs. Miller,**
                                      Warner Bros., 1971

Neider, Charles (1915–   )
    The Authentic Death of   **One-Eyed Jacks,** Paramount,
    Hendry Jones   1961

Noble, Hollister
    Woman with a Sword (1938)   **Drums in the Deep South,**
                                  RKO, 1952

O'Hara, Mary (1895–1980)
    Green Grass of Wyoming (1946)   20th Fox, 1948

O'Locke, Charles
    The Hell-Bent Kid   **From Hell to Texas,** Fox, 1958

O'Rourke, Frank (1916–   )
    The Bravados (1957)   20th Fox, 1958
    The Great Bank Robbery (1961)   Warner Bros., 1969
    A Mule for the Marquesa (1967)   ***The Professionals,** Columbia,
                                  1966

Ogden, George Washington (1871–1966)
    The Duke of Chimney Butte (1920)   Robertson-Cole, 1921
    Trail Rider (1924)   Fox, 1925

Olsen, Theodore Victor (1932–   )
    Arrow in the Sun (1969)   **Soldier Blue,** Avco-Embassy,
                                  1970
    The Stalking Moon (1965)   National General, 1969

Overholster, Wayne Daniel (1906–   )
    Cast a Long Shadow (1955)   UA, 1959
    Law Man (1953)   **Star in the Dust,** Universal,
    [as Lee Leighton]   1956

Paine, Lauran (1916–   )
    The Lawman (1950)   **The Quiet Gun,** Fox, 1957

Patten, Lewis Byford (1915–1981)
    Death of a Gunfighter (1968)   Universal, 1969
    Gun Proud (1957)   **Red Sundown,** Universal, 1956

Perkins, Kenneth
 Desert Voices (1937)   **Desert Pursuit,** Monogram,
             1952
 Three Were Renegades   **Tumbleweed,** Universal, 1953
 Note: Original story for screen: **Relentless** (Columbia, 1948); **Riding
Shotgun** (Warner Bros., 1954)

Peterson, Harry C.
 The Forty Niners (1949)   Warner Bros., 1947

Poole, Richard **see** Wells, Lee

Porter, William Sidney (1862–1910)
 [There were 24 American films based on the character of the Cisco
Kid, but only the two listed under "The Caballero's Way" actually give
credit to the original story. The rest simply say, "Based on a character
created by O. Henry."]
 "The Caballero's Way"   **The Border Terror,** Universal,
  (1904)   1919
             ***In Old Arizona,** Fox, 1929
 "The Double-Dyed Deceiver"   **The Texan,** Paramount, 1930
             The Llano Kid, Paramount,
             1939
 "The Passing of Black Eagle"   **Black Eagle,** Columbia, 1948
 "The Ransom of Red Chief"   ***O. Henry's Full House,** 20th
             Fox, 1952 [one episode of four]
 [The following are films based on the character the Cisco Kid other-
wise unrelated to "The Caballero's Way."] **Beauty and the Bandit**
(Monogram, 1946); **The Cisco Kid** (Fox, 1931); **The Cisco Kid and the Lady**
(20th Fox, 1939); **The Cisco Kid in Old New Mexico** (Monogram, 1945); **The
Cisco Kid Returns** (Monogram, 1945); **The Daring Caballero** (UA, 1949);
The Gay Amigo (UA, 1949); **The Gay Caballero** (20th Fox, 1940); **The Gay
Cavalier** (Monogram, 1946); **The Girl from San Lorenzo** (UA, 1950); **King
of the Bandits** (Monogram, 1947); **Lucky Cisco Kid** (20th Fox, 1940); **The
Return of the Cisco Kid** (20th Fox, 1939); **Ride On, Vaquero** (20th Fox,
1941); **Riding the California Trail** (Monogram, 1947); **Robin Hood of
Monterey** (Monogram, 1947); **Romance of the Rio Grande** (20th Fox, 1941);
Satan's Cradle (UA, 1949); **South of Monterey** (Monogram, 1946); **South of
the Rio Grande** (Monogram, 1945); **The Valiant Hombre** (UA, 1949); **Viva
Cisco Kid** (20th Fox, 1940)

Portis, Charles McColl (1933–)
 True Grit (1968)   *Paramount, 1969

Raine, William MacLeod (1871–1954)

A Daughter of the Dons (1914)	**Burning the Wind,** Universal, 1929
The Desert's Price (1924)	Fox, 1925
The Fighting Edge (1922)	Warner Bros., 1926
The Highgrader (1915)	**Fighting for Gold,** Fox, 1919
Justice Comes to Tomahawk (1952)	**The Man from Bitter Ridge,** Universal, 1955
Man-Size (1922)	Fox, 1923
Mavericks (1912)	**The Ridin' Rascal,** Universal, 1926
Ridgway of Montana (1909)	Universal, 1924
The Sheriff's Son (1918)	Paramount, 1919
A Texas Ranger (1911)	**Pure Grit,** Universal, 1923
Wyoming (1908)	**The Man from Wyoming,** Universal, 1924
The Yukon Trail (1917)	**The Grip of the Yukon,** Universal, 1928

Reese, John Henry **see** Carpenter, John Joe

Repp, Ed Earl (1900–1979)

Empty Holsters (1937) [as John Cody]	Warner Bros., 1937

Notes: Original story for screen: **Call of the Rockies** (Columbia, 1938); **Cherokee Strip** (Warner Bros., 1937); **The Devil's Saddle Legion** (Warner Bros., 1937); **Guns of Hate** (RKO, 1948); **Gunslingers** (Monogram, 1950); **The Lone Prairie** (Columbia, 1942); **Saddles and Sagebrush** (Columbia, 1942); **Silver City Raiders** (Columbia, 1943); **Six Gun Gospel** (Monogram, 1943); **Terror Trail** (Columbia, 1943); **The Vigilantes Ride** (Columbia, 1944); **West of Cheyenne** (Columbia, 1938)

Repp received either all or partial credit for the following western screenplays: **The Devil's Saddle Legion** (Warner Bros., 1937); **Gunslingers** (Monogram, 1950); **Terror Trail** (Columbia, 1943); **The Vigilantes Ride** (Columbia, 1944)

Rhodes, Eugene Manlove (1869–1934)

Bransford in Arcadia; or The Little Eohippus (1914)	*Eclair-Universal, 1914*
	Sure Fire, Universal, 1921
The Desire of the Moth (1916)	Universal, 1917
	The Wallop, Universal, 1921
Good Men and True (1910)	Robertson-Cole, 1922
The Line of Least Resistance [short novel]	**Within an Inch of His Life,** Eclair-Universal, 1914
Paso por Aqui (1927)	***Four Faces West,** UA, 1948

Stepsons of Light (1921)	**The Mysterious Witness,** Robertson-Cole, 1923
West Is West (1917)	Universal, 1920

Richter, Conrad (1890–1968)
The Light in the Forest (1953)	Buena Vista, 1958
The Sea of Grass (1937)	MGM, 1947

Rigsby, Howard (1909–   )
Sundown at Crazy Horse	**The Last Sunset,** Universal, 1961

Roberts, Elizabeth Maddox (1886–1941)
The Great Meadow (1930)	MGM, 1931

Roberts, Kenneth Lewis (1885–1957)
Northwest Passage (1937)	*MGM, 1940

Roberts, Richard Emory
The Gilded Rooster	**The Last Frontier,** Columbia, 1955
Star in the West	**The Second Time Around,** 20th Fox, 1961

Roberts, Stanley
"Riding Monte Cristo"	**Galloping Dynamite,** Ambassador, 1935

Note: Original story for screen: **Curtain Call at Cactus Creek** (Universal, 1950)

Rubel, James L. (1894–   )
Medico of Painted Springs (1934)	Columbia, 1941
The Medico Rides (1935)	**Thunder Over the Prairie,** Columbia, 1941
The Medico Rides the Trail (1938)	**Prairie Stranger,** Columbia, 1941

Ryan, Marah Ellis (1866–1934)
For the Soul of Rafael (1906)	Equity, 1920
That Girl Montana (1901)	Pathé, 1920
Told in the Hills (1891)	Famous Players, 1919

Sandoz, Mari Susette (1901–1966)
Cheyenne Autumn (1953)	Warner Bros., 1964

Savage, Les, Jr.
>   *The Doctor at Coffin Gap* (1949) **Hills of Utah,** Columbia, 1951
>   *Return to Warbow* (1955)   Columbia, 1958
>   *The Wild Horse* (1950)   **Black Horse Canyon,** Universal,
>   1954

   Note: Savage received credit for the screenplay of: **The White Squaw**
(Columbia, 1956)

Scarborough, Dorothy (1877–1935)
>   *The Wind* (1925)   *MGM, 1927

Schaefer, Jack (1907–)
>   *Company of Cowards* (1957) **Advance to the Rear,** MGM,
>   1964
>
>   *First Blood*   **The Silver Whip,** 20th Fox,
>   1953
>
>   "Jeremy Rodock"   **Tribute to a Bad Man,** MGM,
>   1956
>
>   *Monte Walsh* (1963)   *National General, 1970
>   *Shane* (1949) [expanded from *Paramount, 1953
>   story "Rider to Nowhere"]
>   "Trooper Hourk"   * **Trooper Hook,** UA, 1957

Schisgall, Oscar (1901–1984) [as Stuart Hardy]
>   *Sierra*   Universal, 1950

Scullin, George
>   "The Killers" [published   **Gunfight at the OK Corral,**
>   in *Holiday Magazine,* Aug. Paramount, 1957
>   1954]

Seltzer, Charles (1875–1942)
>   *The Boss of the Lazy Y* (1915) Triangle, 1917
>   *Brass Commandments* (1923) Fox, 1923
>   **Chain Lightning,** Fox, 1927
>   *The Coming of the Law* (1912) Fox, 1919
>   *Fire Brand Trevison* (1918) Fox, 1920
>   *The Range Boss* (1916)   Essanay, 1917
>   *Silverspurs* (1935)   **Silver Spurs,** Universal, 1936
>   *Square Deal Sanderson* (1922) Paramount, 1919
>   *Trail to Yesterday* (1913) Metro, 1918
>   *West!* (1922)   **Rough Shod,** Fox, 1922

   Note: Sources unknown: **Fame and Fortune** (Fox, 1918); **Forbidden
Trails** (Fox, 1920); **Treat 'Em Rough** (Fox, 1919)

Shirreffs, Gordon Donald (1914–   )
    Rio Bravo (1956)   *The Lonesome Trail,* Lippert,
                                   1955

Short, Luke **see** Glidden, Frederick Dilley

Spearman, Frank Hamilton (1859–1937)
    The Nerve of Foley and Other   *The Runaway Express,*
      Stories (1900)   Universal, 1926
    Whispering Smith (1906)   Mutual, 1916
                              PDC, 1926
                              Paramount, 1948

Stanford, Harry
    Emporia [with Max Lamb]   *Waco,* Paramount, 1966
    Way Station [with Max Steeber]   *Apache Rising,* Paramount,
                              1966

Stone, Irving (1903–   )
    The President's Lady (1951)   20th Fox, 1953

Storm, Barry
    Thunder God's Gold   *Lust for Gold,* Columbia, 1949

Strong, Harrington **see** McCulley, Johnson

Summers, Richard Aldrich
    Vigilante (1949)   *The San Francisco Story,*
                              Warner Bros., 1952

Sutter, Larabie
    The Gun Witch of Wyoming   *The White Squaw,* Columbia,
                              1956

Swanson, Neil Harmon (1896–1983)
    The First Rebel (1939)   *Allegheny Uprising,* RKO, 1939
    Unconquered (1947)   *Paramount, 1948

Swarthout, Glendon (1918–   )
    "A Horse for Mrs. Custer" [in   *Seventh Cavalry,* Columbia,
      New World Writing #5, 1954]   1956
    The Shootist (1975)   *Paramount, 1976
    They Came to Cordura (1958)   Columbia, 1959

Todd, Lucas
    Showdown Creek   ***Fury at Sundown,*** UA, 1957

Traven, B. (1890–1969)
    The Treasure of Sierra Madre   *Warner Bros., 1948
    (1935)

Tuttle, Wilber Coleman (1883–1969)
    "Assisting Ananias" [in   ***Fools for Fortune,*** American,
    Adventure, April 1, 1920]   1922
    "Ba Ba Black Sheep" [in   ***Black Sheep,*** Pinnacle, 1921
    Short Stories, Jan. 1921]
    "Blind Trails" [in *Adventure,*   ***The Wild Horse Stampede,***
    Nov., 10, 1921]   Universal, 1926
    "The Devil's Dooryard" [in   ***The Devil's Dooryard,*** Arrow,
    Adventure, May 3, 1921]   1923
    "Fate of the Wolf" [in   ***Driftin' Sands,*** FBO, 1928
    Short Stories, June 25, 1925]
    "The Fighting Peacemaker"   ***The Fighting Peacemaker,***
                                        Universal, 1926
    "The Law Rustlers" [in   ***The Law Rustlers,*** Arrow,
    Adventure, Sept. 1, 1936]   1923
    "The Man with the Punch"   ***The Man with the Punch,***
                                        Universal, 1922
    "No Law in Shadow Valley" [in   ***Lawless Valley,*** RKO, 1938
    Argosy, Sept. 26, 1936]
    "Peaceful"   ***Peaceful Peters,*** Arrow, 1922
    The Red Head from Sun Dog   ***The Red River,*** Universal, 1934
    (1930)   [fifteen chapter serial]
    Rocky Rhodes (1934)   Universal, 1934
    "The Sheriff of Sun-Day" [in   ***The Sheriff of Sun Dog,*** Arrow,
    Adventure, Nov. 20, 1923]   1922
    "Sir Peegan Passes"   ***The Cheyenne Kid,*** RKO, 1933
    Spawn of the Desert (1929)   Arrow, 1923
    Straight Shooting (1926)   ***The Border Sheriff,*** Universal,
                                        1926
    "The Yellow Seal" [in *Liberty,*   ***The Prairie Pirate,*** PDC, 1925
    Jan., 10, 1925]
    Notes: Source unknown: ***Wildfire*** (Action Pictures, 1945)
    Original story for screen: ***The Fargo Kid*** (RKO, 1945)

Ward, Brad (1922–1960)
    The Marshal of Medicine Bend   ***A Lawless Street,*** Columbia,
    (1953)   1955

Ward, Jonas (1922–1960)
  The Name's Buchanan   **Buchanan Rides Alone,*
                                          Columbia, 1958

Warren, Charles Marquis
  Only the Valiant (1949)   William Cagney, 1950
    Notes: Original story for screen: *The Redhead and the Cowboy* (Paramount, 1951); *Ride a Violent Mile* (20th Fox, 1957); *Woman of the North Country*
    Warren received either all or partial credit for the following western films: *Hellgate* (Lippert, 1952); *Little Big Horn* (Lippert, 1952); *Oh Susanna* (Republic, 1951); *Springfield Rifle* (Warner Bros., 1952); *Trooper Hook* (UA, 1957)
    Warren also directed the following western features: *The Black Whip* (20th Fox, 1956); *Copper Sky* (20th Fox, 1957); *Ride a Violent Mile* (20th Fox, 1957); *Seven Angry Men* (Allied Artists, 1955)

Webb, Walter Prescott (1888–1963)
  The Texas Rangers (1936)   *Paramount, 1936
                                          The Streets of Laredo, Paramount, 1949

Weidman, Jerome (1913–   )
  House of Strangers   *Broken Lance,* 20th Fox, 1954

Wellman, Paul (1898–1966)
  Broncho Apache (1936)   **Apache,* UA, 1954
  The Comancheros (1952)   20th Fox, 1961
  The Iron Mistress (1951)   Warner Bros., 1952
  Jubal Troop (1939)   *Jubal,* Columbia, 1956
    Note: Original story for screen: *Cheyenne* [aka *The Wyoming Kid*], Warner Bros., 1947

Wells, Lee
  Day of the Outlaw (1955)   Universal, 1957
  The Peacemaker (1954)   UA, 1956
    [written as Richard Poole]

White, Stewart Edward (1873–1946)
  Arizona Nights (1907)   FBO, 1927
  Conjuror's House (1903)   *The Call of the North,* Paramount, 1921
  Gray Dawn (1915)   *The Gray Dawn,* Hodkinson, 1922
  The Killer (1920)   Pathé, 1921

"Two-Gun Man"   *Under a Texas Moon,* Warner
                                         Bros., 1930
The Westerners (1901)   Hodkinson, 1919
Wild Geese Calling (1940)   20th Fox, 1941

Wilson, Cherry
Empty Saddles   Universal, 1936

Wilson, Leon Henry
Ruggles of Red Gap (1915)   Essanay, 1918
                                       Paramount, 1923
                                       *Paramount, 1935
                                       Fancy Pants, Paramount,
                                         1950

Wister, Owen (1860–1938)
Lin McLean (1897)   *A Woman's Fool,* Universal,
                                         1918
The Virginian (1903)   Paramount, 1914
                                       Preferred, 1923
                                       *Paramount, 1929
                                       Paramount, 1946

Wright, Harold Bell (1872–1944)
Helen of the Old House (1921)   *Western Gold,* Principal, 1937
The Mine with the Iron Door   UA, 1924
  (1923)
Recreation of Brian Kent (1919)   *Wild Brian Kent,* 20th Fox,
                                         1936
The Shepherd of the Hills   Wright, 1919
  (1907)   First National, 1928
                                       Paramount, 1941
When a Man's a Man (1916)   First National, 1924
                                       Fox, 1935
The Winning of Barbara Worth   *UA, 1924
  (1911)
     Note: Sources unknown: *It Happened Out West* (20th Fox, 1937);
Secret Valley (20th Fox, 1937)

Wylie, I.A.R.
The Road to Reno   Universal, 1938

Yordan, Philip (1913–   )
Man of the West (1955)   *Gun Glory* Columbia, 1953

[Although Yordan's name appears on all editions of this novel, it was actually written by Ben Maddow who was blacklisted at the time of publication.]

Notes: Original for screen: *Broken Lance* (20th Fox, 1954); *The Bravados* (20th Fox, 1958); *Captain Apache* (Spanish, 1971); *Drums of the Deep South* (RKO, 1951); *The Fiend Who Walked the West* (20th Fox, 1958); *Johnny Guitar* (Republic, 1953); *The Last Frontier* (Columbia, 1955); *The Man from Laramie* (Universal, 1953)

Young, Gordon Ray (1886–1948)
    Tall in the Saddle   RKO, 1945

Bibliography

Adams, Les, and Rainey, Buck. *Shoot-Em-Ups: The Complete Reference Guide to Westerns of the Sound Era.* New Rochelle, N.Y.: Arlington House, 1978.

Adler, Renata. *A Year in the Dark.* New York: Berkley, 1969.

Agee, James. *Agee on Film: Reviews and Comments.* Boston: Beacon Press, 1966.

Arnold, Marilyn. "History as Fate in E.L. Doctorow's Tale of a Western Town." *The South Dakota Review,* Vol. 18, No. 1 (Spring, 1980), pp. 53–63.

Aros, Arnold A. *A Title Guide to the Talkies 1964 Through 1974.* Metuchen, N.J.: Scarecrow Press, 1977.

_____. *A Title Guide to the Talkies 1975 Through 1984.* Metuchen, N.J.: Scarecrow Press, 1977.

Barry, Iris. *D.W. Griffith.* New York: Museum of Modern Art, 1965.

Bataille, Gretchen, and Silet, Charles, ed. *The Pretend Indians: Images of Native Americans in the Movies.* Ames: Iowa State University Press, 1980.

_____. "A Checklist of Published Materials on Popular Images of the American Indian in the American Film." *Journal of Popular Film,* Vol. V, No. 2 (1976), pp. 171–182.

Beacham, Waton, ed. *Popular Fiction in America* (4 volumes). Washington, D.C.: Beacham Publishing, 1986.

Beja, Morris. *Film and Literature.* New York: Longman, 1979.

Bluestone, George. *Novels into Films.* Berkeley: University of California Press, 1966.

Bold, Christine. *Selling the Wild West: Popular Western Fiction, 1860–1960.* Bloomington: Indiana University Press, 1987.

Boyum, Joy Gould. *Double Exposure: Fiction into Film.* New York: New American Library, 1985.

Brauer, Ralph, and Brauer, Donna. *The Horse, the Gun and the Piece of Property: Changing Images of the TV Western.* Bowling Green, Ohio: Bowling Green University Popular Press, 1975.

Brown, Karl. *Adventures with D.W. Griffith.* New York: Farrar, Straus and Giroux, 1973.

Brownlow, Kevin. *The Parade's Gone By.* New York: Ballantine Books, 1968.

_____. *The War, the West, and the Wilderness.* New York: Alfred A. Knopf, 1984.

345

Cagin, Seth, and Dray, Philip. *Hollywood Films of the Seventies: Sex, Drugs, Violence, Rock 'n' Roll & Politics.* New York: Harper & Row, 1984.

Campbell, Russell. "Fort Apache." *The Velvet Light Trap, No. 2.* (August, 1971), p. 8–12.

Calder, Jenni. *There Must Be a Lone Ranger: The American West in Film and Reality.* New York: McGraw-Hill, 1974.

Cawelti, John G. *The Six-Gun Mystique.* Bowling Green, Ohio: Bowling Green University Popular Press, no date.

————. "Zane Grey and W.S. Hart: The Romantic Western of the 1920s." *The Velvet Light Trap,* No. 12 (Spring, 1974), pp. 9–11.

Clark, Randall, ed. *American Screenwriters, Second Series.* Volume 44 of *Dictionary of Literary Biography.* Detroit: Gale Research Co., 1986.

Cline, William C. *In the Nick of Time: Motion Picture Sound Serials.* Jefferson, N.C.: McFarland & Co., 1984.

Colvert, James B. *Stephen Crane.* New York: Harcourt Brace Jovanovich, 1984.

Cook, Bruce. *Dalton Trumbo.* New York: Charles Scribner's Sons, 1977.

Cooke, Alistair, ed. *Garbo and the Night Watchman.* New York: McGraw-Hill, 1971.

Corneau, Ernest N. *The Hall of Fame of Western Stars.* North Quincy, Mass.: Christopher Publishing House, 1969.

Current-Garcia, Eugene. *O. Henry.* Boston: Twayne Publishers, 1965.

Davis, Kenneth. *Two-Bit Culture: The Paperbacking of America.* Boston: Houghton Mifflin Co., 1984.

DeMarco, Mario. *Hoot Gibson,* no credits given.

Dimmitt, Richard Bertrand. *A Title Guide to the Talkies.* New York and London: Scarecrow Press, 1965.

Dobie, J. Frank. *Guide to Life and Literature of the Southwest.* Dallas: Southern Methodist University Press, 1958.

Easton, Robert. *Max Brand: The Big "Westerner."* Norman: University of Oklahoma Press, 1970.

Erens, Patricia. "Jeremiah Johnson: The Mountain Man as Hero." *The Velvet Light Trap,* No. 12 (Spring, 1974), pp. 37–40.

Etulain, Richard W. *Owen Wister.* Boise: Boise State College, 1973.

Etulain, Richard W. and Erisman, Fred. *Fifty Western Writers: A Bio-Bibliographical Sourcebook.* Westport, Conn.: Greenwood Press, 1982.

Etulain, Richard W. and Marsden, Michael, ed. *The Popular Western.* Bowling Green: Bowling Green University Popular Press, 1974.

Fenin, George N. and Everson, William K. *The Western: From Silents to the Seventies.* New York, 1973.

Folsom, James K. *The American Western Novel.* New Haven, Conn.: College and University Press, 1966.

————. "*Shane* and *Hud:* Two Stories in Search of a Medium." *The Western Humanities Review,* Vol. 24 (1970), pp. 359–72.

————. ed. *The Western.* Englewood Cliffs, N.J.: Prentice Hall, Inc., 1979.

Ford, Dan. *Pappy: The Life of John Ford.* Englewood Cliffs, N.J.: Prentice-Hall, Inc., 1979.

French, Philip. *Westerns.* New York: The Viking Press, 1973.

Friar, Ralph, and Friar, Natasha. *The Only Good Indian: The Hollywood Gospel.* New York: Drama Book Specialists, 1971.

Gale, Robert. *Luke Short.* Boston: Twayne Publishers, 1981.

Garfield, Brian. *Western Films: A Complete Guide.* New York: Rawson Associates, 1982.

Gilbert, Julie Goldsmith. *Ferber.* Garden City: Doubleday & Co., 1978.

Gruber, Frank. *Zane Grey: A Biography.* New York: World Publishing Co., 1970.

Hardy, Phil. *The Western: The Complete Film Sourcebook.* New York: William Morrow and Co., 1983.

Harver, Ronald. *David O. Selznick's Hollywood.* New York: Alfred A. Knopf, 1980.

Helterman, Jeffery and Layman, Richard, eds. *American Novelists Since World War II,* Volume 2 of *Dictionary of Literary Biography.* Detroit: Gale Research Co., 1978.

Horwitz, James. *They Went Thataway.* New York: E.P. Dutton & Co., 1976.

Jackson, Carlton. *Zane Grey.* New York: Twayne Publishers, 1973.

Kael, Pauline. *Deeper into the Movies.* Boston: Little, Brown and Co., 1973.

_____. *Going Steady.* Boston: Little, Brown and Co., 1970.

_____. *I Lost It at the Movies.* Boston: Little, Brown and Co., 1965.

_____. *Kiss Kiss Bang Bang.* Boston: Little, Brown and Co., 1968.

_____. *Reeling.* Boston: Little, Brown and Co., 1974.

_____. *When the Lights Go Down.* New York: Holt, Rinehart and Winston, 1980.

Kaminsky, Stuart. *John Huston, Maker of Magic.* Boston: Houghton Mifflin Co., 1978.

Karolides, Nicholas. *The Pioneer in the American Novel 1900–1950.* Norman: University of Oklahoma Press, 1967.

Kauffman, Stanley. *Figures of Light.* New York: Harper & Row, 1971.

_____. *Living Images.* New York: Harper & Row, 1975.

_____. *A World on Film.* New York: Dell Publishing Co., 1967.

Kitses, Jim. *Budd Boetticher: The Western.* A BFI Education Department Dossier, 1969.

_____. *Horizons West.* Bloomington and London: Indiana University Press, 1969.

Lahue, Kalton C. *Continued Next Week: A History of the Moving Picture Serial.* Norman: University of Oklahoma Press, 1964.

_____. *Riders of the Range: The Stagebrush Heroes of the Sound Screen.* New York: Castle Books, 1973.

_____. *Winners of the West: The Sagebrush Heroes of the Silent Screen.* New York: A.S. Barnes and Co., 1970.

Lake, Stuart N. *Wyatt Earp, Frontier Marshal.* New York: Bantam Books, 1952.

Lawrence, D.H. *Studies in Classic American Literature.* London: Secker, 1924.

Leisy, Ernest E. *The American Historical Novel.* Norman: University of Oklahoma Press, 1950.

Lenihan, John H. *Showdown: Confronting Modern America in the Western Film.* Urbana: University of Illinois Press, Chicago, London, 1980.

McBride, Joseph, ed. *Focus on Howard Hawks.* Englewood Cliffs, New Jersey: Prentice-Hall, Inc., 1972.

McCarthy, Todd, and Flynn, Charles, ed. *Kings of the B's: Working Within the Hollywood System.* New York: E.P. Dutton Co., 1975.

McClure, Arthur F., and Jones, Ken D. *Heroes, Heavies and Sagebrush.* New York: A.S. Barnes and Co., 1972.

Macdonald, Dwight. *On Movies.* New York: Berkley Publishing Corp., 1969.

Manchel, Frank. *Cameras West.* Englewood Cliffs, N.J.: Prentice-Hall, 1971.

Magill, Frank, ed. *Cinema: The Novel into Film.* Pasadena: Salem Softbacks, 1976.

_____ed. *Survey of Contemporary Literature, Revised Edition* (12 volumes). Englewood Cliffs, N.J.: Salem Press, 1977.

_____ed. *Survey of the Cinema, First Series* (4 volumes). Englewood Cliffs, N.J.: Salem Press, 1980.

_____ed. *Survey of the Cinema, Second Series* (6 volumes). Englewood Cliffs, N.J.: Salem Press, 1981.

Marcus, Fred. *Film and Literature: Contrasts in Media.* Scranton: Chandler Publishing Co., 1971.

Martine, James J., ed. *American Novelists, 1910-1945,* Volume 9, Parts I, II and III of *Dictionary of Literary Biography.* Detroit: Gale Research Co., 1981.

Mathis, Jack. *Valley of the Cliffhangers.* Northbrook, Ill.: Jack Mathis Advertising, 1975.

Meyer, William. *The Making of the Great Westerns.* New Rochelle, N.Y.: Arlington House, 1979.

Miller, Don. *Hollywood Corral.* New York: Popular Library, 1976.

Miller, Gabriel. *Screening the Novel.* New York: Frederick Ungar Pub. Co., 1980.

Morsberger, Robert E., Lesser, Stephen O., and Clark Randall, eds. *American Screenwriters,* Volume 26 of *Dictionary of Literary Biography.* Detroit: Gale Research Co., 1984.

Nachbar, Jac, ed. *Focus on the Western.* Englewood Cliffs, N.J.: Prentice Hall, 1974.

Nash, Jay Robert, and Ross, Stanley Ralph, ed. *The Motion Picture Guide* (12 volumes). Chicago: Cinebook, 1985-1987.

New York Times Film Reviews 1913-1980 (10 volumes). New York: New York Times and Arno Press, 1970-1981.

Nichols, Bill, ed. *Movies and Methods.* Berkeley: University of California Press, 1976.

O'Connor, John, and Jackson, Martin A. *American History/American Film: Interpreting the Hollywood Image.* New York: Frederick Ungar Publishing Co., 1979.

Parish, James Robert, and Pitts, Michael. *The Great Western Pictures.* Metuchen, N.J.: Scarecrow Press, 1976.

Peary, Gerald. "Selected Sound Westerns and Their Novel Sources." *The Velvet Light Trap,* No. 12 (Spring, 1974), pp. 15-18.

Peary, Gerald and Shatzkin, Roger, eds. *The Classic American Novel and the Movies.* New York: Frederick Unger Publishing Co., 1977.

_____. *The Modern American Novel and the Movies.* New York: Frederick Unger Publishing Co., 1978.

Pilkington, William T., ed. *Critical Essays on the Western Novel.* Boston: G.K. Hall & Co., 1980.

Pilkington, William, and Graham, Don, eds. *Western Movies.* Albuquerque: University of New Mexico Press, 1979.

Place, J.A. *The Western Films of John Ford.* Secaucus, N.J.: Citadel Press, 1973.

Powell, Lawrence Clark. *Southwest Classics.* Los Angeles: Ward Ritchie Press, 1974.

Pratt, George C. ed. *Spellbound in Darkness.* Greenwich, Conn.: New York Graphic Society, Ltd., 1973.

Prozini, Bill, and Greenberg, Martin, eds. *The Reel West.* New York: Doubleday and Co., 1984.

_____eds. *The Second Reel West.* New York: Doubleday and Co., 1985.

_____eds. *The Third Reel West.* New York: Doubleday and Co., 1986.

Rainey, Buck. *Buck Jones.* Nashville, Tennessee: Western Film Collector Press, 1975.

Ramsaye, Terry. *A Million and One Nights.* New York: Simon and Schuster, 1964.

Richardson, Robert. *Literature and Film.* Bloomington: Indiana University Press, 1969.

Ringe, Donald. *James Fenimore Cooper.* Boston: Twayne, 1962.

Robinson, W.R. ed. *Man and the Movies.* Baton Rouge: Louisiana State University Press, 1967.

Sandoz, Mari. *Cheyenne Autumn.* New York: Hastings House, 1953.

Sarf, Wayne Michael. *God Bless You, Buffalo Bill.* New York: Fairleigh Dickinson University Press, 1983.

Sarris, Andrew. *The American Cinema.* New York: E.P. Dutton, & Co., 1968.

_____. *Confessions of a Cultist: On the Cinema, 1955–1969.* New York: Simon and Schuster, 1971.

Schickel, Richard. *Second Sight: Notes on Some Movies, 1963–1970.* New York: Simon and Schuster, 1972.

Seydor, Paul. *Peckinpah: The Western Films.* Urbana: University of Illinois Press, 1980.

Simon, John. *Movies into Film: Film Criticism 1967–1970.* New York: Dell Publishing Co., 1971.

Sinclair, Andrew. *John Ford.* New York: Dial Press, 1979.

Slide, Anthony, ed. *Selected Film Criticism 1896–1960* (6 volumes). Metuchen, N.J.: Scarecrow Press, 1982–1985.

Smith, M.P. "Zane Grey on the Screen." *Western Film Collector,* Vol. 1, No. 4 (Nov. 1973), pp. 23–39.

Thompson, Richard. "Two Rode Together." *The Velvet Light Trap* No. 2 (August, 1971), pp. 19–21.

Tuska, Jon, and Piekarski, Vicki, ed. *Encyclopedia of Frontier and Western Fiction.* New York: McGraw-Hill, 1983.

Vinson, James, ed. *Contemporary Novelists,* 2nd edition. New York: St. Martin's Press, 1976.

_____ed. *Twentieth-Century Western Writers.* Detroit: Gale Research Co., 1982.

Voss, Arthur. *The American Short Story: A Critical Survey.* Norman: University of Oklahoma, 1980.

Webb, Walter Prescott. *The Texas Rangers*. Austin: University of Texas Press, 1965.

Wagenknecht, Edward. *The Movies in the Age of Innocence*. Norman: University of Oklahoma Press, 1963.

Weiss, Jaqueline Shachter. *Prize-Winning Books for Children*. Lexington: D.C. Heath and Co., 1983, 455 pp.

Winchell, Mark Royden. *Horace McCoy*. Boise State University Western Writers Series #51, Boise: Boise State University, 1982.

Work, James C. ed. *Shane: The Critical Edition*. Lincoln: University of Nebraska, 1984.

Wright, Will. *Sixguns and Society: A Structural Study of the Western*. Berkeley: University of California Press, 1975.

Wylder, Delbert E. *Emerson Hough*. Boston: Twayne, 1981.

_____. "Thomas Berger's *Little Big Man* as Literature," *Western American Literature,* Vol. III, No. 4, (Winter, 1969).

Zinman, David. *Saturday Afternoon at the Bijou*. New Rochelle, N.Y.: Arlington House, 1973.

Index

Titles of novels and films are in *italics,* and they are further distinguished by the abbreviation "n" for novel and "f" for film. Titles within quotation marks are short stories unless otherwise designated.